Enlightened Feudalism

Changing Perspectives on Early Modern Europe

James B. Collins, Professor of History, Georgetown University
Mack P. Holt, Professor of History, George Mason University

(ISSN 1542–3905)

Changing Perspectives on Early Modern Europe brings forward the latest research on Europe during the transformation from the medieval to the modern world. The series publishes innovative scholarship on the full range of topical and geographic fields and includes works on cultural, economic, intellectual, political, religious, and social history.

Private Ambition and Political Alliances:
The Phélypeaux de Pontchartrain Family and Louis XIV's Government, 1650–1715
Sara E. Chapman

The Politics of Piety: Franciscan Preachers During the Wars of Religion, 1560–1600
Megan C. Armstrong

"By My Absolute Royal Authority":
Justice and the Castilian Commonwealth at the Beginning of the First Global Age
J. B. Owens

Meat Matters: Butchers, Politics, and Market Culture in Eighteenth-Century Paris
Sydney Watts

Civic Christianity in Renaissance Italy: The Hospital of Treviso, 1400–1530
David M. D'Andrea

Law, City, and King Legal Culture, Municipal Politics,
and State Formation in Early Modern Dijon
Michael P. Breen

Transforming the Republic of Letters:
Pierre-Daniel Huet and European Intellectual Life, 1650–1720
April G. Shelford

Reformation and the German Territorial State: Upper Franconia, 1300–1630
William Bradford Smith

Jenatsch's Axe: Social Boundaries, Identity, and Myth in the Era of the Thirty Years' War
Randolph C. Head

Enlightened Feudalism:
Seigneurial Justice and Village Society in Eighteenth-Century Northern Burgundy
Jeremy Hayhoe

Enlightened Feudalism

Seigneurial Justice and Village Society in Eighteenth-Century Northern Burgundy

Jeremy Hayhoe

University of Rochester Press

First published 2008
University of Rochester Press
668 Mt. Hope Avenue, Rochester, NY 14620, USA
www.urpress.com
and Boydell & Brewer Limited
PO Box 9, Woodbridge, Suffolk IP12 3DF, UK
www.boydellandbrewer.com

ISBN-13: 978-1-58046-271-6
ISBN-10: 1-58046-271-5
ISSN: 1542-3905

Library of Congress Cataloging-in-Publication Data

Hayhoe, Jeremy.
Enlightened feudalism : seigneurial justice and village society in eighteenth-century northern Burgundy / Jeremy Hayhoe.
p. cm.–(Changing perspectives on early modern Europe, ISSN 1542-3905; v. 10)
Includes bibliographical references and index.
ISBN-13: 978-1-58046-271-6 (hardcover : alk. paper)
ISBN-10: 1-58046-271-5 (hardcover : alk. paper) 1. Manorial courts–France–Burgundy–History–18th century. I. Title.
KJW853.44.P38H39 2008
347.44'41–dc22 2008000841

A catalogue record for this title is available from the British Library.
This publication is printed on acid-free paper.
Printed in the United States of America.

Contents

List of Illustrations vii

Preface ix

Introduction 1

Part 1: Seigneurial Justice in Practice

Chapter 1
Tiny Courts, Incompetent Judges? 21

Chapter 2
Justice in the Interests of Lords 45

Chapter 3
Justice in the Interests of the Community 61

Chapter 4
Conflict and Consensus In and Out of Court 96

Part 2: The Winds of Change

Chapter 5
Local Knowledge and Legal Reform:
The Transformation of Justice 135

Chapter 6
Tocqueville in the Village: Seigneurial Reaction and the
Central State 172

Chapter 7
A Popular Institution? Seigneurial Justice in the
Cahiers de Doléances 195

Conclusion: Lords, Judges, and the Self-Regulating Village 211

Appendix A: Police Regulations from the Assizes during the 1780s 219

Appendix B: Class Justice? Statistical Tests 223

Notes 229

Bibliography 277

Index 303

Illustrations

Figures

I.1 Map of Burgundy 14

5.1 Duration of court cases, 1750–59 159

5.2 Duration of court cases, 1780–89 159

B.1 Tax assessments of litigants, 1750–59, regular session 225

B.2 Tax assessments of litigants, 1750–59, Grands-Jours 225

B.3 Tax assessments of litigants, 1780–89, regular session 226

B.4 Tax assessments of litigants, 1780–89, Grands-Jours 226

B.5 Tax assessments of litigants, 1780–89, Grands-Jours, *mésus* cases excluded 227

Tables

1.1 Seigneurial courts in three bailliages 25

1.2 Geography of justice: Villages within the jurisdiction of seigneurial courts, bailliage of Beaune, 1767 25

1.3 Profession of seigneurial judges in three bailliages 34

3.1 Crimes tried in fourteen seigneurial courts 65

3.2 *Arrêts* and edicts read to villagers at Grands-Jours 75

3.3 *Mésus* fines and other activities of eight seigneurial justices 83

4.1 Litigation rates by village, 1780–89 103

4.2 Litigation rates by village, 1750–59 104

4.3 Geographic origins of litigants 107

4.4 Civil cases heard in sampled courts in regular session (non-assize) 109

4.5 Profession of plaintiffs and defendants in regular (non-assize) cases 110

4.6 Cases arbitrated in two official samples 118

4.7 Cases settled by accommodation, before the notary of Messigny 127
4.8 Cases settled in regular session by the seigneurial court of Messigny 127
5.1 Cases heard in Grands-Jours 165
5.2 Tax assessments of litigants 169
5.3 Tax assessments of litigants, *mésus* cases excluded 169
6.1 Lawsuits involving lords 188
6.2 Villagers sued by seigneur 188
6.3 Lawsuits involving *fermiers généraux* as plaintiffs 190
7.1 Influence of presiding seigneurial officers on the contents of parish *cahiers* 197
7.2 Demands and grievances related to justice in parish *cahiers* 199
B.1 Paired t-test for null hypothesis: "Plaintiffs were significantly wealthier than defendants" 224

Preface

Contact with the formal court system in eighteenth-century France was far more common for ordinary people than it is today in the industrialized world. In northern Burgundy most people stood before the judge for one reason or another at least a couple of times a year. The judge oversaw most meetings of the village community. Once a year, the married men and widows in each village assembled in the judge's presence to report on village affairs, have laws pertaining to daily life read to them, and see some minor disputes resolved. With the prosecutor's help the local judge also policed the sale and consumption of alcohol, regulated the grain trade, made surprise raids on pubs, and inspected private homes for fire hazards. In many local jurisdictions all transfers of property had to be reported to the local court to ensure the collection of seigneurial taxes. The oversight of village agriculture required as many appearances before the judge as all other functions of the court combined. After a death the extended family of the deceased generally met at least twice in the presence of the judge. Lawsuits were also common, involving a family on average about four times in a decade; and each of these lawsuits required several appearances before the judge.

The influence of local courts, however, was not limited to those moments when ordinary people found themselves in front of the judge. People spent a good deal of time thinking, planning, plotting, and organizing for the future in ways that were always affected by a desire to stay out of court, and to ensure that they could persuade a judge should the necessity arise. Thomas Kuehn's insight about Italian city-states in the Renaissance applies equally well to eighteenth-century northern Burgundian villages: "[L]aw (itself a multifaceted entity) was implicated throughout society in an Italian city-state. Awareness of legal rules and the operation of legal mechanisms were present on a regular (that is, daily) basis. Law's formative influence was not merely occasional. It came into play not only at moments of trouble. . . . [E]ven when the law was not directly in play it informed the possibilities of a text or a social situation."[1]

Unfortunately, the ubiquity of law and the importance of legal institutions have been insufficiently acknowledged by historians of ancien régime France. French legal historians have devoted much more time to understanding legal doctrine than daily practice, while social historians have analyzed criminal justice in some detail but have left civil justice (which was immeasurably more important for people's daily lives) almost untouched.

One might even argue that an emphasis on criminal justice has actually hindered us from understanding how important law and legal institutions were, since one of the tendencies of this literature has been to deny that ordinary people had much contact with the courts. There has been some important work done using notarial documents, especially on dowries and inheritance patterns. Still, there remains much study to be done on the actual practice of civil law, and on the ways in which ordinary people and village communities interacted with the judicial apparatus of the state.

When I began work on this book in 1997, my research was guided primarily by a desire to understand how seigneurialism worked in practice. I began with a set of questions about seigneurs' exploitation of peasants through the courts and the possible existence of a seigneurial reaction that might help explain peasant dissatisfaction with the seigneurial system. This line of argument remains important in the book (chapters 2 and 6 address the question of a seigneurial reaction in some detail), but while conducting my research I was struck by the role of the courts in policing and administering daily life, the wide variety of affairs judged by the courts, and the high number of lawsuits involving ordinary people. In addition to discussing the nature of the seigneurial system and the sources of peasant discontent, therefore, this book argues that seigneurial courts were true venues of local justice that allowed villages to police themselves by providing the coercion that was sometimes required to enforce communal norms. This argument is presented through the demonstration of four related points: (a) seigneurial justice was relatively popular; (b) the courts generally enforced norms with which most peasants agreed; (c) the courts were fundamental to everyday social interaction between neighbors; and (d) as a result of the determination of the magistrates of the Parlement of Dijon, by the last decades of the eighteenth century, seigneurial justice was working better than it ever had to meet the needs of ordinary people and to help the villages of northern Burgundy keep the peace.

Researching and writing history books is never a solitary undertaking. The number of people who have offered advice, read chapters, helped with computer problems, and offered me generous hospitality is large indeed. Funding for research and writing was provided by the Social Science and Humanities Research Council of Canada and the University of Maryland, College Park. Subsequent research on the topic was supported by funds from the Université de Moncton.

During my stays in France I met and received help from an international group of scholars. Jean Bart, of the University of Dijon, was always willing to discuss Burgundian history, explain regional peculiarities, loan and give me books, and invite me into his home. Part of my time in Dijon overlapped with visits of David Parker. I benefited greatly from his insight into the relationship between property and the law, as well as from weekend trips with him into the countryside. Bob Schwartz shared freely of his time, as well as his research into local politics in Burgundian villages. Chris Corley and Charles Papon, who were both conducting extensive research in Dijon, helped me in so many ways, through long chats about legal, institutional, and social history. I have many times enjoyed Charles's generosity and hospitality in Paris.

The archivists of the departmental archives of the Côte d'Or were always quick to assist, and put a great deal of effort into helping me discover the meaning of obscure, local expressions. The librarians of the Dijon municipal library were equally generous with their time, helping me navigate their massive primary document collection.

During the years when I was first a graduate student and then an underemployed recent PhD, I was able to spend time researching, writing, and revising because of the generosity of family and friends who provided free or heavily subsidized accommodations in Dijon, Paris, Washington, Toronto, Ottawa, and Saint John. My parents (Bruce and Carolyn Hayhoe), Keith and Linda Attoe, my brother Robert and his wife Beth, Tim and Judith Le Goff, Françoise Fortunet, Charles and Frédéric Papon, Rob and Marty Rochon, Bob and Joyce Lyle, Scott and Nancy Cameron, Mats Hong, Danny Allan, and Rob Curran all found space for me in their homes at one time or another.

During the writing of this book, I received help from a veritable host of scholars and friends. James Collins, of Georgetown University, has helped me from the very beginning of the project. His many comments on this book as coeditor of the Changing Perspectives series have been invaluable. Anthony Crubaugh has proven supportive of my work, despite broad disagreement on the nature of seigneurial justice. Jeff Houghtby shared with me his understanding of agricultural history and local institutions. Al Hamscher has been exceptionally helpful and patient in explaining some of the concrete matters of jurisdiction in the Old Regime. I have had many fruitful discussions about conflict resolution with Christian Grosse of the University of Geneva. Fabrice Mauclair kindly sent me a copy of his doctoral thesis. I received generous computer and database help from Mark Allan, Danny Allan, and Rob Curran. Sam Arseneault, of the Université de Moncton, helped with maps and illustrations. Many people have read and commented on the book or parts of it. An incomplete list would include Don Sutherland, James Collins, Madeline Zilfi, Jeffrey Herf, James Henretta (and the members of his seminar on history and narrative), James Frusetta, Jean Bart, Sebastien Evrard, Hervé Piant, Claire Dolan, Bob Schwartz, Julian Swann, Antoine Follain, Tim Le Goff, Jill Maciak Walshaw, and Chris Corley. The anonymous reviewers of the University of Rochester Press were also exceptionally helpful in their suggestions.

My deepest gratitude is reserved for those who mentored me through my career in history. D. Gillian Thompson of the University of New Brunswick first drew my attention to the ancien régime and it was largely her doing that I am a French historian. Tim Le Goff, of York University, directed me through a master's in history. His intellectual rigor and generosity continue to astound me. Finally, Donald Sutherland helped turn a vague interest in rural and legal history into a concrete research project. His thoughtful and careful reading of chapters forced me to think more clearly about the big picture.

INTRODUCTION

Everyday life for ordinary country dwellers in eighteenth-century France was substantially defined by their relationship to their seigneur–even in 1789 lords continued to exercise power over village life and local political affairs.[1] Few historians of rural France still find persuasive Alexis de Tocqueville's view that the seventeenth and eighteenth centuries saw the central state gradually replace the local lord in village affairs, ultimately leading to antiseigneurial revolt in 1789.[2] By demonstrating the depth of peasant frustration and anger over seigneurial authority, analyses of popular revolts in 1789 and antiseigneurial criticisms in *cahiers de doléances* emphasize the continued influence of lords over daily life in the villages of France.[3] Peasants from every region revolted against their lords at some time from 1789 to 1793, and many refused to pay seigneurial dues after the summer of 1789, despite the fact that many dues and rights were not formally abolished until three years later. We also know that antiseigneurial sentiment did not spring out of nowhere in 1789, and indeed was rising in the last decades of the eighteenth century. Analysis of popular revolts in France throughout the eighteenth century shows that antiseigneurial violence, most often directed against lords' attempts to partition commons, enclose meadows, and drain marshes, was over three times more frequent from 1760 to 1789 than from 1690 to 1720.[4] And finally, it is clear from parish *cahiers de doléances* that when ordinary people thought about what was wrong with their society, the injustice and unfairness of their exploitation by lords came immediately to mind.

The continued importance of local lords in village life means that an analysis of seigneurial institutions is indispensable to an understanding of peasant history during the seventeenth and eighteenth centuries. A large literature exists about the seigneurie as an institution for the extraction of economic resources,[5] histories of what feudal theorists in the eighteenth century called the fief.[6] But the other element of the seigneurie, justice, is generally passed over quickly in rural histories, often with the assumption that it was moribund by the eighteenth century, either because lords were too cheap to pay for it or because the central state had taken over the jurisdiction of seigneurial judges.[7]

But is it true that seigneurial justice was decayed or dying in the eighteenth century? Even before I had seen the documents, the idea that the construction of a strong central state meant that royal courts had taken over jurisdiction seemed to me implausible, given the small number of royal judges.[8] The numerical inadequacy of royal judges to hear all lawsuits in the first resort was confirmed in the case of northern Burgundy; to cite one example, the bailliage of Arnay-le-Duc, with a population of about 20,000 inhabitants, had in the middle decades of the eighteenth century only two working judges–one criminal and one civil. Even the Dijon bailliage had only eight judges in 1746, admittedly a period of crisis in judicial recruiting (by contrast there were about 100 seigneurial judges sitting within the same region in 1780).[9] Either there were few lawsuits–which I found hard to believe given the complexity of property rights and the importance of honor and reputation–or a great many lawsuits were being heard somewhere other than in royal courts.

And if it should turn out that seigneurial courts were more active than most historians had previously thought, I hoped that the records might provide some insight into the origins of peasant antiseigneurial sentiment. There are two main interpretations of peasant revolt in 1789, and seigneurial courts play a significant role in both. For Alexis de Tocqueville, peasants revolted because by the eighteenth century lords were no longer providing services, including justice, in return for seigneurial extractions. The jurisdiction of seigneurial courts, he claimed, had gradually been taken over by royal courts, so that by 1789 they were basically defunct. If, as I suspected, Tocqueville had exaggerated the decline of feudalism that resulted from state centralization, maybe the idea of a seigneurial reaction might help explain why peasants revolted in 1789. This theory posits that as money replaced fealty in social interactions, lords became exploitative capitalists determined to squeeze all they could from their peasants. In this case, the cooperation of the local seigneurial judge would be essential for the collection of new dues and the enforcement of new rights.

But lords were not the only judicial clients of seigneurial courts. Indeed, several studies have shown that cases in seigneurial courts that directly involved lords as plaintiffs were relatively rare, often less than 5 percent of cases.[10] A useful analysis of the institution would therefore have to describe and evaluate the role of seigneurial courts in keeping the peace, settling disputes, and protecting the property of ordinary people. As a site of social interaction, the courts provide a useful locus for the integration of lords and their authority into village society and remind us that in the ancien régime the seigneurial system never simply pitted lords against an undifferentiated mass of peasants. One final advantage of investigating the seigneurie through local courts is that, although lords could hire and fire the judges, prosecutors, and clerks at will, these judicial officers were nevertheless in some sense agents of the royal and provincial governments. Examining seigneurial courts therefore allows us to observe the process of state-building, conflicts between royal intendants and provincial parlements, and struggles over the rights of lords to control village life.

Historians and Seigneurial Justice–A Consensus under Fire

Other historians have studied seigneurial justice during the eighteenth century, and the majority of them found little to praise. Because seigneurial courts combined public authority and private property, most of the historians who studied them found in miniature all of the abuses and problems of the ancien régime. It seemed scandalous that in the century of Enlightenment private individuals owned the right of justice and could have their cases tried by judges who were on their payroll. The continued existence of an institution that was profoundly exploitative and beyond the control of government administrators showed why a Revolution was required–that is, to wipe away the last vestiges of an unjust and confused governmental and judicial structure that ensured ordinary people got no justice at all. But historians criticized more than just the theoretical problems with the existence of seigneurial justice; they attacked the lack of government oversight on seigneurial courts, the ways that lords abused justice in their own interest, and the fact that judges, prosecutors, and clerks were more concerned with getting rich than dispensing justice. All of this meant that ordinary people simply gave up on the judicial system and were forced either to accept slights, torts, and unpaid debts or to resort to private vengeance.

The most damning criticism of seigneurial justice has always been the confusing and impossibly complicated nature of the system. André Giffard's classic work on Brittany made this point forcefully. In western France the legal custom linked justice to the fief, says Giffard, which meant that any sale or subdivision of seigneuries automatically created new justices. As a result, there were at least two seigneurial courts per parish in Brittany.[11] The existence of so many minuscule courts caused much confusion about the geography of jurisdiction. Abel Poitrineau cites the example of the mountainous regions of Auvergne, where the subdelegates reported to the royal intendant that they simply had no idea how many justices there were or where one court ended and the next began.[12] Like royal administrators, ordinary people could not figure out which court should hear their disputes, and so they simply stayed away from the official judicial system.

The geography of jurisdiction was so complicated and uncertain, earlier historians of seigneurial justice claimed, that there was little possibility of real oversight by ministers, intendants, and higher courts. The lack of oversight meant that lords and judges could collude to oppress and exploit villagers. Lords worked hard to protect their rights of justice, and they did so because they needed their courts to enforce their rights and collect their dues. By the eighteenth century the courts had become important in the ongoing seigneurial reaction whereby lords increased their revenues. Henri Sée claimed that in Brittany justice was the key for maintaining a lord's authority.[13] Pierre de Saint Jacob similarly argued that in northern Burgundy high justice gave lords the right to control village political affairs to their advantage, including the nomination of village treasurers and tax collectors.[14]

In the eyes of these historians, seigneurial justice was abusive primarily because the officers who staffed the courts were incompetent and greedy. The multiplication of small jurisdictions was supposedly problematic because it made it impossible for lords to find enough capable judges, prosecutors, and clerks. Because administrative confusion meant seigneurial courts were insufficiently supervised, greedy officers could stretch cases on indefinitely, charge prohibitive legal fees (and even accept or demand bribes), and use their judicial authority to construct personal spheres of influence.[15]

Things were apparently so bad that ordinary people stayed away from seigneurial courts by the eighteenth century–but when a peasant did decide to brave this morass, the case often dragged on interminably, which further discouraged litigation. Combier claims, for example, that seigneurial courts were painfully slow, with many cases lasting four or five years.[16] The reason that cases took so long, according to various historians, is that the judges preferred to use costly written procedure for the revenue that it brought them.[17] In 1784 the chancellor Lamoignon complained that "there are almost no cases judged orally [*à l'audience*] . . . [T]his is because those tried with written procedure [*les affaires appointées*] are lucrative and those judged orally produce no revenue."[18] A conspiracy between lords and judges to enrich themselves combined with the powerlessness of the royal government to deprive people of access to justice.

While it is fair to describe this negative view of seigneurial justice as a historical consensus, supporting as it does a triumphalist view of the growth of the central state and lauding the accomplishments of the revolutionaries who abolished the system, there were nevertheless some historians' portrayals that were more positive. Among older works on seigneurial justice, Pierre Lemercier's study of the seigneurial courts in and around Paris stands out for its argument that seigneurial judges were servants of the king–a far cry from the selfish, greedy, and ignorant officers who appear in other works.[19] Jean Bastier's work on the seigneurial system around Toulouse argues both that seigneurial courts remained active up to the Revolution and that most judges were competent and honest.[20]

Although all French provinces had seigneurial justices in the eighteenth century, it seems clear that the extent to which they remained active varied from province to province, based on a multitude of factors including the strength of the seigneurial system, the existence of provincial institutions such as the Estates and parlements, and the vitality of communal political institutions. The debate between critics and defenders of seigneurial justice looks different depending on the region studied. A recently published collection of articles on the institution contains a significant number of regional studies from the center-east and from the northwest, but few from other regions and none from the heart of the kingdom, a geography that is perhaps indicative of the state of seigneurial justice across France.[21] Olwen Hufton has suggested that French provinces can be divided into at least three groups with respect to the vitality of seigneurial justice. In some regions, including northern Burgundy, seigneurial justice remained a viable forum for dispute settlement. Secondly, in much of southern France the village community was powerful enough to impose order through shaming rituals with the assistance of groups of young men. Seigneurial justice therefore remained marginal in these regions. Finally Hufton cites Auvergne as a region where neither the local court nor the village community possessed enough moral authority to impose justice, and where direct confrontation was the preferred mode of conflict resolution.[22]

Regional diversity should not be underestimated. There remains, however, a great deal of research to be done in departmental archives all over France before we can draw an accurate picture of the abusiveness or effectiveness of seigneurial justice. Most of the research on the institution that was published before the 1990s relied on administrative documents to demonstrate how poorly things worked, and thus frequently reproduced the prejudices of administrators. The most important regional study, that of Giffard on Brittany, is largely based on such documents and provides no systematic attempt to determine how much justice cost, how long cases took, or exactly what kind of justice ordinary people received in these local courts.[23]

Over the past decade or so, however, several historians have returned to the archives and analyzed the caseloads of seigneurial courts. Consequently, there have been several new studies of seigneurial justice that challenge the dominant view of its abusiveness and decline. Zoë Schneider presents a vertical slice of the judicial system of Normandy from 1670 to 1740, with cases from parlement, presidials, bailliages, and seigneurial courts.[24] Schneider shows in great detail how ordinary people used the law to their advantage. Similarly, Sylvain Soleil emphasizes the close relationship between royal and seigneurial judicial officers and the extent to which one royal presidial court closely policed and oversaw the activity of the seigneurial officers within its jurisdiction.[25] In addition, a recent conference on seigneurial justice, held at Angers, published a collection of articles indicating a strong movement away from the old, negative view of the institution.[26] Benoît Garnot has more recently argued that seigneurial courts in the eighteenth century generally worked well to resolve the minor disputes of village life, most specifically through the twin responsibilities of policing village politics and agriculture and of administering probate justice.[27]

Anne Zink's work on village communities in southwestern France also does much to challenge the traditional negative view of seigneurial justice. She shows that in this part of France seigneurial justice played an important role in local life, with courts meeting regularly to decide disputes between villagers. She also emphasizes the activity of seigneurial courts in keeping the peace in the village and informing local communities of new laws and regulations that had been passed by the royal and provincial governments. "Seigneurial justice is controlled by royal courts; it works for the good of the commune and respects its customs."[28]

Most recently, Fabrice Mauclair's doctoral thesis goes a long way toward refuting a negative view of seigneurial justice. Mauclair's study of a single large seigneurial court provides specific data about the costs of justice, the duration of cases, and the way that procedure worked in these courts. He demonstrates that justice was not unreasonably expensive, that cases were settled quickly, and that attitudes toward the institution were relatively positive. He finds one main problem: court costs seem to have increased fairly steadily over the eighteenth century, especially in probate cases. Still, seigneurial justice remained faster, cheaper, and closer to local life than was royal justice.[29]

Not all recent research on seigneurial justice argues for the continued vitality of the institution, however. Anthony Crubaugh is the first historian to engage in a rigorous comparison of seigneurial courts with Revolutionary justices of the peace.[30] Crubaugh sees seigneurial justice in the ancien régime as a vital tool for enforcing an inegalitarian social hierarchy and argues that it was too slow, too unfair, and too expensive to be used much by ordinary people, who instead had to settle their disputes through private vengeance. Crubaugh claims that seigneurial courts in southwestern France were used primarily by lords to make recalcitrant peasants pay unjust dues, by wealthy merchants to ruin poor debtors, and by well-off peasants to oppress their poorer neighbors. As soon as the new justices of the peace replaced seigneurial courts, there was a dramatic increase in the number of court cases, which Crubaugh sees as the quenching of a thirst for justice that seigneurial courts in the ancien régime had never satisfied.

While it may have been the case in southwestern France that ordinary people disliked and avoided seigneurial justice and had to wait for the Revolution to create institutions that provided true justice, the situation in northern Burgundy looks rather different. I argue that the negative view of seigneurial justice does not apply in northern Burgundy; an analysis of judicial practice and procedure here suggests that seigneurial courts worked much better than any historian of the institution has previously suggested. Complicated judicial geography did not render the system unusable–all ordinary people knew which court was to hear their disputes. The officers were legal professionals, closer to traveling justices without material connection to their villages than to the greedy, untrained influence-peddlers presented in the literature. Procedure in the vast majority of cases was cheaper and faster than the historical consensus would lead us to expect. And, while it is always difficult to know what ordinary people thought, litigation rates and parish *cahiers de doléances* suggest seigneurial justice was surprisingly popular. Moreover, there was a series of procedural reforms, unique to the province of Burgundy, that broadened access by making faster, cheaper justice available to all.

There is only one aspect of the historical consensus with which I agree—that seigneurial justice was a useful, indeed almost indispensable, tool in administering the seigneurial system, ensuring the collection of dues, and protecting the rights of lords. The same judicial officers who quickly and fairly settled disputes between villagers actively collected seigneurial dues and policed the seigneurie for absent lords. There is also good evidence that ordinary people strongly resented both the uses that lords made of their courts and the role of judges, prosecutors, and clerks as agents of the seigneurie. The increasing visibility of the lord in the court that resulted from a massive increase in the number of cases involving lords as plaintiffs contributed to the delegitimization of seigneurial authority and helped lead to antiseigneurial revolt in 1789. Seigneurs could have prosecuted wood theft, nonpayment, and poaching in royal courts, but it would have cost them far more money and many more offenses would have fallen through the cracks. Ironically, then, it was the strength of the seigneurial system in northern Burgundy that ensured the continued vitality of seigneurial justice as a judicial institution with a popular base of support. The duality in the institution is strongly visible in attitudes toward seigneurial justice as expressed in the parish *cahiers de doléances,* as ordinary people were largely positive with respect to the dispute-resolution functions of seigneurial justice. They appreciated still more the ways the court worked in village affairs, requesting that the local judge be given jurisdiction over all questions that had fallen to the intendant and the Waters and Forests administration. These same villagers, however, strongly criticized the way judicial officers worked to protect the rights and prerogatives of the seigneur.

Seigneurs and Peasants in Northern Burgundy

This book centers on northern Burgundy, what is now the department of the Côte d'Or, with a few forays into other parts of the province. I chose northern Burgundy because I wanted to see how the institution worked in a region of active, aggressive, and modernizing seigneurialism.[31] The seigneurial system and agrarian life in the province have been studied by some of the foremost historians of rural France. With one notable exception, all portray northern Burgundian lords as more powerful than those almost anywhere else in France.[32] Pierre de Saint Jacob's analysis of peasant life and property during the ancien régime lays the foundation for all studies of rural northern Burgundy. Deeply sympathetic to the rhythms of agrarian life and the diversity of local conditions, the work displays a local nuance that sometimes threatens to overwhelm the strength of its conclusions. Nevertheless, the overall picture is clear. Agrarian life in northern Burgundy was governed not only by the changing of the seasons but also by the dominance of lords over village communities and the control of urban landlords. The growing importance of economic factors–caused by population pressures and the rise of physiocratic ideas–had three broad effects: the proletarianization of most farmers as the price of land rose, the dismantling of communal rights and common land, and the intensification of seigneurialism as lords tried to squeeze their peasants for all they were worth.[33]

Régine Robin's social and linguistic history of one northern Burgundian bailliage affirms most of Saint Jacob's conclusions. Robin underlines the increasing importance of money in the countryside and describes the transformation of the bond between lords and peasants it entailed–"personal ties are erased by the spread of financial relations." Robin suggests that peasants paid on average about a third of their income to their lord, and more importantly, that lords tended to become more exploitative as the eighteenth century progressed. This "seigneurial reaction," according to Robin, was characterized above all by lords closing off community access to common land and working to undermine communal rights, especially in forests.[34]

In his analysis of one aristocratic family's administration of its seigneurial estates in northern Burgundy, Robert Forster concludes that this family of absentee lords used agents and over-tenants to squeeze its land and peasants for ever-increasing sums of money. The seigneurial reaction here was a result of the growing tendency of the Saulx-Tavanes family to treat its seigneurie as a cash cow in order to keep afloat in the luxury of Versailles.[35] While supporting Saint Jacob's view of the seigneurial reaction, Jean Bart forcefully reminds us that the eighteenth century was not simply an era of the economic modernization of the seigneurial system. His study of *mainmorte,* a right that allowed lords to inherit from their peasants under certain conditions, argues that lords' commitment to increased revenue is visible in their defense and even extension of this archaic form of extra-economic exploitation.[36]

Finally, Hilton Root examines the triangular relations among the central government, provincial elites, and village communities. Root's intention is to challenge two received ideas: that the growth of the central state throughout the seventeenth and eighteenth centuries was accomplished by undermining the independence and power of village communities, and that the state encouraged the development of capitalism to increase its revenues. Rather, he argues that over the course of these two centuries the central government actually supported the independence of village communities, and more specifically, that royal administrators actively opposed the power of lords, whom they saw as competitors for limited village revenues.[37]

On the eve of the French Revolution, according to Root, northern Burgundian villages were becoming simultaneously more independent from lords and more dependent on the intervention of the royal government to protect them from these lords. Root's view of agrarian life and seigneurial authority in the province is deeply at odds with the views of the other historians mentioned above, and perhaps most so in his claim that through access to royal courts villages managed to protect their communal land and forests. Root's claim that the government (especially provincial intendants) actually reduced the power of lords is not persuasive, notably in the face of his own admission that villages always lost their court cases when they sued lords.[38] But Root makes abundantly clear that neither relations within French villages nor relations between those villages and their lords can be properly understood without reference to the role of the central state.

Some Interpretative and Methodological Obstacles

One of the main purposes of this book is to describe the role of seigneurial courts in village life, and one of my main arguments is that the local seigneurial court was a good deal more popular than most historians, and many eighteenth-century commentators, realized. But how can we know what ordinary people thought about seigneurial justice, what motivated them to go to court or accept a slight, or what they would have changed in the institution if they had had the chance? One excellent source is parish *cahiers de doléances,* and I devote a chapter to their analysis. But these documents tell us almost nothing about the actual experience of going to court; the comments therein center on issues like the abolition/preservation of the institution and the distances that people had to travel. The heart of my analysis is based on the court documents themselves, the frequency with which ordinary people went to court or decided to use another form of conflict resolution, and the experience of going to court in terms of cost, procedure, and judicial outcome.

The records of seigneurial courts, however, present myriad interpretative problems, only some of which are familiar to us. The archives of seigneurial courts contain a wide variety of documents, which have been divided by archivists into two groups: the bound judicial calendars (*registres*) and bundles of *procès-verbaux,* made up of everything that is not part of the register. In general, the registers contain all of the cases that were judged summarily in regular session, while the *procès-verbaux* contain the cases that were judged nonsummarily–major crimes and civil cases that became too complicated to judge orally. In addition, expert reports and other documents generated by the court are housed among the *procès-verbaux*. Probate records (inventories, the affixing and removal of seals, judicial auctions) are generally in the *procès-verbaux,* although assemblies to name guardians for minors can sometimes be found in the registers, possibly depending on whether the assembly was held in the village or at the judge's home. The records of the annual assizes can also be found in both sorts of documents, as can witness depositions.[39]

Most historians who have worked on seigneurial justice have paid little attention to the judicial calendars, which is understandable given the extent to which social historians have focused on criminal rather than civil cases. The calendars are also much more difficult to use than the *procès-verbaux,* since there is no official sentence that summarizes the case.[40] Instead, the narrative has to be reconstructed week by week, a job that would be virtually impossible without using a database's search function. The records are also often depressingly brief–many times the clerk simply notes (after recording the name, profession, and residence of the parties) that the judge had stayed the case for a week or a fortnight at the request of one of the parties.[41] Ignoring the judicial calendars to focus exclusively on the *procès-verbaux* may allow us to analyze the court's role in judging major crimes, but it either misses or vastly underestimates the importance of virtually every other operation of the court and leads to a serious misrepresentation of this local judicial institution.

In this book I analyze the cases recorded in both the bundles of *procès-verbaux* and the calendars. But how much can these cases tell us about life in eighteenth-century villages or about popular perceptions of local courts? What sorts of selection determined the kinds of cases that came to court? Which activities, offenses, relationships, and litigants are absent or overrepresented in the records? Historians of crime, writing from the 1970s through to the 1990s, have demonstrated, with impressive sophistication, the problems associated with the analysis of criminal activity through judicial records. Most fruitful has been the notion of the "dark figure," the number of crimes that go unreported. While undoubtedly very large, the number of unreported crimes is of course unknowable. The problem is greater for early modern France than it is for today, given the possibility of private arrangements for criminal affairs, the purported fear of the judicial arm of the state, and the fact that the most criminal prosecutions were instigated by the victim rather than by the courts.

The idea of a "dark figure" is, unfortunately, of no use in understanding civil justice. The distinction between reported and unreported incidents, upon which it is based, does not apply to noncriminal disputes. The problem is not, as with crime, that we know too little about what "really happened" (the number of murders, for example). Indeed, even if we could reconstruct every conversation and interaction that occurred in a village, we would be no closer to knowing how many disputes actually occurred. The difficulty is that it is the individuals involved, and not the law, the state, or the historian, who define what a dispute is.

The methodological impediments to the statistical analysis of civil justice are intractable indeed. A dispute is not a particular series of events, but rather a situation in which the parties see themselves as being opposed. Elders in a Calvinist consistory would say that the main problem was a sinful state of soul, while a modern psychologist might point instead to combined feelings of guilt and aggression that poison interactions. Happily for the researcher, there are outward signs of disputes, such as the refusal to take Communion, insults, physical attacks, the cold shoulder, and lawsuits. But these outward signs should not be taken for the dispute itself. We can state the problem another way, by suggesting that human relationships–be they between siblings, neighbors, spouses–all contain elements of conflict and dispute, which are more or less open or repressed depending on cultural norms and power relations. It is a characteristic of life in society that we are all simultaneously partly in conflict and partly making peace with each other. And while it may be a goal of modern criminal justice systems to monopolize punishment and retribution for major crimes, it is impossible even to imagine a judicial system designed to settle all disputes, or even all actionable disputes.

We can never know, therefore, what percentage of disputes came to court, was resolved by a notary, or was settled with a fistfight, because the total number of disputes is unknowable. The problem goes deeper, however, in that it is difficult even to know how many disputes were settled in court. This is in part a technical problem deriving from the variety of judicial solutions available in court, including three different kinds of procedure (after the assizes, ordinary or summary, and extraordinary), with boundaries that are often permeable between them. In addition, there is the possibility of bringing up a dispute at the assizes, before the assembled community (this is distinct from the trials that are settled very summarily following the assizes). In Meursault in 1780, for example, the widow Boillot complained to the judge that her neighbor, Joseph Latour, had placed a pile of manure near her garden, which the judge then ordered him to remove. A few minutes later, several unnamed inhabitants told the judge that Anne Flagey, wife of a cobbler, frequently stole grapes, sometimes even when she should be at Mass. The judge fined her 10 livres and ordered her not to repeat the offense.[42]

Perhaps an even greater impediment to counting court cases is the existence of several legal disputes that arise within the context of a single court case. Some cases involved both suits and countersuits, which in the documents are sometimes treated as two separate cases, but more often were settled together. More difficult is the presence of lawsuits where guarantors are called into the case, often disputing their responsibility to guarantee. This is especially problematic in inheritance cases, which can mushroom from a single plaintiff and defendant into long lists of litigants, each with her or his own perspective, and lines of alliances and fractures within the family that are virtually impossible to unpack. In 1753, for example, Claude Battault sued François Battault and Pierre Guillampet (his brother and stepbrother), but by the second session, at the request of some of the parties, the case had expanded to include Pierre Grillet and his wife.[43]

People also sometimes appealed an intermediary procedural ruling of the judge, in which case the original suit would be interrupted, to be taken up again some time later, without always making it clear that the return to the seigneurial court was not a new case. In 1786 Claude Goillet brought suit against Jean Liger, Pierre Harpet, Philibert Ladillon, and Jeanne Creuzefond. This was apparently a continuation of an earlier case that had been interrupted by an intermediary procedural appeal to the bailliage of Beaune. Ladillon and Creuzefond both protested that they could not be involved as defendants since they had not participated in the original preappeal part of the case. The plaintiff protested that they were not being called in the principal case, but in the "cause d'appel" and as a result of the guarantees exercised against them. In the end the judge agreed with the new defendants and threw out the case against them, but the case continued against Liger.[44] The records do not give more detail than this, but we can speculate that in this single court case there were disputes between Goillet and Liger, between Goillet and each of the three guarantors, and between Liger and the guarantors. If the guarantee had actually been carried out against Harpet, Ladillon, and Creuzefond, there likely would have been another dispute over who actually had to pay. Most cases were admittedly less complicated than this one, but the statistics I provide about the number and even the nature of civil court cases nevertheless have to be interpreted with some caution–the figures I cite represent little more than orders of magnitude.

The final problem in trying to evaluate the relationship between disputes, a social phenomenon, and lawsuits, a formal institutionalized resolution, is that not all court cases stem from a dispute. This fact, easily demonstrated, is often forgotten, as we tend to think of a judge's responsibility as being that of settling disputes about torts and disagreements about debts. But one of the primary roles of seigneurial courts was to bring to bear the coercive powers of the state to enforce contracts. The most common example of a disputeless lawsuit is the uncontested debt, where the defendant has neither denied his responsibility nor refused to pay. Despite repeated promises to repay, the money had not been returned. In these cases a successful lawsuit is the first step toward a judicial seizure (the actual seizure will require a second judgment). Indeed, defendants regularly failed to appear in debt cases, and judges universally interpreted a no-show in these cases as an acceptance of the debt.

Analyzing the relationship between a lawsuit and a dispute is, therefore, extremely difficult. Even if all records may have survived for a court, we cannot know how many cases came before the judge. It is often difficult to know where administrative, police, and probate jurisdiction ended and where "contentious" jurisdiction began. It is also clear that most disputes did not come before a judge, in eighteenth-century France as in twenty-first-century industrialized societies. Finally, civil cases differ from crimes in that disputes are not discrete, countable events and are created by the parties themselves when they give expression to the sentiment of having been wronged. These analytical problems do not, however, invalidate the study of civil litigation for historians. When litigation is situated among the multiple forms of dispute resolution, and judicial records are combined with notarial, administrative, and communal archives, civil court cases reveal a great deal about daily life, village sociability, and the balance of conflict and peacemaking that made up social interaction.

This book is based on a variety of judicial, administrative, and financial documents from the late eighteenth century. The heart of the documentation is the cases heard in fourteen seigneurial courts during two decades–the 1750s and the 1780s. This sample includes 3,249 cases in regular session and annual assizes (what contemporaries called "contentious justice"), as well as 1,439 acts of probate justice and the police regulations from 363 annual assizes. For comparative purposes I also sampled in bailliage and parlementary records, usually recording cases from one year in the 1750s and one in the 1780s. This database contains 1,034 cases from various bailliages and 799 cases from the Dijon Parlement.

While the cases themselves contain much that is useful, other sources are required to contextualize seigneurial justice within the village, the seigneurie, and the state. The sources used to fit the court and the fief together include private correspondence, seigneurial accounting records, the stamp tax, sales and transfers of seigneuries (*aveux et dénombrements, reprises de fief*), and published legal arguments in important court cases between lords and vassals. Administrative records in Paris and Dijon, parlementary general *arrêts,* remonstrances and other internal documents from the provincial Estates, and various disputes between administrative and judicial bodies show what the government knew about seigneurial justice and how the courts were overseen. Finally, understanding the relation between the court and the village required the use of a wide variety of sources, including tax rolls, village records of the intendants, communal archives, about 300 parish *cahiers de doléances,* a census, parish civil registers, notarized contracts, and parish vestry records.

The sample that is at the heart of this study is made up of the cases, administrative activities, probate documents, and other records generated by fourteen seigneurial courts spread throughout northern Burgundy. As figure I.1 shows, the bailliage of Dijon and the *plaine dijonnaise* are overrepresented, but the sample contains courts and villages from all northern Burgundian bailliages except Avallon. All but two of the justices in the sample were of small or medium size, and in many instances the justice corresponded either to a single village or to a village with a nearby hamlet. The two exceptions are the justice of the *prieuré* of Larey, a seigneurie held by the religious order

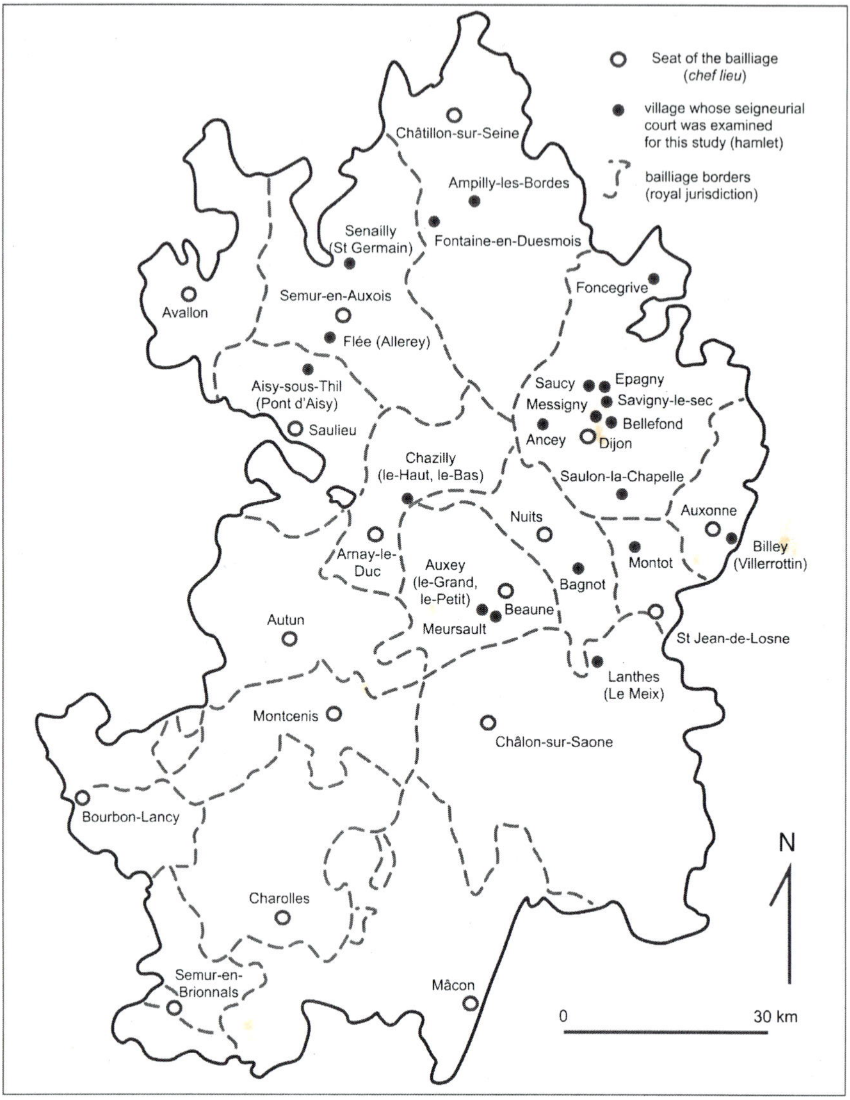

Figure I.1. Map of Burgundy with courts studied (prepared by Samuel Arseneault of the Université de Moncton)

of St. Bénigne, and the justice of Meursault, Auxey-le-Grand, and Auxey-le-Petit. The justice of the *prieuré* of Larey included seven villages within the open-field arable farmland around Dijon, while Meursault, with 1,800 inhabitants in 1786, more closely resembled a small town than a village.

The courts that make up the sample were all high justices, although they saw many more minor civil cases than major crimes pass before them. Because of the work involved to record all cases in a larger court, most of the seigneuries analyzed were composed of a single village. But since even those historians most critical of seigneurial justice have acknowledged that larger multivillage courts continued to function effectively, a bias toward smaller courts is more of an analytical advantage than a problem. All but three of the seigneurs were lay individuals, including both sword and robe nobles, among them counselors in the Chambre des Comptes and judges in the provincial parlement. There were two seigneuries held by religious orders–the large *prieuré* of Larey and the seigneurie of Montot, which belonged to the Sainte Chapelle de Dijon. Finally, the seigneurie of Ancey belonged to the Hôpital général of Dijon.

The villages studied varied in size from the tiny Lanthes and Saucy, with about 100 inhabitants, to Senailly at about 800 and the much larger Meursault. The average size of the communities included in my sample was approximately 400 in 1786. The province of Burgundy was composed of a large number of relatively small villages–in 1786 the average community had 616 inhabitants, but the median figure is much lower, at 414 inhabitants. The sample of villages studied is more or less representative of the size of communities within the province of Burgundy.[45]

There is a lot of variety among the wealth levels and social structures of the villages in this sample, as can be shown from tax records. In the village of Aisy (bailliage of Saulieu) over one-third of the ratepayers are listed as beggars, while two-thirds of the villagers in Billey (bailliage of Auxonne) were either landless day laborers or beggars. The most unequal social structure can be found in those villages around Dijon that practiced open-field farming and where common land had all but disappeared, as in Saulon-la-Chapelle, where there were six times more *manouvriers* than *laboureurs*.[46] Fontaine-en-Duesmois (bailliage of Châtillon) had a more egalitarian structure, with almost as many *laboureurs* as *manouvriers*. *Vignerons* often made up a substantial proportion of the inhabitants, although wealthier wine villages had a great many more employee-vintners than *vignerons* who owned their vines. In Meursault there were 106 *vignerons* who worked the vines of another, and only 11 who worked their own land. This contrasts with the village of Ancey that produced wine for consumption in the microregion, and where there were almost three times more *vignerons propriétaires* than *vignerons pour autrui*.

The sample of fourteen justices and about twenty villages is not entirely representative. It is affected by document survival (many justices were clearly missing too many documents to be included); it is significantly biased toward smaller justices and slightly biased toward small villages; and it slightly overrepresents the area around Dijon. There is nevertheless considerable diversity in terms of village size, social structure, regional coverage, farming practice, and prosperity levels. It reflects what most rural litigants likely experienced when they found themselves before a judge in the courts of first instance in northern Burgundy.

The book is divided into two parts–the first presents the role of seigneurial justice in village life, while the second describes the important ways in which the institution changed during the second half of the eighteenth century. The first and second chapters investigate the oft-repeated criticisms of seigneurial justice. Chapter 1 addresses the idea that the main problem with seigneurial justice was the multiplicity of minuscule courts, for which it was impossible to find competent judges, prosecutors, and clerks. I show that judicial geography was not as confused as many people think and that while most courts were indeed very small, the twin practices of accumulation of functions and of hearing cases in town meant that competent officers could nevertheless be found. Most judicial officers were well trained in legal matters and conscientiously enforced the laws of the nation and the judicial regulations of the province. Chapter 2 finds, however, some truth in the notion that lords used their courts unfairly to exploit their peasants. Seigneurial judges, prosecutors, and clerks did work hard to protect the interests, rights, and property of the lords who employed them, administering and policing the seigneurie to an extent that has seldom been appreciated.

The next two chapters analyze the function of the court within the context of village life. Chapter 3 discusses the "activist" roles of the court in probate, police, and criminal justice. I demonstrate that the courts responded to the will of their clients and were intimately connected to local life. The contrast with the previous chapter suggests a dichotomy (one that first struck me when reading the parish *cahiers de doléances*) between seigneurial justice as used by lords and justice in the service of the community. Judicial officers worked for lords, protected their rights, defended their property, and even participated in an effort to find them more income. But in cases that did not overtly involve the interests of the lord, judges worked as servants of the community.

The last chapter of the Part 1 more firmly situates seigneurial courts within the village by comparing civil litigation to various informal means of dispute resolution. Northern Burgundians were relatively litigious and had frequent contact with the local court. They sued each other over almost every kind of financial, social, and family relationship. Although relatively litigious, the inhabitants of the province were not reticent to settle their disputes out of court, using arbitration, mediation, and private accommodations. These informal means of dispute resolution would, however, have been useless and unenforceable in the absence of a formal legal system. Paradoxically, the prevalence of arbitration, mediation, and extrajudicial settlement illustrates how far seigneurial justice had penetrated into village life. Criticized by eighteenth-century legal theorists and often dismissed by historians as moribund, seigneurial courts were in fact an important forum for negotiating social status and reputation in the villages of northern Burgundy.

Part 2 of the book begins with a discussion of the problem of legal reform. After analyzing the failure of grandiose reform schemes presented by legal theorists, chapter 5 presents a series of seemingly minor procedural reforms implemented by the Dijon Parlement and the provincial Estates. The effect of these small changes was to transform seigneurial justice–comparing procedural indicators before and after the reforms shows that justice became cheaper and quicker, thus broadening social access to justice. Chapter 6 discusses changes in the administration of the seigneurie that occurred in the late eighteenth century. Taking issue with Hilton Root's argument, I show that the provincial intendant's authority over village affairs was limited and did not work in any demonstrable way to limit the authority or pretensions of lords. To the contrary, lords were suing their peasants increasingly often and using their newly reformed courts to intensify their control over villages. This intensification of seigneurialism probably helps explain peasant antiseigneurial sentiment in 1789. Still, the situation differs from what is portrayed as a seigneurial reaction in that there is little evidence of new dues, and no indication that peasants were paying more to their lords than had their parents or grandparents. The final chapter analyzes the parish and bailliage *cahiers de doléances*. Peasants, I suggest, were generally satisfied with the way seigneurial courts resolved ordinary civil disputes. They were virtually unanimous, however, in decrying that lords could and did use their own courts to enforce dues and rights and close seigneurial forests and fields to village herds.[47] My reading of these *cahiers* reveals that peasants made a subtle distinction between the dispute-resolving side of these local courts and a seigneurial institution that had lost all legitimacy by 1789.

Part 1

Seigneurial Justice in Practice

Chapter 1

Tiny Courts, Incompetent Judges?

The village of Jullenay straddled the border between the territories of the Paris and Dijon Parlements. The only high-justice lord of the village, Etienne Philibert Debadier, had one set of officers to judge the village, but these officers theoretically sat over two different courts, depending on the residence of the litigants.[1] In 1741 the lord complained that each time he began a court case against villagers, they "took no time to propose a change of venue [*déclinatoire*], and to maintain that they were from the jurisdiction of the other court." Debadier himself had been the victim of such action in the 1730s, in a case that went all the way to the Royal Council. This expensive case made him decide to have the village surveyed and the borders of the two provinces and justices clearly established.

Geographic jurisdiction was complicated in Jullenay. Many cases led to requests for a change of venue, suggesting not only the lack of rationality in the administration of justice but also the exasperation ordinary people may have felt with the judicial system. This village, then, seems illustrative of many of the criticisms historians have directed against seigneurial justice in the ancien régime. They have complained that geographic jurisdiction was too divided, too irrational, and too arbitrary. André Giffard estimated that in Brittany in the early eighteenth century there was an average of two seigneurial courts per parish and sometimes as many as thirty courts within one parish.[2] Abel Poitrineau reports that in Auvergne seigneurial justice was so complicated royal administrators did not know where one court began and the next one ended.[3] The result was that by the late eighteenth century plaintiffs simply stopped going to court in a system they could not navigate or even understand.

Closer analysis of the strange case of Jullenay, however, allows us to distinguish powerful forces pushing seigneurial justice toward a clear definition of judicial geography. The surveying Debadier commissioned began with an invitation to the villagers to testify to the location of the borders between the two justices. The inhabitants refused, and two villagers responded insolently and were fined for contempt of court by the seigneurial judge. When the surveyors arrived, nine members of the community gathered shovels and pitchforks and forcibly stopped the experts, filled in the hole the workers had dug as border markings, threw stones, and threatened the surveyors. The officers summoned the heads of household–married men and widows–to attend assizes (annual meetings between the court and the village) for each of the two courts, but none came, other than "a horde of women, who had no place at the Jours [assizes], and had come only to cause disorder." More fines seemed to accomplish nothing, so the lord called in soldiers, who were sent packing by a group of men armed with pitchforks and pickaxes. In response to this armed rebellion, the seigneurial court began criminal proceedings against twenty-two men and ordered them all imprisoned pending investigation.

The inhabitants were opposed to what seemed to be the clarifying of geographic jurisdiction in their village. This was not because they preferred one court over the other–the officers and lord were the same, after all. The reason for their violent opposition was that the judicial confusion provided an opportunity to protest the lawsuits their seigneur initiated against them. "This division is more tiresome and onerous for the lord than for the inhabitants, for whom it provides at all times an occasion for disputing."

What is most important in this story, though, is not that the villagers opposed the surveying, but that the lord initiated it. Like all seigneurs, Debadier used his court, staffed by his own choice of judge, prosecutor, and clerk, to collect his dues and protect his property and rights. If the court was rendered useless because of uncertain jurisdiction, the lord's ability to use his court was hampered as much as that of the nonnoble clients of the court. It was the link between justice and seigneurial authority that led to the attempt to bring clarity to a confused situation.

The desire of lords to use their own courts to protect their authority and property rights maintained the vitality of seigneurial justice by ensuring that lords knew not only who their *censitaires* were but who their *justiciables* were as well. In addition, seigneurial courts in northern Burgundy held annual assizes, a practice that had fallen into disuse in much of France. Since all heads of household within the court's jurisdiction were required to attend (the judges took attendance), this meant not only that lords knew what peasants lived within their justice but also that all peasants knew which court should hear their disputes.

There was, then, a practical workability to seigneurial justice that ensured that ordinary people knew what court should hear and settle their disputes. This calls into question the idea, frequently repeated, that seigneurial courts increasingly lost cases to royal courts.[4] This attrition was supposedly part of the strategy of royal administrators to centralize and modernize state institutions. It also occurred because royal courts offered quicker, more reliable service to judicial clients than they would receive in the increasingly abusive seigneurial courts. In opposition to this vision of rationalizing state centralization, this chapter demonstrates that even in 1789 seigneurial courts remained the justice of first instance for most country dwellers, while royal courts were reserved either for appeals or for the urban elite.

While admittedly complicated in theory, jurisdiction in seigneurial courts worked simply enough in practice that most ordinary people could understand it. There were occasional jurisdictional disputes between various high-justice lords, but with an examination of historical title and some surveying, the judges of northern Burgundy's higher courts were always able to settle the matter and draw jurisdictional lines between seigneurial courts. The courts were, it is true, too small to allow a judge to make a decent living, but this did not favor the selection of untrained judges or demands for bribes. To the contrary, lawyers from the cities accumulated several judgeships and continued practicing as lawyers. The relatively small number of judges that sat over a large number of courts also made it easier for the bailliages and parlement to exercise oversight and control over the province's many courts.

The Geography of Justice

Counting the number of functioning seigneurial justices is not an easy task. Seigneurial clerks were supposed to hand over all judicial papers to the state during the early stages of the Revolution, but it is unlikely that the archives of all seigneurial justices ended up in departmental archives.[5] Historians working on other regions of France have used reports prepared by intendants, parlements, and bailliages to count the number of seigneurial courts. In Angers, for example, Sylvain Soleil found a detailed inquiry into seigneurial justice. The officers of the presidial court required each seigneurial court to justify the lord's possession of high justice. They also requested a list of the parishes under the control of the court and the days of the week the court met.[6] Similar enquiries were carried out in Brittany and in the *généralité* of La Rochelle.[7]

No comparable inquiry was ever carried out in Burgundy. There is no mention made of such a report in the administrative correspondence concerning the province in the National Archives, nor is any such report housed in the intendant's files in the Departmental Archives of the Côte d'Or.[8] There is one administrative report that gives an approximate estimate of the number of seigneurial courts in Burgundy, but it is impressionistic and the number is probably inflated. In 1780 Sieur Acher de Montorval, first secretary of the intendance, prepared a report on the administrative powers of the intendant and the way the province was governed.[9] This report begins with a description of the province obviously written to impress the reader with the size, population, and administrative complexity of the province. The intendant sits over a generality of more than twelve hundred square leagues and about "eleven hundred thousand inhabitants."[10] Here is his description of the judicial system of the province:

> There is a Parlement that is also a *Cour des aides*, a *Chambre des comptes*, a *Bureau des finances*, eight presidial seats, 22 royal bailliages of which three appeal to the Parlement of Paris that extends onto part of Burgundy, a *Table de marbre*, nine *maîtrises des Eaux et Forêts*, five *élections* of which three appeal to the *Cour des aides* of Paris, and two to that of Dijon, 35 *greniers à sel* and over 3000 seigneurial courts, nine seats of the *maréchaussée* and 43 brigades commanded by a *prévôt général*.[11]

While the intendant and his staff may have had only an approximate idea of the number of seigneurial courts in the province, the same was not true of the officers of the superior courts, who kept lists of seigneurial courts within their jurisdiction. The Parlement of Dijon frequently issued general *arrêts* on matters of rural police and ordered them to be sent out to all seigneurial courts and read to the inhabitants at the annual assizes, a responsibility that fell on the bailliage officers.[12]

The actual lists kept by each bailliage for this purpose seem to have disappeared, but other documents copied from them have sometimes come to light. An *arrêt* of parlement ends with a list of the "inferior courts that appeal to the bailliage of Beaune."[13] And a letter from a lower officer of the bailliage of Saulieu to each seigneurial court likewise listed the courts to which the letter was to be sent.[14] In addition to these two documents, the *Almanach de la province de Bourgogne* annually published a list of all seigneurial courts in the bailliage of Dijon, along with the names of the officers that staffed these courts.[15] The population, number of parishes, and number of seigneurial courts are presented for these three bailliages in table 1.1. The bailliages of Beaune and Saulieu had approximately the same number of seigneurial courts as they had parishes, while the bailliage of Dijon had almost two parishes per seigneurial court–approximately one court for each 600 inhabitants for the bailliages of Saulieu and Beaune, and about one court per 800 inhabitants in the bailliage of Dijon.

The size of the territory covered by a court varied widely, and a rough average disguises this fact. Still, as many as half of the courts were contiguous with villages. Of the three sources described above, only that for the bailliage of Beaune indicates which villages were under the authority of each court. As we can see in table 1.2, there were 41 courts (53.2 percent) that sat over only one village. There were a few very large courts (five had more than seven villages), and some villages were split between several courts. If a substantial proportion of courts were contiguous with a single village, it is nevertheless true that only about one village in five had its own seigneurial court. Half of villages were part of seigneurial courts that sat over fewer than five villages.

Table 1.1. Seigneurial courts in three bailliages, late eighteenth century

	Bailliage of Dijon	Bailliage of Beaune	Bailliage of Saulieu
Number of parishes[a]	139	77	39
Number of seigneurial courts[b]	90	77	41
Courts per parish	0.65	1.00	1.05
Population in 1786[a]	74,097	41,675	24,648
Courts per 1,000 inhabitants	1.21	1.85	1.66

[a] ADCO L496, Amelot census, 1786.
[b] For Dijon: *Almanach,* 78–98. For Beaune: BM Dijon, MS 1307, "Recueil d'Arrêts du Parlement de Dijon." vol. 4, *arrêt* 11 May 1767. For Saulieu: ADCO B2 424/2, seigneurial justice of Aisy, Pont d'Aisy, letter 30 November 1783.

Table 1.2. Geography of justice: Villages within the jurisdiction of seigneurial courts, bailliage of Beaune, 1767

Villages within the jurisdiction of a seigneurial court	Number of courts	Percentage of courts sitting over the corresponding number of villages	Percentage of villages
1	41	53	21
2	12	18	7
3	9	12	14
4	3	4	6
5	5	6	13
6	1	1	3
7	1	1	4
8	2	2	8
10	1	1	5
13	1	1	7
14	1	1	7

From these figures it is difficult to extrapolate for the province of Burgundy, or even the northern part of the province, but it seems unlikely that Acher de Montorval's estimate of 3,000 seigneurial courts, cited above, is accurate. According to the Amelot de Chaillou census of 1786, there were 1,854 parishes in Burgundy, with a total of 1,105,468 inhabitants. Unless the bailliages of Saulieu, Dijon, and Beaune were exceptional, we would expect closer to 2,000 seigneurial courts for the province.

Most seigneurial courts in northern Burgundy were relatively small, sitting over between 500 and 1,000 inhabitants, or between about 300 and 600 adults.[16] Courts of this size generally saw only a small number of cases each year. The seigneurial judge of Aisy (population 325), for example, heard fifty-four cases between 1780 and 1789, while the judge of Chazilly-le-Haut and Chazilly-le-Bas (combined population 254) saw forty-eight cases pass before him over the same period.[17] The large number and small size of seigneurial courts in the region meant that most courts could not keep a judge, prosecutor, and clerk busy for much more than a few hours a week, nor could they provide these officers with a significant income, as we will see below. Seigneurial courts were likely equally small throughout most of France, with regional variety reflective of the average size of villages and the nature of the seigneurial system.

The size of seigneurial courts may have caused problems to the clients of the courts. One historian has argued that the multiplicity of courts rendered jurisdiction complicated and increased the number of appeals that cases had to go through.[18] It is also possible the courts were too small and judicial incomes too insignificant to attract competent and honest judges. We will see below, however, that these criticisms do not apply in northern Burgundy, as ordinary people had no trouble choosing the right seigneurial court, appeals were limited, and most officers were competent and trained in the law. Indeed, northern Burgundian peasants rarely complained of the size or high number of seigneurial courts in their parish *cahiers de doléances*. Only 3 of 303 *cahiers* explicitly criticized the multiplicity of courts. As we will see in chapter 7, the main criticism of seigneurial justice in the *cahiers* was not the multiplicity of courts but the distance people had to travel to get justice. Most villagers were in favor of reducing still further the average size of local courts by making them contiguous with villages.

One reason the multiplicity of seigneurial courts did not create more uncertainty over jurisdiction is that in Burgundy they continued to hold annual assizes, called Grands-Jours. The officers were to come into the village, read any relevant royal or parlementary *arrêts,* ensure that the village was well policed, see to the election of village officials, and settle any minor cases individuals brought before the court. The clerk took attendance each year, and every head of a household was required to attend, with fines for those not present. This practice may have fallen into disuse in some parts of

France,[19] but in Burgundy the assizes were a thriving institution, and they were reinvigorated in the 1770s. The requirement that each head of household attend this meeting of the relevant local court meant that people knew which court was to judge them. In the case of a dispute with a neighbor, people simply went before the judge whose Grands-Jours they attended.

A picture of the geography of justice must be pieced together from the three lists of courts cited above, from parish *cahiers de doléances,* and from jurisdiction disputes between lords or judges. Consider first the parish *cahiers de doléances.* The villagers of Thoisy-le-Désert and Crécey complained that "in these communities there are seven high justice lords, which frequently makes for cases that continue indefinitely because of the uncertainty in deciding which judge should hear the case, given that the lords each have judges and courts in different places, that it is necessary that there be but one judge who must reside no further than three leagues from the courthouse."[20] But only three out of several hundred extant *cahiers* complained of the geographical complication of seigneurial justice, which suggests this was not a major problem for most country dwellers.

Although seigneurial justice in northern Burgundy was less complicated than extension from Crubaugh's or Giffard's analyses would suggest, this does not mean there were no unclear or uncertain situations. The link of justice to a complex seigneurial system, the fact that justice was patrimonial, and the division of a few parishes among many justices all led to jurisdictional uncertainties. Still, it was always possible to figure these out with a bit of work in the historical and judicial archives of the lord, suggesting that there was a practical workability to this system that is easily obscured by focusing on a few complicated examples.

Jurisdiction during the ancien régime could be territorial, personal, or both–the court to hear a case, in other words, could be determined by the place an offense occurred or by the residence or station of the plaintiff or defendant. Criminal jurisdiction was simplest, in that a nonnoble accused would always be tried in the seigneurial court of the scene of the crime.[21] Pierre Jacquet tells us the accused were always to be tried in the place of the crime rather than their place of residence.[22] In an unpublished manuscript Méllenet describes the jurisdiction of seigneurial high justice over crimes: "the competence of seigneurial judges in criminal affairs is to know all crimes committed within the territory of the court by all nonnoble persons regardless of the social standing of the plaintiff."[23] Crimes were directed against the authority of the lord who owned the seigneurie and so it was his court that tried the case.

Jurisdiction in civil cases was theoretically more complicated. But in practice litigants simply went to the seigneurial court of the residence of the defendant. In 942 cases in fourteen seigneurial courts during the 1750s, only eighty-nine defendants lived outside the jurisdiction of the court hearing the case. But these 942 cases include not only civil but also criminal and police cases, and most of the outsiders were involved in police cases, specifically wood theft, rather than in civil trials. Among plaintiffs, on the other hand, 429 (45.5 percent) lived outside the seigneurial justice hearing the case. No complicated research was required into titles of lords or boundaries of justices–the residence of the defendant determined which seigneurial court should hear a case, and people knew which court this was because of the existence of annual assizes.

Seigneurial courts also had jurisdiction over probate matters. Like regular civil matters, probate justice was considered to be personal. This meant the high justice that properly had the right to see to the settlement of an estate was the justice of the place of residence, rather than the place where the death took place. But this was impractical in cases where a traveler died outside his own parish, and it also undermined the right of each seigneurial court to oversee the property within its area. The practice, then, was that authority over property belonged to the justice where the property lay, while the justice of the place of residence had authority over all personal issues, such as who would be responsible for minor children, how an inheritance would be divided, and which creditors would be paid first.[24]

The conclusion of most jurisdiction disputes was a legal act known as a *bornage,* which described the geographical limits of a seigneurie and justice, and commonly included a map. A drawn-out dispute over Fontaine-lès-Dijon ended in 1741 with a decision that Bénigne Bouhier's seigneurie possessed rights of high justice over the following parts of the village: "from the white cross on the side of the road from Dijon to Fontaine to the street called the Rue de la Confrairie, which road traverses the village and passes in front of the marketplace."[25] When the limits between two seigneuries were unclear, they sometimes marked the land for clarification, as in the case of Saucy and Joussanvaux: "the said justices start to meet at an ancient marker that is almost buried at the *lieudit à la charrière à la Biche,* which has been replaced by a large stone marker at the same place."[26]

Maps and written descriptions such as these are quite common in the seigneurial papers housed in the departmental archives of the Côte d'Or.[27] They can be difficult to interpret in that each presents, at the same time, contradictory evidence of both the complication and the workability of seigneurial justice. They remind us that people sometimes did not know whose court was responsible for a piece of land or a peasant. But they could solve the problem, and with some research draw up an exact map, which suggests things may not have been as complicated as some historians have claimed. This is not to minimize the very real complications that resulted from the feudalization and private ownership of justice. Nevertheless, the fact remains that in most villages of eighteenth-century northern Burgundy people knew to which court they were to take their complaints, and to which officers they answered.

There is one other criticism of the complication of seigneurial justice that is commonly made by both historians and legal commentators from the eighteenth century: that the appeal structure of the ancien régime was highly complex, and worse, that cases often had to go through four or five levels of appeal before reaching the parlement for a final judgment.[28] In the late 1730s Chancellor Daguesseau prepared a manuscript, which he never published, wherein he advocated the reform of seigneurial justice. He complained that plaintiffs and defendants sometimes required seven or eight appeals before reaching a final judgment.[29] The culprit, according to Daguesseau, was the division of seigneuries. When a lord sold off part of his seigneurie, he also sold the right of justice for that part of the seigneurie, but he kept the right to hear appeals from the new court. The solution, the chancellor suggested, was to stop the division of justices, and to outlaw more than one or at most two levels of seigneurial justice. In an antiseigneurial pamphlet, Boucher d'Argis similarly pointed out the "necessity of reducing the degrees of jurisdiction to two in affairs that are of the competence of presidials, and to three degrees in all others."[30]

The appeal structure in eighteenth-century northern Burgundy was everywhere limited to not more than three layers of courts.[31] While the parish *cahiers* frequently complained about the number of appeals (that is, they wanted it to be more difficult to appeal cases), none of them complained about the number of layers of appeal courts.[32] There are examples of seigneurial courts that heard appeals from other seigneurial justices; but in these instances the cases appealed from the seigneurial appeal court would go directly to parlement, still limiting the number of appeals to two.[33]

A sample of civil and criminal cases from the Dijon Parlement and several bailliages bears out the fact that appeal was rare, and that no cases were appealed more than twice. The judgments of the Tournelle chamber of parlement list the courts where the case had already been tried, thus allowing us to see how many court layers the case had come through. In 439 civil and 127 criminal cases from 1785 and 1755, respectively, no case had been tried more than twice before coming to parlement.[34] Similarly, in about 500 civil cases in the bailliage of Dijon in 1755 and 1785, no cases reached the bailliage after being heard in more than one seigneurial court.[35]

Judicial Attrition? Seigneurial Courts as Justice of First Instance

Alexis de Tocqueville's model of state centralization under the ancien régime posits that the royal government successfully orchestrated a transfer of jurisdiction, cases, and clients from seigneurial to royal courts. His view that seigneurial and royal courts competed for the same clients and cases has long dominated the historical literature, as has the view that, in the end, it was royal courts that won.[36] Recent studies of several French provinces, though, have concluded that the antagonism between royal and seigneurial justice has been severely exaggerated. In northern Burgundy seigneurial courts remained the justice of first instance for ordinary country dwellers until revolutionaries abolished them in the summer of 1789. Despite some overlap between the jurisdiction of royal and seigneurial courts, royal courts served urban elites while seigneurial courts remained the justice of first instance for country dwellers. There was a complementary relationship between royal and seigneurial courts. Even in serious criminal matters the accused first came into contact with the local seigneurial court, and only afterward with the royal judge. Even in the 1780s, disputing country dwellers in northern Burgundy went before the local seigneurial judge for arbitration, rather than the distant royal judge.

For criminal cases the complementary relationship between royal and seigneurial justice is especially clear after the reform of 1772. The edict was motivated by the fact that some lords had allowed their criminal jurisdiction to lapse into disorder owing to the possible costs of criminal trials. The remedy was to permit lords to pass some of the costs on to the central government. Seigneurial judges could still conduct a criminal trial through to a final judgment, but the lord would be held financially liable for the costs of appeals to the bailliage and then to parlement, as before the reform. Or the judge could choose to conduct the investigation, hear the witnesses, interrogate the defendant, and then send the case, the paper, and the criminal to the royal court. In the latter scenario the lord would only pay for the costs of the initial judicial investigation, and all costs of the appeals would be borne by the central treasury.[37]

The effect of the reform of 1772 was to transform seigneurial judges basically into *juges d'instruction* in major criminal trials, to make them more explicitly servants of the royal judiciary. This reform effectively continued a process of state-building that was ongoing from the seventeenth century, a process of co-opting rather than replacing competing institutions. The complementary nature of seigneurial and royal justice can be demonstrated in several ways. First, consider a small sample of criminal cases.[38] Of the eighty-four criminal cases in the Parlement of Dijon in 1785 that had a final judgment, seventy-four had begun in a seigneurial or municipal court. Of twenty-one crimes judged in the bailliage of Dijon in 1785, twenty had been investigated and begun in a seigneurial court according to the provisions of the 1772 edict. These included serious criminal matters such as murders, housebreaking, and brutal assaults.

The *monitoire à fin de révélation* also provides a means of illustrating the role of seigneurial courts in judging crimes. This was a judicial procedure whereby a court could use the threat of ecclesiastical sanction to force witnesses to come forward and identify the guilty party. The threat of excommunication could be effective, and it seems that in most cases witnesses testified. In a study of *monitoires* in a Burgundian bailliage (Autun) in the eighteenth century, approximately 60 percent were granted at the request of a seigneurial judge. Alternatively, only about 15 percent were for cases in a royal court and less than half of that group were from bailliages–the others being primarily from *châtellenies,* essentially seigneurial courts attached to fiefs held by the king. Of those *monitoires* used in seigneurial courts, about 6 percent were for murder cases, 7 percent were for assaults, slightly less than 30 percent for thefts, and 12 percent for destruction of property.[39] With little attrition of crimes from seigneurial to royal courts, therefore, most crimes, including serious offenses, continued to be tried in the seigneurial courts of the province.[40]

In theory, seigneurial courts in the eighteenth century possessed jurisdiction over most civil cases. Royal courts' jurisdiction was limited to disputes concerning rights attached to justice such as bastardy, disinheritance, and confiscation; jurisdictional disputes between two or more seigneurial courts; cases involving royal officers; disputes between municipal officers and royal judges; and any case involving "graces and privileges emanating from the king; of the state and quality of persons whose nobility is contested, naturalizations, legitimizations . . ."[41] In addition to this, most Burgundian bailliages had a special chamber possessing the right to register and legalize all documents sealed with the royal seal and jurisdiction over disputes concerning the royal seal.[42] But how did the complementary relationship work in practice? While northern Burgundian royal courts did indeed hear cases that were not appeals, they specialized in serving urban litigants, leaving seigneurial courts as the justice of first instance in the countryside.

Seigneurial justice had not been pushed to the judicial margins. Judges in these courts were not limited, either in theory or in practice, to hearing minor cases. Seigneurial courts that possessed the right of high justice saw no limits on the value at stake in a trial,[43] and they heard cases involving considerable amounts of money. In the fourteen seigneurial courts sampled, during the 1750s in regular sessions the average value of quantifiable disputes judged was 114 livres, while for the 1780s the average was 148 livres.[44] These figures are artificially high, since unquantifiable cases often involved items of little economic value. Still, the fact remains that seigneurial courts did hear many cases involving significant amounts of money. In 1786 in the court of Messigny, the judge ordered Antoine Lescheneaux to pay 1,596 livres that he owed to Bernard Fremyet, who was calling in his loan to Bernard Berger that Lescheneaux had cosigned as guarantor.[45] In the wine-wealthy bourg of Meursault, Touzet, a *négociant,* sued Jacques Bouzereau, also a *négociant,* for repayment of a promissory note of 1,870 livres, plus 1,480 livres from another business deal.[46] Given the poverty in which most country dwellers lived, the majority of disputes involved far less money; but when people had a disagreement that involved everything they owned, they went to the seigneurial judge to moderate the dispute.

The royal bailliages mostly heard cases involving urban litigants. In 1755, 46.2 percent of the 119 cases heard in the court (combining all cases from the bailliage, presidial, and chancellerie of Dijon) involved either a plaintiff or a defendant from the city of Dijon. In 1785 the figure was still higher, with 55 percent of 392 cases involving a Dijonnais. Since in 1786 the city of Dijon contained about 30 percent of the bailliage's population, the provincial capital was strongly overrepresented in the civil cases of the bailliage.[47]

Not only did the bailliage overwhelmingly hear cases involving urban people, these people could hardly be considered "ordinary folk." In the ninety-four nonappeals heard in the bailliage of Dijon in 1785, only nineteen plaintiffs could be considered ordinary people. These included eight artisans, eight agricultural workers, one domestic servant, one innkeeper, and one horse renter. In 1755 the bias toward the wealthy and educated was still stronger: only five of the thirty-five nonappeal bailliage cases had ordinary plaintiffs: three artisans and two agricultural workers. The remaining plaintiffs in these cases were predominantly merchants, nobles, bourgeois, and legal professionals. The residence and professions of the parties in the bailliage cases contrasts sharply with the kinds of people who took their cases to seigneurial courts: in the 1750s in the fourteen courts sampled, 73 percent of plaintiffs and 82 percent of defendants were artisans and farmers. Lower royal courts served a different clientele than did seigneurial courts.

Finally, seigneurial courts heard many times more cases than did royal courts. In 1782 the community of *procureurs* in the bailliage of Dijon met to complain about a significant reduction in their income that resulted from an *arrêt de règlement* of the Parlement of Dijon. In calculating their losses, the *procureurs* estimated that "there are three times more cases heard in inferior courts [i.e., seigneurial courts] than at the bailliage."[48] To verify their estimate, it is possible to calculate the number of cases per 1,000 inhabitants heard in both seigneurial and royal courts. The figures are merely orders of magnitude because of the many problems associated with counting lawsuits, as we will see in chapter 4. In 1785 the bailliage of Dijon heard 412 civil and criminal cases.[49] With a population of 74,097 in 1786, there were 5.6 cases per 1,000 inhabitants.[50] During the 1780s, by contrast, in the seigneurial courts studied the average was 35 cases per 1,000 inhabitants, almost six times higher.[51] There was a great deal of variety among seigneurial courts, but only one of those studied had a lower rate of litigation than the bailliage of Dijon. Seigneurial justice heard many times more cases than did royal justice and remained the court of first instance even on the eve of the Revolution.

Despite all the complaints of legal theorists, understanding the judicial system in ancien régime northern Burgundy was well within the reach of ordinary people. Among the clients of the courts there was no confusion about which court should hear a case. Because of the link of justice to the seigneurial system, lords and judges all knew which people and which pieces of land were under the jurisdiction of their courts. Since parlement insisted on annual assizes in each justice, and since each head of a household was required to attend, ordinary Burgundians were reminded once a year which court they were to use to settle their disputes. The number of layers of courts, including courts of first instance and appeal courts, was everywhere limited to three. Seigneurial justice may or may not have served the needs of ordinary people effectively (the subject of chapters to follow), but any problems that did exist in the judicial system were not, in northern Burgundy at least, the result of confusion as to the geographical jurisdiction of each court.

Legal Professionals or Greedy Amateurs: Who Staffed the Courts?

Although most ordinary people understood which court they should go to, there were nevertheless about two thousand seigneurial courts in the province of Burgundy, most of which were in small villages where no lawyer, procureur, or notary resided. Who, then, staffed the courts? Judicial officers in northern Burgundy, as elsewhere in France, were professionals devoted full-time to the law. Most judges were lawyers, trained in university and qualified to present cases in parlement, the province's highest court. Most prosecutors were either *procureurs* or royal notaries, and most clerks were royal notaries. It is true that judicial salaries were far below what a liberal professional needed to survive, but rather than supplementing their income through suspect business dealings with judicial clients, judges acquired several judgeships and maintained an active legal practice. This meant that almost all were inhabitants of towns and that less than a tenth lived in the villages they judged. We will see in chapter 7 that most parish *cahiers de doléances* expressed the wish for judicial institutions that were close to their villages. The physical removal of justice from the village was one of the most unpopular elements of seigneurial justice in the region, but it was the negative side of the fact that the judicial officers were legal professionals who could not possibly have made a living in a village.

Several kinds of sources allow us to find out who were the officers of seigneurial justices in northern Burgundy. According to royal edict, all seigneurial judges were to register with a royal court each time they were appointed to a new judgeship.[52] The registration was to include a public oath, as well as an investigation into the life and morals of the new officer. While these investigations were entirely perfunctory, they nevertheless name the seigneurie, the lord, the judge, his profession, and his place of

Table 1.3. Profession of seigneurial judges in three bailliages, late eighteenth century

Profession	Parlement (%)	Bailliage of Arnay-le-Duc (%)	Bailliage of Dijon (from the *Almanach*) (%)
Lawyer	46 (66.7)	120 (56.9)	48 (55.2)
Procureur in bailliage	1 (1.4)	8 (3.8)	0
Procureur in Parlement	2 (2.9)	4 (1.9)	8 (9.2)
Royal notary	7 (10.1)	65 (30.8)	8 (9.2)
"*Practicien*"	1 (1.4)	6 (2.8)	0
Stamp tax officer	1 (1.4)	2 (0.9)	0
Municipal officer	2 (2.8)	0	8 (9.2)
Merchant	0	0	1 (1.1)
Unknown	9 (13.0)	6 (2.8)	14 (16.1)
Total	69	211	87

residence. These documents exist in a complete run for only one bailliage in northern Burgundy but can be supplemented by similar documents from the Dijon Parlement.[53] There is also the *Almanach de Dijon,* which lists not only judges but also *procureurs d'office* and clerks for the bailliage of Dijon.[54] There are addresses for the officers–street names if a resident of Dijon, otherwise the village of residence. I was able to match this list for 1780 to lists of *avocats, procureurs,* and *notaires* also included in the *Almanach,* and to tax rolls from villages throughout the bailliage, to find the profession of most of these judicial officers.[55]

The results of this document-matching, presented in table 1.3, demonstrate that most seigneurial judges had significant legal training. Of sixty-nine seigneurial judges registered at the Parlement of Dijon from 1725 to 1789, forty-six (67 percent of the total or 77 percent of those whose profession is known) were university-educated lawyers.[56] This leaves 23 percent of the judges who had not received a university education, but who nevertheless had followed extended legal apprenticeships. *Procureurs* specialized in advising clients on procedural matters, while notaries often acted as informal legal counsel to people who used their service as notaries. The sample provided by the registers of parlement is biased toward larger seigneurial courts, but the list in the *Almanach de Dijon* is exhaustive for one bailliage. Here in 1780 over half of the seigneurial judges within the bailliage were *avocats*–66 percent of those whose profession is known. Only one seigneurial judge in the bailliage of Dijon in 1780 was not a legal professional–Dubois, acting lieutenant in the marquisate of Mirebeau, was a merchant, but his work was overseen by Trouvé, the *bailli,* a lawyer who was also the presiding judge in the *grenier à sel.* Many of the lawyers who judged in seigneurial courts were important men in provincial affairs. Arnoult l'ainé was legal counsel for the provincial Estates, law professor at the University of Dijon, and an administrator of the Collège Godran. The lawyer Daubenton was legal counsel for the Dijon hospital, while Jacquinot the younger and Jarrin were both *procureurs-syndics* of the provincial Estates. Many of the city's legal elite chose to work part-time as a seigneurial judge.

Procureurs d'office in the bailliage of Dijon had less formal training than judges, but they were nevertheless competent.[57] *Avocats, procureurs,* and notaries made up 77 percent of *procureurs d'office* whose profession is known. Only two *procureurs d'office*–one bourgeois and one merchant–had no legal training. The list of seigneurial clerks also contains a high proportion of legal professionals, with 70 percent being lawyers, *procureurs,* or notaries.

Seigneurial justices were staffed by a group of men who had dedicated their lives to the practice of the law. Within the bailliage of Arnay-le-Duc, we can divide judges' oaths into two groups (1710–49 and 1750–89). In the first forty-year period 53.9 percent of judges were lawyers and 31.5 percent were notaries. In the latter period lawyers made up 60 percent of the judges and the share of notaries remained constant at 30.8 percent. While data allowing comparison for a coherent region over a long period of time exists for only this bailliage, the modest increase in the proportion of judges who were lawyers suggests the likelihood of an incremental professionalization of judicial officers over the course of the eighteenth century.

Commentators from the eighteenth century, as well as some historians, have decried the practice of selling seigneurial judgeships to the highest bidder. True venality of office did not exist in seigneurial justice, since lords always maintained the right to remove their officers and since the private sale of the offices from one officer to another was generally not permitted.[58] Nevertheless, it seems that in many parts of France it was a frequent practice for a judge to pay money to the lord when he was hired, effectively buying the office.[59] In the courts of the *duché-pairie* of La Vallière the office of judge sold for as much as 5,500 livres in the late seventeenth century, but here too the lord maintained the right to revoke the office.[60] In northern Burgundy, however, it was not a common practice. Of the 280 swearing-in ceremonies discussed above, only 1 gives a clear indication that money passed hands: in 1765 Jean Claude Gogois paid 200 livres for the office of judge of the seigneurial court of Paisson.[61]

There are several reasons that venality was rare in northern Burgundian seigneurial courts. Firstly, as we will see below, judges' incomes from a single small court were generally insufficient to allow them to pay substantial sums of money to purchase an office. Another reason is the strength of the seigneurial system in northern Burgundy, and the importance of judges, prosecutors, and clerks in administering the seigneurie. Rather than exchange the office for money, most lords preferred to choose officers who could defend their interests. Additionally, one of the functions of venality was to provide some security to the officers, making it more difficult for a lord to fire the judge who had purchased the office.[62] The payment may also have functioned as a guarantee protecting the seigneur, a symbol of the commitment of the officer to his employer.

It is much more difficult, unfortunately, to tell if *procureurs d'office* and clerks paid for their offices. Their oaths of office are spread throughout the records of countless seigneurial justices and are therefore not easily collectible like those of the judges. Jean Bernard was *procureur d'office* in the seigneurial court of Héry, and in 1712 he submitted a declaration to the intendant as part of an investigation into the village's distribution of the tax load. He noted that he paid 130 livres for the office, in addition to 30 livres in fees, probably for the swearing-in ceremony.[63] I have seen few similar examples, however, and it seems likely that *procureurs d'office* did not often pay for their office. Clerks, by contrast, did frequently lease the rights to their office from the lord.

General leases of seigneuries sometimes contained clauses specifying that the *fermier* was entitled to the revenue from the lease of the clerkship. A lease from 1741 of the seigneurie of Foncegrive, for example, specified that Aubin Ladey, the *fermier,* was entitled to "all the seigneurial revenues of Foncegrive," including the price of the lease of a seigneurial mill, the fines pronounced by the court, seigneurial dues, and the "revenue of the clerkship of the said justice that will nevertheless be exercised by the one that I reserve the right to name and appoint."[64] In 1741 Denis Joachim Perrin paid 600 livres to the *fermier* to lease the clerkship of the major seigneurial court of Montrevel.[65] In northern Burgundy, therefore, it was rare that seigneurs received money from the sale of the offices of judge, prosecutor, and clerk. There was, however, money to be made from the lease of the clerkship, a practice that was relatively common.

The Distance between Justice and the Village

Most judges were university graduates chosen for their knowledge of the law and their commitment to defending the interests of the lord. They were legal professionals, not peasants. Since most lawyers and procureurs lived in cities and most notaries either in cities or towns, few judges were members of the communities over which they sat. This distance between the village and the court results from the large number of seigneurial justices and the necessity that, as we will see below, judges accumulate judgeships and maintain an active law practice in order to make a living. Residing in the countless seigneurial courts that sat over one or two parishes was simply not economically viable for a judge and lawyer. Only thirteen of the eighty-nine judges sworn in from 1710 to 1749 in the bailliage of Arnay-le-Duc lived in the village where the seigneurial justice sat. Subtracting the four documents that neglect to give the dwelling place for the judges, this leaves seventy-two judges, or 81 percent, who did not live in their jurisdiction. From 1750 to 1789 the figure is even higher, with 87 percent of the judges living in a nearby town or city and only 11 percent of judges serving in their hometowns. The live-in rate for the bailliage of Dijon in 1780 was even lower. Of the eighty-three seigneurial judges in the Almanach list, fully 77 percent (sixty-four of them) resided in Dijon. Of the remaining nineteen who lived outside the provincial capital, only five lived within the area of their courts. This means that 94 percent of the seigneurial courts had judges who were not locals. The residency rate is similar for procureurs d'office, with 68 percent of them living in Dijon and only 7 percent residing in the villages they served. Clerks tended to be locals slightly more frequently; 15 percent of them lived in villages they served.[66]

Even if judicial officers did not reside in their villages, they may have been involved in business and personal relationships with villagers, which would hamper their impartiality. They may also have taken advantage of their inside knowledge to buy land and other things cheaply. Zoë Schneider discusses the example of lower royal judges in the bailliage of Pont-Audemer who took advantage of judicial seizures and auctions to buy up village property for little money. She argues that this was an important motivation for lawyers to seek out a position as judge.[67] Since these transactions were illegal, the judges hid them as third-party transactions, but the practice becomes visible to the historian because of an extensive judicial investigation into abuse of power by the judges within the bailliage of Pont-Audemer. While there is little doubt that some northern Burgundian seigneurial judges sometimes behaved similarly, it is difficult to evaluate the frequency of such possible abuses. By using tax records from after 1787, though, it is possible to discover whether judicial officers owned land in the villages within the jurisdiction of their courts. The answer, found from matching tax records to lists of judicial officers from the annual assizes, is that judicial officers in the small sample analyzed here owned very little land in their villages.

Tax rolls have to be used with some care. Ordinary *taille* and *capitation* rolls only include nonprivileged residents of the village in question, so other incidental sources must be used to search for these seigneurial officers who lived outside the village. The four kinds of sources that include this sort of data, from most to least useful, are *matrices des sections* prepared in 1791, which list all landowners and estimate their annual revenue; *rôles des privilégiés* done in many villages in 1789 preparatory to the taxing of those who had enjoyed fiscal privilege; *vingtième* rolls, which exist for all villages but are unwieldy to use; and lists of nonresident landowners included in *taille* and *capitation* rolls after 1787.

Out of the thirty-eight known officers who served during the 1780s in the fourteen seigneurial courts studied, five (13 percent) owned land in one of the villages over which they sat. In three of these cases the sources allow us to have an idea how much land the officers owned. In the village of Ampilly-les-Bordes, both the judge and the *procureur d'office* owned land, but the acreage was minimal. The judge's annual income from his land in the village was estimated in 1790 at 16 livres 4 sols, while that of the *procureur d'office* was about twice as much.[68] These officers owned little more than a garden, or perhaps a small parcel of land, probably leased to a local. Of the three other landowning officers, two are only to be found in the lists of nonresident and privileged landowners, giving no hint of how much land they owned.[69] Only Claude Martine, judge of Montot, can be shown to have owned a significant amount of land: approximately twenty-one *journaux* of land, including seven *journaux* of "first-class" land, thirteen *journaux* of second-class land, and one *soiture* of meadows, with annual estimated revenue of 113 livres 7 sols, much higher than the village average of 37 livres 10 sols. Still, there were thirteen people who owned more land than Martine, and the largest landowner in the village earned 982 livres per year.[70] Very little of the income of most judges, prosecutors, and clerks, then, came from renting out land that they had acquired in the villages over which they sat.

As has been noted, there was a downside to the professionalism of the officers: most judges did not live within the jurisdiction of their courts. Since they sat over several courts at once, most judges acquired the habit of hearing most cases in town, either at their own home or at the bailliage courthouse. The court records do not consistently note where a particular case was being heard. There are generally indications given when the judge was sitting "in his townhouse, by loan of territory," but the absence of such a phrase does not indicate that the case took place in the village.

There is evidence that judges heard most cases outside of the village, in the seat of the royal bailliage where most of them lived. In 1772 the *procureurs* of the bailliage of Charolles complained of the number of seigneurial judges that heard cases in their own homes, noting this caused difficulties for them in representing their clients. As a result of their complaint, judges were required to hear their cases in the royal courthouse when they were not judging in the village.[71] A report submitted to the Parlement of Dijon by the community of *procureurs* of the bailliage of Dijon complained of the low wages paid to *procureurs d'office*. In a long list of their unpaid duties, they include the requirement to "transport themselves to the village to inquire into crimes and contraventions." This gives the impression that *procureurs d'office* did not come to the village for regular court sessions, an impression that is only strengthened by the fact that much communication between the court and the village takes the form of correspondence: *procureurs d'office* must also "write continually to the *procureurs* [*syndics*] of the communities, to *messiers* and other local officials."[72] The same community of *procureurs* later described their workweek: "on Wednesday they have the audiences of inferior jurisdictions [seigneurial courts], which because of their multiplicity, occupy them for the entire afternoon . . . on Saturday they have during the morning the audiences of the Chancellerie, and during the afternoon the audiences of inferior jurisdictions."[73] Clearly most seigneurial courts met most of the time in the *chef-lieu* of the bailliage rather than in the village.

The distance people had to travel to see their seigneurial judge could be considerable. For the fourteen courts used in this study, villagers lived an average of about thirteen kilometers from the seat of the bailliage where most cases were probably tried.[74] The inhabitants of several villages (for example, Lanthes and Foncegrive) had to walk more than twenty-five kilometers. All of this obviously caused considerable inconvenience to the villagers. Still, the problem should not be exaggerated. Judges sometimes sat in the village, and if they were willing to wait, people could in any case take their dispute to the annual assizes and have it judged in the village square.[75] Peasants traveled a great deal within the radius of a day's walk, and they made trips to town when they needed to see a notary, pay the stamp tax, or buy salt.

It is not possible to have it both ways, so there will always be a trade-off between quick justice by officers who understand the local situation and impartial professional justice by officers who understand the law. In 1768 parlement ordered that annual assizes were to be held in the bailliage of Bresse. Unlike the rest of Burgundy, Bresse had no tradition of annual Grands-Jours. The deputies of the Third Estate of the city of Bourg protested that this would reduce the professionalism of the legal system by bringing justice closer to the village: "that in abridging the forms, justice will not be as accurately served."[76] Unconvinced, the Parlement of Dijon reaffirmed its committment to the institution of the Grands-Jours in the bailliage of Bresse.[77]

Ordinary people resented the distance they had to travel to plead their cases before the local seigneurial court. In the *cahiers de doléances* of northern Burgundy one of the most frequent demands concerning seigneurial justice is that the court sit in the village. Some villages even went so far as to demand a resident *procureur d'office* in the village to maintain order more effectively. We will see that the Parlement of Dijon brought in reforms that significantly increased the number of cases tried at the annual assizes (in the village) and was working to bring justice closer to the village, but even in the 1780s a substantial proportion of the judge's work took place in town rather than in the village. The suggestion put forth in *cahiers* that all judicial acts could be carried out in the village was, however, highly impractical. Almost all villages were far too small to support full-time officers, and the result would have been to diminish significantly the quality of the justice they received. The distance they had to walk to see their seigneurial judge was the price for having a legal professional as judge.

Judicial Incomes

Judges, prosecutors, and clerks generally did not get rich by abusing their authority, but how much money could they expect to make legitimately from their work? Judicial incomes are difficult to reconstruct, but it seems certain that they were always inadequate, and sometimes derisory. Other than in exceptionally large justices, it was impossible for an officer to make a living from one court. The oaths in Arnay-le-Duc and the list in the *Almanach* support this, with most officers accumulating several offices. In the bailliage of Dijon, 129 people filled 273 offices, an average of 2.1 offices per officer. In 1780 46 percent of seigneurial officers in the bailliage of Dijon worked more than one court, while 51 percent of judges in Arnay-le-Duc accumulated several offices over the eighteenth century. The accumulation of judicial offices was facilitated by the fact that most cases in most seigneurial courts were tried in the seat of the bailliage.

Judicial officers needed to accumulate several offices because their income from a single seigneurial court was insufficient. They received money from two main sources: annual salaries and legal fees. Annual salaries were always insufficient, often amounting to less than 10 livres. General leases of the seigneurie of Montot noted the wages the leaseholder paid the judicial officers: in 1777 the judge, *procureur d'office,* and clerk received annual wages of 7, 5, and 3 livres respectively.[78] A lease of the seigneurie of Foncegrive to Aubin Ladey in 1741 provided for only 10 livres of annual wages for all three officers combined.[79] Only in exceptionally large justices might the officers receive a decent wage; in the barony of Pagny, for example, in 1785 the judge received 500 livres from the lord, and the lieutenant and prosecutor were each paid 300 livres.[80] Jean Finot, a lawyer and judge from Semur-en-Auxois, was exceptionally busy, accumulating as many as a dozen seigneurial judgeships during the 1770s and 1780s. He made on average a total of about 100 livres a year from his judicial salaries, with amounts for individual seigneurial courts varying from 3 to 109 livres per year.[81]

Of course, officers had other sources of income than the pittance they received annually from the seigneur or the general *fermier.* Litigants and those accused of minor crimes paid legal fees when they received their final judgments. The final judgment in civil cases invariably ended with these words: "and to pay the costs of the court case, summarily evaluated by me at [amount to be paid]." These legal fees could be considerable, averaging in regular session over 15 livres. These amounts, however, were not paid to the officers in regular, summary cases. Even in the small number of cases tried using written, nonsummary procedure, not all of the fees paid by litigants went into the officers' coffers. Much of it went to the central government in the form of paper taxes—at least half in major cases tried using nonsummary procedure, according to an anonymous pamphlet from 1788. Are judges to be blamed, the author asks rhetorically, "if the rapacity of *la finance* has overburdened judicial procedure with fees, such as paper taxes, stamp taxes, *contrôle,* fines, *sols pour livre?*"[82]

Judges received money for their work only in nonsummary cases—civil cases involving unusually large amounts of money and criminal cases. Supervising the nomination of experts, deposing witnesses, interrogating the criminally accused, and carrying out judicial auctions were all paid actions of the court. Judges might also be paid a few livres for holding the annual assizes. The most significant source of income for most judges, though, was their participation in probate justice, not only because of the amounts charged but because of the relatively high number of family assemblies to nominate guardians. There were also occasionally *épices* paid judges in nonsummary cases. Even adding all of this together, however, the amounts were small. Jean Finot made an average of about 10 livres a year from legal fees in each of the seigneurial courts over which he sat as judge, although in some courts he made considerably more.[83] We can assume that for an average-sized seigneurial court it would be exceptional for a judge to make more than 100 livres a year—indeed, 50 livres is almost certainly above what most judges made in most seigneurial courts.

Like judges, both *procureurs d'office* and clerks needed to accumulate several offices and remain active in another legal profession (*procureur* in a royal court or notary) to make a living. The fact that clerkships were the only seigneurial office that was frequently leased suggests that clerks may have made more money than either judges or prosecutors. *Procureurs d'office* likely made less money than either judges or clerks. The report prepared by the *procureurs* of the bailliage of Dijon and sent to the parlement to complain of significant reductions in the income of *procureurs* contains several paragraphs specifically about the situation of *procureurs d'office* in seigneurial courts, and is worth citing at length:

> Of all the offices that administer justice, it is without contradiction that of *procureurs d'office* that requires the most respect relative to their functions, which are almost entirely unpaid. They are paid nothing to assist at the audiences, nothing to examine documents that are communicated to them . . . they are paid nothing to exercise *la police,* they are charged to execute freely all of the *arrêts de règlements* of the Court [Parlement] . . . they must correspond incessantly with the *syndics* of the community and with the *messiers* or other local officials, to maintain order.

Probate justice was a more important source of revenue for *procureurs d'office* than for judges, since by the second half of the eighteenth century judges were forbidden from participating in judicial auctions and probate inventories to save money for clients of the courts. "It is only in probate justice that they are accorded rights according to the procedural acts they draw up, but these rights are reduced to almost nothing." The complaints end: "if the *procureur d'office* received wages according to his efforts and care . . . they [the community of *procureurs*] would request no other payments, but he receives nothing other than an amount for the single day he spends at the annual assizes . . . and this is his salary for exercising *la police* and justice throughout the entire year."[84] No judge, prosecutor, or clerk could have lived from the income provided by a single court. An anonymous pamphlet in 1788 asked readers: "set your eyes on all classes of society, will you find one whose fortunes are less rapid and less considerable than amongst those who give themselves to the trying of cases?"[85] Jérôme Pétion de Villeneuve complained in 1782 that lords paid their cooks and coachmen more than they paid their judges.[86]

While the position of seigneurial judge was not a way to get rich, it is nevertheless worth emphasizing that seigneurial judges could make a decent living by seeking nominations in several seigneurial justices and by maintaining a busy law practice. This underlines the importance of the fact that judges generally heard cases in town rather than in the village. In small courts judges generally heard no more than one or two cases at a single session, and if they were to travel to the village, they would lose a day's work each time they had to hear a case. Absenteeism allowed seigneurial judges to reserve a day of the week for judging cases in several courts and to devote the rest of their week to other pursuits such as the practice of law or minor administrative functions in a small city.

Seigneurial judges were part-time professionals, and it is likely that almost all made most of their income from other sources. Jean Finot, of Semur-en-Auxois, made an average of about 250 livres a year from his work as seigneurial judge in nearly a dozen justices from 1770 to the Revolution, with a steady increase each year as his career advanced. But he made a great deal more money from his law practice–more than 1,000 livres a year. Furthermore, in 1779 he managed to have himself named as agent for Chartraire de Montigny, one of the most powerful lords of the province. His salary started at approximately 500 livres a year plus travel expenses, but in 1781 it rose to 3,000 livres per year.[87]

The case of Jean Finot makes clear the ways a young lawyer's work as seigneurial judge could facilitate his insertion into legal and seigneurial networks. In Toulouse fully half of the *avocats* who presented cases in the royal court of the *sénéchaussée* worked as seigneurial judges.[88] Litigants seeking counsel to defend or prosecute a case in royal justice might ask the local legal *practicien* for assistance, and they would be most likely to suggest a lawyer they had met as judge in a seigneurial court. Lords seeking legal counsel on questions of seigneurial law or looking to hire a *feudiste* to redo a *terrier* would prefer someone who had practical experience in such questions.

Economic motivations were doubtless important in the decision to seek out positions as judge in order to make important connections to potential clients and patrons. It would be excessively cynical, however, to dismiss the notion that lawyers sought out the office of judge in order to serve the cause of justice. René Pichot de la Graverie was a judge in the very large seigneurial court of the city of Laval from 1745 to 1764. In his unpublished writings he emphasized the centrality of the law to human affairs and the greatness of the professions of judge and lawyer.[89] It is interesting that although Jean Finot stopped working as a lawyer when he started earning 3,000 livres a year as agent for Chartraire de Montigny, he nevertheless remained active as seigneurial judge despite the relatively low income it provided him and the fact that his reputation was likely already established. While lawyers did undoubtedly seek to enrich themselves, it is also likely that their socialization into the profession predisposed many to seek out judgeships for altruistic reasons.

Conclusion

To us today, the judicial system of the ancien régime may seem almost impossibly complicated, as it did to many enlightened legal theorists.[90] The location of local courts owed more to centuries of seigneurial domination than to rational principles of population density or geography. Some villages were split between two or more seigneurial courts, sometimes even between two bailliages, as in the case of Chazilly-le-Haut and Chazilly-le-Bas, two hamlets under the same seigneurial court but within the jurisdiction of two different royal appeal courts (the bailliages of Beaune and Arnay-le-Duc).[91] Furthermore, most courts were impractically small, with a single small parish within their jurisdiction. The five to ten cases per year that courts judged annually in regular session were not enough to keep a judge, prosecutor, and clerk busy for even part of the year.

It is perhaps not surprising that many historians of seigneurial justice have criticized the system as abusive and concluded that it must have been becoming increasingly irrelevant during the century of Enlightenment. The multiplication of so many small courts certainly could have had the two negative effects that many historians thought to have found, namely, that peasants gave up on a judicial system they could not understand, and that there were not enough competent judges to staff so many courts. In northern Burgundy, however, as this chapter has demonstrated, the situation was rather different. Peasants knew with certainty what court had jurisdiction over them. Almost all courts were admittedly too small to support educated and competent judicial officers, but this did not mean that lords instead found uneducated, illiterate, greedy, and incompetent judges, prosecutors, and clerks. Instead, university-trained lawyers accumulated several seigneurial courts and judged competently while maintaining an active legal practice. The only real problem was that villagers had to travel to get justice. Whether this actually discouraged peasants, who were accustomed to walking great distances for myriad reasons, from going to court, remains a question that can only be answered by examining the cases heard in the seigneurial courts of northern Burgundy.

Chapter 2

Justice in the Interests of Lords

I have been occupied with reading all of the papers of those who have held this position over the past three centuries, to enlighten myself of all the rights attached to your barony, so that in the event that your Highness grants me the favor of this office, I will be in a condition by my own knowledge to maintain all your rights, to which I will give all my attention so that nothing is done contrary to your interests.

–Letter from a lawyer to the baron of Pagny, seeking to be named judge in the barony, 1727

Judges, prosecutors, and clerks in seigneurial courts were trained professionals who understood the law. The problem with seigneurial courts was not that the officers that ran them were unqualified but that they were employees of a lord. Before hiring a judge, *procureur d'office,* or clerk, a lord would need to be assured that he would work hard to protect his rights. While court cases involving the seigneur or one of his representatives always formed a small proportion of cases that seigneurial judges heard, the lord's judicial officers nevertheless played an integral role in the maintenance of the seigneurial system. Seigneurial justice efficiently and relatively cheaply protected the interests of lords. Judges, *procureurs d'office,* and clerks participated actively in the running of the seigneurie, on their own initiative seeking out peasants who had failed to pay.

Was Justice Profitable for Lords?

In 1785 the seminary of Autun described its seigneurie as being made up of dues, rights, and "a justice whose exercise is as expensive as it is difficult."[1] Historians have discussed the question of whether seigneurial justice was economically profitable for lords, and most have concluded that seigneurial justice either barely paid for itself or cost most lords a modest amount of money to run.[2] If we calculate the direct revenue and costs associated with seigneurial justice in northern Burgundy, we see similarly that most lords could at best only hope to break even through the direct exercise of the right of justice. But this does not mean that lords tried to rid themselves of the onerous obligation of justice, since the indirect benefits that accrued to the seigneur made the institution well worth preserving even if it cost a few livres a year to maintain.

The list of expenses in a seigneurial court was not large. Leases of seigneuries commonly enumerated the expenses, since the *fermier général* had to pay them. Generally there were three kinds of costs for lords: judicial salaries, the annual assizes, and the administration of criminal justice. We have already seen that the wages the seigneur or his *fermier général* paid to the officers were minimal, often under 10 livres for simple single-village justices. Lords had to pay the costs of the annual assizes, but this was not a substantial expense: in the village of Montot the assizes cost the *fermier* 18 livres, to fetch the officers in town and bring them to the village and to put them up in an inn if more than one day was required.[3] So the combined cost of the officers' wages and the annual Grands-Jours in most modest-sized seigneurial courts can be generously estimated at between 50 and 100 livres.

By far the greatest single expense was criminal justice. The cost was so great that it sometimes became a hindrance to the pursuit of criminals; the 1772 reform of criminal procedure stated: "[W]e have considered that the fees involved in the pursuit of crimes committed within a seigneurial justice, were for high-justice lords a heavy charge, and sometimes a means to encourage impunity."[4] In 1765 the Parlement of Dijon rebuked the judge of Rougemont for deciding a major criminal case without traveling to the village, adding a reminder of the obligation of judges to "transport themselves in person into the place of the crime and to draw up reports in all cases of homicides, murders, fires and home break-ins."[5] In 1764, despairing that his brother's murder was going unpunished due to the negligence of the officers of the seigneurial justice of Pasilly, Claude Gobley wrote to the controller general in Paris. The royal intendant investigated the charge and decided that the case should be heard in the bailliage due to the negligence of the seigneurial officers.[6]

Lords sometimes had good reason to be wary of the expenses of criminal justice. In 1769 the clerk of the barony of Pagny sent the lord a summary of the costs of a single criminal trial against André Truchart and consorts. This trial for wood theft from the seigneurial forest cost the seigneurie 865 livres 16 sols 10 deniers: 139 livres for the initial civil trial (the case was "converted" from civil to criminal); 458 livres for the time of the officers, witnesses, and experts; 21 livres of executory fees including stamp tax and other royal paper taxes; and 247 livres paid to the arresting police officers and prison guards.[7] Still, while major crimes were expensive to prosecute, most courts heard few of them. In 1759 the clerk of the barony of Pagny sent the lord a list of all the expenses of criminal cases from 1749 to 1753. The twenty-two criminal cases heard in this large seigneurial court over five years cost 889 livres.[8] But even 200 livres a year must be considered exceptionally high, as most medium-sized seigneurial courts rarely judged major crimes of the kind for which lords had to pay.[9]

In northern Burgundy lords did not have to build prisons or courthouses. During their trials, suspects were held at the expense of the seigneur in the nearest royal or municipal prison. Almost half of the accused criminals imprisoned in the bailliage prisons of Beaune and Arnay-le-Duc in the late eighteenth century were there at the request of a seigneurial judge (73 out of 153).[10] An administrative report from 1791 found only one seigneurial prison in the district of Châtillon-sur-Seine: "there is a prison in Leignes belonging to the Madame of Louvois, ex-Dame of Leignes, as possessor of high, middle and low justice. It consists of a small building, humid, unhealthy and in poor upkeep."[11] Most seigneurial courts in northern Burgundy met outdoors or in the home of a resident, when they met in the village at all.[12] The legal author Méllenet noted that in Burgundy "we tolerate that village judges hold their audiences in private homes . . . as long as they abstain from hearing cases in pubs, in seigneurial houses, in the church, and in the cemetery."[13]

For most lords in late eighteenth-century northern Burgundy, therefore, the costs of seigneurial justice were minimal. For an average-sized court covering a parish or two, the total costs of the court, including wages of the officers, the cost of criminal cases, and the Grands-Jours, were almost certainly less than 200 livres a year. Still, this was more money than most took in through the lease of the clerkship, the only real source of direct revenue from the daily running of the court. Considering direct revenue as the only benefit of seigneurial justice to the lord, then, in northern Burgundy as in Brittany, most seigneurs probably broke about even or lost a small amount of money.

Still, the benefit of seigneurial justice to a lord involved more than just the money to be made from the daily running of the court. There were rights and prerogatives attached to high justice. The most important honorary seigneurial right attached to justice was religious privilege. In the local church the high-justice lord and his family were entitled to the place of honor (*banc seigneurial*). This symbolic honor underscored and legitimized the lord's authority by giving him first access to the sacred, emphasizing his paternalism.[14]

There were other seigneurial rights attached to justice, such as confiscation of the goods of people sentenced to physical or civil death, but these were hardly revenue-bearing.[15] A lord could confiscate from a criminal who had "scorned the lord's justice" in committing the crime.[16] The right of bastardy entitled the high-justice lord to inherit from any illegitimate sons or daughters who died without children and had not made a will.[17] Bastardy was a right seldom exercised. There are examples of confiscation, as in the life sentence in the galleys for Benoist Bastien for breaking and entering.[18] But most criminals were poor, and confiscation would almost never offset the costs of the criminal prosecution.

High-justice lords also had rights over the land in their jurisdictions.[19] The right of *épaves* meant that the lord became the owner of any unclaimed farm animals in the village, any unclaimed goods left in a public place, and a third of any buried treasure found.[20] Finally, high-justice lords were the only people entitled to hunt or fish within the seigneurie. These high-justice seigneurial rights over the land resulted from an interesting legal fiction, namely that the owners of the land were entitled only to the result of their labor on the land. Gifts of nature and goods for which the author of the labor was unknown belonged to the seigneur. Hunting and fishing, the harvest of nature's abundance, were the prerogative not of the landowner but of the man responsible to see justice carried out in the village. Even rainwater, when flowing in the streets, belonged to the lord. "Lords," wrote Boutaric, "would have wanted the rain to fall only for them; and if they have not taken the water that falls on the head and land of the poor peasant," it was not for lack of effort.[21] Effectively, then, the right of justice included the right to police or control nature.[22] But this control of nature brought little money into the coffers of these lords. It was, of course, extremely rare for an animal to go unclaimed in a village. When one did, it was sometimes because the animal was diseased; the exercise of this right could thus be more onerous than profitable.[23] Fishing rights in nonnavigable rivers were nominally remunerative, since generally leased to the highest bidder, as in the case of Messigny where the lord got 45 livres in 1788.[24]

The income from hunting was of a different kind. Most experts agreed that hunting was a personal seigneurial right, one that the lord could not lease, give, or loan to another.[25] Furthermore, lords without the right of high justice were, most experts agreed, not allowed to hunt even on their own land.[26] In 1786 the seigneurial court of Belleneuve fined six men 20 livres each. They were hunting within the high justice of Belleneuve, but on the land of the dames Bernardines, a religious order with a non-justice fief in the village. The fact that the men had the permission of the nuns probably helped them get a lower fine, but the judge warned them never to repeat the offense, "on threat of being taken as poachers and devastators following the rigors of the ordinances and *arrêts*."[27] Because hunting was not a right lords could sell or lease, the only income it generated was the fines assessed against poachers, hardly significant amounts–about ten cases in the sample, with fines ranging from about 10 to about 100 livres.

Seigneurial justice cost lords slightly more money to run than the direct revenue they received from the court. Indirect revenue from the rights attached to justice was no higher. Confiscation, *épaves,* bastardy, hunting, and fishing–together these provided minimal income for northern Burgundian seigneurs. This does not mean, however, that paternalism was the main reason the institution survived, or that lords' behavior was economically irrational when they maintained their local courts in activity. As other historians of seigneurial justice have argued, the small amounts of money that it likely cost to run a seigneurial court were amply compensated by the role played by the judge, *procureur d'office,* and clerk in the daily running of the seigneurie.[28]

The Personal Involvement of Lords in the Running of the Courts

The reason that lords were determined to protect their right of justice was that they could use their courts as a means of enforcing and collecting seigneurial dues. Seigneurial courts provided lords with an inexpensive and rapid way of suing peasants who failed to fulfill their seigneurial obligations. More importantly, the officers of seigneurial courts were diligent to protect the seigneurial and property rights of the lords who had hired them, corresponding regularly with them, initiating lawsuits, and levying fines on behalf of the seigneur. Judges, prosecutors, and clerks in seigneurial courts were active and effective defenders of the seigneurial regime.

There is an obvious conflict of interest in allowing lords to use their own courts to sue their peasants. But the law placed a significant limitation on lords' use of their own courts. The seigneurial judge was, according to the civil procedural reform of 1667, entitled to hear "all that involves [the lord's] demesne, rights and revenues, in fiefs as in ordinary land [tant en fiefs que rotures de la terre]."[29] Any other cases involving the lord were to be taken to the relevant royal court; a lord suing a villager to collect land rent would have to take the case to the bailliage, but he could take the same villager before the seigneurial court to collect seigneurial dues. The reason for this distinction is that the law saw the seigneurial system as a kind of public authority, such that failure to give the lord what was due him was in fact a kind of rebellion, a threat to the lord's authority.

Many northern Burgundian lords resided on their estates only during the summer months and had to rely heavily on various agents the rest of the year. The role of the seigneurial intendant in administering the seigneurie has been described, most notably by Robert Forster, but the importance of the judge, prosecutor, and clerk has been insufficiently emphasized.[30] In the ancien régime royal judges performed both judicial and executive functions. This is equally true of seigneurial judicial officers, who not only sued recalcitrant peasants in the interests of lords but also actively administered and collected many seigneurial dues and rights. It was, therefore, important that a lord nominate officers who knew the law and would be diligent to protect his interests. In 1727 a lawyer wrote to the baron of Pagny asking that he be appointed by the lord to replace his recently deceased brother. He had carefully gone through his brother's papers, he says, "to enlighten myself of all the rights attached to your barony, so that in the event that your Highness grants me the favor of this office, I will be in a condition by my own knowledge to maintain all your rights, to which I will give all my attention so that nothing is done contrary to your interests."[31] In 1737 the judge of Corberon wrote to the lord to suggest a replacement for the deceased *procureur d'office.* The judge's nephew, DeBays, though not yet a notary, was a capable young man. Furthermore, family ties would make it easier for the judge to force him to act in the lord's interest. There were other candidates, but over them, the judge said, "I doubtless will not have as much authority to make them act with zeal in all that could interest you."[32]

It was important that lords be able to trust their officers in matters concerning the seigneurie, but lords were not content simply to leave matters in the officers' hands. Letters between lords and seigneurial judges, prosecutors, and clerks demonstrate that lords were active in their control of their courts, and that the courts were active in overseeing the seigneurie. Because such letters were the private property of the lord and his officers, when they were not destroyed over the intervening centuries they remained in private archives until donated to the Departmental Archives. Correspondence such as this therefore exists for only a small number of seigneuries, hidden among thousands of uninventoried letters. But every seigneurial court studied heard many cases involving the lord. The dame of Meursault, for example, sued Jean Lallé and Joseph Marnet in 1785 for damages they committed in the seigneurial forest.[33] The *procureur d'office* must have forwarded to her the report of the forest guard, after which she initiated the lawsuit. Multiple examples of this kind could be given for every court, suggesting that the correspondence that survives for a few seigneuries originally existed for almost all, demonstrating that lords knew what was going on both in court and in the village and wrote to advise, reprimand, cajole, praise, and criticize their officers.[34]

Most correspondence was concerned with issues that affected a lord's authority or income. These included farming and forest offenses, police offenses, and criminal cases. In 1764 the *procureur d'office* of Thenissey sent a summary of the records he had sent over the past two years, almost exclusively lists of fines handed out for villagers stealing from the lord's forest or pasturing illegally in village fields.[35] In the barony of Pagny, the *procureur d'office* sent a letter to the lord each time the forest guard caught villagers or animals in the seigneurial forest.[36] Letters describing the fines collected by the court were the most common type of communication that took place between lords and their officers, since they indicated how well the court was protecting the lord's fields, forests, and rights.

Procureurs d'office actively advised lords and took action on their behalf. In 1781, for example, the *procureur d'office* wrote the baron of Pagny and complained that people too often appealed their fines to the bailliage. Since the seigneurial officers defaulted at the bailliage, villagers could thereby escape paying their fines. The *procureur d'office* asked permission to pursue the appeals, so that "the delinquents, fearing your power still more, will become more timid."[37] He went on to suggest that, instead of trying offenses against the lord as police matters, they should pursue the cases civilly, which would also allow the judge to sentence the defendant to pay the court costs, saving the lord money.[38] It is suggestive that in the village of Saffres when the inhabitants got together to demand that the lord show them evidence that they really owed him certain seigneurial dues, they first went to the *procureur d'office,* who then communicated the request to the lord.[39]

On one hand, because lords were in constant direct communication with their judicial officers, they heard when the court convicted people for criminal offenses, when villagers disturbed public order, and when inhabitants trespassed in seigneurial forest and field. In normal civil cases, on the other hand, lords left the judicial officers alone to decide cases according to the law; the correspondence between lords and their judicial officers suggests that lords had little influence over regular civil cases.

Judicial officers occasionally resisted the authority of the seigneur who had hired them. In 1777 the seigneurial agent of Agencourt wrote to the lord. He wanted to proceed judicially against some villagers who had begun their own grape harvest on the first day after the opening of the harvest, a day reserved exclusively for the lord's harvest. But the judge and prosecutor refused to proceed with the case, and the agent reminded the lord that "the judge and *procureur d'office* behaved themselves badly against our *fermier* last year at the Jours."[40] He wanted to have the lord fire the officers, but was cautious because of their legal connections and their reputation as "very rancorous people."[41] There is some evidence that both lawyers and *procureurs* may have resented the authority that the seigneur had over them when they worked as seigneurial judges and prosecutors. The *cahier de doléances* of the community of lawyers of Beaune, as well as those of the communities of *procureurs* and royal notaries (the same people who sat as the seigneurial judges, prosecutors, and clerks), all demanded that seigneurial judges not hear any cases involving the interests of the lord.[42] However much a few leading lawyers, *procureurs,* and notaries may have disliked the mixture of private authority and justice, it is nevertheless clear that most judicial officers were effective servants of the lord. And no matter how much a few judges and even prosecutors may sometimes have resented seigneurial control, the possibility of destitution and the availability of more pliable judges and *procureurs d'office* effectively gave seigneurs the upper hand in any power struggles of this sort.

The Daily Practice of Seigneurialism in the Courts

Lords and prosecutors initiated lawsuits against peasants in all seigneurial courts studied. Of a total of 3,429 cases heard in these courts in the 1750s and in the 1780s, in both regular session and in the Grands-Jours, 267 (7.8 percent) involved the lord or his representative as plaintiff. Regular session cases involving lords made up about 10 percent of all cases (194 out of 1,972 cases). Only a minor proportion of cases involved the lord or his representative, which reinforces the argument that seigneurial justice worked primarily to allow village communities to regulate themselves, enforcing norms that most ordinary people agreed with. Northern Burgundian lords nevertheless used their courts more frequently than lords did in most other parts of France.[43]

Lords and their agents sued ordinary people over a variety of offenses, which is not surprising when we consider that seigneurial authority was multifaceted, extending over individuals, families, communities, and their land. The most important category of cases involving the lord was offenses committed by villagers in seigneurial forests and fields. These cases were divided almost evenly between wood or grass theft and illegal pasturing.[44] Interestingly, in Jean Nicolas's sample of revolts and popular disturbances from 1661 to 1789, the most common popular violence against lords also involved disputes over land and rights, which became especially prevalent after 1760.[45] There would have been still more of this kind of court case, but for the organized efforts of villagers to outwit the forest guard. They posted sentries who called out to alert woodcutters that the guard was approaching. In Senailly the prosecutor complained that "the vigilance of the guard is insufficient to discover the perpetrators due to the precautions they take to watch him and to inform the delinquents by signals when he approaches the forest."[46] In Billey on one occasion the inhabitants did more than notify each other that the guards were coming. After two forest guards caught Claude Grivault cutting wood in the seigneurial forest with an ax, they arrested him (his two accomplices escaped), but a mob of women, headed by the parish priest, came out to stop them from continuing their rounds. When the case came to court, the village closed ranks against the court, providing alibis for the women and the priest.[47] Lords' enforcement of their property rights in forest and field was one of the least popular forms of seigneurial authority, as well as one of the most significant ways in which seigneurial courts worked to the advantage of lords.[48]

Seigneurial guards also caught villagers hunting and fishing, both violations of seigneurial prerogatives. The guards patrolled the forests looking for animal traps, for villagers with guns, and for other evidence of hunting. As with wood theft, people got to know the forester's schedule and could outwit him. Hunting and especially fishing were common practices, but prosecution was much rarer than for wood theft. According to the royal ordinance of 1669, judges were to hand out 100-livre fines for first-time poachers. Those caught a second time were to be fined 100 livres again, and the third time they were to be put in stocks in the public square for three hours and then banished from the parish for three years.[49] But judges rarely came down this hard on hunters, generally choosing to "moderate" the fine to far less than 100 livres, and never banishing recidivist hunters. Fishing was easier to police than hunting, given the more sedentary nature of the activity. But lords and their guards generally tolerated unlicensed fishing in the many streams that ran through the countryside; most of the small number of fines handed down involved people fishing instead of attending Sunday Mass or other such special circumstances.

Seigneurial justice was an important tool in maintaining a lord's control over the purchase and sale of property in the village by enforcing the twin rights of *retrait féodal* and *lods et ventes*. *Retrait féodal* meant that, so long as he acted within a year and a day of a land sale, a lord could force the buyer of any land to sell to him at the price he had paid. *Lods et ventes* was a seigneurial tax that all buyers of land in the village had to pay the lord. The rate varied by seigneurie–in Fontaine-en-Duesmois the lord collected *lods et ventes* "à raison du sol par livre," a rate of 5 percent, while in Flée and Allerey the rate was 20 deniers per livre.[50]

Although *retrait féodal* was important as a symbol of the lord's control over land ownership and property transfer, it was not a significant impediment to the land market. In the sample of court cases there are no disputes over *retrait féodal*, and no evidence that the lords exercised this right during the period. The registers of the *contrôle des actes* record all contracts that were subject to the stamp tax, and any use of the right of *retrait féodal* should appear in these registers. In fact, they are very rare. During the year 1783, for example, in the circumscription of Baigneux-les-Juifs, there was not a single case of the exercise of *retrait féodal*.[51] There are occasional references to *retrait féodal* in private seigneurial papers, but few from the late eighteenth century.[52]

Lods et ventes were financially important for northern Burgundian lords, who used their courts extensively to enforce and collect these dues. In most villages the buyer had to report the acquisition of land, not to the lord or his seigneurial intendant but to the clerk of his court. In the village of Senailly the inhabitants reported and paid on 106 land purchases during the 1750s.[53] These land parcels had a total value of 7,936 livres, which at a tax rate of 5 percent brought in 397 livres to the lord. In the smaller village of Aisy-sous-Thil, the reported property transactions totaled 2,398 livres in the 1750s and 4,054 livres in the 1780s.[54]

Seigneurial officers sued villagers who failed to report their transactions and pay the *lods*. A common way for villagers to avoid payment of the *lods et ventes* was to exchange pieces of land, since the tax only applied to cash transactions. Because two pieces of land were rarely exactly equivalent, there was generally a payment of *mieux-valeur,* the difference between the value of the two parcels. The judge of Meursault ordered François Batault to pay 25 livres to the lord on the difference, plus a fine of 3 livres 5 sols for not having reported the exchange.[55] In some cases the *procureur d'office* prosecuted more than one person for not paying. In 1789 in the justice of Senailly the judge fined 28 people 3 livres 5 sols each for not having reported property purchases to the court. These acquisitions of land went back into the 1770s, indicating that in the late 1780s this lord and his officers conducted an investigation into land sales in this village.[56]

Courts helped lords collect other seigneurial dues, such as annual cash payments like the *cens* and the seigneurial *taille* and in-kind payments such as the tithe. There are seventeen cases involving the *cens* among those studied from the 1750s and 1780s, fifteen cases involving the tithe, and six lawsuits involving the seigneurial *taille.* Both the *cens* and the seigneurial *taille* were collected in cash, at rates fixed long before the eighteenth century, and rendered less significant by several centuries of inflation. The amounts that lords received from these dues also varied enormously. In Epagny, for example, the lord annually collected a total of only 6 livres 10 sols in *cens* and 14 livres from the seigneurial *taille.*[57] In many cases the seigneurial *taille* could be much higher, as in Fontaine-en-Duesmois, where the villagers together paid 75 livres annually. The amount in Ampilly-les-Bordes was 60 livres per year.[58] James Collins estimates that within the bailliage of Châtillon-sur-Seine the seigneurial *taille* generally amounted to about 50 livres, although amounts up to 100 livres per year and more were not rare.[59] The cases involving the seigneurial *taille* in the courts studied were sometimes directed against individuals who had not paid, and sometimes against either the community as a whole or the tax collectors who were to collect the seigneurial *taille* at the same time they collected the royal tax of the same name.

Lawsuits over the seigneurial *taille* were comparatively rare, because it was generally collected along with the *taille royale* and paid by the village as a lump sum. In 1784 the *fermier* of Ampilly-les-Bordes sued the *syndics* (elected village officers) for 60 livres, the total amount of seigneurial *taille* owed each year for the whole community. The *syndics* contested the idea that the community as a whole was responsible, claiming instead that, while they were responsible to determine how much each household paid based on the rolls of the royal *taille,* the lord or his agent was then responsible to collect the tax from each individual.[60] Formalized means of collection and the legal fiction of collective responsibility all meant that lawsuits over this due were rare.

Like the seigneurial *taille,* the *cens* varied a great deal, although it seems safe to assume that it was generally lower than the *taille.* In Saulon-la-Chapelle the *cens* added up to a paltry 8 livres per year, but in the tax inquiries of the late seventeenth century some villages paid similar amounts in *cens* as they did in seigneurial *taille*.[61] While the total *cens* paid to the seigneur by all villagers could be considerable, the amounts paid per hearth were relatively low. This explains why lords often sued for payment only after several years of delinquency. Almost all the lawsuits over *cens* involved arrears of at least ten years, and often as many as twenty-nine years, the legal maximum,[62] as in 1785 when the judge of Meursault sentenced Jean Baptiste Ginot to pay 147 livres 17 sols of arrears in *cens*.[63]

In northern Burgundy many lords also possessed a seigneurial tithe, the right to collect a fixed proportion of the harvest. Where it existed, the seigneurial tithe was one of the most profitable of all seigneurial dues. In Epagny, for example, the *terrier* stated that the lord was entitled to a twelfth of all grains harvested, including wheat, barley, oats, and legumes. He also collected one-twenty-fourth of wine produced when the grapes were pressed on the communal press, and one-sixteenth when they were not, as well as a tithe of all newborn lambs.[64] In Allerey the seigneur collected a tithe of 3 percent on all grains and legumes.[65] The seigneurial tithe varied by seigneurie, and often the rate was different within the seigneurie. In Montot, for example, land in the *lieu-dit* known as *les fins de Tonge* paid a tithe of one-fifteenth, whereas the rest of the seigneurie paid only one-thirtieth of the harvest.[66] These tithes were generally not true seigneurial dues, but rather the classic ecclesiastical tax that had been purchased by the seigneur on condition that he pay a salary to the parish priest. The *champart,* a theoretically distinct right, could sometimes also be referred to as a seigneurial tithe, a fact that further complicates matters.[67] Lawsuits involving the seigneurial tithe were relatively infrequent because of the formal means of collection and the prohibition on moving grain from field to barn until the tithe had been paid. Harvesting or carting grain after dark was illegal, and the act carried with it the assumption of the intent to defraud the tithe collector. Pierre Languereau in 1783 was fined 30 sols for having "removed and carted a load of wheat" after the sun went down.[68]

Many lords in the province possessed the right of *tierce,* which entitled them to a significant proportion of the harvest on some land, generally a ninth, although it could be as low as a fifteenth and as high as a fifth.[69] The right often applied to common land that had been converted to arable, but it could equally apply to land that had been recovered and cleared by individuals over previous centuries.[70] Suits over the *tierce* were not common in the courts studied. The only instance was when Jean Labbé, *fermier général* of the seigneurie of Flée, complained to the court that many inhabitants hid their sheaves of wheat to hinder him from collecting. He added that unknown inhabitants had even stolen some of the proceeds of the *tierce* from his barns.[71] It is unclear why there were not more cases involving the *tierce,* although it may be because it applied to less land and fewer peasants than most of the other seigneurial dues and rights discussed herein.

Forced work duties, or seigneurial corvées, were among the most important of seigneurial rights. Collected in kind, they had not diminished in value with monetary inflation. The number of days that a lord was entitled to collect varied from none to six, with three days per year being the most common.[72] In the villages of Bellefond, Billey, and Villerrottin the corvée amounted to only one day per year, whereas in Ancey the inhabitants owed three days of free work per household per year.[73] Households headed by *laboureurs* owed corvées of plowing or carting, while others provided manual labor, working for the lord or his *fermier général* during the planting and especially the harvest. In wine villages the villagers worked for the lord to bring in the grape harvest, which was made simpler by the fact that most lords had the right to start their *vendanges* one day before the inhabitants. Court cases over *corvées* were not frequent in the courts studied, with five such cases over the twenty years analyzed. Interestingly, four of the five cases were from the 1780s, and only one was from the 1750s. While the sample is too small to conclude definitively, it could be that more peasants sought ways to avoid their forced work duty by the last decades of the eighteenth century. The fact that the entire community worked on the same day no doubt made it difficult to escape the *corvée*, however, and the very small number of such cases indicates the vast majority of northern Burgundian peasants remained subject to this seigneurial right.

Lords and *procureurs d'office* frequently sued peasants over more than one kind of due or right at a time, as was the case in thirty-eight of the ninety-two lawsuits over seigneurial dues. These lawsuits were frequently an attempt to take advantage of change in the life of the vassal. When a vassal died, for example, the lord might sue the new heir for twenty-nine years' worth of dues, forcing him or her to provide proof that the deceased had paid all his seigneurial dues over the past twenty-nine years. In 1785 Jean Jobard, Jean Laplanche, and Jean Baptiste Batault were able to show receipts to the judge proving that they had paid their "rentes, cens et *redevances*."[74] In 1759, by contrast, the recently widowed Françoise Leclerc Saulx and her son were unable to produce receipts proving that her husband had paid his dues, so the court ordered her to pay twenty-six years of a *cens* of oats, an annual chicken, and several other annual payments in grain.[75]

Seigneurial milling and baking monopolies (*banalités*) also provoked lawsuits. Many lords possessed the right to monopolize these two processes, and a few had monopolies over the pressing of grapes to make wine. An eighteenth-century seigneurial *manuel* from Meursault noted that the lord owned an oven where "the inhabitants are obliged to bring their dough and to pay the fee to the *fermiers* . . . of a twentieth part of the dough."[76] Accompanying these various seigneurial monopolies was the right to take a proportion of the wheat, dough, or wine, a tax that often came to about 5 percent, although the amounts varied.[77] Lords never exercised these monopolies personally, choosing instead to lease the rights to enterprising villagers.[78]

Banalités were partly a form of public service.[79] The seigneur effectively agreed to ensure that villagers had access to an oven, a mill, or a wine press. The price of this guarantee was the proportion of the flour, dough, or wine that people produced. Most seigneuries with a village oven heated it once a week, which was probably about as often as people wanted to bake bread. By the late eighteenth century it is clear that these seigneurial rights/responsibilities caused considerable inconvenience to many inhabitants. Using the seigneurial flour mill sometimes meant paying more for the service, and people also complained that the millers stole wheat from them. In one case the mill in the village shut down for much of the summer due to falling water levels, but the miller still tried to force the villagers to wait until the water rose instead of taking their wheat elsewhere.[80] The main disadvantages with the seigneurial grape presses were the possibility of contamination of the must, either from other grape varieties or from bacterial growth caused by inadequate cleaning.

In some seigneuries the monopolies had fallen into disuse, though where they still existed the local seigneurial courts enforced them with vigor. Pierre de Saint Jacob suggests that lords sometimes abandoned the communal oven, since they had to provide the wood to fire it, which became increasingly onerous as the price of wood rose in the eighteenth century. But lords did not often give up their rights over the mill or the press, which were generally more profitable.[81] Where the right survived, the officers of the local seigneurial court frequently conducted annual visits of each house to ensure that there were no private ovens. In August 1789 the judge fined Charles Macherat for not letting the *échevin* of the community into his home to inspect his chimney and search for an oven, evidence that here the court forced the village to police itself for ovens.[82] In 1782 the judge of Fontaine-en-Duesmois fined Nicolas Berthelemet 50 livres for having built a bread oven.[83] Both ovens and grape presses were impossible to hide, and carting loads of flour and grain to a mill in another village could hardly go unnoticed.

Seigneurial *banalités* provided a kind of public service, but other seigneurial rights were more overtly exploitative. The seigneurial right of *mainmorte,* particular to the county and duchy of Burgundy (Burgundy and Franche-Comté), limited the ability of peasants to pass on their property. The lord inherited from any *mainmortable* who died with no direct descendant living communally with him or her. Some results of this, predictably, were that extended families were more common in villages of *mainmorte,* that marriage contracts in these villages more often contained clauses establishing a community between the new couple and one set of parents, and that more property changed hands before death–all ways of trying to get around the *mainmorte* restrictions.[84] Jean Bart shows that this seigneurial right did not disappear or become less harsh in the late eighteenth century. Despite a few high-profile manumissions, most notably by Louis XV, most lords who possessed this right protected it jealously.[85]

Not all lords possessed this seigneurial right. Jean Bart cites a 1918 estimate by the head archivist of the Côte d'Or that 3,241 of 9,331 parishes in the province of Burgundy were subject to *mainmorte*.[86] Three of the fourteen seigneurial courts studied sat over villages of *mainmorte*.[87] In these three villages there were only two disputes over *mainmorte* in the court records of the 1750s and 1780s. In 1751 Bridot Cornotte, a *laboureur* from Senailly, asked the court to allow him to inherit all of his wife's property. In 1734, he pointed out, they had passed a "mutual and reciprocal bequest" whereby the surviving partner of the marriage would receive all property of the deceased.[88] The judge chose to view this donation as an attempt to defraud the lord of what was legitimately due him: the donation, he wrote, in an uncharacteristic explanation of the reasons behind a decision, had "all the characteristics of a *donation à cause de mort* prohibited by the Custom to folks of *mainmorte*."[89]

The lack of lawsuits over *mainmorte* is evidence of the strength rather than the weakness of this right and emphasizes that peasants were powerless to challenge the seizure of their property under the relevant circumstances. That lords placed a great deal of value on *mainmorte* is indicated in a letter from a lord to his seigneurial agent. The day after the heady night of August 4 when the National Assembly reformed the seigneurial system and abolished *mainmorte,* Chartraire de Montigny was alarmed at the "loss of the right of *mainmorte* that is suppressed without any compensation whatsoever." Montigny wondered if the annual lease of his seigneurie might drop by as much as 1,000 livres and asked his agent to speak to the *fermier* about the matter.[90]

Seigneurial courts played a vital role in administering *mainmorte,* and among the probate records of seigneurial justices where the lord possessed the right there are always several *échutes de mainmorte,* documents that record the seizure of the property to the benefit of the lord. The officers of the court, called in to conduct a probate inventory, would notify the lord that he was entitled to disinherit the family and initiate the seizure. Lords generally did not actually take possession of the property, usually choosing instead to offer the seized estate up for public auction in the village. The judicial officers conducted the auction as well as the seizure, so that lords received the revenue from the exercise of the right with almost no personal involvement. When Claude Beurdeley opposed the seizure of his wife's estate in 1789, he was careful to specify that it was the *procureur d'office,* and not the lord, who was claiming that the estate was subject to *mainmorte*.[91] Certainly lords knew of and approved the seizures, but they heard about them from the judicial officers, who remained in charge of the operation until the end.

The lord of Senailly and St. Germain got 3,936 livres from *échutes de mainmorte* from 1734 to 1775. The fifteen peasants whose heirs were disinherited ranged from Philibert Moreau, who was so poor that nobody came to the auction (the lord gave the goods back to his sons), to Jean Canian the younger, whose estate brought in 2,880 livres.[92] Most of the estates sold for less than 200 livres, suggesting that most *mainmortables* who died with no direct heirs living with them were at the lower end of the village social scale, if not the very poorest. Most often a relative of the deceased got the property, usually for less than its estimated value (and preauction estimates were always conservative, generally about half of the market value), suggesting that villagers did not bid the property up to its market value out of sympathy for the family.[93] Lords must have accepted that their decision to auction the estate meant the family would get the property for less than its value.

Judges, *procureurs d'office,* and clerks were effective administrators of the seigneurie. This fact is amply reflected in the parish *cahiers de doléances* that exist for northern Burgundy. As we will see in chapter 7, these were significantly more positive with respect to seigneurial justice than are *cahiers* from other regions of France, containing frequent requests for the extension of the authority of seigneurial judges. The *cahiers* in northern Burgundy were, however, unanimous in decrying the authority that lords had over the judicial officers. The villagers complained that judges had no choice but to decide in favor of the seigneur. They requested solutions such as allowing the king to name the officers, forbidding seigneurs from firing judges, and requiring that a royal bailliage court hear all cases involving the seigneur. They understood that the right of justice was fundamental to the entire seigneurial system and one of the most important reasons why they could not escape the authority of the lord.

Conclusion

Seigneurial courts in northern Burgundy were not overwhelmed by cases involving the interests of the lord. Small seigneurial courts that sat over one or two villages heard no more than a handful of civil, criminal, and police cases per decade that pitted the lord against his peasants. As we will see in the following chapters, the vast majority of judicial officers' time was spent maintaining order between village inhabitants, protecting their property, ensuring the transfer of property between generations, and policing agriculture.

The small number of court cases over seigneurial dues does not tell the whole story with respect to the role of judicial officers. One of the most important functions of seigneurial justice was to limit the number of lawsuits involving lords. Frequent communication with the *procureur d'office* kept lords up to date about their seigneuries and allowed lords to see that their rights were maintained. Lords used their courts to keep villagers out of their forests and off their land and to collect dues such as the seigneurial tithe, the seigneurial *taille,* the *cens,* the *lods et ventes,* corvées, and *mainmorte.* No doubt the threat of a court case was more important than the number of cases would suggest, especially given that most peasants must have known that they stood little chance of winning a case against the lord in his own court.

Lords who used their own courts to pursue peasants for failing to pay dues or respect their authority could have taken these same cases to the royal court, where, with longer time delays and more procedural formalities, they would likely still have won. The greatest benefit from seigneurial justice for lords was the knowledge of local conditions that their judicial officers could provide them. It is true that most judicial officers lived several hours' walk from the villages, and they often heard cases in town rather than in the village. They nevertheless met with all household heads each year in the assizes, where they would be apprised of most of the major questions and issues involving the village. Their authority over probate justice provided them with knowledge that allowed them to enforce *mainmorte.* Through the farming fines they knew when animals had been seized in the lord's forests and could therefore begin civil proceedings against the villagers for damages. Most officers in seigneurial courts knew what went on in their villages and used that information to ensure that the lord's rights and property were protected. They had, in fact, been hired specifically for that purpose.

The small number of cases involving the seigneur does not mean that the seigneurial system remained popular or widely accepted among the inhabitants of northern Burgundy's villages. While there are incidents of opposition to seigneurs, especially those who sought to impose new burdens on peasants, in northern Burgundy, as in lower Maine, lords generally did not have a great deal of difficulty to "compel their vassals."[94] The fact is, however, that beyond minor resistance techniques of exchanging land rather than selling it, of hiding part of the harvest, of pilfering grass and sticks from the seigneurial forest, and of drawing up inheritance documents that sought to circumvent *mainmorte,* there were few effective ways of opposing the authority of the lord. Any villager who refused to pay a seigneurial due quickly found himself summoned before the local court, ordered to pay, and ultimately threatened with debtors' prison or a judicial seizure of his movable property. As plaintiffs in their own courts, lords were able to use the authority of the judges they had appointed to ensure the survival and economic viability of their seigneurial estates. Faced with such an effective and efficient means of enforcement, nothing short of organized widespread resistance to the seigneurial system had much chance of succeeding.

Chapter 3

Justice in the Interests of the Community

Seigneurial judges helped maintain lordly authority, but this was not their only role. Indeed, fewer than one case in ten directly involved the lord's interests. In a general way the court was responsible to keep the peace in the village and protect both the property and the honor of its clients. The local court continued to play a significant role in administering and policing daily life and local politics in the village. In addition to judicial authority, seigneurial judges had both legislative and executive functions, being responsible to establish norms in the village and to oversee the enforcement of these norms. There were three main ways in which judges intervened without necessarily having been solicited by judicial clients. In probate affairs judges protected the interests of minors and ensured that property went to creditors and heirs. In police matters the court worked to protect village property and rights, kept the peace in the community, and ensured broad participation in local affairs. Finally, in criminal justice courts provided people a means of compensation for theft and redress for physical assaults.

Historians of seigneurial justice have argued paradoxically that by the late eighteenth century the institution was both increasingly moribund and irrelevant and increasingly intrusive and abusive. The importance of seigneurial courts was declining primarily because of state centralization—competition with royal courts and the extension of the authority of the provincial intendants over village affairs. At the same time, however, lords were attempting to increase their revenue and solidify their authority. Seigneurial courts served the needs of ordinary people less and less, and that of lords more and more.[1] There may be some truth to this portrayal of seigneurial justice; Anthony Crubaugh's work suggests that civil caseloads in the Aunis and Saintonge were gradually declining over the eighteenth century while lords were nevertheless using the court to renew their *terriers* and sue their peasants.[2] We have seen that in northern Burgundy the local court was a vital means of enforcing

Parts of this chapter have been published in modified form as "Neighbours before the Court: Crime, Village Communities, and Seigneurial Justice in Northern Burgandy, 1750–1790," *French History* 17, no. 2 (2003): 127–48; and as "La police aux Grand-Jours dans la Bourgogne du nord: Pouvoir des seigneurs ou auto-régulation?" in Brizay, Follain, and Sarrazin, *Les justices de village,* 205–18. I am grateful to Oxford University Press and Presses universitaires de Rennes for permission to reproduce the material here.

seigneurial authority and of administering the seigneurie. The question of a seigneurial reaction is difficult to evaluate and I discuss it in a later chapter, but it is clear that the number of cases involving lords and their agents increased in northern Burgundy as the eighteenth century drew to a close.

For northern Burgundy it is, however, inaccurate to portray seigneurial justice as declining or abusive. The seigneurial court's authority over local political matters, its ability to pursue and convict criminals, and its oversight over property transfer between generations remained central both in terms of the caseloads of seigneurial courts and in terms of the courts' influence over village life. While litigation between individuals was surprisingly common in northern Burgundy, ordinary people came into contact with the local seigneurial court most often through its probate and especially its police activities. Furthermore, in all of these active interventions of the court, it was truly the interests of the court's clients that were paramount–seigneurial judges, prosecutors, and clerks fulfilled their responsibilities with diligence.

Criminal Justice and the Self-Regulating Community

One of the primary functions of a judicial system is to protect people's property, honor, and physical safety by punishing criminal acts. Despite what some historians have claimed, in northern Burgundy the seigneurial courts did so relatively effectively. It is true that the local judge and prosecutor only rarely investigated and pursued criminal cases entirely of their own initiative. Most criminal cases came before the court because the offended party reported it to the clerk, and most criminal cases were prosecuted jointly by the *procureur d'office* and a plaintiff who was seeking reparation. It is also true that in most criminal cases the convicted defendant was sentenced to pay court costs that could be considerable indeed–the seigneur only paid the legal fees for major crimes where there was no plaintiff other than the prosecutor acting as public party. Therefore, villagers who were involved in violent disputes or who suffered a theft of their property at the hands of a neighbor most often managed to settle the matter without going to court, primarily because the costs of criminal justice could be very high. The seigneurial judge nevertheless played an important role in keeping the peace and protecting the property of ordinary people, who trusted the judge to settle these disputes. What is most important is that judges treated violence and minor thefts between neighbors as basically civil affairs, with restitution, a payment for damages, and a small fine being the usual outcome. Seigneurial judges played a vital role in the self-policing of northern Burgundian villages.

Most cases in northern Burgundian seigneurial courts were civil, and of the small percentage of cases that involved crimes, most were minor.[3] The local court generally pursued criminal cases only because the victim asked it to. Ordinary people were willing to use the courts to arbitrate their violent disputes over honor and property because they were largely satisfied with the job their judges did. Procedure in the seigneurial courts of northern Burgundy remained oral, simple, and within the grasp of ordinary people, and the courts processed cases relatively quickly.

The most important factor in explaining recourse to the local seigneurial court in criminal affairs is that the judges basically left the plaintiff in charge of the case. Most cases came to the attention of the court only because a participant to the event called it in as arbitrator. The judicial system of the ancien régime was almost entirely victim-driven. In the courts sampled, only one criminal case in the 1750s and four in the 1780s were directed by the *procureur d'office* acting as public prosecutor without the existence of a private individual as coplaintiff. This means that most criminal cases were instigated and prosecuted by the victims with the assistance of the *procureur d'office*.

The court generally involved itself as sole party in criminal cases only when the perpetrators were either unknown or from outside the village. In 1751, for example, an officer of the *maréchaussée* stopped a suspicious-looking stranger in the fields of Billey. He searched him and found a sheet and a shirt in his possession. The officer took him into the village where he discovered that a guest at the local inn was missing the linen in question.[4] Most of the other cases involving the public prosecutor also concerned strangers caught by public clamor and imprisoned for theft. There were also several cases where the perpetrators were unknown, as in 1784, when the court got involved because vandals broke into the parish church of Belleneuve and stole candles, silver crosses, and holy vases.[5]

Seigneurial judges were content to leave plaintiffs more or less in control of minor criminal cases because they agreed with ordinary people that minor crimes were best settled through restitution rather than punishment. Equally important is the fact that judges and prosecutors were looking out for the interests of the lords, their employers. As we have already seen, one of the most onerous responsibilities attached to the right of high justice was that lords had to pay all costs of criminal prosecutions for cases when the public, represented by the *procureur d'office,* was the only plaintiff.[6] These legal fees could be considerable indeed, as in the trial of André Truchart and consorts for wood theft in 1769, where the lord had to pay 865 livres for the court costs.[7]

By accepting the victim as coplaintiff, the court could sentence the loser of the case (normally the defendant) to pay court costs. The rule was that the lord had to pay the costs of all criminal prosecution where there was no coplaintiff requesting restitution. In 1763, for example, in response to a seigneurial judge who charged court costs to the defendant, the Parlement of Dijon issued an *arrêt général* that "prohibits all judges within the jurisdiction of the court, from condemning [the defendant] to pay the costs of the procedure, when the public party is sole plaintiff."[8] This is why the public prosecutor of the barony of Pagny wrote to the baron requesting permission to pursue wood thefts as civil rather than criminal matters. His reason was this would allow "the condemnation of the delinquents to pay the expenses."[9] The judicial officers saved their employers money by allowing the injured to be named as coplaintiffs in minor criminal affairs, as when the judge of Bagnot sentenced Louis Simon and his daughter Claudine to pay 30 livres to Françoise Baudelier for beating her up, plus 68 livres for the costs of the court.[10] One of the forces encouraging villagers to carry their criminal disputes before the seigneurial court was that judges in minor criminal matters were primarily concerned with restitution. An important reason for this was judges preferred to treat the cases as essentially civil matters, so that the litigants rather than the lord would have to pay legal fees.

In minor crimes where the guilty had to pay court costs, this was frequently the most onerous part of the sentence, even if costs were usually lower than in the major crimes for which lords had to pay. Court costs were especially high in violent disputes where the court had to hear from many witnesses in order to decide who had started the violence. Defendants Jacques Bertin and his wife, Désirée Conot, paid 72 livres in court fees resulting from multiple interrogations of the accused, the hearing of witnesses, and six meetings of the court, after which the judge found them guilty of attacking another villager.[11]

The costs of criminal justice doubtless acted as a deterrent to going to court, and to a much greater extent than in civil justice. Not all criminal cases, however, involved high court fees. The judge of the village of Bagnot sentenced Claude Rousselet to pay 50 sols for the furniture he had stolen from Jean Baptiste Pierret. Admittedly the court costs, at 18 livres, were high enough to deter going to court, but this was far from the amount charged in major crimes.[12] Similarly in an assault case Pierre Poulet only had to pay 14 livres in legal fees, as he admitted his fault and no witnesses were needed.[13] Criminal disputes settled summarily at the assizes could involve court fees of no more than several sols, as when François Saussier was ordered to restore the three measures of wheat he took from a neighbor's cart, and to pay two sols for the court fees.[14]

Approximately two-thirds of the crimes tried in the sampled courts were offenses against persons (assault and defamation), while the other third were crimes committed against property (see table 3.1).[15] The thefts fall into two distinct categories, one of which will be more familiar to historians of crime. The first category is thefts perpetrated by outsiders–either passers-by or local troublemakers who over time made themselves intolerable to the point that the community called in the court to excise them by banishment, galleys, or death. These are the kinds of crimes that historians have used to argue that local communities dealt with their own through informal kinds of pressure. Those passing through the village were obviously difficult to influence

Table 3.1. Crimes tried in fourteen seigneurial courts

	Assault/defamation (%)	Theft (%)	Other (%)
1750–1759	32 (71.1)	12 (26.7)	1 (2.2)
1780–1789	25 (65.8)	13 (34.2)	0
Total	57 (68.7)	25 (30.1)	1 (1.2)

through communal sanction and were often treated with suspicion in any case, which meant that controlling them required the participation of the court. Take, for example, the case of Jacques Girardot (known as Grosjacques). At his trial for housebreaking it became clear that he was a real troublemaker, who had frequently stolen from inhabitants over several years. He was often drunk in public, apparently cheated at cards, and threatened the life of a suitor who competed for a young woman's affections.[16] It is clear in this case that the community had indeed tolerated this man's bad behavior for some time.

Criminal cases like this one, where the accused was convicted of a long list of offenses that had gone unreported for many years, while abundant in bailliage and parlementary archives, account for only a small proportion of crimes tried in the seigneurial courts of northern Burgundy. Most property crimes in seigneurial courts belonged to a second category, in which inhabitants called in the court to get restitution of things stolen by a neighbor.

Restitution was the primary concern of plaintiffs in the vast majority of minor property crimes. In 1759 Jean Perrot the elder accused Claude Malardhier and Jean Baudouin of stealing 12 livres from him in a *cabaret.* The final decision of the court is missing, but all that Perrot wanted was his 12 livres back, and possibly an apology. Doubtless the parties settled out of court with Malardhier and Baudouin paying him back the money.[17] The same desire for simple restitution was true even in more serious criminal cases. There are several cases of inheritance theft where disgruntled heirs or neighbors pilfered from the estate before the legitimate heirs arrived. In 1757 when Léger Jacottot came back to the village to collect his deceased wife's property, he found that almost everything she had left in the village was missing. Suspecting that his wife's sister and her husband had taken it all, Jacottot began criminal proceedings for theft against Nicolas Ladey and Claudine Fevre. Still, all he asked for was 300 livres, which he estimated to be the value of the goods. Ladey and Fevre offered him an unspecified amount far below that, which the court ordered him to accept.[18]

In 1782 the *fermier* of Fontaine-en-Duesmois noticed that two of his sheep were missing. He asked around and found that they had been sold at last month's market day in the nearby town. The purchaser identified François

Gabiot fils, an inhabitant of the village, as the seller and thief (and testified that the animals had carried the *fermier*'s brand). Etienne, the *fermier,* began criminal proceedings against Gabiot. Gabiot's parents accompanied him to court at the second session and told the judge that although their son had done this without their knowledge or help, they wanted to settle the matter out of court. In the end the Gabiots paid 24 livres for the legal fees and promised 19 livres in restitution (the estimated value of the sheep), to be paid by Easter. Etienne agreed to accept this money as restitution, and the judge finalized the agreement, noting that as a result of the payments, "this case remains finished, ended, and as if never begun."[19] Despite the seriousness of the crime, and the real possibility of asking for corporal punishment, Etienne wanted nothing more than restitution. Furthermore, the judge was willing to allow the victim to decide the outcome, and even to participate in an extrajudicial settlement without any punishment or even a symbolic fine.

Many of the thefts tried in these courts were for wood stolen. Most often these were settled with a simple order of restitution and an equivalent fine (so that the offenders basically paid double the value of the stolen wood) without any real use of criminal procedure.[20] Sometimes when the thefts were from the lord's forest, the court treated these cases seriously, with imprisonment during the trial, the use of inquisitorial procedure, and threats of corporal punishments. In the end, though, the court and plaintiff always backed off, with a payment of damages and a fine being the final outcome; in the sample there are no examples of the kinds of exceptionally high fines and corporal punishment allowed by the Waters and Forests edict of 1667. In 1781, apparently frustrated by the frequency of wood pilfering, the *procureur d'office* of Foncegrive instigated criminal proceedings. The court heard from eighteen witnesses, and it eventually imprisoned Nicolas and Mathieu Ladey, François Febvre, and Louis Aubry. After extensive interrogations where they all admitted to having taken some wood, the court sentenced them–to nothing more than fines and civil damages.[21] Even serious wood thefts in the lord's forest, treated as criminal affairs, then, did not lead to anything more than restitution of damages and a fine.

Property crimes between neighbors fit into two broad categories. Firstly, in most cases the offended party called in the court soon after the offense, presumably after asking for the property back. Secondly, occasionally the victim and other villagers had apparently tolerated irritable property loss and violence until it became unbearable, only then reporting it to the court. When it came to offenses committed by neighbors, villagers were reluctant to bring to court cases that might lead to serious punishment of the accused, who would often have friends and supporters within the community. Victims might have to endure a certain level of discomfort until the accused became enough of a troublemaker to motivate someone to report him to the court. Most cases, though, were not like this; since judges were willing to order only restitution for minor thefts and property offenses between neighbors, villagers could use the courts with confidence. There was clearly a point at which a dispute became intolerable and one party lodged a formal complaint, but the calculations that plaintiffs used to decide to go to court remain unknown to us. This decision, though, was little affected by any notion that the court would impose an unfair or foreign justice–people trusted the court to rule in a way that would provide restitution without overly disrupting village harmony.

The majority of criminal cases tried in the seigneurial courts of northern Burgundy involved matters of honor. During the 1750s, combined assault/defamation affairs accounted for 71 percent of criminal cases. For the 1780s the figure was a bit lower, with this category comprising about two-thirds of criminal cases. I place assault and defamation cases in the same category: despite our present-day tendency to think of the former as a civil and the latter as a criminal matter, these courts treated them essentially the same. Indeed, they were often indistinguishable, since many of the assaults caused no physical harm to the plaintiff. An apology and the award of damages was the usual outcome in both cases, although if a surgeon could certify that injured parties had been forced to take to bed as a result of the attack, they would also receive compensation for workdays lost. Assault cases generally began with the exchange of insults, with escalation to physical blows. Both insults and assaults were attempts to win a dispute with the other party. In physical altercations the chief goals of each party were to hit the other's hat off and knock him or her to the ground, both important symbolic actions involving honor.[22]

The court case was an attempt to restore honor by reversing the power relationship established by a loss either in a fight or an exchange of insults. This comes through clearly in the requests by victims that the court examine their cases. In 1784, for example, François Bourgoin submitted to the court his demand that Antoine Clere be held responsible for his actions. He wanted Clere publicly to apologize, admitting that it was "wrong, meanly, and with the intention of harming the reputation of the plaintiff that he called the plaintiff . . . a beggar and thief, and attacked him on the road." He wanted Clere to recognize him as an "honorable man" and to have to pay 100 livres in "pious works."[23]

Disputes could escalate into severe physical altercations, but sometimes the parties brought to court defamation suits where no violence had occurred. Honor mattered to ordinary northern Burgundian peasants enough to bring to court those who insulted them. The affronts that ordinary villagers threw at each other in the heat of passion were impressively varied and expressive.[24] As elsewhere in early modern Europe, the most common insults against women attacked their sexual virtue, while it was the financial honesty of men that insults most commonly called into question. These were serious, targeted insults that could cause material harm to ordinary men and women. A man reputed to be dishonest could find himself cut off from village and regional credit and market networks, while a single woman believed to be promiscuous might have trouble finding a marriage partner. Genret l'ainé called Anne Pruielle a "bitch and whore" and accused her of having "conducted an illicit commerce with someone."[25] A typical example of an insult said to a man is that directed at François Garcenot, the *fermier* of Bellefond, who, according to Elizabeth Loppin, was a "beggar, thief, and bankrupt."[26] Blaize Roux, in a dispute that continued despite a prior judgment of the court, said publicly that Claude Perrot "was an old dog, an old receiver of stolen goods, a damned rascal, a damned thief, [and] that the said Perrot stole with impunity whenever he found occasion."[27]

While these defamation and assault cases were important to ordinary people because their personal and family honor was at stake, there were often concrete property matters lurking behind the fistfight or the calumny. Unfortunately for the researcher, plaintiffs took pains to hide the larger context from the court, in order to portray themselves as innocent victims. In 1787 Jeanne Piedferré and her husband, Antoine Andriot, complained to the court of the insults and violence they experienced at the hands of Anne Mongin. Since June, they said, their neighbor daily insulted and threatened them, "although the supplicants never gave her cause." The day before the complaint, she attacked their seven-year-old son, who was playing quietly in front of the house. Mongin also submitted a request to the court. She claimed that Jeanne Piedferré and her mother had insulted her daily for months, calling her a slut, whore, thief, and keeper of a bawdy house. A few days ago, she wrote, "without the smallest cause of provocation," the mother and daughter attacked her with stones, injuring her so badly that she had to stay in bed.[28] Clearly there was a larger dispute here than simply sexual insults and stone throwing. The case may have begun with an argument over property boundaries, an unpaid debt, even a paternity dispute between the families, and then escalated slowly to the point of violence. In the narratives that each presented to the court, though, neither party could make reference to the larger context since doing so would undermine the contention that the one was totally innocent and the other party entirely guilty.

Occasionally some of the issues behind a dispute came out in the course of the case. A series of assaults and knockdown fights between Claude Perrot and the Roux father and son is illustrative. In 1756 the parties came before the court in an insult case. Blaize and Nicolas Roux publicly insulted Perrot, calling him a thief and a reseller of stolen goods.[29] About a year later they came before the judge again. This time there had been a fight in the local *cabaret,* with the Roux pair attacking Perrot for refusing to sell them wine. Threats, blows, and graphic sexual insults followed. Not until the final judgment of the court do we see the concrete issues behind the fight. The court ordered the Roux pair publicly to apologize for the insults, admit that these were untrue, and ask forgiveness. Significantly, the judge ordered them to give up the two *journaux* of vines that they had taken and not to use the land at all during Perrot's lifetime.[30] This fight, in other words, was an inheritance dispute, a struggle over a piece of land that the Roux pair thought they deserved to inherit.

In highlighting this particular case's context, the intention is not to suggest that mere honor was unimportant to ordinary people in northern Burgundy or that property was the only thing worth fighting over. Indeed, the dichotomy between honor and property is largely artificial, as people doubtless felt insulted when their neighbors stole from them and as an insult could harm one's ability to get credit. Honor, honesty, and sexual virtue were important commodities, and an attempt to undermine reputation would lead to a search for redress, either through escalation or a court case. These court cases point to the simple truism that peasants did not insult and fight each other for no reason. Despite the posture of all plaintiffs, peasants were not so irrational as to attack a neighbor, either verbally or physically, "without reason or provocation." Violence and insults, then, were usually the extension of an old dispute by other means–and the court case the continuation of that dispute.

On a June day in 1784, Jean Normand and Jean Ladey each appeared separately to accuse the other of assaulting him the day before. Normand's story was that Ladey and his domestic servant came into Normand's barn, threw themselves on him, beat him with a stick, dragged him around the barn, and tried to strangle him. Ladey, for his part, claimed that Normand had long nursed a violent hatred against him, often threatening him with violence, and on the day in question he grabbed Ladey by the hair, threw him to the ground, punched and kicked him repeatedly, and even scratched his face with his fingernails. It was only with the help of neighbors who came running that he managed to escape without more serious injuries.[31]

In this case it was Jean Normand who first reported the crime to the court–but only by a few hours. Ladey told the judge that he was "surprised to learn that Normand had the audacity to give you, sir, his request for judicial inquiry against the supplicant. This was doubtless to cover himself from those [inquiries] that he knew the supplicant was about to begin against him." The court case included a report from a surgeon, who visited Normand (none of the Ladeys had any significant physical injuries). The surgeon described a large bruise on Normand's head, another on his neck, and some damage to his hand. He estimated that these wounds would take about six days to heal. The court heard the testimony of 37 witnesses. Because the barn door had been closed, no one had seen the fight, but most of the witnesses heard Normand's screams and reported that he staggered out of the barn and called the gathering crowd as witness to the violence. Despite apparent premeditation and real violence (evidence suggested that Ladey's son had used a hammer, as well as the stick), the judge's final decision involved no more than 24 livres in damages for Normand's recovery time in bed, and a fine of 5 livres. By far the most onerous part of the sentence was Ladey's responsibility for court costs of 125 livres.

Although the violence in this fight was more extreme than in many other disputes, the Ladey-Normand dustup illustrates many of the themes of criminal disputes between neighbors in northern Burgundy. Neither Ladey nor Normand perceived seigneurial justice as a kind of exterior, foreign, elite justice to be used only against outsiders, but rather as a forum for the airing and resolving of disputes between neighbors. There was clearly long-standing animosity between them, but the dispute came before the court on the first occasion that it became physically violent. The case also illustrates the common practice whereby both parties to a dispute deposited their complaints before the court, often within the same day, each claiming to have been wronged by the other.[32] This would involve a race to reach the clerk of the local court, both because the first to report the offense might have some advantage in local opinion and because financial damages depended on a surgeon's report.

Villagers involved in disputes used the local court wisely, positioning themselves as the victims of a malicious and contentious attacker. Even before appearing in front of the judge, they worked to stage themselves and the dispute. During the heat of the moment in a physical fight, people had the presence of mind to yell "à l'assassin," to call out for witnesses, and to get onlookers to agree to testify on their behalf–all things that suggest that the court itself was an important arena for disputing. Françoise Maillard, for example, testified to the court that when she passed a neighbor's house she heard Jean Baptiste Demay's wife call out loudly for witnesses to the insult Claude Ardiot had just said to her husband.[33] When Richard Roget ran toward the commotion he heard coming from a neighbor's front yard, the fight between the couples Burgiard and Bertin was over, but he saw and heard "the said Burgiard who was buttoning his trousers and held those present as witnesses for the hand down his trousers."[34] Parties to fights or exchanges of insults, then, tried to construct a narrative of victimhood for the local seigneurial court and sometimes tried to use the local court to escalate their disputes.

Going to court often involved a decision to escalate a dispute, with hope of victory through concessions forced by the costs of going to court or by judicial decision. We should not lose sight, however, of the fact that going to court could also represent an attempt to end a dispute and bring about reconciliation, a return to normality, or at least the deescalation of the dispute.

Among historians of crime in France, a view has emerged of the relationship between the village community and the judicial arm of the state that tends to emphasize their profound separation. Primarily because peasant communities were suspicious of the intervention of urban elites–but also because official justice was too expensive, slow, and complicated–only a small proportion of crimes came before the courts. The combined effect of the government's refusal to provide viable judicial settlement and the penchant of village communities to deal with their own internally motivated people in early modern France to resolve their disputes through various forms of "popular justice," such as the mediation of elites, the intervention of the community, or further confrontation between the parties. While scholars disagree about whether people used unofficial methods of settlement primarily because they chose to or primarily because the official judicial system was so poor, most nevertheless see eighteenth-century villages as primarily self-regulating in criminal matters. The only crimes where communities actively requested the intervention of the judge were those involving criminals who were outsiders (vagrants, people passing through) and hence unreachable through communal sanction, and those where local inhabitants repeatedly refused to submit to attempts of the community to intervene.[35]

This vision of the rural community is partially vindicated by the analysis of the criminal cases of northern Burgundian seigneurial courts. It is clear that many minor criminal disputes over honor and property did not come before the seigneurial court. There were doubtless many more physical fights and exchanges of insults than the handful that most small seigneurial courts heard over the course of a decade. Certainly the high cost of criminal justice would have provided incentive to put up with some violence, dishonor, or loss of property.

The majority of criminal cases nevertheless involved neighbors rather than outsiders. Communities, disputants, and judges all agreed on the priority of restitution over escalation or humiliation. Seigneurial courts therefore worked as an instrument of autoregulation for the village, and ordinary people perceived it as such, rather than as the instrument of an external authority imposed on them from outside the village. In criminal cases the seigneurial courts of northern Burgundy were a profoundly local institution. Far from serving only to police the uncontrollable and the foreign, seigneurial justice settled the criminal disputes of ordinary people. Northern Burgundians called in the court to settle disagreements that had led to the exchange of insults or blows. The instrument of neither an urban elite nor a civilizing state, seigneurial justice was fundamental to the relationships among ordinary northern Burgundians. Rural communities mostly policed themselves, it is true, but the seigneurial court was a vital part of this self-policing.

The findings presented here point to the conclusion that criminal justice cannot be understood on its own. Historians of crime have long suggested that criminal justice has to be understood within the context of various informal ways of settling criminal disputes, although the promise of notarial documents in the analysis of "arrangements" is only beginning to be fulfilled.[36] More significantly, however, criminal and civil justice have to be understood together. The relationship between criminal and civil justice is closest in lower courts, since the process of appeal filtered out the minor crimes that most resembled civil disputes. One of the problems is the difficult nature of the sources in seigneurial courts, with almost all civil cases (and many criminal ones) buried in the registers in a week-by-week description of each session, without a final summary in the final judgment (there are separate sentences only for those cases tried with written, nonsummary procedure, less than 5 percent of cases). A short time spent in the registers of seigneurial courts reveals that the distinctions legal theorists made in the eighteenth century between civil, criminal, and police justice fall apart when we are faced with analyzing actual disputes involving the property, lives, and privileges of ordinary French men and women.

Police Authority in the Interests of the Community

While cost may have been a consideration in criminal cases, the same cannot be said of police affairs, which judicial officers conducted without collecting fees. The responsibility for policing village life remained significant in the eighteenth century. La Poix de Fréminville listed the responsibilities of the *procureur d'office* of seigneurial courts: among other things, the court officer had to uphold religion, "make commerce flower and enrich the subjects of the king."[37] Maintaining good order within the jurisdiction of the court included policing the physical space of the seigneurie: oversight of roads, houses, buildings, and chimneys. It also included ensuring the smooth operation of the agricultural system and the protection of fields and forests belonging to inhabitants, to the community, and to the lord. Judges were also to ensure the orderly behavior of villagers: this charge included stopping blasphemy, prostitution, and usury, policing alcohol and inns, and ensuring respectful deference to the lord and to the court itself. The court also supervised local markets (the grain trade, weights and measures), village political affairs, and local farming practices.[38] The police authority of seigneurial judges was primarily a form of autoregulation, with judges responding to the concerns of inhabitants.

Most police activities of seigneurial courts took place at the Grands-Jours (annual assizes). Generally the judge announced the date for the assizes a week or two ahead of time, usually through the parish priest. In Belleneuve the court officers had the priest read the following notice to the inhabitants:

> Master Jean Baptiste Hucherot, *procureur* in the presidial of Dijon and *d'office* in the lands and seigneuries of Belleneuve, Savolle, the Mottes d'Ahuy and of the Fontaine d'Ahuy, of Lambelin, Savolles and Beauvais, makes known to all the inhabitants of the said places, that the Grands-Jours will take place Monday the twenty-ninth of the present month of

> October 1759 at Belleneuve the seat of the justice at nine o'clock in the morning, where the inhabitants are invited to find themselves or be fined [*sous peine d'amende*].[39]

At the date, time, and place set by the officers, the court would meet in the presence of all heads of households. The most common time of year was from late August to the end of the year, with four-fifths of assizes being held in these months. The assizes could be held almost anywhere, other than in the lord's castle. It seems to have been most common to hold the assizes outside, in the village square, although they sometimes used inhabitants' homes, rotating among those that were big enough to hold the community and court.

The first order of business was always the roll call. Reading from village tax rolls, the clerk made sure that each household was represented at the assizes, with fines for those who were absent without a good excuse, usually 3 livres 5 sols, sometimes moderated to 10 sols. The only acceptable excuses for nonattendance were absence from the village since the time of the announcement, or sickness. While few inhabitants defaulted entirely—attendance rates were very high—some did try to sneak back to the fields before the end. In Senailly when the judge called back Guillaume Bresseau as he snuck out after the roll call, Bresseau "answered in an arrogant tone, that each had his own affairs, that we had our affairs here, and that he had his own elsewhere." The judge fined him 3 livres 5 sols for his contempt and irreverence.[40] Doubtless it did not help matters that the majority of assizes in northern Burgundy were held in the late summer or early fall, the busiest time of the year in these farming communities.

After taking attendance and fining those absent, the court proceeded to lecture the inhabitants on their behavior, beginning with the general and proceeding to the particular. The first order of business was to read parlementary rulings that affected village life. These could include anything from the royal edict permitting enclosure to repeated injunctions against shivaree. Then began a veritable litany of things that the inhabitants were required to do or forbidden from doing.

The regulations given to the inhabitants of Fontaine-en-Duesmois in 1755 serve as a good example of the kinds of police issues that concerned seigneurial judges, although any session of any other court would do as well. The judge started with the most general. The inhabitants were not to drink in the village pubs (public drinking in the countryside was for travelers only), were forbidden from "swearing the holy name of God," and had to attend religious services regularly and with "all appropriate modesty." He reminded them that they were not allowed to hunt under any circumstances. Their dogs had to wear sticks around their necks to protect rabbits, pigeons, and other small game. Except animals used to work the land, all cattle were to be put in the communal herd. Finally, they were to keep their animals out of the lord's forests except where they had permission to graze.

After these general regulations, most of which came directly from parlementary general *arrêts,* the judge moved on to specifically local matters. Individuals were not to cut any trees in the communal forest until after the division of the land into lots by the judicial officers. People who owned goats should keep them at home; the guards would kill any they found in the fields or forests. Villagers were reminded that they should not cut through planted fields, make new paths, or damage hedges. It was forbidden to light fires near the seigneurial or communal forests. Children should not pick grass and flowers in the pasture, and parents and masters would be held responsible if they did so. Any who dug for slate, granite, or marble must fill in the holes. Finally, the judge told them not to throw stones (presumably those picked off their fields) onto the roads.[41]

We can more systematically reconstruct the list of police regulations that villagers heard at the annual assizes, since after 1780 the judges in the province all read the same *arrêts* to the villagers, reading from one of two pamphlets published with parlementary approval. We can divide the *arrêts* in these two booklets by category to see how the Dijon Parlement wanted to use seigneurial courts to keep order in the countryside.[42] The results, presented in table 3.2, reinforce the argument that seigneurial justice was a form of autoregulation in northern Burgundian villages. By far the largest number of regulations concerned agriculture in the village, the protection of the fields of villagers and the community. Procedural questions were also significant, as the court reminded people of the new procedure for trying farming torts or that their lord was responsible to maintain the seigneurial court in activity. Questions of morality also came up, including, for example, the attendance of Mass, blasphemy, and gambling. Finally, the court also reminded villagers of their responsibility to their seigneur. This points to the assizes' dual function: to provide an annual assembly of the village household heads to decide village affairs, and to reinforce the lord's authority over the village.

One of the crucial functions of the assizes was to regulate the election or appointment of local village officers. The inhabitants in each village had to nominate as many as ten village officials every year. The most important position was that of *procureur syndic* (also called *échevin*). Villages had two *syndics,* who were responsible for convoking assemblies of the community when necessary. Although they had no more formal authority than any other members of the community, *syndics* had access to the purse strings of the village and represented the community to the outside world. Villages also had to appoint two *asséeurs,* who assessed each family's tax contribution and drew up the tax rolls for that year. Since the assessors did not collect the taxes, the village also needed to appoint two tax collectors who then took the

Table 3.2. *Arrêts* and edicts read to villagers at Grands-Jours

Compilation	Agriculture, roads	Morality	Authority and rights of lords	Local politics	Judicial procedure
Capel, 1779	23	6	4	13	14
Causse, 1786	31	10	4	9	4

rolls drawn by the assessors and collected the money.[43] To police its fields, the village needed two *messiers*. These *messiers* were responsible to roam the fields and capture any animals caught in the seeded fields before the end of the general harvest. Some wine-producing villages also nominated two *vigniers*, who policed the vines in the same way. After 1773 the village also had to appoint two *prud'hommes*, who were to evaluate damages in harvest and pasture disputes. In all northern Burgundian villages, therefore, the inhabitants had to appoint at least eight and sometimes as many as a dozen officials each year.

The local seigneurial court was responsible for ensuring that every village filled all of these positions. It was crucial for the central state to have legal representatives with whom to deal in various situations. Rather than dealing with the village as a group, the government required the appointment of representatives who would be personally responsible. The provincial Estates needed tax assessors and collectors in each village in order to ensure the payment of the *taille* and *capitation*. The collector was made personally responsible for paying the taxes for the village: in the event that an inhabitant failed to make his payments, the collector himself would have to pay and then take the deadbeat to court to recoup. The same was true for *syndics*, who had to answer in person for the use they made of village funds. Even *messiers* and *vigniers* were personally responsible for any unreported farming torts that occurred on their watch. In our sample, fully 178 out of 603 civil trespass torts tried in the fourteen courts in the 1780s saw civil damages assessed against the *messiers* rather than the owners of the wandering animals. Local officers in the ancien régime served as intermediaries between the village and the state. They simplified tax collection, oversight on local fiscal matters, and the policing of fields, thereby allowing authorities coercive power without having to investigate who was actually responsible.

This legal fiction of the personal responsibility of local officers gave seigneurial judges a great deal of authority over local political matters. The central state had no stake in disputes between collectors and villagers who refused to pay. In the end the collector would have to pay, and then take the case before the local seigneurial judge. This hands-off approach to the administration of villages gave seigneurial courts a great deal of authority over local political matters, and it made sense for the same seigneurial judges to ensure that these local officers were legally appointed, fit for the position, and had sworn to do the job. The seigneurial court oversaw the appointment and swearing-in because the same court would have to hear cases where the judge had to determine actual responsibility.

Another important purpose of this oversight was to ensure that each village did indeed have responsible officers, and sometimes even to protect these officers from abuse by the community. The judge of the barony of Gemeaux intervened in 1757 to order the community to assemble and nominate *échevins* after the village officers from the past year complained that no one attended the assemblies they convened to elect their replacements: they "notice easily that [the inhabitants] want to extend their service since the inhabitants try not to appear at the assemblies and that as soon as they hear the bell ring those that are around the municipal hall leave, doubtless so as not to be present at the assembly."[44] Local office was considered onerous, and the seigneurial judge ensured that all village men shared in the burden.[45]

Judges did not themselves name the village officials. A general *arrêt* of the Parlement of Dijon from 1768 specified that at the assizes the judge "will accept the oath of the *messiers, asséeurs, collecteurs, procureurs* [*syndics*] or *échevins* who will be chosen and presented by the community for the next year."[46] Sometimes the community had met before the assizes to select the officials and then simply presented the names to the judge, but in other instances the vote took place at the assizes. In the seigneurial courts studied there are only two examples of a judge overturning a village's nomination for local office. One involved the appointment of a blind invalid, clearly incapable of carrying out the duties. In the other case a village tax collector was found guilty of erasing notations on the tax rolls that people had already paid. In addition to assigning a hefty fine and requiring a public apology, the seigneurial judge declared him "unfit in the future for exercising the functions of collector and all other community offices."[47] Given the villager's blatant fraud, it is unlikely that the inhabitants resented this judge's authority over village politics.

After the judge had read aloud the police regulations that affected the village and seen to the nomination of local officials, he then asked the assembled community if anyone had complaints or comments to make. People brought up a wide variety of complaints and comments to the judge, which suggests they had widespread confidence in the ability of the court to regulate their local affairs.

Especially common were complaints brought before the court concerning communal farming. Maintaining common land was a continual uphill battle for villages in northern Burgundy. Much has been written on *triage,* the right of lords to force the community to hand the seigneur a third of the common land.[48] Equally important, though, was the gradual but steady usurping of common land by local inhabitants. All villages in the region periodically had to go on the offensive against those who appropriated common land. In Aisy in 1789, for example, the inhabitants complained to the judge that, despite the survey done several decades ago, people recently had usurped so much of the common land that it was now hardly wide enough for one cart to pass. The court ordered the community to appoint experts to investigate the encroachment and authorized it to take back the land in question.[49]

Other agricultural issues came up as well, such as requests that sheep or goats be expelled from common land, complaints that gleaners began before the harvest was complete, or that wandering children damaged crops. The poor state of roads was another common complaint. In Ancey, for example, villagers informed the judge that the road in front of Germain Carré's house was higher than the rest of the road, leading to flooding that was especially harmful during the winter freeze. The judge ordered the community to change the slope of the road and rebuked Carré for pushing the edges of his garden onto the road and thus contributing to the problem.[50]

The use and division of communal resources was also regulated by judges at the assizes, usually at the request of the inhabitants. Village-owned forest presented some problems. To ensure that the wood was put to use by members of the village, judges forbade the inhabitants from selling any part of their share of the communal wood to people from outside the village.[51] One common arrangement was for the officers of the court to accompany several forest experts into the communal forest and divide that year's harvestable part of the forest into equal lots, after which the inhabitants would draw straws and cut the wood themselves.

Most of the discussion at the assizes concerned agricultural matters, and in many cases the judge simply responded to the requests of the inhabitants. The assizes had the character of a communal assembly headed by the local judge. Each household was to send one person to the assizes. As heads of households, widows and spinsters attended in significant numbers.[52] Married women were excluded, although everyone could show up at the end of the assizes for the hearing of summary civil cases. The presence of all household heads meant that any decision reached by those assembled would have a quorum of "the sane and major part of the inhabitants" and could be validated by the judge.[53] The action of the court in police matters most often resulted from complaints of inhabitants, rather than the imposition of the morality of the judges or the will of the lord, but sources do not reveal which villagers spoke at the assizes. Without naming the speaker, the judge of Fontaine-en-Duesmois fined Jean Legendre 3 livres 5 sols, "on the complaints made by the inhabitants that the said Jean Legendre had a separate herd, as well as Pierre Desarbre."[54]

If it is likely that the voices of the better-off inhabitants counted the most, it is nevertheless certain that the poorer settled members of the community (*manouvriers* and *journaliers*) had a better chance of being heard in the assizes than they did in regular communal assemblies. Attendance records from village meetings, on the one hand, reveal that propertied landowners and bigger tenants dominated, and that the less wealthy rarely even attended. At the assizes, on the other hand, forced attendance meant at the very least that the judge could solicit the opinions of the less well off. When the community of Foncegrive deliberated before the judge to decide when to divide the forest, the judge took the votes of all twenty-nine people present–twenty-one were in favor of splitting it that year, and eight favored waiting.[55] When the same village met in a general assembly to decide whether some of the communal pasture should be set aside for hay (rather than used as pasture), only nine people were present.[56] A wider spectrum of villagers got to discuss local political affairs and provide input at the Grands-Jours than in regular general assemblies of the community.

Although most police matters in these courts involved farming or local politics, occasionally issues of morality came before the court. About half a dozen people had to pay fines for working on Sunday without the permission of the priest or the court. In these cases it was probably the priest or a pious parishioner who reported the infraction to the court. There were also two men publicly rebuked by the court for disorderly conduct, including public drunkenness and wife beating. When the *procureur d'office* of Ancey reported to the judge that Antoine Mercenot caused frequent public scandal in the village, the inhabitants concurred. It seems that the Friday before the assizes Mercenot got drunk in the local *cabaret* and "mistreated" his wife when he got home. Without the intervention of neighbors, he would have rendered her unconscious. Etienne Mortureux was worse still, they claimed, for repeatedly abusing his wife and for forcing her outside on two separate occasions, once during a rainstorm. He also abused and mistreated those who came to his wife's rescue.[57] The judge fined both men 25 livres. This kind of reaction to behavior deemed immoral, associated more with consistories in Protestant regions, was in fact quite rare in the seigneurial courts of northern Burgundy. Despite broadly defined police authority–including the power to punish irreligious, blasphemous, and immoral behavior–seigneurial judges in northern Burgundy intervened almost exclusively in agricultural and village political matters, and usually at the request of the inhabitants.

Seigneurial judges also had police authority over the production, sale, and measure of various foods in the village. No villagers were to sell wine without the permission of the high-justice lord or his officers. The requirement that *cabarets* register with the court gave the officers the opportunity to verify that drinkers were not being defrauded, as the verification of weights and measures was to be carried out before issuing a license.[58] In 1786 two *cabaretiers* in Billey were fined for selling wine without permission and without having their measuring units verified by the court.[59] The court was to guard against the possibility of watering down the wine and to stop those who would sell "one wine at two prices."[60] The power to issue and withhold local liquor licenses also gave teeth to the courts' attempts to police public drinking.

Local courts also oversaw the production and sale of bread and meat. Judges set prices for bakers and butchers, ensured that the merchants had enough food to meet the needs of the villagers, and verified their weights and measures to protect the consumers from fraud. Most villages were too small to support a baker or butcher–of the villages in the sample, only three (Bagnot, Messigny, and Meursault) had butcher shops and only five (Aisy, Auxey-le-Grand, Bagnot, Messigny, and Meursault) had a resident baker.[61] Still, where there were butchers or bakers, the court did step in. In 1784 the inhabitants of Meursault complained that their butcher was selling poor meat. The court appointed the local blacksmith as village meat inspector and ordered the butcher not to sell any meat that the smith had not inspected.[62] Judges also had authority to set the prices of both bread and meat. Informed that the price of meat in the region had dropped below the 5 sols per pound that the butcher charged, one local judge ordered a reduction in the price. After haggling back and forth, the judge and butcher settled on 4 sols 6 deniers per pound for all meats.[63]

Seigneurial judges also had broad authority over the grain trade. Judges regularly reminded villagers that they were not to interfere with the free passage and commerce of grain. In 1770 the parlement ordered that anyone who wanted to participate in the grain trade was to register with the seigneurial court that policed the market nearest to his home.[64] Judith Miller has shown the way that royal administrators during the eighteenth century worked to ensure the provisioning of cities without seeming to interfere with the free working of the market. Under normal circumstances officials let the market set grain and bread prices, intervening only in times of crisis, and even then doing so as inconspicuously as possible.[65] The same seems to have been true in the few villages that had bakers; seigneurial judges mostly stayed out of price regulating, but occasionally intervened at the request of the inhabitants in times of dearth, as in 1784 when the judge of Aisy ordered the village baker to sell bread at the price set by the nearby city of Saulieu.[66]

Seigneurial courts enforced rules with which most people agreed. Only with respect to judges' attempts to limit the consumption of alcohol do we see evidence of a clash between the court and the village as a community. But the total failure of the attempt underlines the extent to which most interaction between the court and the community was based on consent and cooperation. According to a parlementary *arrêt* of 1718, reiterated in 1778, no *cabarets* were to serve alcohol to any inhabitants of the village, and no one could enter a *cabaret* within less than a league (about 5 km) from his home.[67] The Parlement of Dijon was serious about the enforcement of this policy, and the officers of seigneurial courts were to be the main defense against public drinking in the countryside.

Seigneurial judges and *procureurs d'office* tried to enforce this rule, but it was an uphill battle. Fines to innkeepers, barflies, parents, and masters remained ineffective deterrents, since nobody in the countryside agreed with the *arrêt.* Villagers never reported local consumption of alcohol in the *cabaret* to the court unless it led to public violence, and each time the officers of the court made surprise visits to the village pubs they found locals downing their wine. When the judge of Messigny ordered the local officials to check the *cabarets* occasionally for inhabitants, they flatly refused. That the local officials "even excited the major part of the inhabitants to retire [from the Grands-Jours] with emotion and scandal," is suggestive of the unpopularity of this law.[68]

The responses of *cabaretiers* brought before the court sometimes reveals the sense of frustration they felt toward this senseless policy. The small hamlets of Chazilly-le-Haut and Chazilly-le-Bas had an embarrassment of riches, with four unofficial *cabarets.* When the judge called them before him to answer charges that they sold wine to locals, they answered "that they needed to earn a living, [and] that they were obliged to give to those who requested it."[69] In Flée Dominique Mercier was fined 50 livres for selling wine to locals one Christmas Eve. He acknowledged that he had sold them wine but said that they drank it "without noise or scandal," and argued "that he does not think to have caused any harm."[70]

Evidence that villagers routinely ignored the injunctions of parlement and their local judge against drinking in the village can be seen in the depositions of witnesses in court cases over tavern brawls.[71] A tavern fight sometimes led to a civil and minor criminal court case. In the course of the investigation courts inevitably heard the testimony of locals who were drinking in the tavern when the fight broke out. In one case a few of the witnesses apparently felt obliged to explain their presence: Hugues Lavieille claimed to have entered only because Jean and Nicolas Carré forced him to witness a business transaction between them and another party.[72] Local taverns, in other words, were filled with locals drinking wine together and participating in village sociability.

When the *procureur d'office* of Foncegrive voiced his frustration with his inability to stop village drinking, he could have been speaking for every other prosecutor and judge in northern Burgundy:

> [W]hatever exactness he puts into the execution of the *arrêts de règlement* of the court concerning the interdictions of frequenting *cabarets,* he has not been able to stop the course of offences that are committed in the said village of Foncegrive. Innkeepers, to the prejudice of the regulations read at the Grands-Jours, do not cease giving to drink during the day and at night to several persons from this village.[73]

The rule limiting public drinking in the countryside to travelers only, he realized, was disregarded by virtually everyone. This legislation is a good example of a failed attempt to impose behavioral norms, and as such it offers a good contrast to the normal function of seigneurial justice in police matters, where the judge enforced behavioral norms with which villagers agreed.

After reading parlement's *arrêts* and hearing the complaints of the inhabitants, and before settling civil suits and sending people home, the assizes continued with the assigning of fines. These included penalties for trespass in the seigneurial forest, for hunting, for working on the sabbath, and for destruction of small game by wandering dogs. The vast majority of the fines, though, involved communal agriculture within the village. These were fines for wandering cattle, for harvesting before the appointed time or beyond the field boundary, for theft from the communal land, and for illegal pasturing of all kinds.

The fines assigned for pasturing contraventions provide further evidence that seigneurial justice was an important form of autoregulation for village communities in northern Burgundy. Common land and communal farming practices, so important to the working of agriculture in this open-field system, functioned effectively because of the combined vigilance of the community and the local seigneurial court. The vast number of fines assigned for breaking the rules of communal farming points to the conclusion that, while most people benefited from these rules and almost nobody wanted to abolish communal farming, everyone in the village tried ceaselessly to bend the rules to his own advantage. Without the police authority of the local seigneurial court, communal farming would have degenerated into chaos.[74]

Farming fines were treated separately from the civil side of the trespass offense, where the guilty party had to pay civil damages for the wheat, barley, rye, or hay trodden down. There was often both a separate civil lawsuit for the damages and a fine for the same offense, although there were many more fines than civil lawsuits for farming torts. What interest did the state have in keeping cattle out of illegal pasture? The answer to this is closely related to the nature of open-field agriculture and the existence of communal rights over privately owned land. After the general harvest of a crop, the fields planted in that crop were opened up to communal pasturing. Cattle (or sheep) could roam the unenclosed harvested fields, feeding on the remaining stubble. This was an important source of feed in many parts of France. Before the general harvest was complete, it was illegal to send any animals into the fields, even your own, given the risk they would stray onto nearby partially harvested land. In 1755 the court of Bagnot fined a certain Baudot 35 sols for five of his own horses caught feeding in his own oats (in other words, no damage had been caused to anyone's fields but his own).[75] So long as a single inhabitant had not cleared his fields, no animals were allowed onto the fields. The rest of the year the *messiers* also worked to protect arable land from cattle wandering onto it from nearby pasture or fallow land. This was especially a problem when parents entrusted their animals to the care of children, who were "sometimes more inclined to amuse themselves than to look after their cows."[76]

For farming torts there was often a civil trial for the damages caused, especially after the 1773 reforms. Though based partly on the *messiers*' report, the civil tort was handled separately from the offense against the system of communal agriculture. For every civil trial involving a farming offense (called *mésus* in Burgundy) there was a fine assessed, but there was not a civil trial for all *mésus*. In fact, only about an eighth of farming fines in the 1750s and a quarter in the 1780s were accompanied by a civil trial.

The usual fine against the owners of the wandering cattle was 7 sols. If the court wished to fine more than this amount, the judge needed more evidence than simply the unsubstantiated word of the *messiers*. There were doubtless good reasons to limit the authority of *messiers*, given that over the course of several decades over half of the married men in the village would perform the function for a year. This limit of 7 sols also had serious drawbacks, though, as it was insufficient to be an effective deterrent. The *procureur d'office* of the barony of Gemeaux complained to the judge of the insignificance of the fines; the *procureur* was especially worried that so many of the animals caught were guarded by children and domestic servants. Apparently concerned about the message this relative leniency sent to these minors about respecting the law, he said, "Men and women who conduct their cattle into the said roads and paths do not fear to pasture illegally under the eye of these children in the wheat, meadows, clover, and vines, trampling the roots underfoot, and to say that their cattle eats well for seven sols of fines."[77]

Fines in pasturing offenses were by far the most common kind of judicial activity carried out by the courts. Because of the work involved and the diminishing returns of further research, I did not record the details of the thousands of farming fines for all the courts studied. I did, however, count the number of fines for eight of these courts.[78] Table 3.3 compares the number of fines assigned by the judges to various other activities of these eight courts. The fines outnumbered every other legal action. In the 1750s the fines outnumbered all civil and criminal cases by a factor of three! In the 1780s, with the civil prosecution of so many more civil farming torts, the fines approximately equaled the number of civil and criminal disputes (1,711 cases and 1,625 *mésus* fines). The policing of open-field agriculture was one of the most important functions of seigneurial courts.

Mésus fines, though frequently assigned by these courts, did not provide a significant source of income to seigneurs. The court in the sample that assessed the highest number of these fines was the seigneurial justice of Billey. The judge of this village of 370 inhabitants fined 469 people for wandering cattle in the 1750s and 569 in the 1780s.[79] These fines more than doubled the 101 and 249 civil and criminal cases settled in the 1750s and 1780s,

Table 3.3. *Mésus* fines and other activities of eight seigneurial justices

Court activity	1750s	1780s
Mésus fines	1,638	1,625
All cases in regular session	324	530
All (civil and criminal) cases in Grands-Jours	220	1,181
Gracious acts of justice	365	578

respectively, in both the regular sessions and the Grands-Jours. Even this most aggressive court, though, brought in a pittance to the lord from the farming fines–at 7 sols per fine, less than 20 livres per year. The seigneurie of Billey, which sold in 1769 for 42,000 livres, likely brought in 2,100 livres of annual revenue (at a conservative estimate of 5 percent).[80] The lord's revenue from the fines, then, was but a drop in the bucket. Far from being a source of revenue for lords, the policing of agriculture was a seigneurial responsibility, a service the officers of the court had to provide for free to the community to keep the system of communal agriculture running smoothly.

Lords and judges could have used seigneurial justice to mold more submissive, more religious, more disciplined subjects. Judges, after all, annually read aloud edicts and rulings on morality; they forbid blasphemy, shivarees, the ringing of bells to ward off storms, even *veillées*. But judges did not try at all to enforce these rules. The sole example of a civilizing law that judges tried to apply was the policing of alcohol sales and consumption–which the more sensible attitude of peasants made unenforceable. What these courts did well, indeed very well, was respond to the complaints and comments of the inhabitants and help the community resolve the disputes and problems that would otherwise threaten it.

Probate Justice–Expensive but Necessary

While some people may have lived without appearing before the local judge as a plaintiff or defendant in a lawsuit, and a few may even have avoided getting fined for violating agricultural regulations, no settled inhabitant of a village could avoid the exercise of the court's jurisdiction over his or her estate after death. In ancien régime France probate justice was referred to by legal theorists as gracious justice (because, unlike contentious justice, it did not pit two adversaries against each other), or *juridiction volontaire*–a bit of a misnomer, since most operations of the court in probate affairs were not voluntary for the families or for the court. At death, the local seigneurial court had legal responsibilities toward an estate, including to look after the interests of minor children, creditors, and any absent heirs before the property could be passed over to the family for partition. There were problems with the administration of probate justice, notably the cost that was sometimes incurred in complicated cases. The costs of probate justice were, furthermore, regressive in that smaller estates generally cost proportionally more to settle than did larger ones. Still, the overall picture with respect to probate justice remains moderately positive. With some foresight most families could get through the process having paid about 20 livres in legal fees. For estates overburdened with debts or in cases involving stepparents and half-siblings it is unlikely that things could have been done much more cheaply, given that this was a system where the user paid.

In an important synthesis on seigneurial justice in the eighteenth century, Benoît Garnot points out that probate justice remained one of the primary responsibilities and activities of seigneurial judges right up to the Revolution. Anthony Crubaugh presents evidence from the southwest to support this idea, with 44 to 66 percent of all judicial decisions or acts in his sampled courts coming from probate cases (seals, inventories, guardianships, auctions).[81] While it is certain that drawing up probate acts to protect heirs and creditors occupied a significant amount of time for judicial officers, in northern Burgundy all seigneurial courts resolved a much larger number of lawsuits (i.e., contentious justice) than probate inheritance matters (i.e., gracious justice). Statistics are less helpful than we might think here, because of the problems associated with counting lawsuits, and because most estates that passed before the judge required multiple acts. We can estimate, however, that most seigneurial courts heard four to five times more lawsuits than the number of estates that they settled for families through probate, and that for every judicial act of gracious justice most courts heard at least two civil lawsuits.

Upon hearing of a death in the village the court clerk, accompanied by a village notable (often the schoolmaster), placed seals on the goods of the deceased. They locked all trunks and doors to ensure that family members did not divide up the estate until the court had completed the necessary steps. This was an essential part of the process of property devolution, designed to ensure that the right people (as defined by the legal Custom of Burgundy, by parlement, and by the testator) got the property. The court had to act quickly to ensure that family members did not defraud each other, as sometimes happened. In 1783 the presumptive heirs of François Gigot appeared before the court to request an inquest into a possible theft from the deceased. The court-conducted inventory listed goods worth only 183 livres. Where, they wondered, were the "money in cash, wheat, kitchen utensils, dishes, linen of all kinds, notes of credit, things, brandy, and firewood" that they knew he owned?[82] The judge conducted an inquiry into the matter but discovered nothing suspicious.

Once the estate was sealed, the court's primary responsibility was toward surviving minor children.[83] The court made certain that the family met to appoint two guardians for the children. The court also intervened in any major transactions affecting the property of the minors, such as leases of land or the auction of the harvest. And finally, the court was there at the end of the guardianship to ensure that the ward got as much of the estate as she or he was entitled to–the original amount, plus the revenue, minus the expenses of looking after him or her.

The first step was for the court to oversee the appointment of two guardians. In Burgundy minority continued to the age of twenty-five, so guardians had to be appointed for any unmarried sons and daughters under that age.[84] The extended family met and then reported its choice of a *tuteur* and *curateur* to the judge, who would ratify the decision and administer an oath to the guardians. Normally one of the guardians was from the mother's side and the other from the father's. Except when he or she was incapable through age or sickness, the family nominated the surviving parent as tutor. When the minors were orphaned, families chose uncles as tutors in 44 percent of cases and siblings (brothers, stepbrothers, and brothers-in-law) in 34 percent of cases. The assembled family also appointed a curator, who acted as a check on the tutor, the main guardian. By far the most common curators were uncles, although there were some cousins, brothers, and brother-in-laws. There were also several "*oncles à la mode de Bourgogne,*" first cousins of the parents.[85]

Women, except as mothers of the minors, were forbidden from being nominated as tutors or curators, a rule based on a woman's legal inability to conduct property transactions without her husband's permission.[86] But 20 percent of tutors for orphans were listed as *beau-frère, oncle à cause de sa femme,* and *cousin germain à cause de sa femme*–men standing in for their wives. It was the couple that acted as guardian, and families would never appoint an unmarried man in any case.

The guardians had two main responsibilities: to see to the clothing, feeding, and education of the minors; and to safeguard their property. The minors would normally live with the tutor, although occasionally he might pension them off to the lowest bidder. In 1756, for example, the tutor of Antoinette and Jean Baptiste Bréon advertised after Mass in the local church that he was looking for someone "who would be willing to take [the children] in pension . . . for three years." In this instance the only bidders were two uncles of the children, one of whom offered to look after Antoinette for 12 livres a year, while the other took on Jean Baptiste for 20 livres a year.[87] In 1787 Pierre Ferret pensioned off Barbe and Reine Ferret, his nieces. Any takers had to agree to "feed, sleep, warm, bleach, teach them their religious duties, and give them a good education, to treat and maintain them in cleanliness in their clothes that will be given them by the said tutor."[88]

Judicial oversight over the administration of the property of minors continued after the appointment of guardians, as all major property matters came before the court for ratification. Guardians were not allowed simply to lease land to whomever they wanted, since this would provide too many opportunities to defraud the minors. Land they held in trust was leased in public auctions conducted by the court.[89] Also common was the sale of the harvest from land already planted. In Aisy, for example, the tutor of Pierre Guichard's children sold that year's product from three *journaux* of grains to the lord of Precy for 49 livres.[90]

The most potent form of judicial oversight was the *compte de tutelle.* At the end of a guardianship–that is, at the majority or marriage of the ward–the tutor was required to give an account of his administration of the goods and revenue from the estate.[91] The tutor could do so before arbitrators or before the local seigneurial court. While some accounts were amicable, wards frequently sued guardians to force them to account for their "management and administration." Judges always agreed, and the tutor would submit a written account to the court. The judge would go through it item by item, crossing out or reducing expenditures that he thought to be illegitimate or inflated.[92]

Sometimes, instead of nominating guardians, families decided to emancipate the minor from parental authority. Unmarried minors in their early twenties or late teens could be freed from parental authority as represented by the tutor and curator. Since emancipations were a royal prerogative, the normal procedure was that the family first applied to the *chancellerie* of the Dijon Parlement, which had authority over the royal seal for the province of Burgundy. The family would then meet in the presence of the seigneurial judge, who would read the letter of emancipation, hear the opinions of all family members, and officially ratify the emancipation. The family of Pierre André Masson praised his maturity: Masson had proven himself "for several years and especially since the death of his father, having comported himself in such a way as to show himself capable of administering his goods, that he is of a regular conduct and that we can without danger confer on him the administration of his goods and movables and the revenue from the immovables."[93]

Emancipation by royal letter and family agreement did not free the minor from all parental authority, even by proxy through the *tutelle.* As Masson's family stated, the emancipation gave Masson outright possession of his "goods and movables," but he only had access to the revenue from immovables (e.g., land, buildings). He therefore could not sell or alienate the land inherited until marriage or the age of twenty-five.[94] In addition, an emancipated minor was still assumed to need assistance in court, and so at the emancipation the family would appoint a *curateur en plaids* to assist in court cases.

In northern Burgundy few families opted to emancipate orphaned minors. There were only five emancipations in the sampled courts in the

1750s and four in the 1780s. At the same time, families appointed tutors for 125 and 168 men and women in their twenties during the 1750s and 1780s, respectively. In other words, less than 5 percent of twenty-something minors were emancipated by their families. There are several reasons why emancipations were rare in northern Burgundy. Unlike regions of Roman law in southern France, parental authority was held to end with marriage or majority, with these events bringing about "tacit emancipation." So the vast numbers of emancipations that filled many courts in southern France were unnecessary in northern Burgundy. The cost and time associated with emancipations is not known but included trips to Dijon, court fees to the *chancellerie,* and meetings of the family. Finally, the Parlement of Dijon did not easily grant emancipations. Jean Bouhier, jurist and first president of the Dijon Parlement, noted that although emancipations are common in many parts of France, "we make things difficult in our parlement."[95]

After the family had appointed guardians for minor children, or immediately after sealing the estate when there were none, the next step in the settling of estates was a complete inventory of the goods, money, and papers of the deceased. The probate inventory (*inventaire après décès*) had many functions, all of them related to the protection of the heirs, creditors, and minor children. Minors needed an accurate record of the value of the estate to ensure that their tutor and curator did not take advantage of them. The partition of the estate among the surviving heirs would be based partly on the inventory done by the seigneurial court.[96] Finally, an important function of the inventory was to see if the estate was capable of paying the creditors. If the cash on hand and money owed to the estate did not outweigh the debts, the court would order a judicial auction of the movables.

The court did not inventory the estates of all who died. The childless had no need of an inventory, since customary law divided the goods between the parents and the surviving spouse based on their marriage contract. Unmarried people also had little need of an inventory, except when heavily indebted. And finally, if a surviving spouse could demonstrate to the court that the married couple had no minor children and that the estate was not overburdened with debt, the court would often allow the family to dispense with the inventory. In 1750 Andrette du Condé argued against the other presumptive heirs that there should be no court-conducted inventory of the estate of her husband, a merchant, since "her husband left no minors from his marriage, and all the heirs of her deceased husband are here present."[97] The judge ordered an inventory, but only because the other heirs demanded it.

When there were surviving minor children, the court had a serious responsibility to see that the children got their due at majority, though it was possible to avoid an inventory even in these cases. Sometimes the family reached an agreement and avoided the inventory. Charlotte Gradelet, for example, informed the court that she and the rest of the family, including her deceased husband's siblings, had agreed that no inventory was needed. Instead Gradelet agreed to feed, clothe, and keep her children until they reached majority, to instruct them, and have them learn a profession. At majority each would receive 15 livres. The other family members informed the judge that this was a beneficial arrangement for the three minor children–in other words, that the 15 livres was equal to or greater than what their share of the inventoried movables would have been–so the court did not do the inventory.[98]

In many instances the inventory was the last contact the court had with the estate. The clerk kept a copy of the inventory in his archives and passed several other copies to the families (and to the tutor and curator). Unless there was a significant amount of money owed by the deceased, the *procureur d'office* would then request that the judge discharge him of his responsibility toward the estate. If there were no debts, if the cash on hand was enough to pay the debts, or if the heirs promised to guarantee the debts and were wealthy enough to do so, the judge would discharge the *procureur d'office* and order the seal removed, and the family would move on to divide the inheritance.

Sometimes creditors opposed the lifting of the seal from the estate. In 1780 two *procureurs* and a *fille majeure* appeared in court to protest the lifting of the seal on the estate of Jean Baptiste Gallinet. They all claimed that Gallinet died indebted to them. Despite the *procureur d'office*'s advice that the estate was so small that the costs of a judicial seizure and auction would eat up all of the movables, the judge ordered an inventory, a sale, and a subsequent distribution of the revenue in order of privilege–the church, court costs, noble creditors, and then everyone else.[99]

The court's main responsibility was to creditors and minors, but it also had to look after the interests of the various heirs. The court's role here was smaller, since, unlike minors, adult heirs were legally responsible, and unlike creditors, they were likely to know of the death and actively participate in the settling of the estate. Still, before the judge would allow the removal of the seal and the discharge of the *procureur d'office,* he was to ensure that none of the presumptive heirs opposed the discharge. This meant that all heirs had to be present before the court or send written permission for other family members to represent them. If one of the heirs protested the way the family was planning to divide the goods, or if one of the presumptive heirs was absent, the estate would remain open. In 1788 the court refused to discharge the *procureur d'office,* to remove the seal, and to execute the will of François Dumery because his three children were not present (two lived in Paris and one in Lucenay-le-Duc). Things remained in this uncertain state until their mother submitted proof of power of attorney (*procuration*) from the children, about six months later.[100]

The route from probate justice to civil litigation in inheritance matters was an easy one. At every procedural step the court required the agreement of the family members. When siblings, parents, grand-children, and spouses disagreed about who should be nominated guardians, whether there should be an inventory, or who would get what, the estate would then move into regular civil litigation so the judge could decide the question. François Gauteret requested that the seal be removed from his brother's goods, while his two sisters and their husbands opposed this. It seems that François lived together with his brother, Claude, and before his death Claude had sold his portion of the shared goods to François for 200 livres. François therefore claimed that the court had in fact sealed a house and goods that belonged exclusively to him, and that all Claude owned at death was the 200 livres, which could be divided between him and his sisters. The sisters saw the sale as an attempt to defraud them of their rightful inheritance and claimed a third of Claude's share of the goods he possessed in community with François. The dispute continued until the siblings reconciled among themselves, with François agreeing to pay each sister 120 livres. It was only then that the judge could order the lifting of the seals and the transfer of the estate to the heirs.[101]

Apart from protecting minors and heirs, the court actively participated in the division of estates. In some instances heirs presented a will to the court and asked the judge to order its execution. The judge would read the testament and verify that it was written by a notary, signed, and witnessed. Then he would order it to be carried out. In 1751, for example, the widow of Daniel Deroye, a merchant who had died suddenly while she was away working in the vineyards, requested that his testament be verified and executed, which the judge did.[102]

The validation of a will was a voluntary service that the court offered to villagers, but few took advantage of it, with no more than a handful of "homologations" per decade in any seigneurial court. There are several reasons for this. The first is that official validation was not required to execute a will. Only when there was dispute over the will was it necessary for the heirs to have the seigneurial judge order its execution. In addition, most people did not write wills. This is revealed through study of the inheritance patterns of Messigny, a small village north of Dijon. Court cases from the seigneurial court of St. Bénigne, combined with parish death records and notarial documents, allow us to see how families in Messigny chose to settle their estates and what roles the court, arbitration, and simple agreement played in the transfer of property from one generation to the next. We are fortunate in that the village of Messigny possessed its own notary (most villagers had to travel to town for a notary) and most inhabitants conducted their legal business with him.[103]

Most inhabitants of Messigny did not write wills. From 1780 to 1789 there were sixty-eight adult deaths recorded in the parish registers of Messigny. In the same period the village notary recorded only twenty-six wills, including testaments, *donations à cause de mort,* and *partages* done before death.[104] Some of those who died in the 1780s may have written a will earlier, but it is unlikely that many did so, since virtually all testaments were written by people who thought they were on their deathbeds. Most contain a clause similar to that of François Chaussenot's will, which notes that he was "abed, indisposed in body, nevertheless of a sound mind *[sain de jugement].*"[105]

How were will writers different from those who died intestate? The first assumption would surely be that those with more property to leave behind were more likely to prepare a formal, written, notarized will. There is some evidence to support this, but the relation between wealth and will writing is not strong. Of the twenty-six who wrote wills, it was possible to match fifteen with tax payments from 1784. While the average tax assessment in Messigny for 1784 was 13.7 livres, the average will-writer (among the fifteen identified) paid 16.1 livres. But this exaggerates the role of wealth, as those who could not be located on the tax rolls include several domestic servants, as well as poor day laborers who boarded with family and so paid no taxes. If we included these poorer inhabitants, the average wealth level of will-writers would probably be approximately equal to the overall average for the village.

Gender was a significant factor. Fourteen of the twenty-six will-writers were women, including five unmarried women. There are several reasons that women were overrepresented in the population of will-writers. The first is that unmarried women, with neither children nor husband, had total freedom to hand out their money as they saw fit. Marie Sauvestre, *fille majeure journalière,* left everything to her brother Jean.[106] Claudine Fleury, a domestic servant, chose to leave all her earthly possessions to her master.[107] The overrepresentation of married women is more difficult to explain. It could be related to the fact that many women outlived their husbands. Since the Burgundian Custom left the husband's estate wholly in his wife's hands until her death, giving her usufruct rights over his property and actual ownership and authority over her own, the member of the couple who died first could have been more likely to die intestate. The surviving spouse, who would then divide the estate among the children, would write a will.

More significantly, the married women who wrote wills were more concerned with avoiding contention and dispute within the family than were male will-writers. Of the wills written by women, half of them mentioned that she was writing the will to avoid possible dissension in the family. Men who wrote wills mentioned family harmony only twice (in 15 percent of wills). Etiennette Marchand, a bourgeois widow, noted that she, "desiring to prevent all difficulties between her children and grand-children, has done the division of goods among them in the following manner . . ."[108] Anne Drouard wanted to "avoid the contests that could arise between her children and grand-children on the subject of her future succession."[109]

In Messigny there were several groups of will-writers. Among married men and women with children, those who wrote wills were better-off than average, and thus slightly more likely to write wills because they had more property. The unmarried were another important group of will-writers, since they were freer to do what they wanted with their property. Finally, women felt more personally responsible than men for harmony within the family and wrote wills to preserve it.

For those who drew up wills, what role did the seigneurial court play in the division of the estate? Most of the will-writers had their estates settled without court intervention. Of the twenty-six who wrote wills, only three came before the court for legal confirmation, and none of them generated any real disputes among the heirs. The five inheritance disputes actually judged by the court all concerned the estates of villagers who had died intestate. The concern of female will-writers to maintain harmony and goodwill clearly bore fruit: the preparation of a will made it far less likely that the heirs would dissipate the estate in legal battles.

Where the deceased had died without leaving a will, the estate would be divided equally among the children, regardless of birth order or gender. Any gifts given to children at marriage or at other times would be subtracted from the total given to each child.[110] The family had several means of partitioning the estate. The heirs could simply reach an agreement, divide the land, and then sign an accord before a notary. This was the easiest and most desirable way to divide an estate, but it only worked when the heirs could get along. Alternatively they could ask the judge to perform the division. With the help of experts and input from the family, the judge would divide the buildings, land, and goods into equal portions and then have the heirs draw lots. Finally, families could take their disputes to arbitrators, who would divide the estate the same way a judge would.

Those who did not write wills needed more intervention from the local seigneurial court, and the settlement of estates could become especially expensive when the family members fought over the property. The average court costs to litigate an inheritance dispute in the fourteen courts studied was 55.9 livres in the 1750s and 87.9 livres in the 1780s, about 3.5 and 5.5 times more than other kinds of cases.[111] The high cost of inheritance disputes was related to the complexity of the cases, which typically involved marriage contracts, many witnesses, and multiple plaintiffs and defendants each with their own programs. They were also expensive because, when the judge reached his decision, the division still had to be carried out, which execution carried additional costs. Mothers who wrote wills to maintain peace within the family were wise–they not only avoided posthumous ignominy but also saved their heirs a great deal of money.

Even when the heirs did not fight among themselves, the court's involvement could be costly. Estate auctions were bad news. The costs of the court–by the time the seal, the *tutelle* (when there was one), the inventory, the sale, and then the distribution were over–were high indeed. On average it cost 83 livres to settle an estate that went to auction in the 1750s and 137 livres in the 1780s. This represented an average of 11 percent of the value of the movables from the estates.[112] Of estates with movables worth less than 1,000 livres, the court costs took 15 percent in the 1750s and 24 percent in the 1780s. Court costs ate up a sizable amount from the estates of the poor: 57 percent when the goods auctioned were worth less than 200 livres in the 1750s, and 38 percent in the 1780s. When the *procureur d'office* of Ancey suggested a sale of the estate of Anne Laveille, the family protested against "the fees of the sale that would be done and would absorb the major part of the revenue."[113] It is unsurprising that, whenever possible, heirs tried to avoid court-ordered auctions. Estates that had to go to auction to pay creditors lost a great deal of the movable property to the court. Families had to pay in court fees at least a tenth of the revenue from the auction, and as much as half of small estates.

It is important to note here that, as was also the case with criminal cases, the money paid to the court in probate justice did not all go into the pockets of judicial officers. The law fixed the amounts that judicial officers were entitled to for these services. The judge received 20 or 30 sols for affixing a seal (30 sols for the estate of a bourgeois) and 30 or 45 sols for a *tutelle*. For judicial auctions the judge received 3 livres for estates worth less than 100 livres, and 30 sols more per 100 livres of value to a maximum of 10 livres for estates worth over 600 livres.[114] Generally the fees paid to *procureurs d'office* were about half, and to clerks slightly less than half, of the amounts paid to judges. The amounts increased slightly in 1747 when the Parlement of Dijon authorized judges to collect 3 livres for the nomination of guardians for minors. In addition, to save money for the clients of the courts, after 1747 judges were forbidden from participating in estate auctions, which were to be conducted by the clerk assisted by the *huissier* of the justice.[115] Estate auctions were expensive because the court used a great deal of taxed paper, prepared all documents in multiple copies, published the auction, registered the legal acts prepared, and contacted presumptive heirs and creditors. While probate justice was certainly the most significant source of income for judicial officers, the amounts that found their way into the coffers of the judge, prosecutor, and clerk were much smaller than the amounts paid by the clients of the courts.

It is more difficult to know the court costs involved when there was no sale of the estate. Auctions were exceptional, with only about 13 percent of estates requiring this type of court intervention to protect creditors.[116] The rest settled for far less money, since an estate sale generally required the presence of court officers (after 1747, only the clerk) in the village for one or two full days. Unlike the cases in regular contentious session, the records of probate acts of justice do not systematically contain statements of the costs, presumably since the court waited until the end to add up court fees. There is no doubt that the inventory and the sale cost the most.

Most *tutelles* were done either at the judge's townhouse or immediately after the annual assizes if the family sought to avoid a trip to town. The *tutelle* took only a few minutes, since most families had made up their mind before coming.[117] If you could avoid an inventory by agreeing to feed, clothe, and raise the children, costs could be quite low. In Chazilly, for example, the posing of the seal and the *tutelle* for the estate of Anne Bonnard was done for only 8 livres 8 sols.[118] In 1786 the *procureur d'office* of Chambolle and Morey initiated a lawsuit against a dozen people who had not paid court fees for probate justice over the previous ten years. Here a *tutelle* cost 7 livres 7 sols 6 deniers, of which 3 livres went to the judge, while the *procureur d'office* received 2 livres 5 sols and the clerk 2 livres 2 sols 6 deniers.[119] When the family managed to avoid costly inventories and sales, and could stay out of contentious justice, the entire settlement of estates generally went through for less than 20 livres, often less than 10, an amount that surely compares favorably to twenty-first-century probate costs.

The local seigneurial court was often heavily involved in the settlement of estates, and it was required by law to seal the estate until the court was satisfied that the minor children, creditors, and absent heirs were protected. Sometimes this was very expensive, but in many cases families could see to the devolution of property between generations with only a minimum of contact with the court, saving them a great deal of money. Still, of the various functions performed by seigneurial courts, probate justice was by far the most expensive. Realizing this, the Parlement of Dijon tried to limit these costs. In 1747 it issued a restatement of the fees that seigneurial judicial officers were allowed to charge for services. To save heirs money, the *arrêt* specified that the court was to place seals on estates in only four situations: when the family expressly requested it, when there were minor children, when one or more presumptive heirs were absent, and when there were creditors opposing the partition of the estate.[120]

We will see in chapter 5 that court costs declined appreciably in civil cases in the late eighteenth century. This, however, was not the case in probate matters. If we compare court costs and procedural indexes for inheritance matters between the 1750s and 1780s in the courts studied, it is clear that the settling of estates actually became more expensive and time-consuming. During the 1750s the 337 estates that came before the court for any services (mostly for *tutelles*) generated 562 separate legal acts, or 1.67 acts per estate. In the 1780s the 482 estates needed 872 acts, or 1.81 legal acts per estate. In probate justice northern Burgundian seigneurial courts became slower and more procedural. In the very large seigneurial justice of La Vallière in western France, the cost of voluntary justice similarly increased markedly over the course of the eighteenth century. Most notably, judges charged about four times more for guardianships in the 1780s than in the 1690s. The increase was less for seals and inventories but was still significant.[121] The increase may have been less spectacular in northern Burgundy, but it was clear nevertheless. It is possible that the judicial officers of the 1780s used probate procedure to recoup the legal fees they lost through parlement's inauguration of faster and cheaper procedure in contentious justice.

Still, the cost and slowness of probate justice should not be exaggerated. The majority of estates did not require a court-ordered auction, and most siblings did not fight over their parents' property. With a little foresight parents could ensure a relatively painless transfer of property to the next generation. The expense of probate justice was mostly due to the nature of the cases themselves, especially with disputes and auctions, both of which involved a lot of the court's time. In the *cahiers de doléances* of 1789, some people complained that they had to make trips into town to have guardians nominated. Other than this, most seem to have recognized that there was no cheap way to protect the interests of minor children, adult heirs, and creditors.

Conclusion

Seigneurial courts participated effectively in local affairs. There was a problem, however, in the considerable costs involved in probate and criminal cases. It is clear, in fact, that these were among the most expensive of all cases that came before seigneurial judges. Minor criminal cases could sometimes cost the accused 100 livres or more, an amount that represented several months' income even for better-off peasants. Probate cases for estates that were overburdened with debts or where the heirs could not get along were also expensive, but this is probably the case in all judicial systems. High costs doubtless discouraged some victims of minor thefts or physical violence from going to court. Ordinary people nevertheless developed strategies that were effective in minimizing costs while using the services of the court. In criminal cases it was common to use the threat of the court case to force an opponent to settle privately–to apologize and provide restitution. In probate matters high costs could be avoided in several ways, of which the most common were writing a will and avoiding a probate inventory by settling an amount to be paid when children reached their majority. The Parlement of Dijon, as we will see, was trying to improve the situation by limiting court fees. While there was a significant reduction in overall court costs, the changes involved primarily the use of a new procedure for minor cases. For criminal and probate cases, it is the considerable complexity of the cases–the need to hear witnesses and to protect the financial interest of minors–that explains the high costs. Only if the monarchy had agreed to pay legal fees for judicial clients could the problem have been solved.[122]

Despite the costs of justice, seigneurial courts were a significant and active force in these largely self-regulating villages, ensuring the protection of property and honor, the smooth functioning of village politics, and the transfer of property between generations. Judges took seriously their responsibilities toward individuals, families, and communities and generally fulfilled their functions reliably. The fact that judicial officers enforced the seigneurial system and allowed absentee lords to maintain their profits should not blind us to the positive ways in which seigneurial courts intervened in local life. Apart from cases that very directly involved the lord's interests, most judges seem to have worked in the best interests of their clients.

Seigneurial courts remained active in criminal cases. Their judgments generally were neither too harsh nor too mild, and focused on restitution rather than humiliating punishments that might escalate the dispute. The judge's control over local political matters and agricultural life was likewise effective and relatively popular. For local politics (presiding over village assemblies, ratifying local elections) the judge's main role was to provide a measure of equality and ensure that local positions were filled. While people may sometimes have resented the fines they had to pay for pasture and harvest offenses, the court's intervention ensured the effective functioning of the agricultural system. In probate cases the courts worked to protect the economic interest of minors, presumptive heirs, and creditors and to ensure that the deceased's wishes were carried out. Local courts were active, interventionist, and overall a positive force in the northern Burgundian countryside.

Chapter 4

Conflict and Consensus In and Out of Court

In most police, probate, and criminal cases seigneurial courts responded effectively to the wishes of their clients and enforced norms with which most people agreed. This is, of course, still truer of civil litigation, since plaintiffs would generally not sue unless they felt they had something to gain. The main purpose of this chapter is to analyze the meaning of lawsuits within the context of rural society in eighteenth-century northern Burgundy. Ordinary people in northern Burgundy, as we will see, were litigious, with more lawsuits per capita than many other societies in different times and places. It is difficult, however, to know what litigation rates tell us about a society. Court records and litigation rates need to be interpreted with care. The main challenge is to understand the relationship between a lawsuit, a dispute, and a perceived slight or tort. Attempts by sociologists and legal theorists to determine what rates of litigation reveal about the contentiousness of contemporary American society have made this point forcefully. For a disagreement to become a dispute and then a lawsuit, the injured party must first perceive the injury ("naming"), attribute responsibility ("blaming"), and finally go to the person responsible and demand restitution ("claiming").[1] Only when the person that the victim holds responsible refuses to offer compensation or repay something owed does a tort or debt become a dispute. Many actionable disputes never come to court because the injured party often does not complete the process of naming, blaming, and claiming.[2]

Not all unpaid debts or actionable torts become disputes, and not all disputes end up in court. To evaluate the willingness of people to use the courts in contemporary America, Michael Saks argues that scholars need to know the number of the following: actionable injuries, decisions to claim, cases presented to lawyers, lawsuits filed, settlements negotiated, trials begun, trial verdicts, amounts of awards, appeals, and compensation actually paid.[3] At each stage the number of cases declines drastically. In his

A small part of this chapter has appeared as "L'arbitre, intermédiaire de justice en Bourgogne vers la fin du XVIIe siècle," in Claire Dolan, ed., *Entre justice et justiciables: Les auxiliaires de la justice du moyen âge au XXe siècle* (Quebec: Presses de l'Université Laval, 2005), 617–26. It is reproduced here with the permission of the publisher.

investigation of medical malpractice, Saks suggests that only 10 percent of the victims of bad doctoring choose to sue. Of these, an infinitesimal proportion reach a final verdict in court, with some cases filtered out by lawyers who refuse to take the case, and many more being settled out of court, either with the judge's help or through the initiative of the parties following the threat of a lawsuit.[4]

The fact that only a tiny proportion of disputes ever came before the court is a truism that could doubtless apply to every society that has ever existed. It is nevertheless true that to understand the social function of the lawsuit and local courts in northern Burgundy we similarly need to know something about the way that disputing was conducted outside of court. As in twenty-first century America, an important function of lawsuits in the eighteenth century was to encourage the opponent to get serious about settling the dispute outside of court.[5] Ordinary people in northern Burgundy plotted out their strategies for victory, threatened and then instigated court cases when a neighbor went too far, but were always willing to settle if the other party was amenable.

The private settling of disputes is crucial to understanding seigneurial justice–not, as some have argued, because it shows that people preferred that these local courts leave them alone, but because bringing about reconciliation between the parties was the ultimate purpose of the court case. Judges did not perceive non-judicial methods of settlement as competing with official justice, but rather frequently encouraged parties to reconcile themselves, to use the mediation services of a neighbor, or to take their disagreement to arbitrators.

While there was a host of formal and informal methods of dispute settlement in eighteenth-century northern Burgundy, seigneurial justice was at the heart of the way that ordinary folk resolved their disputes.[6] I do not mean to suggest that a majority, or even a substantial proportion, of theoretically actionable disputes came before the local judge–there is little question that the number of court cases was an insignificant percentage of the instances in which people disagreed.[7] But when people reached a resolution of a dispute, the local court generally played a role, even if it was only through the unstated threat to go to court. Whether it was through the threat of the costs of justice, the possibility of having an agreement enforced by the court, or the ratification of arbitrations by the court, most informal ways of bringing people together depended for their effectiveness on the local seigneurial court.

This chapter is about the ways that ordinary people disputed and resolved their conflicts both in and out of court. In it I make two distinct but related arguments. Continuing with the main theme of this study, I present seigneurial courts as true local justices, with a role in everyday life that was far greater than judicial institutions have today. There were many informal ways of settling disputes, but arbitration, mediation, negotiation, conciliation, and private settlement were effective precisely because of the involvement or threat of involvement of the official justice system through the local seigneurial court. There were no entirely unofficial or informal means of conflict settlement, but rather a scale of more or less formal means of resolution, all of which depended on the existence of a formal court system. This leads to the radical conclusion that court records are essential for understanding social relations not only because they provide evidence of the kinds of social bonds that existed and broke between individuals, but because local courts provided some of the context for the elaboration and construction of social bonds.

The other main argument here is a corollary to the notion that seigneurial justice played an important role in everyday social relations. In this litigious society, court cases did not generally lead to the severance of normal social bonds (in contrast to the situation in contemporary industrialized societies), and with the notable exception of private family matters, there was little public dishonor associated with calling in the local seigneurial court to mediate between disputing parties.

The Uses of Litigation

What motivated people to come to court? How did people decide to submit their dispute to the arbitration of a judge? These questions are, unfortunately, impossible to answer with certainty. Judges never asked litigants to justify themselves, and if people occasionally explained their motives for coming to court, we will see below that these statements were part of a legal strategy rather than reliable indications of motivations. It is not possible to situate the point at which a dispute became significant enough for the parties to go to court–the thousands of calculations people made about how to continue or end the many disputes and conflicts that made up daily life are irretrievably lost to us.

Historians have suggested several explanations for why people went to court in the past. Some see the court case as part of a victory-seeking strategy rather than a serious attempt to end the dispute. Isabelle Carrier analyses the lawsuits of a family of local notables in southern France. Continually in dispute with each other and everyone else, it is very clear that for these men and women the lawsuit was simply one more step in ongoing and endless disputing. None of the lawsuits ever truly ended the dispute, and it seems unlikely that any of the parties even imagined it could do so.[8] Daniel Lord Smail claims that lawsuits were motivated primarily by hatred, and that litigants cared little about the ultimate outcome of the case: the lawsuit "was intended primarily as an inimical gesture, a public warning, a sign to all and sundry of budding animosity."[9] Gregory Hanlon agrees that emotion was an important part of the reason that people had for going to court, but he argues that people were looking for justice. They sought equalizing redress for what they had suffered at another's hand. Unlike Smail, Hanlon argues that the judge's decision, rather than the simple fact of suing someone, was the ultimate goal for most litigants.[10]

Other historians have suggested that the decision to go to court was always taken only after all other possible means of dispute resolution had failed. Since ordinary people perceived judicial institutions as foreign and strange, the story goes, they called in the court only as a last resort. Because of the popular Christian emphasis on living peaceably, disputers ended up in court only after trying to resolve their conflicts with the help of the priest, a local notable or a family assembly. Nicole Castan cites the peasant maxim that "a poor agreement is better than a good lawsuit." Terrified by the official justice system, peasants tried every possible alternative before coming to court.[11] Jean Quéniart argues that "the most common sentiment was that villagers had nothing to gain from frequenting the judges, and that one took the risk of making enemies rather than friends." He further claims that a few villagers (only the wealthiest) willingly used the courts, some merely tolerated it, but the majority avoided it whenever possible. Going to court, then, was shameful evidence that more peaceable solutions had failed.[12]

Certainly when they stood before their judges, many litigants were quick to point out that they came to court only as a last resort. This was especially true when lawsuits involved family members. In 1790 Jean and Joseph Renier submitted a complaint to the seigneurial court of Flée. When their sister Anne died, they claimed, Jean-Michel (the other living sibling) took her entire estate, refusing to give them their share. They waited seven months before bringing the matter before the court, hoping that Jean-Michel would come to his senses. His failure to do so was why "they find themselves forced to take the extreme path" of coming to court.[13]

This desire to avoid lawsuits between family members is especially apparent in the wills that people wrote. The Custom of Burgundy provided that the estate of non-nobles who died intestate would be divided equally among all children, regardless of birth order or gender.[14] Many parents who wrote wills followed this equitable partition, so the heirs got the same part of the estate as they would have had the parent not written a will.[15] Anne Auclair, for example, divided her estate among her three children while she was still alive. Together they estimated the value of all the land and property, divided it into three equal lots, and then drew straws. Since her will followed the customary intestate division, her reason for writing a will was not to ensure that her wishes were carried out after her death. Her will also did not reduce the costs of settling the estate (providing that her children remained friendly after her death). Her reason for writing a will was to maintain peace within her family: she wanted to "maintain after her death the union and the sweet intelligence that rules between her children and to remove all difficulties that could arise in the division of her property and that of her husband."[16]

Unrelated defendants and plaintiffs also made a point of noting that they were not litigious and that it was only the obstinacy of the other party that brought them before the judge. In 1751 François Pelletier sued Emilland Blondeau for damages committed by Blondeau's geese in Pelletier's barley. Blondeau told the judge that he was not civilly responsible since the field was bounded by the road but was not enclosed by a fence or hedge. He nevertheless offered to pay Pelletier a measure of barley plus 24 sols for the court costs, explaining that he "does not like to use a court case to end the matter."[17] In a case over an assault, the accused, Jean Grenot, informed the judge that, although his accuser would never be able to prove his case, "nevertheless desiring to live in peace and union with everyone and to have no lawsuits," Grenot offered to pay the plaintiff's court costs and medical fees for his treatment.[18]

Examples such as these seem at first to support the views of historians like Nicole Castan that peasants were ashamed to go to court and that they did so only after exhausting non-judicial avenues of settlement. There are, however, several reasons to be suspicious. First among these is the fact that many such statements to the court occurred in cases that involved members of the same family. There is no question that village opinion held that families should be able to manage their own affairs without recourse to the law. Indeed prevailing notions of paternal authority tended to conflate a husband and father's power over his wife and children with a monarch's absolute power over his subjects, thus closing the family off from outside interference.[19]

Statements that litigants appeared in court only after exhausting all other avenues are much rarer in non-family lawsuits. More importantly, such statements have to be understood as part of a strategy used to win the lawsuit. Plaintiffs did their best to convince the court that the defendant's obstinacy had forced them to bring the matter to the court. Responding to a lawsuit over the *cens* from the widow of a previous *fermier* of the seigneurie, Claude Genglaire noted that if the "Sieur Margin [the old *fermier*] would have been willing to see reason there would have been no lawsuit between them."[20] Genglaire portrays Margin as a man unwilling to see reason, to live peaceably and even to defend the logic of his case. Implicitly he presents himself to the court as eminently reasonable and amenable to a peaceable solution. Plaintiffs tried to avoid being seen by the court, the community, and their families and friends, as litigious.

Defendants similarly tried to present themselves as the peaceable victims of unreasonable, litigious neighbors. In some ways it was easier for defendants than for plaintiffs, since they were the passive recipients of summons issued by the plaintiffs. A common strategy of defendants was to claim to the court that they had already offered to settle the case. Pierre Gille, for example, protested the involvement of the court in a farming dispute with Jean

Bitousset. He claimed that he had offered to pay "amicably" an amount to be estimated by two experts for the damages caused by his horses in Bitousset's land. This strategy involved admitting responsibility, but was an attempt to avoid having to pay court costs. The judge either did not believe or did not care that Gille had offered to pay–in his final judgment he ordered him to pay the two measures of hay for the damages, plus court costs of 33 livres.[21] The self-portrayal of litigants as peaceful neighbors driven to litigation by the intractable stubbornness of the other party to the dispute was primarily a strategy to win their case, and tells us little about litigants' real motivations for going to court.

The final reason for not believing litigants who said they used the court reluctantly is the number of villagers who passed through before the judge. Hervé Piant, in an innovative discussion of ordinary people's willingness to use the courts, suggests that most ordinary people believed in a vision of village solidarity, and therefore felt obliged to explain why they were disrupting it. But this vision of village society was a myth, and in any case it hardly hindered people from going to court regularly: "it is astonishing to see the extent to which court registers are filled with enemies of litigation."[22]

In the end, we can never know with certainty what motivated ordinary people to decide to go to court. There were undoubtedly many different reasons to do so, and it would not be difficult to find examples of people who lodged a court case simply to make public the fact that they had been wronged. And certainly some people lived their whole life without going to court, preferring to accept slights or use violence rather than risk appearing before the judge. The evidence from northern Burgundy in the eighteenth century, however, suggests that in most cases people were primarily interested in having a dispute resolved so that normal life could resume. In any case, northern Burgundians testified of their desire to live at peace with their neighbors, but they nevertheless ended up in court relatively often. Rates of litigation in most of these small northern Burgundian villages are significant, suggesting that, whatever litigants told the judge, they were not highly reticent to call in the judge to settle their disputes and conflicts.

It does seem likely, though, that litigation rates in the eighteenth century were well below levels that characterized the sixteenth and seventeenth centuries, when most of Western Europe likely experienced a massive increase in the volume of litigation.[23] In the courts of the English town of King's Lynn, for example, the number of lawsuits in the advanced stage of pleading increased sixfold between 1563 and 1640.[24] In the King's Bench and Court of Common Pleas, the number of cases began to soar in 1560–by 1640, when the number of cases began to level off, there were about fifteen times more lawsuits than there had been in the 1490s.[25] At the height of the litigation craze (the late sixteenth century), almost every household in King's Lynn may have appeared in court each year.[26]

From these high rates of litigation, English courts saw a gradual decline through the late seventeenth century, reaching a low-point at about 1750, after which there was a slow rise into the 1830s.[27] Richard Kagan finds in early modern Castille the same pattern of sharp rise in the sixteenth and early seventeenth centuries followed by a decline through the late seventeenth and eighteenth centuries.[28] For France we have few studies of litigation or caseloads over the true *longue durée,* but Jonathan Dewald found that the seigneurial justice of the barony of Pont-St-Pierre had about three times fewer cases in the 1780s as it had in the late sixteenth century.[29] Similarly, John Dickinson found a rapid decline in levels of litigation in the late seventeenth century in the bailliage of Falaise, followed by stagnation to the middle of the eighteenth century and a slow rise to the Revolution.[30] Caseloads in the Parlement of Paris were also in gradual decline over the course of the eighteenth century.[31] Fabrice Mauclair demonstrates that the same overall pattern can be found in the large seigneurial justice of the *duché-pairie* of La Vallière, although in another large seigneurial justice, the barony of Huban in the Nivernais, caseloads remained more or less constant throughout the eighteenth century.[32]

As we see in tables 4.1 and 4.2, many northern Burgundian seigneurial courts heard no more than a few cases per year. Fontaine-en-Duesmois is the most extreme case, with only 13 and 12 cases for the 1750s and the 1780s, respectively, but several others were only slightly higher, like Montot. There is a large diversity among the villages studied, with litigation rates varying in the 1780s by as much as a factor of ten between the most and the least litigious villages. In the 1750s there was slightly less variety in litigation rates, but the differences were nevertheless significant, varying by a factor of about six.

Keeping in mind the wide distribution of data, we can nevertheless calculate average rates of litigiosity for the villages studied. In the 1780s the seigneurial courts settled a total of 2,455 cases between individuals (both the vast number of fines and gracious probate justice are excluded here and I have excluded two villages that had multiple seigneurial courts). The population in these villages was, according to a 1786 census, 7,020. There was, therefore, about one lawsuit for every three inhabitants of the villages during the 1780s, or 35 lawsuits per 1,000 inhabitants per year. But these population figures include children, who were much less likely than adults to appear before the judge in civil affairs. The figures also ignore the fact that a lawsuit involved an average of 2.5 individuals. The adult population of the villages can be estimated at about 5,000, while the number of people involved in contentious court cases was about 6,150. On average, then, individual northern Burgundian adult villagers were involved in 1.2 court cases per decade after the reforms of the 1760s and 1770s.[33] During the 1750s the calculations are complicated by the lack of population data, but if we multiply the number of households by 3.6, the number of adults per household in 1786, we

Table 4.1. Litigation rates by village, 1780–89

Village[a]	Population in 1786[b]	Hearths	Cases in regular session	Cases in assizes	Total cases[c]	Lawsuits per year per 1,000 people	Lawsuits per household over the decade
Aisy	325	66	54	0	54	16.6	0.81
Ampilly	211	25	36	5	41	19.4	1.6
Ancey	361	79	21	76	97	26.9	1.2
Bagnot	354	59	76	159	235	66.4	4.0
Bellefond	201	40	60	65	125	62.2	3.1
Billey and Villerrottin	370	45	32	298	330	89.2	7.3
Chazilly	254	50	30	18	48	18.9	0.96
Epagny	192	44	31	103	134	69.8	3.0
Flée	297	42	25	1	26	8.8	0.62
Foncegrive	231	46	53	119	172	74.5	3.7
Fontaine-en-Duesmois	361	62	12	0	12	3.3	0.19
Lanthes	100	23	104	13	117	117	5.1
Messigny	650	138	68	272	340	52.3	2.5
Meursault and Auxey[d]	1,858	371	496	24	520	28.0	1.4
Montot	271	72	19	4	23	8.5	0.32
Savigny-le-Sec	222	57	31	66	97	43.7	1.7
Senailly	762	112	81	3	84	11.0	0.75
Total	7,020	1,331	1,229	1,226	2,455	34.9	1.8

[a] I excluded the villages of Saucy and Saulon-la-Chapelle, both of which belonged in part to the religious chapter of St. Bénigne. Both were divided between several seigneuries, making the calculations impossible.

[b] ADCO L496, Amelot census, 1786.

[c] The number of cases includes all cases heard in regular session, including criminal cases and fines and (overwhelmingly) civil litigation; all private disputes heard in the assizes (i.e., pasturing disputes, but not fines for illicit pasturing). It does not include either the pasturing fines from the assizes or instances of probate justice. If all police and criminal cases were excluded, the total number of cases would drop about 10–15 percent.

[d] The number of court cases for the seigneurial court of the barony of Meursault are partly estimated. This court was more active than I first realized. Compiling all cases over two decades would have been too time-consuming, so I calculated five years' worth (i.e., 1750–55 and 1780–85), then doubled the number of cases heard in each five-year period.

Table 4.2. Litigation rates by village, 1750–59

Village[aa]	Hearths, 1750s	Cases in regular session, 1750s	Cases in assizes, 1750s	Total cases, per family (i.e., hearth)	Lawsuits per decade (1750s)
Aisy	71	17	0	17	0.2
Ampilly	26	41	1	42	1.6
Ancey	62	19	50	69	1.1
Bagnot	36	93	25	118	3.3
Bellefond	22	11	16	27	1.2
Billey and Villerrottin	62	68	54	122	2.0
Chazilly	45	35	0	35	0.78
Epagny	28	9	6	15	0.54
Flée	45	101	2	103	2.3
Foncegrive	37	20	3	23	0.62
Fontaine-en-Duesmois	43	13	0	13	0.30
Lanthes	12	20	1	21	1.8
Messigny	165	27	45	72	0.44
Meursault	343	530	2	532	1.6
Montot	48	30	0	30	0.63
Savigny-le-Sec	47	12	18	30	0.64
Senailly	94	158	2	160	1.7
Total	1186	1204	225	1429	1.2

[a] As in table 4.1, I have excluded the villages of Saucy and Saulon-la-Chapelle.

can estimate similar figures. During the 1750s individual adults could expect to be involved in about 0.8 court cases.

Are these figures high or low? Clearly the number of court cases does not represent a majority of the disputes, conflicts, and disagreements in which ordinary people were involved. Only a tiny proportion of inhabitants were involved in a lawsuit at any given time. The number of court cases is nevertheless high enough to challenge the notion that ordinary people perceived the local seigneurial court as an exterior authority that was to be avoided at all costs. Most property-owning families could expect to be involved in a court case at least once or twice per decade, and virtually everyone likely had a friend or relative who have been to court within the previous year or two.

How do northern Burgundians compare to other societies in terms of the frequency of their recourse to justice? Unfortunately there is a paucity of comparative data on litigiosity rates. In the American West in the late nineteenth century, JPs in one county heard one case per year per 111 inhabitants, one case per year per 25 inhabitants in another, or litigation rates of 10 and 40 cases per 1,000 inhabitants.[34] William E. Nelson suggests that in most towns of Plymouth County there was about one lawsuit between inhabitants of the same town per 1,000 people per year, and that over fifty years in the eighteenth century only about 5 percent of the towns' inhabitants passed before the judge.[35]

The best source of comparison is the national data presented by Bernard Schnapper for nineteenth-century France for both civil tribunals and justices of the peace.[36] There are many problems involved in comparing his analysis to the data presented in tables 4.1 and 4.2. The jurisdiction of JPs was not identical to that of seigneurial judges. JPs sometimes functioned as a Reconciliation Office, a fact that is not reflected in Schnapper's data. His analysis includes urban courts, which had higher rates of litigation than rural courts, so the exclusive focus on villages (and one small bourg) in the sample of seigneurial courts is also problematic. There is also a large unknown in the fact that Schnapper did not include commercial courts, whereas seigneurial justices heard such cases. On the positive side, both seigneurial courts and JPs resolved the civil side of farming torts, so the large number of such cases in seigneurial courts should not present a problem.[37]

With these caveats in mind, it is nevertheless clear that eighteenth-century peasants were litigious by nineteenth-century standards. The very highest rates of litigation in mainland France before JPs in 1856–60 was 29.5 per 1,000 inhabitants, with a national average of about 11.[38] Rates in the civil tribunals were far lower, averaging between 1 and 7 cases per 1,000 inhabitants, with a national average that varied over the century between 2 and 4 per 1,000 inhabitants. With an average of 35 lawsuits per 1,000 inhabitants in the 1780s and between 20 and 25 per 1,000 inhabitants in the 1750s (depending on the multiplier used for family size), northern Burgundian peasants frequently asked the court to intervene to settle their disputes. They may even have been more litigious in the 1780s than in the nineteenth century, as average litigation rates for cases before JPs in the Côte d'Or were between 17 and 18 per 1,000 inhabitants in the mid-nineteenth century.[39]

If, instead of calculating litigation rates, we wanted to consider the way the local seigneurial court immersed itself in local life, we would have to increase the figures dramatically. As we saw above, pasturing and other agricultural fines, which have been excluded in the number of cases, outnumber all contentious cases combined. We would also have to include the court's role in administering estates and looking after minor wards of the court. If we were to include these instances, we could estimate that after the reforms of the 1760s and 1770s each household could expect to come before the seigneurial court on average almost every year and in the 1750s they might appear three to four times over the decade. This was in addition to the required, and enforced, attendance of all household heads each year at the annual assizes of these local justices that were so integral to the regulation of daily life in northern Burgundian villages.

Undifferentiated litigation rates of the sort given above, though indicative of the level of involvement of the court and of the contentiousness of social relations, conceal almost as much as they reveal. The biggest problem with these figures is that in many of the civil court cases the plaintiff was not from the same village as the defendant. A case in which, for example, the court ordered Messigny merchants Claude and Antoine Gilbert to pay the 57 livres they owed Pierre Chaperon, a roofer from Dijon, tells us little about social relations within the village of Messigny, and more about business practices, the structure of credit and economic relations between the town and countryside.[40] Credit in the early modern period always depended to some extent on personal social relationships (viz. the double meanings of "credit" as reputation and money owed), so there can be little doubt that some kind of social bond tied Chaperon and the two Gilberts, if only something as insignificant as the sharing of a carafe of wine to seal the bargain. Still, the intertwining of social and economic relationships was strongest between men and women who were neighbors as well as creditors, debtors, and business partners. To understand the role of the court in village life it is necessary to separate court cases into those where the plaintiff and defendant had to continue to have daily social interaction from those where the parties could break their social and economic ties more easily.

Seigneurial courts in northern Burgundy were not only for country dwellers, as we can see in table 4.3. Approximately 60 and 70 percent of cases in the 1750s and 1780s, respectively, saw two litigants from the same village. While a significant number of cases involved urban dwellers, the proportion of such cases declined by half between the 1750s and 1780s. While the evidence remains merely suggestive since based only two years in a single

Table 4.3. Geographic origins of litigants

	Plaintiff and defendant from same village (%)	Plaintiff from another village (%)	Plaintiff from a town or city (%)
1750–59, regular session only	524 (54.4)	273 (28.3)	166 (17.2)
1750–59, assizes	172 (76.1)	32 (14.2)	22 (9.7)
1750–59, total	696 (58.5)	305 (25.7)	188 (15.8)
1780–89, regular session only	518 (51.9)	356 (35.7)	124 (12.4)
1780–89, assizes	1,084 (88.1)	103 (8.4)	44 (3.6)
1780–89, total	1,602 (71.9)	459 (20.6)	168 (7.5)

bailliage, urban dwellers may have acquired a preference for royal justice by the late eighteenth century: the proportion of civil cases in the bailliage of Dijon that involved an inhabitant of the capital increased from 46 percent in 1755 to 55 percent in 1785.[41] The proportion of cases involving the inhabitants of two separate villages also declined between the two decades studied, although here the decline is relative and not absolute. In any case, the change in the clientele of seigneurial courts is indicative of the fact that the institution was increasingly specializing in regulating village life, reinforcing its position as a form of auto-regulation for northern Burgundy's villages.

The incidence of inter-community litigation is nevertheless indicative of the economic interdependence of the countryside. In northern Burgundy, as in much of France, city folk owned a great deal of farmland that they rented to tenant farmers. There were other economic ties between town and country, such as the *bail à cheptel,* a sharecropping lease that was a form of credit whereby the owner loaned a herd of sheep to the lessee.[42] Finally, peasants sold their crops to and bought their supplies from urban merchants. When any of these financial relationships soured, when one party was unable or unwilling to meet established conditions, these contracts and deals could end up before the local seigneurial judge.

Inhabitants of the many small villages of northern Burgundy also sued and were sued by folks from neighboring villages. About a quarter of cases in the 1750s and a fifth of those from the 1780s involved a plaintiff and defendant from two different villages. These lawsuits resembled intra-village litigation in that most cases saw plaintiffs and defendants of approximately equal social and economic standing. They are evidence of the degree of geographic mobility within regional limits and of the existence of social and economic bonds beyond the village. Through marriage, families were often spread over several parishes and villages. A demographic study of the village of Messigny found that only half of marriages united two inhabitants of the village. Most of the other marriages were between a local and someone from a nearby village, although some of the brides and grooms were from surprisingly far away.[43]

People also loaned money and conducted business with inhabitants of villages other than their own. Recent work in notarial archives has illuminated the extent of rural credit markets all over France. Of course, people often borrowed as well from neighbors and family, and Gilles Postel-Vinay estimates that only about a tenth of loans passed through notaries.[44] Unnotarized loans generally involved much less money, as when Gabriel signed a promissory note agreeing to repay the 43 livres that Louis Villereau had loaned him.[45]

Despite the frequency of lawsuits between inhabitants of different towns and villages, the majority of lawsuits in the seigneurial courts of northern Burgundy nevertheless involved two or more residents of the same village. This is important in that it contradicts the idea that peasants called in the local court as mediator only in disagreements with those over whom the community had no control. More importantly, the kinds of cases and the people involved in those cases shows that seigneurial justice was truly a local institution, used by inhabitants to settle their minor disputes and regulate their disagreements. Virtually all kinds of people in these villages called the court in to arbitrate their disputes that sprang from almost all kinds of activities.

The following discussion uses figures taken from all civil court cases heard in regular session in the fourteen sampled seigneurial courts. This involves conflating all litigation generally with litigation within the village.[46] This conflation overestimates the importance of debt disputes and underestimates the importance of most other kinds of lawsuits. Farming disputes, trespass offenses, land disputes, fights over the use of common land and communal pasture, and village political affairs were all most likely to occur between residents of the same village, since physical proximity was required to generate the dispute. Indeed, a quick categorization of the civil cases heard in the sampled courts, presented in table 4.4 suggests that there were few facets of life that escaped the purview of the local seigneurial courts.

Keeping in mind, then, that the percentages given in table 4.4 inflate its importance, debt nevertheless remains by far the most significant category of disputes between villagers–at least 40 percent of all civil disputes even between inhabitants of the same village. Ordinary people borrowed not only through notaries from strangers, but also small sums of money from neighbors. It would be difficult to overemphasize the importance of credit in village social relations. Sometimes the debtor signed a promissory note, but often the parties apparently relied on memory and neighborliness to ensure repayment. This lack of written proof was why Jean Baptiste Sarrazin and Etienne Amoignon had to go to court to have a debt settled. The judge had to hear from three witnesses to the transaction to decide that Amoignon

Table 4.4. Civil cases heard in sampled courts in regular session (non-assize)

Type of case	1750–59 (%)	1780–89 (%)
Debts	464 (53.7)	461 (56.7)
Farming torts	73 (8.4)	21 (2.6)
Inheritance	101 (11.7)	91 (11.1)
Common land/farming	24 (2.8)	21 (2.6)
Land/building disputes	39 (4.5)	53 (6.4)
Farming disputes	11 (1.3)	11 (1.3)
Village affairs	51 (5.9)	33 (4.0)
Tithe	5 (0.6)	4 (0.5)
Breach of promise/paternity	5 (0.6)	5 (0.6)
Unknown	91 (10.5)	123 (14.9)
Total	864	823

indeed owed the plaintiff the 6 livres that he demanded.[47] When Claude Cuillerey loaned 58 livres to Roch Paperet, he got him to sign a note. The court saw Paperet's signature and summarily ordered him to pay the money.[48] Innkeepers, village merchants, and artisans extended credit to villagers as a matter of routine, and the examples of neighbors loaning small sums of money to each other are virtually unending.

The peasants of northern Burgundy also came to court a great deal over issues that concerned land boundaries and the use to be made of that land. They asked the court to adjudicate boundary disputes, to settle minor farming offenses, to determine whether one party was allowed to build onto his home, and to help decide matters of communal farming. Some of these functions of the court have already been discussed above, but the importance of seigneurial justice in keeping property rights and boundaries clear for villagers needs some emphasis. The local court ensured that people had the peaceful use of the land they owned and rented, plus fair use and access to communal resources, as defined by local custom and parlementary *arrêts*.

The third largest category of court cases in northern Burgundy was inheritance disputes. Family members preferred to settle inheritance matters without going to court, both for financial reasons and to keep the peace within the family. Still, when a dispute was too complicated or too bitter for amicable settlement within the family, people could rely on the court to help solve the problem. The use of the court was most common in cases where

Table 4.5. Professions of plaintiffs and defendants in regular (non-assize) cases

	Plaintiffs, 1750s (%)	Defendants, 1750s (%)	Plaintiffs, 1780s (%)	Defendants, 1780s (%)
Unknown	17 (1.9)	53 (4.3)	32 (3.1)	86 (6.0)
Agriculture				
Laboureur	155 (16.9)	400 (32.8)	149 (14.6)	392 (27.3)
Manouvrier	42 (4.6)	97 (7.9)	64 (6.3)	134 (9.3)
Vigneron	89 (9.7)	203 (16.6)	80 (7.8)	235 (16.4)
Merchant				
Merchant	195 (21.3)	155 (12.7)	238 (23.3)	168 (11.7)
Cabaretier	24 (2.6)	8 (0.7)	22 (2.1)	25 (1.8)
Bourgeois	13 (1.4)	9 (0.7)	23 (2.2)	19 (1.3)
Artisan	98 (10.7)	108 (8.8)	158 (15.4)	166 (11.6)
Domestic servant	3 (0.3)	0	5 (0.5)	6 (0.4)
Villages, officers				
Community	8 (0.9)	43 (3.5)	9 (0.9)	47 (3.3)
Local officer	18 (2.0)	41 (3.4)	11 (1.1)	8 (0.6)
Lord and his men				
Fermier	73 (8.0)	14 (1.1)	64 (6.3)	30 (2.1)
Seigneur	20 (2.2)	2 (0.2)	32 (3.1)	3 (0.2)
Seigneurial officer	20 (2.2)	8 (0.7)	6 (0.6)	16 (1.1)

Liberal professions				
Officer	5 (0.5)	0	14 (1.4)	14 (1.0)
Legal professional	51 (5.6)	9 (0.7)	56 (5.5)	7 (0.5)
Priest	13 (1.4)	9 (0.7)	8 (0.8)	7 (0.5)
Teacher	3 (0.3)	0	6 (0.6)	6 (0.4)
Surgeon and doctor	12 (1.3)	16 (1.3)	10 (1.0)	9 (0.6)
Unmarried (men and women)	56 (6.1)	46 (3.8)	37 (3.6)	58 (4.0)
Married women[a]	38 (4.1)	47 (3.8)	50 (4.9)	50 (3.5)
Widows	58 (6.3)	82 (6.7)	64 (6.3)	66 (4.6)
Total	915	1,221	1,024	1,436

[a] Married women and widows are counted according to the profession of their husbands in this table. I also provide here, however, the number and percentage of litigants who were married women and widows–the percentages add up to more than 100 for this reason.

the deceased had children from more than one marriage, as when Marguerite and Catherine Moingeon appeared in court opposite Jean Baptiste and Pierrette Duvergey to have the court divide the estate of their mother.[49]

This brings us to the one area of life where seigneurial courts almost never intervened–social relations within the family. Families used the courts to settle property disputes, but kept other matters private. There are, for example, no lawsuits for spousal abuse. There are two instances where, during the assizes, the community complained that a husband abused his wife, but they were both cases where the abuse spilled out into the public square.[50] Urban courts in the ancien régime did sometimes deal with spousal abuse in their resolution of cases of physical or property spousal separation.[51] Marie Cathenet told the judge of the bailliage of Dijon that for eighteen months her husband abused her, dragging her by the hair, threatening to kill her and locking her outside on four separate occasions.[52] But while a few wealthy urban women had the family support and sense of independence to ask the court for separation from an abusive husband, rural women almost never did. The sentiment in the countryside seems to have been that the court had no business in family life other than in cases that directly involved property–and even then it was best to keep the peace without the court.

Seigneurial courts in northern Burgundy heard a wide variety of cases touching on almost all areas of social life. They also settled disputes between all kinds of people, as the above table illustrates. Men and women from all over the social spectrum brought their disagreements to the local court. The only inhabitants excluded from the courts of northern Burgundy were the propertyless. Those listed in the tax rolls as beggars never appear, and agricultural day laborers (*journaliers*) appear only rarely.[53] This is not surprising, given that the business of the court was to regulate the use, transfer, and ownership of property. The courts also dealt with issues of honor, but the honor of the very poor was worth little, partly because of the link between honor and property. The only contact the propertyless generally made with court was at death, when the clerk sealed the estate and inventoried the pitiful goods left behind.

Although the propertyless were excluded from the seigneurial courts, the poorer settled members of the community were not. *Manouvriers* made up about 5 percent of plaintiffs in both the 1750s and the 1780s, while artisans made up closer to 10 percent of plaintiffs. Certainly *manouvriers* were underrepresented in the court cases–in the tax rolls of the villages studied, a quarter of the families in the 1750s and 30 percent in the 1780s were headed by *manouvriers*. But this is not simply because of class biases in the administration of justice. It should come as no surprise that merchants are by far the most frequent plaintiffs in the list, or that *laboureurs* are the second biggest social category. Most court cases, after all, were generated by market transactions and merchants transact more often than anyone else, buying, selling, borrowing, and lending.

The overrepresentation of merchants disappears when we consider only those court cases heard between inhabitants of the same village. In fact, in court cases within the village, the average client of the court was only about a fifth richer than the average ratepayer. Perhaps more important is the fact that plaintiffs and defendants paid approximately the same amount of taxes. In regular session, during the 1750s plaintiffs and defendants paid almost exactly the same amount, while in the 1780s plaintiffs were wealthier, but only by 14 percent. This seemingly negative change in the 1780s is probably the result of procedural changes that attracted some of the poorer plaintiffs to the assizes and away from the regular session. The tax assessments of defendants and plaintiffs are presented graphically in appendix B, and a paired t-test demonstrates that plaintiffs were not significantly wealthier than defendants. Seigneurial justice was not simply a tool of the village elite. It did more than provide local *coqs de village* with a way of exerting their authority. Furthermore, these courts settled disputes over property from all kinds of villagers, although those with more property naturally needed to go to court more often to defend it.

The seigneurial courts analyzed here saw a broader spectrum of village society pass before them than other similar courts elsewhere in France. Anthony Crubaugh argues that seigneurial courts in Aunis and Saintonge were primarily used by wealthy plaintiffs against poorer defendants. And indeed, among "frequent litigants" ordinary peasants are much more likely to be present as defendants than as plaintiffs (*laboureurs* appear as defendants about three times as often as they appear as plaintiffs).[54] In the large seigneurial court studied by Fabrice Mauclair, only about 20 percent of litigants worked in agriculture, and most of these were wealthier *laboureurs* and seigneurial over-tenants.[55] In the seigneurial court of Sablé in western France, agricultural professions accounted for only 15 percent of plaintiffs and a quarter of defendants–the list of users of the court is skewed toward artisans and especially merchants.[56] In the northern Burgundian courts studied, on the other hand, the percentage of litigants (in regular session) working in agriculture is about half (48 percent), a figure that would increase dramatically (to at least two-thirds by the 1780s) if we were to include the minor cases judged at the assizes.

Northern Burgundians went to court relatively often, displaying a willingness to go to court that applied to most social categories, albeit in degrees that varied somewhat according to the amount of property that they had to protect. Ordinary farmers, artisans, and merchants in the villages of northern Burgundy frequently went to court when they saw their property threatened. Seigneurial courts worked to maintain the property rights of villagers. They also kept the economy running smoothly by enforcing property transactions and thereby helped maintain the peace among the inhabitants of the province. Recently an historian of seigneurial justice has suggested that the institution created social tension and contributed to the outbreak of the Revolution.[57] In northern Burgundy, to the contrary, seigneurial courts simply mirrored the tensions that existed–judges reacted to social tensions and helped resolve crises and dissipate tension.[58]

Private Arrangement, Official Justice

Even if people went to court on average every few years, there should be no illusion that the court resolved a majority of villagers' disputes. For every court case there were surely hundreds (thousands? tens of thousands?) of times that people settled a conflict themselves, a neighbor intervened to broker a solution, disputants buried the hatchet, or a villager took another route to his field so as to avoid confrontation. There were, in other words, many ways to deal with a dispute other than a court case. In this second part of this chapter, I analyze a few of these informal means of dispute resolution, with an eye to understanding the role of the local court in village society by contrasting the kinds of disputes that people willingly submitted to the judge's arbitration with the kinds of disputes that were more likely to be solved in other ways. We examine three quasi-informal means of dispute resolution that all involved the intervention of a third party, to see if judges were more or less effective than local elites and neighbors at bringing disputing parties together.

The official justice system compares favorably to binding arbitration, mediation, and private arrangement of disputes. Each of the informal means of dispute resolution specialized in a small range of cases–arbitrators decided accounting questions, mediators generally intervened only in disputes that threatened to disrupt the peace in the village, and private arrangement before a notary was primarily reserved for disputes within the family. While the local seigneurial judge could have heard all of the cases so settled, there were real advantages in using less formal means of dispute resolution. Arbitration was quicker and cheaper for very complicated accounting problems such as dividing debt and profit between business partners; mediation was quicker and especially more private than the local court and thereby probably better able to de-escalate disputes that were engulfing the village community; and private arrangement was seen as less shameful for conflicts between family members.

Arbitration

There was one judicial institution in ancien régime France that in some ways resembled the formal court system, an institution that has generally been portrayed as a viable competitor to the judicial system: arbitration. Many historians see arbitration as an extra-judicial procedure used by those who mistrusted the official judicial system. Hervé Piant argues that seigneurial judges had to work hard to maintain the confidence of their clients, since they faced stiff competition from non-judicial methods of settlement, including arbitration.[59] Yves Jeanclos insists that arbitration was neither the first stage of institutional justice nor even a form of public authority. It resulted from private agreement and so existed in competition with the court system.[60]

Arbitration was, in fact, a form of public authority and a legal institution. By the eighteenth century this was an institution whose procedure and nature were regulated, and whose decisions were upheld, by royal law. More importantly, arbitrators did not compete with judges because the law limited their competence and forbade them from deciding questions of law. Arbitrators performed accounting operations and left the business of law to the province's judges.

The analysis of arbitration is complicated by the fact that historians often use the word to apply both to official, government-regulated arbitration, and to the friendly intervention of neighbors, social elites, priests, and seigneurs in disputes. Indeed we can find the same confusion during the eighteenth century. *Le Dictionnaire critique de la langue française* (in both the 1762 and 1694 editions) defines *arbitre* as one who helps end a disagreement, without emphasizing the fact that arbitrators have the authority to enforce their decisions: "He who is chosen by persons on one side and the other to end their disagreement. To take, to name, to choose someone as *arbitre*. To agree upon *arbitres*. To relate something to *arbitres*. To end a case through *arbitres*. To compromise through *arbitres*." In 1787, on the other hand, *Le Dictionnaire critique de la langue française,* makes an interesting distinction between the *arbitre* ("judge chosen by the parties, who give him the authority to end their disagreement") and the *arbitrateur,* a mediator who brokers a friendly agreement (one who is chosen "to end a disagreement amicably").[61] The principal difference between the *arbitre* and the *arbitrateur* is that the authority of the first resides in the agreement of the parties to respect his decision, which can be executed in court, while the authority of the second resides uniquely in his ability to convince the parties that his decision is fair. We will discuss the role of those described as "arbitrateurs" later in the chapter, in the section on mediation. As used in this chapter, the terms arbitrator and arbitration refer uniquely to official, binding arbitration, as regulated by the law.

The normal procedure for arbitration was that each party named an arbitrator, who examined the evidence from the dispute, most often papers such as marriage contracts, wills, donations of property, and contracts of business partnerships. The arbitrators then hammered out just how much each party owed the other and reached a final judgment. Their decision was binding, as long as the prescribed procedure was followed and the nature of the case was one that the parlement defined as subject to the possibility of arbitration.

Zoë Schneider suggests that arbitration dwarfed the regular judicial system, with many more cases being settled this way than before the courts.[62] Since, as Schneider points out, the documents of arbitration are scattered throughout notarial, judicial, and private archives, it is impossible to have a reliable count or even close estimate of the number of cases adjudicated by arbitration. In northern Burgundy, though, it is nevertheless clear that arbitration was far less common than taking disputes to court. There are several structural and institutional reasons for this, the most important of which was the policy of the Parlement of Dijon with respect to arbitration. In 1766 this parlement published an *arrêt général* regulating arbitration. In the preamble the magistrates noted that of all the things that threaten the rights of royal judges, the most significant was that disputants often chose private parties as their judges. Ordinary people did this because "arbitrators have long had the habit of attributing a universal jurisdiction to themselves to the prejudice of the Edict of the month of August 1560," which permitted arbitration only for "the fact of merchandises, divisions of successions between near relatives, and *comptes de tutelle*."[63] In their *cahier de doléances,* the inhabitants of Ogny requested that people be permitted to use arbitration for all kinds of cases, further evidence of the real limitations placed on the institution: "that litigants will be free to choose arbitrators to decide their disputes in all circumstances, and for all cases, at the first written request of one of the parties."[64]

The existence and effectiveness of arbitration depended on the support of the province's judges. Of course parties may have nominated two impartial men to settle a dispute between them and then carried out their suggestions. Without the authority of the regular court system behind it, though, there was no possibility of coercion should one disputant dislike the decision. If the province's courts would not uphold the arbitrators' decision, the arbitration itself ceased to be binding and depended solely on the ability of the arbitrators to bring the parties together. An illegal arbitration is no arbitration at all, but rather a mediation. This is more than semantics since what characterizes arbitration is the fact that the parties agree to abide by the arbitrators' decision, and that neither party can back out after the final decision has been rendered. Arbitration, in other words, could exist and remain effective only in so far as the judges of the regular judicial system enforced it. Arbitration is closer to the official judicial system than to a range of unofficial, infrajudicial practices.

The fact that arbitration was a legal institution that depended on the courts for its existence can be seen in the Dijon Parlement's registers of minor cases.[65] People often came before parlement to have their arbitration contracts ratified by the province's highest magistrates. A quarter of the summary court cases heard in parlement using oral procedure in 1755 and 1785 were ratifications of the decisions of arbitrators.[66] In 1785 siblings Claude and Claudine Arnoux appeared in parlement to request ratification of the arbitration done by Vernissy and Bretin (two lawyers from Dijon who specialized in arbitration). The court ordered the judgment of the arbitrators to be executed, and expressly gave the arbitrators authority to decide any subsidiary matters that came up in the next two months, until the final division of Claude and Claudine's parents' estate.[67]

Sometimes parties came before parlement because one of the disputants refused to submit to the arbitration. In 1785 Elizabeth Joly appealed a decision that held her responsible to pay 388 livres to Antoine François Simon, a merchant. The judge dismissed her appeal, ratified the arbitration and fined her 12 livres for bringing a merit-less appeal before him.[68] The Dijon Parlement very rarely overturned the decisions of arbitrators: in the 59 requests for ratification over these two years there is only one case where the magistrate judging the matter failed to uphold the arbitrators' decision.[69]

Almost all of the cases settled by arbitration in the second half of the eighteenth century fit into the categories defined by the 1766 *arrêt* as subject to the possibility of arbitration. We can show this by combining the parlementary sample of appeals and ratifications with runs of arbitration records that exist in the archives of several bailliages, most likely compiled by the courts to ensure that arbitrators were limiting themselves to those cases the law allowed them.[70]

The disputes arbitrated in northern Burgundy almost all fit into three categories, as we can see in table 4.6. In both samples only about 3 percent of cases fell outside the parlement's narrow definition of cases where arbitration was allowed. In the parlementary sample there were two ratifications of arbitrations in cases of marital separation of property, but both were done before parlement's *arrêt* of 1766. In the cases ratified in 1785 there were no illegal cases, nothing other than inheritance and business partnership disputes. The two irregular cases in the bailliage sample involved village communities that had used arbitration, and one happened before 1766, while the other occurred in 1790. The cases sent to arbitration, and especially after 1766, fit into the narrow categories defined by parlement.

By far the most important category of arbitrations was inheritance, a category that accounted for over four-fifths of arbitrated disputes. These fall into two broad sub-categories: division of estates and calling guardians of minors to account. In the division of estates the arbitrators divided the estate into portions of appropriate value (often equal) and then assigned the portions to the family members. This was complicated, and often involved, for example, deducting dowries or other large gifts that had advantaged one heir. When the father or mother had re-married the division was often especially difficult and time-consuming. The arbitrated inheritance dispute between Barbe and Suzanne Noblot and their mother Pierette Pruffin over the estate of Jean Noblot is a good example, since Pruffin had a son from her first marriage to Simon Fairet. The parties to the dispute provided the arbitrators with the following

Table 4.6. Cases arbitrated in two official samples

Type of case	Bailliage (%)	Parlement (%)
Business disputes	8 (10.8)	5 (8.5)
Inheritance (division of estates)	35 (47.3)	43 (72.9)
Inheritance (guardianship disputes)	29 (39.2)	5 (8.5)
Others	2 (2.7)	2 (3.4)
Unknown	0	4 (6.8)
Total	74	59

documents: the marriage contract of Truffin and Fairet, the court-conducted inventory of Fairet's estate, any contracts showing property acquired during this first marriage, the marriage contract of Truffin and Jean Noblot, contracts for acquisitions in this marriage, the marriage contract of her son from the first marriage, a resume of the expenses and revenue of the estate since Noblot's death, and marriage contracts for Barbe and Suzanne.[71]

The other form of inheritance disputes settled by arbitration was demands for the settling of accounts by guardians of minor children (*comptes de tutelle*). At the end of a guardianship the tutor was to justify to his wards that he had not dissipated the property and revenue entrusted to him by the family. Doubtless some of these were done orally, but many of these *comptes de tutelles* appear in notarial, arbitration, and court records. In 1788 Marie and André Garcenot appointed two Dijon lawyers to arbitrate between them. Marie had recently married, thus ending André's guardianship. André told the lawyers exactly how he had looked after Marie's inheritance from her mother, noting all expenses and revenues of the estate. The arbitrators in the end decided that the revenue of the property exceeded the expenses by 561 livres 7 sols, the amount that they ordered André to pay her.[72]

The last category of cases sent to arbitration was business disputes. These were always cases where both parties owed some money. The arbitrators tallied the credits and debts of each party. Sometimes these cases involved business partnerships. Nicolas Magnien and Claude Vallon had formed a partnership to lease the ponds of the village of Chaugey, and arbitrators had to decide what expenses the two partners had each paid over the past year and to how much of the profits they were each entitled.[73]

The magistrates of the Parlement of Dijon were largely successful in their attempt to limit official arbitration exclusively to specific kinds of inheritance disputes and to complicated debts. The cases settled by arbitrators were essentially accounting problems. Arbitrators did not decide matters of law–they divided property and debt between people who already agreed on the proportion of the total to which each was entitled. They did not, for example, decide whether the division of an estate was to be equal–rather, once the court or the heirs had decided, the arbitrators figured out how much each heir had already received and divided the estate according to the wishes of the deceased or the order of the court. In business partnership cases they decided how much each partner had paid and received and split the profit (or debt) among the partners according to the formula already established by the court or the parties. Judges could, and sometimes did, perform services like verification of the *compte de tutelle* or settling business disputes–but these were often time-consuming operations that could be more conveniently handled by arbitrators.

Judges sometimes ordered litigants to use arbitration to settle their dispute, evidence that arbitration was a well-oiled cog in the judicial system of eighteenth-century northern Burgundy. In Bellefond in 1782, for example, Denis Gruardet demanded that his mother and stepfather, as his tutor, account for their administration of his property. They must have refused to give account of the property, forcing Gruardet to bring them to court. The seigneurial judge of Bellefond ordered them to provide Gruardet with a *compte de tutelle*. Four months later the judge told them to take the case to arbitration.[74] In this case the judge seems to have abandoned his control of the case, letting the arbitrators take over. Sometimes, though, as in the dispute between Jeanne Creuzefond and Antoinnette Veau, the judge ordered them to report back with the final arbitration.[75] In cases that seemed suited to it, one party to a dispute would also sometimes ask the judge to order his opponent to use arbitration.[76]

Judges settled most cases themselves without ordering arbitration. Still, of those cases arbitrated, a significant proportion was there by judicial order. Judges had ordered 33 of the 79 arbitrated disputes in the sample from the bailliages, including 24 from a seigneurial or municipal court (i.e., a non-royal court of first instance), and six from a bailliage. The other 41 arbitrated disputes had gone straight to arbitration and were based on arbitration contracts passed before notaries rather than court orders. Courts played an important role in arbitration and in many cases arbitration was in fact the continuation of, and not an extra-judicial alternative to, a court case.

According to law any adult male of free status could act as arbitrator. In Burgundy this meant that no *mainmortable* could arbitrate disputes, since his ability to contract was limited. In Normandy, women sometimes acted as arbitrators despite the formal denial of their right to do so, and the provincial parlement normally upheld their decisions.[77] The records of arbitration in northern Burgundy during the last half of the eighteenth century contain no examples of women acting as arbitrators, although Yves Jeanclos found women arbitrators there in the Middle Ages.[78] By the late eighteenth century disputers in northern Burgundy most often named two lawyers as arbitrators. Among the 81 records of arbitration found in the bailliage sample described above, which include the names and professions of about 162 arbitrators, only about a dozen were not lawyers–these include *procureurs,* royal notaries and a few surveyors. Arbitrators, then, shared the same social origins as seigneurial judges–legal professionals, and especially lawyers. What's more, lawyers sometimes worked as seigneurial judge in one village, and could pick up arbitration work in other villages. Jean Finot, for example, lawyer from Semur-en-Auxois and judge in a large number of seigneurial courts, arbitrated an inheritance division between the widow Gabrielle Chevanne and her step-son in 1773.[79] The choices that people made when selecting arbitrators suggest that ordinary people saw arbitration as a semi-formal legal institution best reserved for those with legal experience and knowledge.[80]

Arbitration in northern Burgundy was not an extra-legal solution for those who wanted to avoid the formal legal system. It was part of the judicial system of the ancien régime. The Dijon Parlement decided what kinds of cases were subject to arbitration, limiting arbitrators only to accounting matters. Recourse to arbitration was limited. Parties often went to the parlement for appeals and ratifications of arbitrations. Local seigneurial and royal courts sometimes ordered the plaintiff and defendants in court cases to submit their problems to arbitration and return to the court with the decision.

Mediation

While official arbitration was limited to very few kinds of cases, people could ask the local lord, a priest, or a respected neighbor informally to mediate almost any kind of dispute. Several historians emphasize the frequency of informal mediation. Eric Wenzel, for example, discusses the importance of the local parish priest in settling disputes: "royal justice is consulted only after the failure of the mediation of the presbytery."[81] Nicole Castan and Steven Reinhardt both place a great deal of emphasis on private settlement, arguing that people preferred it because of the cost, slowness, and antagonistic nature of official justice.[82]

Mediation in northern Burgundy was less common than we might expect, and was primarily reserved for those cases that threatened to upset broader social relations within the village. In the majority of cases, involving money owed, roaming cattle, and unmet obligations, the parties went to court without rancor, and maintained normal neighborly relations through and after the court case. Neighbors had little incentive to intervene, and the parties themselves no reason to invoke their help, given the rapidity, reliability, and cheapness of official justice. In protracted inheritance disputes and exchanges of insults and blows between feuding families, on the other hand, local elites, neighbors, and the community as a whole had considerable incentive to intervene.

The fact that most disputers did not make serious attempts to involve a neighbor as mediator, choosing to use the court as soon as it became clear that the parties themselves could not reconcile, does not mean that mediation was unimportant in the villages of northern Burgundy. There were plenty of instances in which family members and local elites attempted to intervene, but in all of them except one the dispute was visibly causing rancor within the village. The only exception is a dispute over rent for land where the defendant requested two weeks delay in the case to "finish with the said [litigant] by the said mediation of the priest." Although there was no apparent public disorder, there was likely emotion and clamor that remain hidden to us.[83]

More typical is the example of Anne Gallinet, a young unmarried woman who named Jean Baptiste Viard as father of her baby. Viard not only denied paternity, but he and his mother both were frequently heard to say that Gallinet was too promiscuous to know who the father was.[84] In this case a plethora of villagers tried to reconcile the couple. Denise François, the 58-year-old wife of a local merchant, testified that she advised Viard's mother "that she would do well to arrange this affair." Another woman advised Viard's mother to marry her son off, but got only threats and insults for her trouble. Françoise Maréchal, a 60-year-old *manouvrier*'s wife, offered her home as a place for the two families to meet to work out an agreement, but they could not agree on the amount of compensation and almost came to blows.[85] All of these attempts at reconciliation (and several others mentioned in the depositions) failed to bring the parties together, and Viard married another local woman. Still, there is no final judgment of the court, so neighbors probably managed to persuade them to agree on financial compensation.

Depositions of witnesses in assault cases illustrate just how physical fights and disputes over honor disrupted the life of the community, and help us understand why elites and neighbors intervened in these cases, but not in most other disputes. Antoine Clere testified that Jeanne Piedferré and Anne Mongin "never cease, to the great scandal of the region, to insult each other publicly, calling each other bitch, whore with the dirty word, and other similar insults."[86] After Jean Latour and Claude Bouzereau fils got into a shouting match in the local *cabaret* over money that Claude claimed to be owed, Jean Boillot, a 45-year-old *vigneron,* testified to the court that all those present were "scandalized by their swearing." Indeed Boillot helped the innkeeper throw the troublemakers out.[87] Both of these cases settled out of court after several initial sessions before the judge. It is likely that one or more of the scandalized neighbors and villagers intervened. If it is implausible that the parties involved ever became friends or even truly set aside their differences, it does seem that friends or neighbors convinced them to stop their public insults and fist-fights. Public disputes like these, incidents that disrupted the peace, contrast greatly with most court cases, private disputes that generated no scandal and so did not motivate neighbors or elites to intervene.

Some disputes aroused such emotion in the village that the leadings inhabitants could not remain idle. In 1754 Blaise Roux's mother failed to negotiate his marriage to Jeanne Fremyet's daughter. Fremyet and her sons continually insulted Roux, calling him "misnamed [*mal-nommé*], which in the village of Ancey means a witch and hinders a boy from finding a wife." After a violent confrontation and several more insults, several local elites intervened to persuade them to end the dispute. Roux presented the judge with an agreement whereby the widow and her sons apologized for their insults and agreed to stop. The treaty, he told the judge, was done "at the invitations of Madame Canablier dame of Ancey and of Monsieur Patote parish priest of the said place, and of several other charitable persons of the same village of Ancey who intervened to encourage him to end the civil lawsuit amicably."[88] With two families at each other's throats, this case spilled out into the public arena and threatened the social fabric of the village.

Cases between the village community and an inhabitant were relatively frequent, especially those involving tax assessment or the use of common land. These cases were sometimes settled privately, generally through the intervention of a notable who was not a member of the community, such as the seigneur or the priest. In the village of Corgengoux, the priest wrote to the *procureur d'office:* "I have learned that you were ordered to come to the village for the case that Cotin has against the community. I think that your trip will be useless, unless you have the intention to come and see us, which would give us great pleasure, because I have mastered the affair to end it amicably [*car je me suis rendu maître de cette affaire pour la terminer à l'amiable*]."[89] There were incentives to settle these cases out of court: cases involving the community were very slow and expensive, requiring multiple village assemblies, consultations with lawyers, the permission of the intendant, and multiple trips to town for the *syndics.* They also disrupted the peace in the village.

The contrast between the cases where other villagers felt they had something at stake, and the majority of lawsuits, shows that most court cases did not signal an end of social relations between the plaintiffs and defendants. Indeed litigants sometimes appeared in court more than once against each other, apparently continuing to loan, borrow, rent, buy, and sell to each other after the lawsuit. A 1780 disagreement over the price of a horse did not stop Jean Lavieille from loaning François Masson 27 livres in 1781.[90] Similarly the fact that Catherine Ecart had to take Claude Rousselet to court to get the 240 livres he owed her did not stop her from loaning him 265 livres soon after.[91] The use of the formal justice system did not mean that they could no longer conduct business with each other.

This judicial system was different from the contemporary American court system, where most court cases are between people who anticipate no future relationships.[92] This helps explain the rarity of attempts at mediation by neighbors–since ordinary court cases generally did not threaten to explode into bitter feuds or disrupt social relations, the respectable members of the community had no reason to involve themselves. Court cases were only shameful and to be avoided when they involved family members or when rancor and bitterness seemed likely to result.

We might posit a rigid separation between an official justice that attempts to decide questions of guilt, and informal mediation that works to bring the parties together and restore social interaction. In reality, though, one reason why neighbors did not often intervene to reconcile disputing parties is that the judges of northern Burgundy worked hard to bring litigants to a mutually satisfactory solution. When passing sentence, judges frequently noted that the defendant agreed with their decisions. When the judge of Senailly ordered René Bressseau to pay his old domestic servant 30 livres for back-wages, he noted that the payment was being ordered "with the consent of the defendant," a phrase that recurs frequently in the records.[93] The judge of Meursault used the exact same words when sentencing a *vigneron,* Denis Titard, to pay 72 livres to a *négociant* from Beaune.[94] It is significant that the judges often noted that they had procured the agreement of the defendant and were basically ratifying an agreement by the defendant to pay the plaintiff.

Sometimes we can more directly observe the judge overseeing and mediating a process of negotiation and compromise between the parties. In Meursault, for example, Jean Baptiste Ressort, a lawyer from Beaune, sued two *vignerons* for damages committed in his fields by their animals. At the first meeting of the court, Charles Veau and Martin Robiteau (the *vignerons*) offered Ressort 6 livres for the tort, which he accepted. The judge accordingly threw the case out and ordered the defendants to pay court costs of 8 livres.[95] Instances like this, where the parties negotiated before the judge, are numerous. In a defamation case, the judge managed to convince Jean Laverné, the defendant, to apologize publicly in the courthouse, and then threw out the plaintiff's request for monetary compensation.[96] In 1757 Pierre Regnier demanded repayment of the 12 livres François Princet owed him. Princet told the judge that he had only spent nine livres, and managed to convince Regnier that this was indeed so. Accordingly, the judge ordered Princet to pay the 9 livres, plus costs.[97]

Sometimes the judge worked together with the parties and a mediator to reach a satisfactory settlement. In one complicated inheritance dispute the judge suggested that the parties convene a family assembly. When they next appeared before him, they reported the result of the family assembly, and brought a neighbor with them, who told the judge that, "the parties to the case having reported to him to get his decision on their disagreement," he had found in favor of the widow.[98] In this case the formal court system interacted with less formal methods of settlement like family assemblies and neighborly intervention. Far from jealously defending their right impartially to decide between parties, seigneurial judges encouraged the plaintiffs and defendants to come together, advised them to enquire of other family members, and were ready to legalize the "extrajudicial" decision.

In northern Burgundy ordinary people sometimes had the help of family members, social elites, and neighbors to settle their disputes. This kind of intervention, though, was mostly limited to those cases that threatened the social life of the community. Most often disputers did not need the services of a neighbor because the official judicial system met their needs relatively well. In any case, most court cases did not threaten to end normal social relations between the parties. Plaintiffs and defendants could use the judge to oversee negotiations, to examine the fairness of their offers and counter-offers, and in the end to ratify any agreements they might make. Unofficial mediation, then, appears to have been relatively uncommon, with inhabitants of villages mostly leaving parties to friendly disagreements to work out their own solutions with the help of the local judge. One of the much-touted judicial reforms of the Revolution was the development of *bureaux de paix,* where the JP tried to mediate cases, bringing about reconciliation before hearing the case as judge.[99] In fact disputants were required to attempt official mediation before commencing litigation. Requiring the use of mediation was indeed a revolutionary innovation, but it should not blind us to the fact that under the ancien régime seigneurial judges often sought to reconcile disputing parties.

"Accomodation sur procès"

One of the crucial functions of the court case, in the eighteenth century as today, was to put pressure on the other party to settle amicably. Jonathan Dewald argues that this was the most important role played by seigneurial courts, and that private settlement was primarily motivated by the costs of justice.[100] The threat of the cost of going to court certainly helped encourage plaintiffs and defendants to get together to settle their differences, but equally important was the public shame involved in certain categories of disputes, notably those within a family. This is revealed by comparing the kinds of cases settled in court with those cases where the parties reached an agreement out of court, usually settling it with a contract drawn up by a notary. Cases settled "amicably" out of court overwhelmingly involved family members, and especially inheritance matters–cases on which other villagers were likely to look disparagingly.[101] Most other kinds of lawsuits the litigants were likely to see through to the end. The cost of justice was not the most important factor driving accommodations, and in most cases normal social relations could continue despite the lawsuit.

Although the private arrangement of disputes was common in northern Burgundy, the rates of settlement before official justice are amazingly high. In regular court sessions 57 percent of cases in the 1750s saw a final judgment rendered by the judge, while in the 1780s the figure is 67 percent of the cases. If we include the cases settled in the assizes, where the rate of settlement was close to 100 percent, the totals rise to 85 percent in the 1780s and 65 percent in the 1750s.[102] Most cases that got as far as a first hearing before the local judge, then, were settled in court. This rate is appreciably higher than that found in most other studies of local courts. Christopher Brooks estimates that, of the cases that began in the court of King's Bench in seventeenth-century England, about half of them reached the "stage of advanced pleading." Of these, Brooks gives no data on how many actually finished in court.[103] Both Anthony Crubaugh and Zoë Schneider comment on the high percentage of cases that began in court but then settled privately.[104] The high rate of official success in the seigneurial courts of northern Burgundy is the result of the high speed of the judicial system, with the majority of cases seeing settlement in one session–the threat of a court case becomes less effective in forcing private settlement as defending a case in court is less onerous.

The first kind of source useful for examining accommodation is the records of court cases themselves. Unfortunately most of the 15–30 percent of cases that settled out of court left little evidence in the records. Most simply disappear from the registers, leaving us to assume that accommodation was how they ended. Jeanne Claude Roussey, the widow of a *laboureur,* sued the owner of the local wood mill for 159 livres for wood she sold him, and she also demanded payment for the labor provided by her children over two years.[105] The judge granted a delay of a week, but the parties never appeared again. In the absence of a default judgment, the widow and miller must have settled on an agreeable payment and ended the dispute.[106]

Occasionally the litigants appeared in court to inform the judge that they had settled their dispute–and they sometimes negotiated their settlement in the presence of the judge. This most often occurred in instances where the case involved estimation of value or repayment of damages in a tort, since they could use the judge to ratify their agreement. In 1786 Nicolas and Louis Lambert (*manouvrier* and his minor son) complained to the court of the shameful way that Nicolas Dalay and Madelaine Rouget had treated them. Because the Lamberts had reported Dalay and Rouget for wood theft in the lord's forest, they threw Nicolas Lambert into the river, and later Madelaine attacked his son with a hammer. After hearing the long report read out in court, the parties reached an agreement. Dalay agreed to pay 12 livres damages, plus all medical and legal costs the Lamberts had incurred, apologize publicly, avoid insulting or assaulting them again, and finally, agreed to "repeat the said declaration to Madelaine Rouget his wife if necessary."[107] The judge ratified their agreement and the case ended that day.

Court records, however, are of only limited use in evaluating private settlement of disputes. This is because often villagers settled their disputes at the threat of the lawsuit, so that many never appeared in court. Fortunately, however, they frequently made use of a notary to record the agreement. Among the countless thousands of sales of property, wills, and marriage contracts housed in notarial archives, there are many private settlements of disputes, variously called "*transaction sur procès,*" "*arrangement,*" "*accommodation.*" These are contracts testifying that the plaintiff and defendant had agreed to end a court case, and stating the terms to which the parties consented. They are fascinating in that they illuminate much about social relations in the countryside, and also a great deal about popular attitudes toward official justice. Historians have made little use of these sources, though a recent resurgence in the use of notarial records bodes well for the future.[108]

A few historians have written about accommodation, but virtually all have focused on the arrangement of criminal cases. Alfred Soman, for example, has studied these records in settling criminal cases, especially witchcraft.[109] This emphasis is understandable, in that the private settlement of murders, robbery and other major crimes forces serious re-thinking of the boundaries between civil and criminal affairs. By the late eighteenth century, though, virtually all of the accommodations were for civil affairs. Of 57 cases settled before a notary from 1780 to 1789 in the village of Messigny, only four were criminal affairs, and all of those were minor assault/insult cases. Given the penetration of the state into local life, and the efficient running of seigneurial and royal courts in northern Burgundy, few major crimes were settled by arrangement between the parties by the late eighteenth century.

The records of the notary of the village of Messigny provide a good run of documents from the late eighteenth century. Because the inhabitants conducted all of their legal business with the local notary, we can compare the cases settled privately to those judged by the local seigneurial court, presented respectively in tables 4.7 and 4.8.[110] The most obvious difference between the two samples is the overwhelming importance of inheritance disputes in the private settlements. In the court of Messigny inheritance disputes made up only about 7 percent of the cases, while they account for no less than half of the private accommodations. The reasons for this are easily apparent and give some insight into the nature of accommodation. Families chose to settle their inheritance disputes by agreement before the notary because of the dishonor involved in quarreling within the family. The high price of settling these very complicated cases before the judge also contributed.

While parties often ended court cases by accommodation, inheritance contests where one party had merely threatened legal action were far more common. Typical in this respect was the agreement reached between Simone

Table 4.7. Cases settled by accommodation, before the notary of Messigny

Type of case	1750–59	1760–69	1770–79	1780–89	Total (%)
Inheritance	7	1	13	31	52 (50)
Assault/insult	1	0	2	4	7 (6.7)
Debts	2	2	0	8	12 (11.5)
Contracts	1	0	0	6	7 (6.7)
Retrait lignager	1	2	1	3	7 (6.7)
Communal affairs	1	0	2	2	5 (4.8)
Pregnancy	1	1	0	2	4 (3.8)
Land/building disputes	3	1	2	0	6 (5.8)
Farming torts	1	0	0	0	1 (1)
Engagement	0	1	0	0	1 (1)
Unknown	0	1	0	1	2 (1.9)
Total	18	9	20	57	104

Table 4.8. Cases settled in regular session by the seigneurial court of Messigny

Type of case	1750–59	1780–89	Total (%)
Inheritance	4	3	7 (7.4)
Debts	13	44	57 (60)
Contracts	0	1	1 (1.1)
Land disputes	4	3	7 (7.4)
Assault/defamation	2	1	3 (3.2)
Communal affairs	3	3	6 (6.3)
Pregnancy	1	0	1 (1.1)
Seigneurial	0	1	1 (1.1)
Unknown	0	12	12 (12.6)
Total	27	68	95

Febvret, widow of a *manouvrier,* and her three stepchildren. They agreed that "to avoid the proceedings that these were on the point of beginning against the said Simone Febvret concerning the inheritance of the said Michel Nardot," they would leave her alone on the condition that she give them some of the land and an annuity worth 200 livres principal.[111] The heirs of François Vernier wrote in an agreement "that they were on the point of entering into a contest between themselves on the subject of several claims and pretensions that most of them claim to have on the estate of the said François Vernier." They added that the costs of the case would absorb much of the estate, and that they had been advised to settle the contest amicably. So they agreed on a partition of the estate, noting that they were all satisfied with the settlement, "without being able to make claims on each other in any manner."[112]

Most accommodations of inheritance disputes resulted from threatened lawsuits, but in some cases the parties simply feared that they might fall into disharmony in the future. In 1760, for example, Marie Sauvageot divided her estate between her children. She did this before her death to make up for the unequal dowries she had given to her two daughters. "These two establishments," she noted, "unequal in dowry, combined with other circumstances known to the said *demoiselle,* make her fear that some disagreements and lawsuits may arise to consume in legal fees the greatest part of her estate."[113]

Inheritance cases, though by far the largest category, are not the only kinds of cases where disputing parties came together to reach an agreement. As can be seen in the many debt court cases that begin in court but disappear from the records, it was not uncommon for extra-judicial agreements to occur in debt cases–though parties in these settlements would rarely use a notary to record the settlement. The debt disputes settled by arrangement were complicated, and included mortgages, perpetual annuities, and money owed from various other contracts. Also, debts settled by arrangement had often reached the stage of a judicial seizure, making speed of settlement crucial, in addition to the dishonor involved in having allowed a dispute to degenerate so far. In 1785 Bernard Lambry and Catherine Pocherot contracted with François Pauthenet to end "all difficulties that they have together, on the subject of a seizure that the said Pauthenier has done." They agreed to let him keep the wheat he had seized from their barns, and to pay him the 11 livres that was the difference between the value of the seizure and the original debt.[114]

One of the most interesting kinds of cases arranged in northern Burgundy involved the right of *retrait lignager.* This was a customary right whereby family members took precedence over non-relatives for the purchase of land. Whenever someone sold a piece of land, within a year and a day any near relative could force the purchaser to sell him or her the land for the original price paid, in effect invalidating the sale in order to keep the land within the family.[115] Family members sometimes used the courts for a kind of blackmail involving this right. The general practice was for a family member to approach the buyer of the land and inform him that he intended to exercise his right and retake the land. He threatened a court case to force the transfer of land, at which point the buyer gave in, and offered a payment in exchange for the family member agreeing not to exercise the *retrait.* When Christine Deschamps's brother Claude sold land to the Deveaux widow, Christine managed to get five mesures of wheat worth about 10 livres in exchange for agreeing not to exercise her right of *retrait.*[116]

Another important kind of arrangement was the settlement of paternity disputes. All unwed pregnant women were to declare their pregnancy either before the local judge or before a notary. Most women preferred to use a notary for this, probably because he could provide more privacy. Declarations of pregnancy were a means of discouraging premarital sexual activity by ensuring that all pregnancies came to term. This should not obscure the fact that the declaration of pregnancy could be a powerful instrument for protecting the unwed mother. In the vast majority of declarations the young mother requested a copy of the document, evidence that she intended to use it to get reparations from the father.[117] In 1763 Catherine Vernier noted that she was reporting the pregnancy both to satisfy the law, and "to proceed against the said Gaspart Gilbert to place the child or the children with whom she is pregnant and for the damages and interests resulting to her in this respect."[118] The presence of such clauses means that all declarations of pregnancy have to be seen as the beginning of a legal dispute and a court case.

The fact that most of the declarations of pregnancy contained clauses noting that the woman intended to use the document to ensure she got what was due her reminds us of the difficulty involved in defining and counting disputes. Disputes, after all, are defined through perception. We can say that in the 1750s the villagers of Messigny went to court about 27 times (68 times in the 1780s, or more than 300 if we include the assizes) and settled 18 disputes by accommodation (57 in the 1780s), some of which had begun in court and some of which had only seen legal action threatened. These figures are highly problematic, though, because of the blurred line between accommodations and other notarial acts and because of the difficulties in separating court cases that involved disputes from those that did not. Should pregnancy declarations be considered the beginning of court cases, since all implicitly threaten judicial action should the father not meet his responsibilities?

Documents generated to determine the division of an inheritance make this point more forcefully still. Few would think of wills as evidence of a dispute, but a number of testaments contain a clause noting that the testator feared that the heirs would fall on the estate like jackals, dissipating the property in endless court fees. Some might think that these clauses are simply part of the standard form of a will, and therefore represent the notary's stylistic flourish rather than originating from the will-writers themselves. This, however, is not the case. Admittedly the phrase "to avoid the contestations that might arise between her children and grand-children on the subject of her future succession" occurs several times, notably when the practice of Messigny was owned by the notary Forneron.[119] But in other cases the wills specifically mentioned the source of the feared dispute, such as dowries given to daughters, sons who had stolen from parents, or the existence of step-siblings. Furthermore, the mention of a dispute crops up in only a small percentage of wills and other inheritance-related documents. In the village of Messigny, during the 1750s and the 1780s, the inhabitants had 37 wills drawn up, of which only six clearly mention a worry about a dispute. If we include all inheritance documents (*partages, donations,* renunciations, etc.), there is explicit mention of a dispute in eight out of 81 documents. The notary may have provided the words, but the idea to mention the fear of a dispute came from the testator herself, rather than being inserted or even suggested by the notary.

The fact that the testator had reason to fear family conflict of this sort suggests that disagreement had already reared its head–perhaps at some family gathering the matter of the dispersal of the parents' property had come up and led to some disagreement over who would get the house, the silver, or a choice piece of land. What's more, most wills actually followed intestate division of property, which further reinforces the argument that these documents were sometimes intended primarily to avoid a dispute that may have already begun, rather than to ensure that the deceased's wishes were followed with respect to the division. In declarations of pregnancy the simple fact that the couple had not married points us to the conclusion that a dispute was already underway between the man and woman and explains why the woman asked for a copy of the declaration. With *retrait lignager* the family member would threaten legal action, but almost never carry it out. Conflict and cooperation continuously coexist in all human relations, and it is illusory to imagine that we can understand one without the other.

Conclusion

Robert Ellickson has argued that legal scholars seriously overestimate the importance of the law: "large segments of social life are located and shaped beyond the reach of law." In his study of how Californian ranchers and farmers resolve cattle trespass cases, he found that the institutions of the state are almost never involved. Instead neighbors apply their own norms. The community expects trespass victims to notify the owners of the animals immediately and to assist the rancher to remove his animals. The owner of the animals should reimburse for the damages, but generally in kind rather than in cash by offering, for example, to allow the injured party to take a few bales of hay from his barns. Most interestingly, the norms that the rural inhabitants apply are not the same as those imposed by the law–community norms universally hold the owner of the animals responsible, whereas the law makes distinctions based on the presence or absence of a fence and between counties that are "open" and those that are "closed."[120] Ellickson elaborates a general theory of how people select a controller of behavior to enforce rules, choosing among the self, express contracts, informal social forces, hierarchical private organizations, and the state. He argues that transaction costs generally determine which controller people select, and adds that "a rational utilitarian would be more willing to confer rulemaking functions upon the state if the state had a comparative advantage over norm-makers in generating rules supportive of cooperative outcomes."[121]

Ellickson's insights are helpful in understanding the ways that ordinary people in eighteenth-century northern Burgundy carried on their disputing and agreeing. Peasants chose different forms of dispute-resolution based on the nature of the dispute, with a keen eye to the relative advantages and disadvantages of various forums. Transaction costs go a long way to explaining recourse to arbitration for complicated business disputes and inheritance divisions, and to private arrangement before a notary for inheritance cases. The intervention of neighbors to help broker a peace through mediation was used to deescalate disputes that were disrupting village life and therefore had lower transaction costs in both time and honor lost for the parties and their family and friends.

While it is true that ordinary peasants resolved their disputes without involving the court most of the time, the frequency of recourse to the official judicial system is nevertheless striking. This is largely because, by contrast to twentieth-century northern Californian ranching communities, in northern Burgundy there was general agreement between the norms applied by the community and those applied by the court–everyone, judges included, agreed that the peace could best be kept by avoiding harsh punishments and awards of heavy damages, and by seeking to procure the assent of those involved. Seigneurial judges were "supportive of cooperative outcomes," which made ordinary people more willing to confer enforcement functions on the local court. Ordinary people saw seigneurial justice as a form of self-regulation for the community and used it primarily as part of the village's system of conflict resolution.

While villagers resolved many of their disputes among themselves, the evidence presented here suggests that norms of neighborliness in northern Burgundy were not powerful enough in the eighteenth century to keep the peace by themselves, if indeed they ever had been. Seigneurial justice functioned as a form of self-regulation, but it was also the only dispute-resolution institution in the village that had the authority to impose its decision when the parties could not be brought together. The use made of informal means of dispute-resolution paradoxically underlines the importance of seigneurial justice by showing that, even when people did not go to court, the possibility and threat of using the court was behind many informal resolutions of disputes and even ordinary agreements. Arbitration, mediation, and the private arrangement of disputes, then, were not forms of sociability and dispute resolution that competed with seigneurial justice, but logical outgrowths of an institution whose judges saw the reconciliation of disputing parties as one of their main responsibilities.

Part 2

The Winds of Change

Chapter 5

Local Knowledge and Legal Reform

The Transformation of Justice

The question of reform provoked a great deal of public debate in the eighteenth century. Philosophes, physiocrats, agronomists, and populationists all argued for the necessity of profound institutional change, claiming it would bring about national regeneration. Seeking to solidify its tax base and bring more prosperity to the kingdom, the monarchy implemented many of their suggestions for reform.[1] A few minor national legal reforms succeeded, such as an increase in the authority of presidial courts, and a procedural change allowing royal courts to try serious criminal cases after the seigneurial judge had completed the investigation.[2] But because of resistance by magistrates in the kingdom's parlements, the most ambitious attempt, the standardization of inheritance law and the form of testaments, went nowhere, and the overall verdict with respect to legal reform is unimpressive.[3]

Seigneurial justice did not escape the eighteenth-century reform impulse. Many legal theorists were deeply critical of seigneurial justice, generally favoring the abolition of these local courts that they associated with innumerable abuses. And these jurists seem to have had the ear of the royal government–certainly by the 1780s the royal ministry was favorable to the notion, and the royal coup d'état of 1788 that abolished the parlements was clearly designed to cause seigneurial courts rapidly to wither away.[4] Despite the considerable volume of books, pamphlets, and tracts that demanded legal reform, however, the eighteenth century saw no major national reforms of civil procedure, and no substantial national institutional changes affected seigneurial justice.

The lack of effective national reform of seigneurial justice does not mean, however, that the institution stagnated over the course of the eighteenth century. In a society based on privilege, the reforms that worked best were regional rather than national, a fact that the monarchy recognized during the 1760s and 1770s by passing edicts allowing the enclosure of private land and

---

Part of the material presented here appeared in Benoît Garnot, ed., *Les juristes et l'argent: Le coût de la justice et l'argent des juges du XIVe au XIXe siècle* (Dijon: Éditions universitaires de Dijon, 2005). It is reproduced here with the permission of the publisher.

the division of commons on a provincial basis, and always after a request from the province in question. In Burgundy the Parlement of Dijon and the provincial Estates brought about a series of procedural reforms that changed seigneurial justice in important ways. The new laws put a strong emphasis on the rapid, summary, and inexpensive resolution of minor disputes and profoundly transformed for the better the way that many villagers experienced contact with the judicial system. While these reforms left intact the authority of lords over the nomination of judicial officers and the ability of lords to use the courts in their interest, the Parlement of Dijon put substantial checks into place that signaled to lords that seigneurial courts were under the control of royal appeal courts. Limited as they were to one province, and dealing with procedural minutiae in very minor cases, these reforms have completely escaped the attention of historians, just as they seem to have escaped the attention of most eighteenth-century authors.[5] Nevertheless, the changes underline the considerable capacity for reform that existed even within an institution that represents so many of the contradictions and problems of the ancien régime. Furthermore, a majority of those bringing about the reforms, magistrates in the parlement and delegates in the provincial Estates, were themselves high-justice lords. The reforms therefore offer an excellent example of change from within the system and demonstrate how reform in the ancien régime could benefit the people and simultaneously protect the rights and privileges of the elite.

Legal Reform in Antiseigneurial Pamphlets

In the eighteenth century many authors turned their attention to seigneurial justice, suggesting major reforms or outright abolition.[6] But their suggestions generally left intact seigneurial authority through the court, the element which, as we will see in examining parish *cahiers de doléances,* was most abhorrent to ordinary people. At the same time proposals would have diminished the close connection between the court and the village, the element that the *cahiers* suggest was the most popular. Jurists argued that the mixing of personal property and public power in the judiciary was inappropriate, and called for the abolition of seigneurial justice. They began from the premise that the existence of seigneurial justice was inappropriate within a state where sovereignty emanated from the king. From there they theorized that the private ownership of justice should be ended, and all judicial authority transferred to the king. But this very mixture of the private and public, of property and authority, placed significant limits on what was thinkable for these theorists. Despite their apparent hostility to seigneurial justice, they all called either for the indemnification of lords, or for leaving a kind of feudal justice in the hands of lords. The pre-absolutist or feudal nature of the

French state, in other words, so deeply confused property and power that the abolition of seigneurial justice was only thinkable within the context of a profound remaking of the state.[7]

By far the most important ancien régime works on seigneurial justice were Charles Loyseau's *Traité des seigneuries* and *Discours sur les abus des justices des villages*.[8] All authors who wrote about seigneurial justice in the eighteenth century made reference to his works–indeed, some of them apparently knew nothing more about seigneurial justice than what they learned from Loyseau, since all their examples are drawn from his work.[9] Loyseau's attitude toward seigneurial justice is more complicated than most pamphleteers realized, and most eighteenth-century authors took only two things from his work on seigneurial justice: his colorful examples of abuses and the absolutist notion that the king was the only legitimate holder of judicial authority.[10]

Loyseau's main interest was the nature of public authority. In his treatises on seigneuries, offices and orders, he showed how this was exercised through the system of office-holders, the seigneurial system, and the society of orders. He began from the premise that public authority was the prerogative of the prince who, as perfect lord, supreme officer, and only sovereign, could confer his authority to underlings.[11] The seigneurial system, venality of offices, and the social hierarchy of the ancien régime all had their origin in the person of the king. Loyseau made an important distinction, though, between the state, which "owned" sovereignty, and the king, to whom this sovereignty was communicated by the state. As head of state the king had both the authority and duty to make the law, create offices, wage war, act as supreme dispenser of justice, and mint money.[12]

Charles Loyseau was a defender of absolute monarchy. Seigneurial justice for him was not a part of the seigneurie, which was a form of private power, but was a public right.[13] But if justice were a form of public authority emanating from the state, why was it exercised as though it were personal property, in the name of the lord? Loyseau's answer was that important lords, dukes, and counts seized the right to administer justice from the king, and that the king had never retaken it from them.[14] His solution to this absurdity of public justice administered like private property was ambiguous. At one point he expressed his wish for the suppression of seigneurial courts,[15] but in the rest of his works he called instead for reform. His suggestion was that judges administer justice in the name of the king, and therefore be considered royal officers. Prosecutors and clerks could continue to be named by the lord, since in effect they acted in the lord's interest and so were more closely attached to the fief than to justice. The other reform that he suggested was that seigneurial judgeships be made permanent, so that judges could decide all cases according to the law, without fear of being dismissed by a malicious lord.[16]

Theorists who used Loyseau's work generally took from it his scathing examples of seigneurial judges who were illiterate drunkards holding court in the tavern, or of places where plaintiffs had to go through five or six levels of appeals before getting a final judgment. But these abuses were not Loyseau's main point. He wanted to show that justice was a form of public authority that properly belonged only to the state, and that the real problem with seigneurial justice was a theoretical one–that justice was in the hands of private individuals. Of a host of late eighteenth-century authors who used Loyseau, only Boucher d'Argis noticed this. In a pamphlet listing the everyday problems with seigneurial justice and suggesting reforms, Boucher d'Argis says of Loyseau that his main goal had been to "discover the usurpation and the abuses of seigneurial justices and to show clearly that they are against all laws, and if he entered into a few details of the vices of the actual administration of justice in these subaltern tribunals, he did it very superficially, and did not even propose a remedy."[17]

All authors who wrote on seigneurial justice in the seventeenth and eighteenth centuries referred to Loyseau and his work, but it was only late in the eighteenth century that his thinking was carried through to its logical conclusions. Many theorists had agreed with Loyseau that justice belonged to the state and was therefore held by the king, and that seigneurial justice originated in a usurpation of public authority by seigneurs. Until the late eighteenth century, though, no one was willing to conclude from this that seigneurial justice should be abolished. In his unpublished manuscript, Chancellor Daguesseau vigorously denounced seigneurial justice and the terrible abuses with which he thought it was rife.[18] He then noted that if "the true principles of public law" were the only consideration, the best solution would be to abolish these local courts.[19] But instead of following these principles, Daguesseau suggested reforms that, with one exception, were thoroughly banal. He called for an end to the creation of new seigneuries following the division of fiefs, and the simplification of procedure, notably through a reduction in the use of written procedure. More radically he suggested, un-dogmatically ("it could be good to command"), the possibility of uniting surrounding seigneurial courts in the hope of making it easier for lords to find good officers to staff the courts.[20]

The reason that even radical critics of seigneurial justice stopped short of calling for abolition was respect for property rights. The confusion of private property and public power was what made so many critics hesitate to call for abolition. This was partly rooted in the distinction made by Jean Bodin between *imperium* and *dominium*. A sovereign's absolute authority over his subjects does not, for Bodin, give him the right to "take nor give another man's goods without the permission of the owner."[21] This distinction meant that even commentators who were deeply opposed to seigneurial justice stopped short of calling for suppression. An anonymous book written in 1789 in the form of advice to the Estates-General is a good example of this. The author's analysis began with the principle that justice in the countryside should be "as simple as the inhabitants, as uncomplicated as the objects [of the lawsuits] are minor." A good judicial system would reduce the number of trials by encouraging amicable arrangement of disputes, whereas the current system, he said, is endlessly complicated, with an incredible number of minuscule courts.[22] The untrained practitioners who staff these courts encourage an already litigious peasantry to drag on the smallest dispute with endless legal wrangles. After painting this rather standard picture of the abuses of seigneurial justice, the author proposed setting up an experienced legal man over a circumference of twelve to fifteen leagues, who would arbitrate and conciliate in all cases where both parties agreed to come before him. The author suggests this solution in order to protect the property rights of lords, who would still have a court in their seigneuries.

Fouquau de Pussy, in a similar pamphlet written for the Estates-General, made all the same complaints about seigneurial justice, but reached a different conclusion. More theoretical than the above author, Fouquau began by discussing the abuses in the origins of seigneurial justice–that lords usurped a royal prerogative from the king, and that seigneurial courts "are even opposed to the constitution of the state, to the interests of the king and his subjects."[23] The principle of usurpation, though, was less important to Fouquau than the abuses in practice, abuses that he listed almost identically to the anonymous pamphlet cited above. His solution to this morass was to suppress all seigneurial courts and return this authority to the king. In their place he would establish royal bailliages in each city or large town, with a circumference of a dozen parishes.[24] Still, he respected the property of lords in their justice. To safeguard their property, the crown must either buy the right of justice from them, or allow the lords to lease the new royal bailliages.[25] In the end, despite all the talk about lords illegitimately snatching justice from the crown, Fouquau's reforms either leave lords in charge of justice or redeem this illegitimate and abusive right from the very people who in the mists of the past had stolen it from the king.[26]

Very few authors managed to break free from assumptions that safeguarded seigneurial justice as private property. The only author writing before about 1788 to call unequivocally for the abolition of seigneurial justice without suggesting redemption was S.-N. H. Linguet. In a book published in 1764 he strongly condemned the entire French judicial system and especially seigneurial justice. "Seigneurial courts are usually staffed by peasants who are very intelligent and respectable, as long as they direct a plough, but who are unfit, it seems, to become the mouthpiece of Themis."[27] Linguet called feudalism barbaric and claimed that it plunged all of Europe into centuries of ignorance. Accordingly he had no sympathy for lords who might lose their right of justice if the king suppressed the institution. Linguet was an exceptional figure in that he liked nothing better than to swim against the intellectual current.[28] He had an intellectual advantage over most eighteenth-century authors in that his view of politics was essentially Hobbesian, so that it was irrelevant to him whether justice properly belonged to the king or to lords.[29] The government was not appointed by God, but rather it was set up to protect people from violence. Laws and judicial system that were not fulfilling their job of "providing for citizens the free and assured possession of their goods" must be changed.[30] Seigneurs owned justice because they were the strongest and most violent in the past, but with political changes the king was strong enough to take it from them. According to a leading authority on Linguet, this book recommending judicial reform was un-saleable and had virtually no impact on the discussion among the literate classes, demonstrating how far outside the mainstream his views on the judicial system were.[31]

Linguet was the lone voice crying for the abolition of seigneurial justice in the eighteenth century. It was not until 1788 during the uncertainty associated with the abolition of the parlements that others began to call for the suppression of seigneurial courts without indemnification. M. Mézard anonymously published an essay suggesting reforms to France's judicial system. He began the book by discrediting the idea that what France needed was better, more exact laws and legal procedures. There had been countless attempts to reform procedure, and some of these, like the Civil Ordinance of the late seventeenth century, were enlightened and intelligent. The solution was the abolition of seigneurial justice, a system that gave not only lords, but also judges, a personal interest in the misadministration of justice. Like Linguet Mézard was quite utilitarian: "judges are made for justice, and justice for the people."[32]

It is interesting that the judicial reorganization undertaken by Maupeou in 1771 does not seem to have called seigneurial justice into question. Many of the justifications offered in pro-Maupeou pamphlets were highly critical of feudalism. But this was a way of speaking about aristocratic despotism rather than a criticism of seigneurial authority. Indeed, a leading expert on the Maupeou coup d'état suggests that only one of Maupeou's apologists (Charles-François Lebrun) recommended the abolition of seigneurial justice.[33]

Critics of seigneurial justice were most opposed to the general idea that public authority could be owned by private individuals. This is why it can be useful to analyze seigneurial justice in the context of the criticism of venality, the system that allowed public office to be bought and sold (with various taxes and fees paid to the king). Indeed it seems that most critics of venality wrote almost exclusively of the purchase of judicial office, hardly mentioning finance or other offices. William Doyle argues that what is most striking is the relative lack of criticism of venality and the fact that even the Enlightenment did not create any substantially new critiques of venality. And as with seigneurial justice, those advocating abolition believed that the king would have to buy back the offices sold, which would be prohibitively expensive.[34] Almost everyone criticized venality, but few could see any clear alternative to it, especially by the later eighteenth century in the context of growing fears of unchecked royal authority.

Even when money changed hands, the offices of seigneurial judge, *procureur d'office* and clerk were, however, not truly venal, in that the payment of money did not protect the officer from destitution by the lord. Because he feared the authority that lords had over judges, Loyseau maintained that any seigneurial judge who had paid money for his office could not be dismissed by the lord without just cause–the office became "inamovible" with the payment of money.[35] It is unlikely, however, that this was ever practiced: the Ordinance of Roussillon specified that seigneurs can "according to their pleasure and will, revoke and remove their judges from their charges and their offices," and Loyseau admits that with respect to this question "usage has overtaken reason."[36] In his commentary on the Burgundian legal custom, the province's greatest eighteenth-century jurist, Jean Bouhier, argued that the only thing that changed when money had been paid for a seigneurial office was that the lord would have to reimburse his judge if he dismissed him.[37]

The main problem with venality was that it gave too much power to those who held the offices, while the main problem with seigneurial justice was that those who held the offices did not have enough power, but were rather forced to render decisions favorable to the lord. This is why most critics of seigneurial justice do not seem to have linked venality with seigneurial justice. Loyseau is again exceptional in this regard, at least in part because he wished to argue that lords could not dismiss judges at will. Most writers, as I have suggested, were a great deal more pragmatic than Loyseau in their criticisms of seigneurial justice. Most were incapable of imagining the abolition of seigneurial courts because they saw them as property that belonged to seigneurs.

The conservatism of antiseigneurial authors that had protected seigneurial justice as private property was abandoned by the National Assembly on the night of August 4, 1789, as it abolished the institution without indemnification. The delegates accepted and were willing to take to its conclusion Loyseau's idea that "usurpation was the main origin of seigneurial courts." A report presented in 1791 to the Committee of the Judiciary explained that lords had not been indemnified because they had created the right of justice "with their own hands." The difference, of course, was that by this point sovereignty was held to reside in the people so that even a monarch could not choose to alienate public authority without the consent of the nation.[38]

Keith Baker has argued that the way people thought and spoke about politics changed after 1750. "First in the dispute over the refusal of sacraments, then in the institutional conflicts over the grain trade, and then in the Maupeou crisis, French politics broke out of the absolutist mould."[39] This judgment applies in many ways to the discourse about seigneurial justice. After 1750 the number of legal thinkers who wrote critically about seigneurial justice increased. In inexpensive pamphlets that made their arguments accessible to a public who may never have heard of Loyseau, they complained about abuses in the origins, and especially the practice, of seigneurial justice.

The seigneurial system so profoundly confused property with public authority that only two or three of the most radical authors before August 4, 1789 could take to its logical end the notion that the ownership of justice was illegitimate. The central government did not seriously try to take back its public authority from high-justice seigneurs until 1788. Indeed it is important not to overestimate the degree of antiseigneurial sentiment within royal and ministerial circles. David Parker has recently argued that Louis XIV was antiseigneurial neither in theory nor in practice.[40] In any case, virtually all authors who called for suppression of seigneurial justice wanted reimbursement, thus implicitly legitimating the usurpation of justice by lords. Only with the start of the French Revolution did it become possible to think through Loyseau's notions that venality, the seigneurial system, and the society of orders were illegitimate brakes on an undivided sovereignty, whether held by the king or the nation.

It is instructive to compare the criticisms of legal theorists with those that ordinary people expressed in the *cahiers de doléances*. As we will see in chapter 7, most villages foresaw the preservation of seigneurial justice, even requesting that local judges be given the authority of the intendant and the Waters and Forests courts. They were, however, deeply critical of the ways that lords could influence justice, decrying the fact that lords were in some sense both judge and party. There is a striking similarity between the *cahiers* and the pamphlets, in that both agree that justice belonged to the king and should be administered in his name only. Villagers offered much more practical solutions to this problem, however, requesting that all officers be named by the king, or at the very least that the lord not be able to remove officers whose ruling displeased him. There is an important difference, as well, in that the villagers in the *cahiers* were largely satisfied with the competence and level of professionalism of their judicial officers, whereas legal theorists portrayed them as incompetent, illiterate, and greedy. Ordinary people, the clients of seigneurial courts, surely understood how the institution worked better than did urban-dwelling legal theorists. In northern Burgundy the largely positive attitudes of ordinary people was substantially the result of an important series of procedural reforms brought about in the province through the cooperation of the parlement and the provincial Estates.

The Parlement of Dijon and Legal Reform

Grandiose schemes calling for the creation of a parallel system of royal courts of first instance that would provide better justice and thereby slowly replace seigneurial justice, of allowing the king to appoint seigneurial officers, or of outright abolition of seigneurial courts all led nowhere during the eighteenth century. The reasons for the failure of these reform plans are twofold. First, as we have seen, respect for private property safeguarded the institution to the point that few theorists could even imagine abolition before 1789. The other major impediment to national legal reform was the legal diversity that existed within a society based on the principle of privilege. Judicial reforms that were national in scope, or that were seen to undermine the property of lords, were probably doomed to failure before revolutionaries abolished the worst parts of the seigneurial system and found the political will to bring administrative standardization to the nation.

Institutional and procedural reforms brought about by the Dijon Parlement and the Estates-General of the province starting in the late 1760s stand in stark contrast to those suggested by most legal theorists. Because of their practicality, these reforms were a resounding success. Using a practice that was peculiar to eastern France, the annual assizes, seigneurial courts were brought much closer to the village, and procedure for minor cases was vastly simplified and rendered a great deal cheaper. With respect to the authority of seigneurs, the element upon which most grandiose reform schemes fell apart, the record is somewhat mixed. Certainly the reforms did not undermine the seigneurial system, and the link between justice and seigneurialism was possibly even strengthened–most parlementary magistrates and delegates to the provincial Estates were high-justice lords, after all. Still, the reforms did subject seigneurial justice more strictly to judicial oversight and verification by royal judges and clearly indicated that the primary allegiance of seigneurial judges was to the parlement rather than to the lord who had hired them.

Until recently historians have tended to emphasize the fact that royal officers had no real oversight or knowledge of seigneurial justice, and that there were few checks in place on the cupidity and laziness of seigneurial judges.[41] This was certainly not the case in northern Burgundy, and seems unlikely to have been true even of other parts of France. Others have already noted that seigneurial courts functioned as part of the judicial arm of the central state. Sylvain Soleil emphasizes the fact that bailliage officers knew what went on in seigneurial courts, while Zoë Schneider goes as far as to consider bailliages and seigneurial courts together as "lower courts."[42] In northern Burgundy seigneurial courts were part of the complex of institutions that linked subject to king. Local seigneurial judges were not left alone to do as they wished, but were subjected to rigorous oversight by the magistrates of Burgundy's highest court, the Parlement of Dijon.

By the eighteenth century, seigneurial courts in northern Burgundy worked consistently, met regularly, and enforced the relevant laws as established by the highest court and royal edict. During the 1760s, however, the Dijon Parlement initiated a series of reforms designed to ensure the survival and efficiency of seigneurial justice by establishing closer observation of these lower courts. Indeed, a broad coalition of Burgundian ruling elites, including the Dijon Parlement (before, during, and after the Maupeou reforms), the provincial Estates, and (to a lesser extent) the intendant, worked together to make procedure more rapid and less expensive and to broaden access to the justice of first instance in the countryside. The reforms were impressively effective, leading to a doubling of the number of lawsuits, and the presence of poorer inhabitants as litigants.

As highest court in the province, the Parlement of Dijon had the closest contact with, and most direct oversight of, seigneurial justice. The judges of the parlement heard appeals from bailliage and seigneurial courts, and issued rebukes in the form of general *arrêts* to judges, prosecutors, and clerks whose personal behavior brought disrepute to justice. In 1747, for example, parlementary magistrates annulled the decision of the seigneurial justice of Meilly because the judge ate and drank with one of the parties in the case.[43] For gambling with villagers, the prosecutor of Chanceaux was forbidden from practicing as *procureur d'office* in any court for three years, and fined 500 livres.[44] Another case in 1768 was annulled because the clerk of the seigneurial court moonlighted as an innkeeper.[45] In 1776 the Dijon Parlement told the officers of the seigneurial court of Bagé to have its hearing at a regular time and day each week, and to do so "in robes and with appropriate decency."[46]

The magistrates of the Parlement of Dijon intervened to ensure that seigneurial courts did not try to cut corners to save money for lords or judicial officers. Sometimes clerks tried to save time by writing up the transcripts of the trial before the court met, filling in blanks after.[47] Because it provided them with more revenue, seigneurial judges sometimes tried minor cases using expensive written procedure rather than summary oral procedure. In a minor criminal affair one prosecutor had insisted on hearing many witnesses, and used full criminal procedure including the confrontation of witnesses. The Dijon Parlement annulled the procedure, and the prosecutor had to pay all the costs of the original case from his own pocket.[48]

The province's highest court also saw to it that the interests of lords did not corrupt the practice of justice. In cases where the plaintiff was the "public party" the lord who owned the court was obliged to pay court costs, as part of his responsibility to maintain order in the seigneurie.[49] This was why in 1763 the behavior of a judge provoked an "*arrêt* of the Parlement of Burgundy that forbids all judges of its jurisdiction, from ever condemning the guilty to pay the expenses of the case when the public party is named as the sole plaintiff."[50] Another problem in criminal cases was that seigneurial judges sometimes tried to save the lord money by avoiding the mandatory visit to the village to see the place of the crime.[51]

Throughout the last half of the eighteenth century, the Parlement of Dijon exercised considerable oversight over the seigneurial courts within its jurisdiction. The magistrates of Burgundy's highest court used their authority of appeal to make sure that judges did not behave in unseemly ways when they went to the village, that lower courts used proper procedure, and that the fiscal interests of officers and lords did not lead to overt injustices. From the late 1760s, however, the Parlement of Dijon became much more involved in the administration of seigneurial justice. From 1766 to 1775 this provincial court systematically both brought in new regulations for seigneurial courts and reissued and enforced requirements that had long existed. These magistrates became determined to root out abuses in the administration of seigneurial justice and to ensure that ordinary people all over Burgundy had access to a quick, cheap form of justice.

The Dijon Parlement made its first move in affirming its authority over seigneurial justice in 1766. This was a formal reminder, in the form of a general *arrêt,* that all judicial officers had to register their offices and be sworn in by a royal judge.[52] This was not a new practice, and there is no way of knowing if it had fallen into disuse, but by re-issuing the original royal edict of March 1693, this reminded seigneurial judges all over Burgundy that they were responsible to the parlement.

The next general *arrêt* affecting seigneurial justice came only a few weeks later and directly concerned criminal cases. It is interesting that this *arrêt* predated the royal reform of criminal procedure in seigneurial courts by about six years. Like the royal edict, this too was designed to ensure that regular procedure was followed, and that the automatic appeal of major crimes to parlement took place. The Dijon Parlement commanded all seigneurial and royal judges under its authority to send in biannual reports on the criminal activity of their courts. Each January and June all courts had to send a summary of all criminal proceedings, including the names of the accused, the date and length of their detention, and the current state of the prosecution.[53] This would ensure that all major crimes were automatically appealed in the parlement, and would allow the magistrates more closely to control what went on in the province's lower courts.

In 1768 the Dijon Parlement issued its most thorough general reform of seigneurial justice. Again, it was more of a restatement than an innovation, but parlement made clear that it intended closely to examine the working of seigneurial justice. In March 1768 parlement ordered all lords who possessed the right of justice to make sure that they instituted officers who resided within the relevant bailliage.[54] The *arrêt* reminded lords of their responsibility to pay the officers a salary and to ensure that by these officers "justice is administered to their subjects, on pain of prosecution and of arbitrary fine paid to the King." Most importantly, the officers were required to hold annual assizes, where the villagers heard new laws and rules read aloud, the judge tried minor cases cheaply and summarily and exercised his oversight over village politics. The *arrêt* ended by describing the ways in which the parlement meant to ensure the execution of the rules. The parlement would nominate a judge, *procureur d'office,* and clerk in all seigneurial courts that were not staffed within a month of the *arrêt.* The lord would have to pay these officers salaries of 100, 75, and 66 livres to the officers, amounts which were at least ten times more than average judicial salaries. The same rule would also apply whenever a judicial office became vacant. Each high-justice lord was required to send proof to the parlement that he had appointed officers, and that these officers had held assizes within the previous year. There were also two general *arrêts* issued in 1770 and 1772 that regulated legal fees in seigneurial courts, formally setting wages for sergeants, *huissiers* and legal practitioners who acted as solicitors (*procureurs postulants*).[55] It is worth noting that the Maupeou Parlement in place from 1771 to 1774 pursued the same policy of reforming seigneurial justice by bringing the institution closer to the villages, a fact that further underlines the considerable consensus among the province's judicial and administrative elite that justice needed to become more summary and less expensive.

By the late 1760s the Parlement of Dijon had issued most of the general reforms having to do with seigneurial justice. The next decade saw mostly clarifications of the issues raised by the *arrêt* of 1768. Because the assizes were to become more frequent and more reliable, this meant that judges could intervene more regularly in village affairs. In 1772 there was a re-issuing, with additional comments, of an *arrêt* from 1695 that ordered seigneurial judges to verify the accounts of the parish vestry boards each year. At the end of the assizes, the seigneurial judge was to meet with the parish priest, the "principal inhabitants" of the village, and the elected vestry officer to go over the financial accounts of the vestry. The judicial officers were to do this after the assizes, and never in the presence of the entire community.[56] This was necessary to ensure that the vestry officers did not embezzle funds, but could be avoided if the bishop or archbishop had visited the parish within the year. By the 1780s every seigneurial judge in the sample did indeed examine the vestry accounts after the annual assizes. In 1773 the parlement ordered all villages to appoint a guard for the communal forest each year. The judge was to make certain that the village instituted a guard, and that he carried out his responsibility to watch that the forest resources of the village were not pillaged. If the community refused to nominate a communal guard, the judge had to appoint one himself from among the inhabitants. The *arrêt* also ordered the judicial officers to follow up the reports given them by these guards and to fine the guilty.[57]

In order to ensure that the new laws and reforms were understood by ordinary people and enforced by seigneurial judges, the Dijon Parlement participated in the gathering and publication of the general *arrêts* of parlement and royal edicts that affected seigneurial justice. In 1779, with the "approbation and permission" of parlement, an anonymous Dijonnais lawyer published a handbook for seigneurial officers. The *Règlements généraux pour les justices seigneuriales* listed all of the reforms of the 1760s and 1770s, as well as many of the older laws concerning procedure and especially policing by seigneurial judges. The small, portable handbook served both to remind seigneurial judges that the province's high court was watching over them, ready to intervene, for example, if they misused written procedure, and to underline the responsibilities they had toward the clients of their courts.[58] In fact it became standard for judges to have their clerk read this book aloud to the assembled villagers each year at the assizes.[59] In 1786, another similar handbook was published, this time with more overt support from parlement.[60] The publication, and apparent widespread diffusion, of these pamphlets helps explain the success of parlement in bringing seigneurial justice further under its authority.

Most of the general *arrêts* issued by the Parlement of Dijon were restatement of preexisting policies. Still, they signaled clearly the commitment of the Dijon Parlement to oversee the provincial judicial system. More importantly, the *arrêts* reminded lords of their responsibility to ensure that their seigneurial courts were staffed and active. But by far the most significant part of the general *arrêts* was the fact that they contained concrete oversight provisions, most specifically the requirement that lords send proof that they had hired officers and that these officers held assizes annually. While the actual letters that lords sent in do not survive in the archives of the Dijon Parlement, we can find a few examples in correspondence kept by the families of parlement and bailliage officers. In an undated letter sent to a parlement officer, for example, a *procureur d'office* named Nicolas stated: "I have the honor also to attach to this letter the certificate of the convocation of the assizes in the four parishes of this justice." The letter continues with a short description of three criminal affairs judged in the seigneurial court "since the re-establishment of the court."[61] In another letter sent to the Dijon Parlement, Poulin the elder, a seigneurial judge who sat over six courts, stated that he "repeated to the *procureurs d'office* of my justices . . . to see to it that each year the Jours will be held, or to advise you of the obstacles that could have prevented it."[62]

The Dijon Parlement was not the only administrative body working to reform seigneurial justice in the 1760s and 1770s. By the second half of the eighteenth century, the provincial Estates were also greatly concerned to reduce the costs of justice for ordinary people. The result of their intervention was to make seigneurial courts much more effective at protecting the property of northern Burgundians. At their request the king granted two important procedural reforms in 1773.

In Burgundy seigneurial judges had jurisdiction over *taille* assessments, and they therefore heard cases where individuals challenged the decision of the village officials. For much of the eighteenth century the provincial

Estates had worried about the amounts that ordinary people spent on legal fees to pursue cases that led at best to a reduction of a few livres. The first major change that the king granted at their request came in 1752. The ruling established that people could only challenge their assessment if it increased by more than a twelfth over that of the previous year. The king renewed this rule every three years, but the Estates continued to complain that these *procès en surtaux* still cost too much.

The repeated requests of the Estates led to the king issuing a declaration in 1773. The king noted that he looked favorably on the request to "simplify by a procedural ruling in the matter of *tailles,* just as we have done in the *pays d'élections* by our declaration of the 27th of January 1772." The one-twelfth rule remained in place, but with several additions. Seigneurial courts would only accept challenges of assessments for three months after the village completed its tax rolls. The parties were forbidden from submitting formal legal arguments, and had to limit themselves to a simple declaration of their property and revenue. The declaration specifically encouraged plaintiffs to pursue the case without legal representation. Judges were forbidden from naming experts to evaluate the request, and had to perform the calculations themselves without fees. If the documents submitted were not detailed enough to allow the judge to decide, he was to visit the village and speak to the local officials, especially the tithe-collectors who would know most about the value of the fields. All documents were to be exchanged without using the services of court officers, using instead a simple messenger. As defendant, the community had only three weeks to meet and determine whether the inhabitants approved the assessment and wished to defend the case in court. Costs were to be strictly limited: judges only received twelve livres, and then only if they visited the village. If the plaintiff hired legal representation, he could only charge 3 livres plus 20 sols for each copy of the *mémoire* presented. And finally, appeals of these cases were to go directly to parlement, bypassing the bailliage in order to save time and money. Here too costs were limited, judges received no money, and the *procureurs* of the parties could charge no more than 18 livres.[63]

The new rules concerning *surtaux* signaled the determination to reduce the formalities of justice, to encourage people to plead their cases without costly legal representation, and to make efficient use of local judges who were "more likely [than royal judges] to know or to be informed of the faculties of ratepayers" because of their intimate connection to the village.[64] Similar reform impulses are to be found in the change in the way that local courts tried *mésus* after 1773. This reform, also accomplished in 1773 by royal declaration at the request of the provincial Estates, turned out to have the most profound impact on seigneurial justice of all the changes of the late eighteenth century, making justice almost free for minor cases and excluding the costly intervention of sworn experts and *procureurs* for these same minor cases.

This reform was a direct result of the new emphasis that parlement placed on the assizes. The provincial Estates requested that minor farming disputes be settled only at the assizes "which, according to an *arrêt de Règlement* of your Parlement of Dijon of the twenty-sixth of March 1768, must be held at least once each year by the officers of high-justice lords." In the remonstrances they sent to the king in 1773 the Estates complained that these *mésus* cases were ruinously expensive and slow. They described the normal procedure. First the offended party reported the offense to the court, and the plaintiff and defendant each appointed one expert to examine the fields. These experts were sworn in by the court and usually made a second trip for the investigation. Before the judge decided the merits of the case, one party often demanded a new report. After all this written procedure, the Estates wrote, these cases where the amount involved was rarely more than five to six livres often cost the loser as much as 800 livres in court fees.[65] Their suggested solution: "we have thought, sire, that it would be simple to decide these sorts of cases without fees or formalities, by bringing them to the assizes." The king answered in the margins that he was pleased with the interest of the Estates for the well being of his Burgundian subjects, and that he would quickly issue a declaration inaugurating the new procedure.

"Our intention is to simplify procedure in all kinds of ways," said the preamble of the declaration that the king issued within months of this remonstrance.[66] All *mésus* cases that did not involve violence were to be settled every year at the annual assizes. Each year at the Grands-Jours the community was to name three experts for the year, called *prud'hommes.* Most villages already nominated *prud'hommes* to decide the dates of the opening of the harvest, so the reform attached new duties to an existing institution. The offended party went directly to the *prud'hommes* and asked them to visit the piece of land in question. These experts reported orally to the clerk with an estimation of the damages. The clerk kept these reports until the next assizes, where the judge would pass judgment. The officers of the court received no money for these judgments, so the dispute would be settled for five sols, the salary of the *prud'hommes.*

The Parlement of Dijon registered the new law without comment. The magistrates demonstrated their commitment to the reform by issuing a general *arrêt* one day before registration, which ordered all villages to "name a sufficient number of *prud'hommes,* to estimate farming torts committed in the fields."[67] The explicit approval of the new procedure, and the fact that the Estates requested it as a result of the 1768 general *arrêt* of parlement suggest that the administrative and judicial leaders of these two institutions, who so often competed and fought, agreed on the kinds of functions that should be fulfilled by seigneurial courts and were determined to simplify procedure, broaden access to justice, and make these courts more explicitly tools of the central and provincial governments.

Why Did Provincial Authorities Reform Seigneurial Justice?

The Dijon Parlement and the Burgundian Estates worked to reform seigneurial justice for several reasons, including an enlightened determination to make the province's institutions work better. Equally important, however, was the fact that many of the representatives in the Estates, and most of the magistrates in the parlement, owned fiefs with the right of high justice attached. Since seigneurial justice was a crucial tool in the enforcement and policing of lords' rights and revenues, these lawmakers profited materially from the reforms that made seigneurial justice more efficient and more connected to local life.

All three chambers in the provincial Estates had significant material stakes in the maintenance, even strengthening, of seigneurial justice. The representatives of the first Order were important clerics from the province's religious orders, all of which owned seigneuries with the right of justice. The nobles belonged to the social group that owned most seigneuries. There was even an attempt within the Second Chamber of the Estates to limit access only to those who owned a seigneurie with the right of justice.[68] Although most representatives of the Third Estate did not own seigneurial courts, most of them were mayors of towns. Municipal justice was essentially a special kind of seigneurial justice where the town possessed the right of high justice. In a dispute between the municipal court and bailliage of Dijon, the parlement noted that "the right of justice being only seigneurial and not royal . . . seigneurial rights and high, middle and low justice belong to the city."[69] The provincial Estates of Burgundy, therefore, had material interest in the preservation of seigneurial justice.

Just how deeply was seigneurialism rooted in the Parlement of Dijon? In his analysis of the Parlement of Dijon in the late eighteenth-century, Albert Colombet claims that most parlementaires owned seigneuries with the right of justice attached, and were highly effective as managers of their estates.[70] Most parlementary judges were continually on the lookout to acquire new seigneuries. In the classified advertisements of the *Affiches de Bourgogne,* where people often posted seigneuries for sale, Colombet found not a single instance where a parlementaire wanted to sell a seigneurie, but there were 45 acquisitions of seigneuries by these same magistrates.[71] Colombet also claims that profit from their estates made up the single most important source of revenue for all of these families.[72]

It is impractical in a study on seigneurial justice to investigate at length the way that parlementaires administered their seigneuries, but the number of magistrates who owned seigneuries can be determined. This was done through comparison of two different sorts of tax documents for the years 1747 and 1786: the records of *capitation* for office-holders, and the records of the *dixième* and *vingtième* for Burgundian seigneuries.[73] It should be noted that the proportions given below represent minima, given the problems associated with document-matching through name recognition.

The Parlement of Dijon was full of high-justice lords. In 1746 there were 77 presidents and counselors in the parlement. Together these officers owned no fewer than 110 seigneuries, an average of 1.4 seigneuries per parlementaire. Not everyone owned a seigneurie, though. In fact 27 parlementaires (33.8 percent) were not lords, at least in Burgundy. The more important a parlementaire was, the more likely it was that he owned a seigneurie. Most parlementaires owned between one and four seigneuries, but the first president, Fyot de la Marche, was the proud owner of 18! There were nine presidents in the parlement in 1746, and only one of these did not appear in the list of seigneuries in Burgundy. Together the nine presidents owned 34 seigneuries, or 3.4 per president. In 1787 the feudalization of the Parlement of Dijon remained a significant factor, but with some minor changes from 1746. In 1787 there were 71 presidents and counselors, who together owned 78 seigneuries, or 1.10 per person. Twenty-five officers of the parlement owned no seigneuries (35.2 percent). Among the presidents, again one of the nine did not own a seigneurie. The other eight presidents owned 18 seigneuries between them.

In 1787, as in 1746, most parlementaires owned at least one seigneurie (approximately 65 percent in both years, 90 percent of presidents). On the other hand, the total number of seigneuries that these parlementaires owned had decreased from 110 to 78. This drop in ownership of fiefs by members of the Parlement of Dijon is best understood with reference to changes in recruitment in the late eighteenth century. After 1775 parlement recruited increasingly from outside the province. Of 50 new counselors received after 1775, ten were not from Burgundian families. These 50 counselors came from 37 families, of which nine families were still commoners at the time of inception of the young counselor.[74] Both the lower social status and the tendency to recruit from outside the province help explain the drop in the ownership of seigneuries. Families of lower social standing might often not have enough money to afford seigneuries, especially after sinking 30,000 livres into the purchase of an office of counselor.[75] The families of counselors who had recently arrived in Dijon might have owned seigneuries in their own provinces, but this is not taken into account in the figures above.

Most parlementaires owned seigneuries with the right of high justice attached. This meant that they understood how seigneurial courts worked in practice and were unlikely to be taken in by the negative stereotypes associated with the institution. Royal administrators, since at least the early eighteenth century, had resented seigneurial justice as a hindrance to the full authority of the king. They were also convinced that the institution was full of abuses and routinely failed to provide justice to the king's vassals. This was why Daguesseau suggested abolishing the institution as early as the 1720s–and also why the king took advantage of the crisis of 1788 to undermine seigneurial justice.[76] Parlementaires in Dijon, on the other hand, had orchestrated the judicial reforms of the 1760s and 1770s and as lords, had witnessed first-hand the extension of cheap, efficient justice to the inhabitants of the province.

A combination of the self-interest of magistrate/seigneurs and humanitarianism explains much about the policies of the Dijon Parlement with respect to seigneurial justice. The (self-proclaimed) role of the parlement as the defender of provincial liberties and privilege was another important factor. Jean Bart describes the collective attitude of the Dijon Parlement in the late eighteenth century as a kind of provincial patriotism. The magistrates of this court strongly opposed both the spread of Parisian customary law and Roman written law from the South.[77] This was their way of protecting Burgundian legal particularism, strengthening provincial autonomy, and giving more authority to the parlement itself. The protection, defense, and reform of seigneurial justice here was part of this same process.

The Dijon Parlement was determined to protect the province's privileges, institutions and legal particularities from being abolished by royal ministers–and seigneurial justice was central for parlementary magistrates' understanding of their own authority and of provincial privilege. We will see in chapter 6 in a discussion of one of the most protracted disputes between the parlement and royal ministers, concerning the auctions of village communal resources, that provincial magistrates viewed the pretensions of the intendant as an attempt to rob the province of its privileges by undermining the authority of seigneurial judges. The same was true of the Varenne affair, which had led in the middle of the century to the imprisonment of the secretary of the Estates by the provincial parlement and his repudiation by the king.[78] This concerned seigneurial justice, since the parlement's opposition to the *élus* of the Estates arbitrarily setting tax assessments of local elites was in part a defense of its authority to hear appeals of the decisions of seigneurial judges concerning *taille* assessments.

The centrality of seigneurial justice to the Dijon magistrates' conception of provincial privilege can be seen in their response to the royal reforms of 1787–88.[79] The royal edict of 1788, forcibly registered by the Parlement of Dijon on May 10, provided for the creation of so-called *grands bailliages*.[80] These courts replaced the parlements in civil and criminal affairs, while the parlements also lost their right of registration and remonstrance to a newly created plenary court. The nation's parlements were left with no more than criminal cases involving the privileged and a few important civil cases.[81] Naturally the magistrates of the Parlement of Dijon objected to what amounted to the abolition of the province's highest court. These changes would make parlement nothing more, they noted in a published criticism of the reforms, than "the passive witness of all the disorder that could arise, without being able to remedy the situation at all."

The edict also affected the administration of seigneurial justice, since plaintiffs and defendants were given the choice of attending the local seigneurial court or going to the *grand bailliage* in all civil and criminal cases. Furthermore, lords were to be required to have a judge, *procureur d'office,* clerk, prison and courthouse in the seat of all justices. While allowing plaintiffs to choose their judges was a threat to seigneurial justice, it is likely that the institution could have survived such a change given the relative popularity of the institution in northern Burgundy. But requiring resident judicial officers in each justice would have been absolutely catastrophic for the institution, making it impossible to staff the many hundreds of small courts with competent officers. This is why the magistrates of the Parlement of Dijon were concerned about how the reforms would affect lords. "This ordinance," they explained, "threatens equally the property of all lords, who are robbed of their right of justice, in authorizing their vassals to go directly to the bailliage in all cases."[82] Similarly the magistrates of the *Chambre des Comptes* noted that "the ordinance on the administration of justice poses a threat to the property of the lords, vassals of His Majesty, who . . . must be maintained in all their Rights, whether revenue-bearing or honorific."[83]

If seigneurial courts in northern Burgundy were reformed through the diligent oversight of the provincial parlement, was the same thing true in other parts of France? Was Burgundy the exception in a country whose local courts were gradually becoming obsolete? There is evidence from many different parts of France that during the second half of the eighteenth century judicial oversight by parlementary magistrates and bailliage judges over seigneurial courts became more effective. Jean Bastier has shown that the Parlement of Toulouse actively involved itself in policing seigneurial courts by verifying cases, conducting enquiries, and generally halting abuses.[84] The result was to increase public confidence in seigneurial justice. The same was apparently true of the Parlement of Besançon, and of the area under the control of the *présidial* of Angers.[85] In fact the enquiries undertaken by parlements, bailliages and intendants into the functioning of seigneurial courts, and used by historians critical of the institution suggest that in Brittany, in Aunis and Saintonge, and in Auvergne there was a generalized push for judicial reform within the context of the preservation of seigneurial courts.[86] Still, it is likely that Burgundy was exceptional because of the strong emphasis on the assizes and the invention of a new summary form of procedure for farming torts. The new emphasis that parlement placed on the Grands-Jours and the hearing of minor disputes summarily, combined with the procedural reform instigated by the Estates, put seigneurial justice in a position to improve the speed and lower the cost of the justice that ordinary people received at the hand of the province's judicial institution. Whether it worked, of course, would depend on the way that the reforms were carried out by judges, prosecutors, and clerks.

The Effects of Reform

In 1778, a few scant years after the judicial reforms, a farmer wrote a letter to a magistrate in the parlement complaining of the lack of execution of the reforms in his local court. De Prey, the author of the letter, had heard it whispered that the judge, owner of a large farm administered by his 30-year-old daughter, benefited enormously from illegal pasturing of his animals and so refused to allow villagers easily and quickly to sue each other for damages. The result was that over 100 measures of grain and 12 cartloads of hay were lost to the law-abiding farmers.[87] This letter reminds us that if the procedural reforms were to have an impact on the judicial system it would only happen if many hundred seigneurial judges decided to follow the letter of the reform and actively encouraged villagers to use the Grands-Jours as a forum for the settling of minor disputes.

Court costs and a host of procedural indicators demonstrate that most seigneurial judges agreed with the province's legislators on the need for faster and more summary justice for minor affairs. In 1771 the seigneurial judge of Coulanges la Vineuse and Val-de-Mercy, concerned that procedure was often too slow, issued an ordinance that he had the clerk read aloud to the villagers. In it he explained that minor cases should be judged without the submission of written arguments or evidence. Many solicitors, he said, submit long written complaints to begin their cases, rather than simply reporting orally to the court and having a summons issued. To remedy this, the judge informed the villagers that he would not allow *procureurs* to charge for any writings except in major cases.[88] Although local ordinances of this kind do not exist for any of the fourteen seigneurial courts sampled, we can see from the declining average time elapsed per court case that judges all over northern Burgundy worked to reduce formalities and get cases through more quickly. In other words, seigneurial judges not only encouraged litigants to use the assizes for minor cases, but went further than parlement, settling cases more quickly even in regular session.

There were significant changes in the regular running of the courts, but by far the most important changes occurred at the annual assizes. The new procedure for farming torts, combined with a willingness among judges to hear many minor civil cases at the assizes, meant that the total number of cases almost doubled as a result of the reforms. What's more, the availability of cheaper justice meant that poorer people in the village had access to justice. Anthony Crubaugh has argued that in one region of the Bordelais the judicial reforms of the Revolution (most significantly the abolition of seigneurial justice) sated a thirst for justice that ancien régime courts had only aggravated. The largest change was in the vast multiplication of minor farming disputes, which before the Revolution had apparently gone unsettled. Furthermore, Crubaugh argues that seigneurial courts were an instrument of class justice while justices of the peace allowed even the poor to go to court. Although northern Burgundy's seigneurial courts look a great deal less abuse-ridden than those Crubaugh describes, it is interesting that in northern Burgundy the reforms of the 1760s and 1770s had identical effects to those that in other parts of France had to await the intervention of Revolutionary legislators.

Procedure in Regular Session

Taking a lawsuit before a seigneurial court in the eighteenth century was not difficult. The procedure involved was simple and mostly oral.[89] Many plaintiffs and defendants chose to use legal counsel (a *procureur postulant*), but it was possible for litigants to present their case without assistance in summary affairs, and they did so in regular session in about one case in ten.[90] The case began with the plaintiff stopping in to see the clerk to register the complaint. That day or the next, the clerk would write up a summons, to be delivered by the sergeant of the seigneurial court.[91] Courts did not keep copies of summons, and few of these survive, but an example can be found in the records of the provincial intendant: "13 March 1774. The *syndics* and inhabitants of the community of Senailly, joined by M. Jean Labbé *procureur d'office* in the local justice. By this they give notice to Jacques Drouhin miller at Vizerny, in the office of M. Guyot his *procureur,* of the audience in the justice of Senailly, next Thursday, to hear the matter."[92]

On the day set for the first session the judge would hear the arguments, presented orally, and either reach a decision or tell the parties to appear again in a week or two. The judge would sometimes order the litigants to prove their contentions by calling witnesses or by presenting documentary evidence. The plaintiff, the defendant, and their legal representatives all presented the case through oral argument. Even when parties presented written evidence, the procedure generally remained oral, with the parties or their counsel explaining the significance of the written evidence (generally written contract or expert's report). In a dispute over rents in 1751 the judge ordered the defendant to present written argument for his side of the dispute. This was only after six previous sessions of purely oral argument in a case that had become very complicated.[93]

It is important to emphasize the oral nature of the procedure used in the seigneurial courts of northern Burgundy, since several historians have argued that legal procedure during the ancien régime was mired in formality and relied heavily on complicated written documents and argument.[94] But the Civil Ordinance of 1670 mandated the use of summary, oral procedure for a wide variety of cases. Louis XIV implemented this reform, in the words of the preamble, "to re-establish [justice] by the authority of our laws in the interior of our kingdom, after having brought peace by the strength of our weapons." In seigneurial courts all private matters that involved less than 200 livres were to be tried exclusively with summary procedure (the maximum was 400 livres in royal courts), as well as all police cases involving less than 1,000 livres and most inheritance and probate matters. The judge was to hear the oral pleadings of the parties, who were entitled to represent themselves without legal counsel (that is, without an *avocat*), and his decision would be reached "without procedure of formality."[95] According to an eighteenth-century commentary on the ordinance, the section on summary affairs was the most important part of the entire reform, since it functioned to "abbreviate the exercise of justice . . . because of the simple procedure that is observed in the relevant cases, which are the most common."[96] While seigneurial judges in other parts of France may have ignored the provisions of the ordinance (in the Bordelais, for example), in northern Burgundy, the close attention and control of the provincial parlement meant that written procedure was highly exceptional.

The use of oral procedure encouraged ordinary people to use the local court to settle their disputes. Even if only about 10 percent of defendants in regular session appeared before the judge without legal counsel, almost nobody had to consult a lawyer. The *procureurs postulants* who assisted plaintiffs and defendants had some legal training, perhaps through clerking for a notary. They knew how seigneurial justice worked and could coach their clients in procedural issues. It is difficult to reconstruct the amounts that these village practitioners charged, since the amounts are not included in the court costs listed in the final judgment. Parlementary *arrêts* regulated the amounts that *procureurs* charged for various procedural acts and activities, but we do not know when *procureurs* may have done each type of act.

The Parlement of Dijon did act in 1777 and then again with more force in 1781 to reduce the amounts that *procureurs* charged their clients. The total reduction brought about by these two reforms is difficult to evaluate, but that of 1781 provoked a strong negative reaction from the *procureurs* of the province. While the general *arrêt* reduced the amounts charged by *procureurs* in both royal and seigneurial courts, the change was much greater for cases tried in seigneurial courts. In order to evaluate the effects of the changes, the communities of *procureurs* in the province added together the costs of all operations for which they charged fees in both royal and seigneurial courts. This calculation does not represent in any way the amounts that real clients would have paid. But since, as they argued, "the reductions apply to the most common activities in procedure," the calculation reveals significant trends. Activities carried out in royal courts diminished from 39 to 31 livres as a result of the reform, while those in seigneurial courts dropped from 26 to 15 livres. Some of the activities that *procureurs* had charged for before the reform were to be done for free after 1781, such as the delivery of letters and opposition formed against the division of an estate among heirs.[97] Here again we see that the Parlement of Dijon was concerned with reducing the costs of justice, and that it was more important for them to do so in seigneurial courts than in royal courts.

We can attempt to reconstruct the costs of legal representation by using court cases between *procureurs* and their clients for services rendered in seigneurial courts. Judges before whom such cases appeared frequently sent the matter to the community of *procureurs* in the relevant bailliage. These officers would read over the papers provided by the *procureur* and decide how much the client really owed. The register of deliberations of the community of *procureurs* of the bailliage of Dijon contains a number of these decisions, of which 29 were for services rendered in a seigneurial court (they also performed similar operations for cases heard in the bailliage, in the Waters and Forests court, and before the provincial intendant).[98]

In this small sample of disputes, the average amount paid by the client to the *procureur* was 29.5 livres. One exceptionally expensive case (300 livres) skews the sample, however, and if we eliminate it the average drops to 16.4 livres. The median amount charged, more representative of what most clients paid, was significantly lower, at 7.1 livres. Nine of the 29 cases involved a village community as either plaintiff or defendant, and if we exclude these to concentrate on those cases that involved only individuals, the average amount was 13.5 livres and the median cost was five livres. Are these costs representative of the amounts that most villagers paid to hire judicial representation in seigneurial courts? Most of the disputes settled by the community of *procureurs* came from the 1780s, after the Parlement of Dijon had reduced the amounts that *procureurs* could charge, and costs were likely higher earlier in the century. On the other hand, these cases come to our attention precisely because the *procureur*'s client felt that he or she had been overcharged.

In general we can estimate that a peasant could hire a *procureur* in a simple case involving a debt or an unmet obligation for no more than a few livres, as when the *procureur* Robelot represented the *fermier général* Thomas in the seigneurial court of Echirey against a merchant for two livres six sols. More drawn-out cases could cost twenty livres or more, and very complicated cases, such as inheritance disputes or any case involving the village community, might require paying the *procureur* fifty livres or more. While hardly likely to bankrupt most litigants, the cost of hiring legal counsel was a factor that ordinary people had to take into account before deciding to go to court, and it certainly provided incentive to settle complicated cases privately. By reducing the amounts that *procureurs* could charge, and especially by encouraging villagers to plead without representation by using the annual assizes for minor cases, however, the Parlement of Dijon and the provincial Estates were both working to reduce the costs associated with legal representation in seigneurial courts. By the 1780s the *procureurs* of the province of Burgundy had appointed two members whom they sent to Paris to prepare an appeal in the Royal Council, complaining that the reforms of the parlement had so reduced their fees that they could hardly make a living. It is instructive that in order to prepare their arguments for the appeal, the two deputies wrote back to Dijon requesting copies of the 1773 changes in the procedure for *mésus* and for *surtaux,* two reforms that together worked to exclude *procureurs* from a large proportion of cases.[99]

Just how summary was the procedure used in seigneurial courts in northern Burgundy? The following figures refer only to cases tried in regular weekly sessions, which was slower than the assizes, but which nevertheless compares favorably to other judicial systems. It is true that the amount of time elapsed before the first session before the court could be considerable. In the one court where I recorded the date of the summons, on average in the 1750s 98 days elapsed before the first session (82 days in the 1780s).[100] On average, in this one seigneurial court, it took three months for a case to proceed from first complaint to first court session. But if we eliminate the 38 cases in the 1750s and the 60 cases in the 1780s where more than three months elapsed, the average time between summons and initial court-date was 22.5 days in the 1780s and 23.7 days in the 1750s–about three weeks from complaint to court date.

Once a case began in court, the judges of northern Burgundy generally expedited it through quickly, and the speed of trials increased notably after the reforms. We can see this first in the number of times a case appeared in front of a judge before final judgment, which is presented graphically below. In the 1750s in the sample, cases that reached a final settlement in court came before the judge an average of 2.1 times. During the 1780s, on the other hand, parties appeared an average of 1.9 times before the court before receiving a final judgment, about 10 percent fewer appearances in court. While this change may seem insignificant, there were more major cases being tried in regular session in the 1780s, with many more minor cases filtered through to the assizes after the reforms.

The improved efficiency of these courts can be seen also in the length of time elapsed between the first and final appearances in court. In the 1750s the average court time for cases that reached a settlement was 64 days, while the figure for the 1780s was 61 days, but of cases that settled in less than 90 days, the average time from first session to settlement was 10.5 days in the 1750s and 7.7 days in the 1780s. Of cases that settled in less than a month, the average time was 4.4 days in the 1750s and 3.0 days in the 1780s. In the 1750s 84.3 percent of cases saw a settlement in less than three months, and 74 percent in less than one month. During the 1780s 86.8 percent of cases took less than three months, while 78.3 percent were judged in less than one month.[101] It should be emphasized that these statistics confound civil and

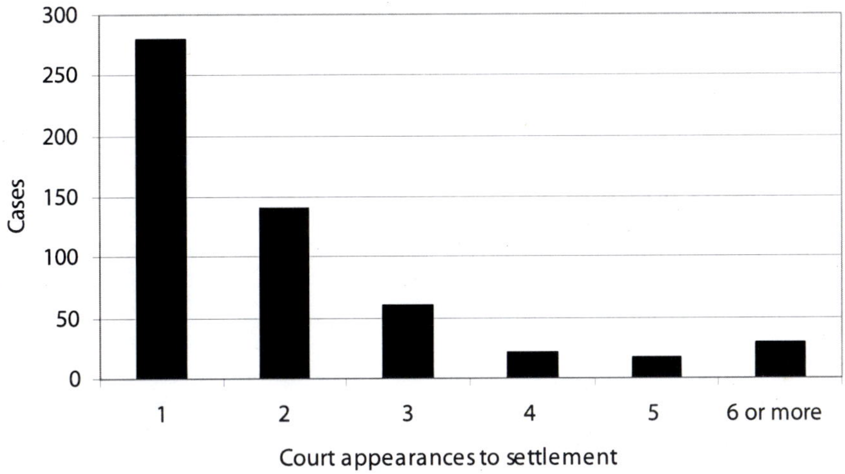

Figure 5.1. Number of appearances in court before final judgment, regular session (1750s)

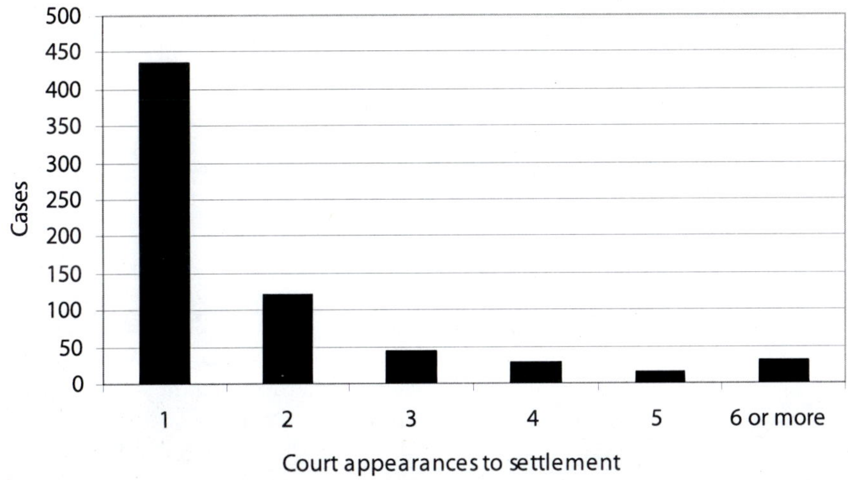

Figure 5.2. Number of appearances in court before final judgment, regular session (1780s)

criminal cases, and include all cases tried using both written and summary procedure in regular session.

The course of justice in late eighteenth-century seigneurial courts in northern Burgundy can hardly be described as slow and circuitous. Justice was reasonably swift and was becoming swifter. The biggest change between the two periods was in the number of cases settled in one session. In the

1750s 53.3 percent of cases were settled on the same day they began, but by the 1780s the proportion rose to two-thirds of cases (see figures 5.1 and 5.2). The average length of time spent in court may have decreased only slightly, but the number of plaintiffs and defendants who spent very little time in court increased significantly. In the 1780s, in other words, parties in minor disputes could anticipate a rapid settlement, while the parties in more complicated cases could expect to wait a long time (longer than in the 1750s) for a final decision.

Justice in regular weekly session was relatively swift, but was it cheap? At the end of court cases, judges stated how much the case had cost and sentenced the loser to pay. During the 1750s average court costs were 19.8 livres. But most court cases did not cost 20 livres to settle, and the presence of a few very expensive cases skews the average. Median court costs, more indicative of what most people could expect to pay, were far lower, at 7.5 livres. In the 1780s disputes cost an average of 23.6 livres in court fees. Again, though, the median court costs were lower, at 12.0 livres per case. Given that the price of wheat increased 55–65 percent from 1726–41 to 1785–89,[102] the rise in court fees was minimal. We must also remember that in the 1780s many more minor cases were being settled at the assizes, leaving behind a higher proportion of complicated and expensive cases in the regular session.

How do the costs and duration of cases in seigneurial justice compare to other judicial systems? In Richard Kagan's study of lawsuits in sixteenth- and seventeenth-century Castile, court cases in the *Chancilleria* of Valladolid took an average of two to three years from complaint to final settlement, but this was a superior appeal court and so comparison with the duration of cases in seigneurial courts are less than helpful.[103] John R. Wunder's study of justices of the peace on the American frontier may provide for more accurate comparison. In the late nineteenth century in these local courts the average length of time from first court action to final settlement was 9.36 days.[104] In northern Burgundy in 85 percent of cases that ended within three months, the average duration was 7.7 days in the 1780s, or comparable to Wunder's JPs.

Several recent studies allow us more helpfully to compare northern Burgundian seigneurial courts to similar local justices in France. The first comparison is with seigneurial courts of Aunis and Saintonge, studied by Anthony Crubaugh. Here the average duration of court cases in five seigneurial justices ranged from six months to two and a half years, and the average costs varied from 21 to 106 livres per case (median costs ranged from 13 to 39 livres).[105] In the *prévôté* of Vaucouleurs, on the other hand, average court costs in a sample of 233 cases tried using summary procedure amounted to 10 livres.[106] Fabrice Mauclair provides a large number of statistics about speed and costs of justice in the large seigneurial court of the *duché-pairie* of La Vallière. Here the average cost of a civil lawsuit judged using nonwritten procedure was a mere 5.5 livres. Between 24 and 50 days elapse between first session and final judgment in two seats of this large justice, and between 53 and 75 percent of cases were settled in a single session.[107] The small seigneurial courts studied in northern Burgundy, therefore, were much cheaper and more efficient than those studied by Crubaugh. The comparison to the *duché-pairie* of La Vallière and the prévôté of Vaucouleurs, however, is only vaguely helpful: the figures cited by both Mauclair and Piant include only civil cases tried using oral procedure, while the costs I cite also include criminal cases and civil cases tried using written procedure, both of which were vastly more expensive and lengthy. All things considered, the northern Burgundian courts studied nevertheless seem to have been slightly more expensive and slower than these two courts. But this is partly explained by the fact that here the simplest cases were tried at the assizes, leaving relatively more complicated cases to be heard in regular session.

Ordinary inhabitants of northern Burgundy's villages became more confident and willing to make use of their local courts because procedure was cheaper and faster than before. The most significant change was that litigants chose to settle out of court less often in the last decade of the century. In regular session there was a 10 percent decline in the number of cases where the parties began the case in court and then settled privately, with 67 percent of cases pursued through to final judgment in the 1780s. The increased willingness of ordinary people to take their cases to court and to wait patiently for the judge to decide the case was partly the result of the fact that the judge took less time to reach that decision and that the whole thing cost less than it would have before. People turned to more formal methods of dispute settlement because better formal dispute settlement was available to them.

Seigneurial justice worked relatively well in late eighteenth-century northern Burgundy. Judges generally settled cases quickly and without using elaborate written procedure. Procedure remained almost exclusively oral, and within the grasp of most ordinary people. A sizeable proportion of litigants (about a tenth, defendants about twice as often as plaintiffs) fought their disputes without legal counsel, and those who had legal help and advice did not have to go bankrupt to pay for it. In most cases the parties received a final judgment from the court less than two weeks from the first session of the dispute.

Civil justice in regular session was also less expensive in northern Burgundy than eighteenth-century commentators claimed, with median court costs for all disputes judged in regular session situated around ten livres. Civil court costs nevertheless remained a problem in northern Burgundy. For the one in ten litigants who went to court without counsel, the 10 livres would represent a total amount. But in most cases we would have to add the amounts paid to the *procureurs postulants* of both parties. The amounts they charged are difficult to estimate, and the court cases between *procureurs postulants* and their clients likely exaggerate the costs involved. We can nevertheless estimate that those who won a lawsuit in regular session likely paid between five and fifteen livres (to a *procureur*), whereas the loser would have paid this amount plus about ten more livres directly to the court.

The New Procedure at the Assizes

The moderately high costs of civil justice in regular sessions helps explain why the provincial Estates and the Parlement of Dijon brought in reforms encouraging ordinary people to take advantage of very cheap justice after the annual assizes, without the need for legal counsel. Indeed the most significant changes in speed and cheapness of justice occurred not at the regular weekly sessions, but at the annual assizes. This was primarily because of the new procedure to be used in the trial of civil farming disputes, which were to be settled once a year, at virtually no cost. Predictably, country dwellers in northern Burgundy took advantage of these reforms, with a massive increase in the number of farming torts tried. The assizes also became a forum for the settling of minor civil lawsuits of all kinds, providing cheap and fast justice for the poorer inhabitants of the province.[108]

From an occasional meeting of the court with the community every few years, the assizes in northern Burgundy became reliably annual by the last decades of the eighteenth century. We might expect that the Dijon Parlement's *arrêt général* of 1768 ordering all lords to ensure that their judges held annual assizes was simply the kind of blustering that ancien régime institutions periodically engaged in to preserve the rights and prerogatives of their officers. But after the reforms most seigneurial courts did indeed hold assizes much more regularly. In the fourteen courts sampled the judges held assizes in 22 villages.[109] During the 1750s there was a total of 138 assizes, or an average of 6.3 per village over the decade. In the 1780s these same courts held 201 assizes, or 9.14 per village per decade.[110] Before the *arrêt* of 1768, then, villages had Grands-Jours only slightly more often than every other year. No fewer than four villages only had assizes once during the 1750s. By the 1780s most villages held assizes each year. Seventeen of the 24 villages had either nine or ten assizes over the last decade of the ancien régime, and because of the uncertainty of 1789 these can be considered to have not missed a year. Only one court had fewer than eight (Saulon-la-Chapelle had four). By the end of the eighteenth century, then, ordinary people here could count on their judge to have assizes each year. This encouraged people to bring civil cases to the Grands-Jours, since they could be confident that they would not have to wait two or three years because of the slackness of the judicial officers.

Before the reforms of 1773, which inaugurated simplified procedure for farming torts, most minor farming disputes were never brought before the court. During the 1750s in the sample of cases, there was a paltry 73 of these cases tried in regular session and 16 in the Grands-Jours. By the 1780s, on the other hand, there were 23 in the regular session and a staggering 575 settled in the Grands-Jours, an increase by almost a factor of seven. The procedure required before the reform was too time-consuming and costly for most peasants. If an over-zealous farmer harvested a row or two too far onto his neighbor's field, the peasant who lost a bit of wheat, barley, or hay might have to get his own harvest in quickly–he would not have time to wait for the court to order town-dwelling experts to evaluate his loss. Once he harvested, all evidence of the damage was destroyed. After the reform, the wronged party could have the village *prud'hommes* evaluate the damage the same day he discovered it and harvest the next day.

Minor boundary problems over harvest, trespass, pasturing, and seeding on another's land were absolutely ubiquitous in the open fields of the province. Peasant holdings were divided into unfenced micro-parcels of land–individual farmers often had dozens of plots spread throughout the fields of the village. Claude Caillet, *fermier général* in the village of Corgengoux, possessed several hundred micro-parcels of land when he died in 1733. The average size of his fields was about 0.03 hectares.[111] The small size of the plots, many of which were no more than a meter or two in width, explains why there are so many fines for "retours," damage done when turning the plough, as well as why after the creation of the new procedure for *mésus,* the number of civil cases increases so massively.

Two examples, one from 1752 and another from 1780, underline the difference the 1773 reform made in practice.[112] In the village of Meursault, Michel Guenot, a *manouvrier,* sued Etienne Lapierre, a *laboureur* and *vigneron,* for damages caused by his animals (probably horses) in Guenot's field of hay. Fortunately Lapierre admitted responsibility, which saved Guenot the expense of calling witnesses. Still, the parties nevertheless had to appoint experts to examine the damages and submit a report to the court. The damage was minimal–Lapierre had to pay 30 sols or 10 sheaves of hay. But he also had to pay the court costs, which amounted to 32 livres, or about 20 times the value of the damages recovered.[113]

The example from 1780 saw about three times as much awarded in damages, but court costs were far less, despite a further legal complication. Toward the end of the Grands-Jours, the judge of Auxey-le-Grand and Auxey-le-Petit proceeded to hear cases between private individuals. He was presented with a report from the *prud'hommes,* which stated that damages committed in Pierre Touillier's field were worth 4 livres 16 sols. The judge asked Touillier who was responsible for the damages, and he indicated Jean Marillier, a barrel-maker from the village. Marillier apparently denied responsibility, to which Touillier responded by calling on two (unnamed) villagers from the assembled crowd who had seen Marillier's animals in the field. The judge ordered Marillier to pay the assessed damages, plus court costs of 25 sols 3 deniers.[114] Since this court held its assizes in August, as did many courts, and the animals trespassed in the fall, Touillier had to wait almost a year before receiving his money for damages, but the court settled the case in one session, quickly, efficiently, and above all cheaply.

These examples are representative of court costs and complication of simple farming torts under the two systems. In *mésus* from the 1750s that reached settlement, the average costs were 41 livres. In those settled in the Grands-Jours in the 1780s, the average cost was 11 sols, or 1/75 the cost of such cases in the 1750s. The settling of *mésus* in the 1780s was almost free, and people took advantage of this by bringing their minor farming disputes before the court in vast numbers without ever having to pay to consult legal counsel, since *procureurs postulants* did not participate in the cases settled after the assizes.

In an undated letter written by the clerk of a justice of the peace, the author compared the way that the pre-Revolutionary seigneurial courts settled *mésus* with the procedure used in the new Revolutionary courts. "In the ancient order, the officers of the so-called seigneurial justices at the assizes annually chose three *prud'hommes* who were exclusively charged to investigate and evaluate the *mésus* in seeded property." In the courts of the JPs, much like in the prereform seigneurial courts, the plaintiff addressed himself to the judge, who then appointed experts to evaluate the damages. This was an improvement over the prereform system that let the parties name their own experts. Still, the author notes, the "fear of leaving his work forces [the proprietor] to renounce all visits of the fields, which works in the delinquent's favor." In this letter to the administration, the clerk suggests that all justices of the peace nominate two or three *prud'hommes* in each village who could estimate the damages. "If your decision conforms to my opinions," he ends the letter, "we will end an abuse that makes people yearn for one of the institutions of the Ancien Régime."[115] In the private papers of University of Dijon law professor Antoine Jacquinot there is a personal note he made to himself, most likely for a lecture on rural policing under the new legal system. He notes that "it would be good to return to the regulations given in the past at the Jours [assizes]; there are useful things that have been omitted in the rural code."[116] In the Bordelais the Revolution for the first time provided ordinary people access to fast, cheap, and effective judicial services, evidence of which can be seen in the sudden multiplication of minor farming disputes in court.[117] In northern Burgundy, on the other hand, the reforms of the Revolution made it more difficult to settle these minor farming dispute, and seigneurial justice in the last two decades of the ancien régime provided an effective means for settling these disputes.[118]

Table 5.1. Cases heard in Grands-Jours

Type of case	1750–59	1780–89	Factor by which the number of cases increased/decreased
Unknown	1	23	–
Debts	105	290	2.8
Mésus	16	575	35.9
Police	45	68	1.5
Land disputes	17	64	3.8
Farming disputes	0	58	–
Local politics	6	49	8.2
Wood theft	0	49	–
Inheritance	5	10	2
Contracts	0	10	–
Seigneurial (dues)	21	8	0.4
Crimes (minor)	5	3	0.6
Taxes	5	19	3.8
Tithe	0	5	–
Total	226	1231	5.4

The settlement of all kinds of minor civil matters also became simpler by having them heard at the assizes, a fact that helps explain the general increase in the number of cases tried at the Grands-Jours (see table 5.1). After *mésus,* the second most significant kind of civil dispute in the Grands-Jours of northern Burgundy was debts. The number of debts settled in the annual assizes almost tripled between the 1750s and the 1780s, with 105 in the earlier and 290 in the later decade. As with *mésus,* the settlement of debt disputes in the assizes was both simple and inexpensive. In Epagny, for example, Jeanne Baron, the widow of Jean Michel, sued Nicolas Ménétrier for money she claimed to be owed. The court ordered Ménétrier to pay thirty livres, after hearing reports from several of the assembled villagers that they had overheard the parties discussing the debt, and that Ménétrier had agreed to owing for food and lodging provided by Baron. The court costs were virtually non-existent, with Ménétrier sentenced to pay 2 sols for legal fees.[119]

The debts settled in the Grands-Jours generally involved minor amounts of money and often pitted a poorer creditor against a better-off debtor. Many of these debt cases were for money owed for farm labor or domestic service. In Foncegrive in 1785, for example, Antoine Fevre fils brought suit against Jean Ladey, a *laboureur* and one of the elite of the village, for threshing he did for him two years ago. Fevre asked for 8 livres 10 sols for the work, but the judge, apparently after asking the villagers about the labor market that fall, awarded him five livres for the work. Court costs were one livre.[120] In Messigny the court awarded eleven livres to Bernard Fremyet, *manouvrier,* for two months of domestic service that his son had provided to Henry Dupuis, *vigneron.*[121] In 181 debt cases that were settled in the Grands-Jours and where we have information on the court costs the loser had to pay, the average court costs in the 1780s was less than 8 sols. Because court costs were so low in the assizes, the village poor could bring suit. The cheapness of this justice, combined with the new emphasis that judges placed on the Grands-Jours, motivated many to bring their minor debt cases to the assizes.

The fact that these cases were conducted in public, in the full view of the community, also probably encouraged the poor to bring their cases. In his study of class relations in an agrarian village in Malaysia, James C. Scott underlines the way in which the oppressed classes take advantage of a discourse of reciprocity in their acts of everyday resistance. The poor expect the local elite to display a certain amount of generosity and to provide assistance and work opportunities, while the wealthy expect the poor to be suitably humble, to defer and to provide labor. Although in private (Scott's "hidden transcript") the poor gripe about the rich, and the wealthy see the poor as lazy parasites, in public they are more cordial.[122] The Grands-Jours of late eighteenth-century northern Burgundian villages brought disputes over wages and minuscule debts into the public sphere.[123] This likely increased the power of the subordinate in these economic relationships, due to shared assumptions about behavior. The elites may have been reluctant to be seen disputing in public against a social inferior, especially since the amount involved was small. Furthermore, the community itself could hear all the evidence and reach its own decision, and a wealthy farmer would want to avoid getting a reputation for bilking his day laborers and domestic servants.

The presence of inheritance disputes at the assizes may seem surprising, given that these were for the settling of minor affairs. But the inheritance disputes settled at the assizes never involved the division of assets, which was too complicated (and private) to be settled summarily in public. Rather, these were generally cases where one or more family member had not met his responsibilities toward other heirs. Especially common were disputes over pensions that adult children had agreed to pay a parent, usually in exchange for an early inheritance. In 1755, for example, Simonne Perrot sued the spouses of her children (by then deceased) for an annual pension. She cited the "general renunciation she did of all her goods," and the "impossibility of earning her living, being 78 years old." The judge ordered the heirs to pay her twenty livres every three months, plus court costs of five sols.[124] In 1783 the court ordered the children of Claude Pain to provide him with a pension, in addition to feeding, lodging and looking after him.[125] In 1788 Bernard Logery asked the judge to decide how much his children should have to pay him–the court set the amount at 48 livres a year.[126]

These cases were like the debts owed by employers in that the sympathy of the assembled villagers would almost certainly be on the side of the aged parent. The children, who may have griped in private, would be forced to acknowledge their responsibilities in front of the judge and community. The same was true in several cases where family members intervened to see to the well-being of minors who had lost a parent. Jean Modot of Ancey was the curator of the minor children of Louis Jovinget. Their mother had died, and the extended family had assembled and decided that their father, as tutor, could look after the children. As curator, Modot was responsible to ensure that the tutor did not squander the property they were to inherit from their mother at majority. During the Grands-Jours Modot informed the court that in the fifteen years since his wife died, Jovinget had done no repairs to the buildings he held in trust for the children. The court ordered the father to "do the necessary repairs in the home of his minor children."[127]

Another major category of lawsuit settled in the Grands-Jours was disputes over land use and ownership. The court decided who had the right to use a piece of land–disputes over boundaries were generally heard at regular session, given the necessity for surveying. Since the procedure in the Grands-Jours was summary, the records are brief, often not giving enough details to understand these cases. In 1784, for example, the court ordered Bénigne Frochot to give to Simon Thévenard the "40 perches in question," without explaining the matter further.[128] Most of the land disputes concerned either the terms of verbal leases or questions of inheritance. Another common form of land dispute concerned rights of passage through another's field, as when the judge ordered Henry Dupuis to re-open an ancient passage through his field, at the request of a neighbor.[129]

The new emphasis on the annual assizes profoundly changed the institution of seigneurial justice. Perhaps nowhere is the change more clear than in the costs that litigants had to pay to take their cases to court. We have seen above that in regular session court costs either remained about the same or were slightly higher after the reforms. But it was at the assizes that most minor cases were being settled by the 1780s. Including all of the cases tried in both regular session and at the assizes, we can calculate a rough average court cost for all cases. This provides a truer picture of seigneurial justice and reveals just how good the institution had become at settling the minor disputes that made up daily life in the village communities of northern Burgundy by the last decades of the eighteenth century. By the 1780s in the courts studied median court costs in all civil disputes[130] had dropped to only 1.5 livres, an amount that was within the reach of all but the very poorest villagers.

Poor Litigants and Their Access to Justice

The lower costs of justice after the reforms indeed encouraged more of the poorer villagers to instigate lawsuits. By matching litigants to their annual *taille* payments, we can see that the radical decline in the amount of red tape required and the reduced court fees brought people from lower on the social scale into the court. Tax assessments provide a reasonably reliable guide to the wealth and property structure of the village. There are doubtless examples of local village elites who used their political leverage to procure a lower assessment, but this was hindered in several ways. The local seigneurial judge had the authority to hear any disputes over taxes and to set the assessment by act of court. Furthermore the provincial Estates had the power to set tax-payments for local elites when there was reason to fear undue influence over the process. Finally, there was the fact that each year saw the appointment of two new assessors. A rural bourgeois who imposed his will on one set of assessors would have to do so each year, so that the reduced tax burden would necessarily become common knowledge.[131]

Though tax records are generally reliable for judging relative wealth within a village, the matching of tax and court records contains some biases. The document matching tends to miss non-household heads that appeared in court, thereby excluding women other than widows, minors, and those who boarded with other inhabitants. Missing married women probably does not affect the conclusions here, since there is no reason to think that married women who came to court were poorer than married men who did so. On the other hand, minors and those without their own homes were certainly poorer than average, so that the document-matching makes litigants seem wealthier than they were.

The new emphasis on the Grands-Jours for lawsuits did allow a poorer group of people access to the local seigneurial court, but the massive increase in *mésus* cases overwhelms this change–in table 5.2 we see that litigants in the 1780s were actually wealthier than those in the 1750s, and litigants at the assizes were wealthier than those at regular session. This is because those who owned, rented, or worked more land and had more animals tended to come before the court in *mésus* cases more often, inflating the average assessment. Owning more land meant, of course, that there were more possibilities for neighbors to harvest a row too far or for villagers to tramp down a field, while bigger herds meant more animals to look after and a better chance an animal might stray onto illicit pasture. Since these cases account for well

Table 5.2. Tax assessments of litigants

	Number of cases	Cases where litigants could be found on tax rolls	Average tax assessment (*taille* and *capitation*), in livres	
			Plaintiffs	Defendants
Regular session, 1750s	964	189	25.9	25.7
Assizes, 1750s	226	40	22.9	24.2
Regular session, 1780s	1,008	201	29.3	25.7
Assizes, 1780s	1,231	392	33.0	28.2

Table 5.3. Tax assessments of litigants, *mésus* cases excluded

	Number of cases	Cases where litigants could be found on tax rolls	Average tax assessment (*taille* and *capitation*), in livres	
			Plaintiffs	Defendants
Regular session, 1750s	889	176	26.1	25.8
Assizes, 1750s	210	38	22.9	24.2
Regular session, 1780s	944	195	28.8	25.7
Assizes, 1780s	651	180	20.5	19.6

over half of the assize cases in the 1780s, the explosion of these cases overwhelms any subtle changes in the clientele of the courts in other cases.

Disregarding the *mésus* cases from all samples, as I have done in table 5.3, reveals that the new emphasis on the assizes did indeed open the court up to a greater proportion of villagers. In non-*mésus* cases in the 1780s, in regular session plaintiffs' tax-assessments averaged 29 livres and defendants' averaged 26 livres. In the assizes, plaintiffs paid on average 21 livres and defendants paid 20 livres. In other words plaintiffs in the assizes paid almost 30 percent less taxes than plaintiffs in regular session, while defendants paid 24 percent less. Since the average tax contribution in these villages (from tax-rolls, irrespective of court records) was 21 livres in the early 1780s, the average customer of seigneurial justice in the assizes of 1780s was, economically at least, an average inhabitant of the village. The same was true, although to a lesser extent, of the assize cases of the 1750s. Again disregarding *mésus* cases, in the assizes plaintiffs paid taxes of 23 livres and defendants 24 livres, or 12 percent and 6 percent less than plaintiffs and defendants in regular session in the 1750s. Even in the 1750s, then, the courts sitting in assize heard lawsuits involving villagers who on average were poorer than the clients of the regular session.

Conclusion

The emphasis on the annual Grands-Jours opened seigneurial justice to a larger group of people. Although seigneurial justice had never been simply a tool of the village elite, in the assizes of the 1780s villagers from all over the social spectrum took their minor disputes to the court. Cheap justice and no formalities made it easier for the less well-off to come before the judge. The assizes in northern Burgundy became a more important forum for the settlement of minor disputes of all kinds. At the Grands-Jours the village poor could use a combination of the law and social pressure to force the better off to pay them handfuls of pennies owed them, and aging parents could make recalcitrant and ungrateful children support them. Judges also settled land and farming disputes, both of which would be considerably expedited by the presence of all household heads, who could report orally both on local farming practices and land usages. Most importantly, the changes in procedure for *mésus* truly revolutionized the settlement of minor farming disputes and brought many cases to court that before would simply have gone unsettled. These cases of all kinds the judges of northern Burgundy settled for almost no money and without legal counsel. Legal fees were always under a livre and sometimes as little as a few sols. Most of these were cases that in the 1750s had to be tried in regular session and would have cost at least ten times more to settle. Because of the small amount of money involved, many of these cases would simply have fallen through the cracks of the judicial system of the 1750s.

The Parlement of Dijon acted to bring seigneurial justice more closely under its control, making the hundreds of judges, prosecutors, and clerks in the province more directly agents of the central government by ensuring that justice was administered the way that the magistrates of the parlement required. What is most significant, however, is the extent to which the reforms brought seigneurial justice closer to the village, especially once the provincial Estates brought in the new procedure for *mésus*. With the annual assizes reinvigorated, the local court was better able to oversee the use of common land, communal spaces, and village politics, responding to the wishes of the inhabitants. Seigneurial courts by the 1780s administered true local justice, as more and more minor cases came before the judge to be settled virtually for free.

The reforms of the parlement and the estates in the late 1760s had a profound impact on northern Burgundian seigneurial justice. The judges in seigneurial courts shared the desires of parlementaires that procedure be less cumbersome and less expensive. In regular session they settled more cases in one session, ordered witnesses in fewer cases, and generally expedited suits through the courts more quickly. The judges of northern Burgundy also encouraged people to take advantage of more summary justice in the Grands-Jours, where judges resolved minor disputes farming torts for people from across the social spectrum.

Although the faster procedure in the assizes benefited most people, and was generally lauded in the *cahiers* (see chapter 7), for some people these changes went too far. The lightning-fast procedure for settling farming torts occasionally caused some outcry in court. In about two hundred assizes from the 1780s, there are ten instances of various inhabitants being fined for "rebellion and irreverence committed to justice." All of these instances arose out of *mésus* cases that the judge had settled summarily based on the reports of the *messiers* and the *prud'hommes.* In Ancey the court fined Etienne Mortureux ten livres for his insolence and his public vow to continue pasturing his animals on others' land.[132] Several times judges fined people for shouting out in court that they intended to appeal a decision in a *mésus* case (appeal was forbidden according to the new summary procedure for these cases).[133] In Ancey, Nicolas Dubois the younger apparently felt strongly enough about the matter to stand up and tell others "that one did not have to pay despite the said judgment."[134] These fines remind us that faster and less procedural justice must inevitably lead to the judges missing some of the subtleties in a few cases.

But the main problem with the reforms was not that procedure was too summary or that litigants in minor farming torts could not lodge appeals. The close links between justice and seigneurial authority raised the possibility that more efficient courts could better enforce the seigneurial system. Like every other litigant in the village, a lord could use the new procedure for collecting bushels of wheat, barley, or hay from those whose animals had committed the offense. The regularity of the assizes after the reform meant that lords could count on being able to collect fines for wood and pasture theft committed on seigneurial forest and fields, and the increased amount of local knowledge among officers made them better able to see to the collection of dues and corvées. As plaintiffs in their own seigneurial courts, the magistrates of the province's highest court stood to benefit as much as anyone from the increased speed and efficiency of the seigneurial courts of the 1770s and 1780s.

Chapter 6

Tocqueville in the Village

Seigneurial Reaction and the Central State

In the wine-growing countryside outside of Mâcon, in southern Burgundy, on the 26th of July 1789, church bells rang out to summon the inhabitants of Igé for a meeting. A water fountain to which the villagers claimed title was enclosed within the seigneurial park, and despite drought conditions that spring and summer the lord continued to refuse them access. The inhabitants went as a crowd to the castle, tore a hole in the wall around the park, entered the castle, and terrorized the lord and his family before leaving. The next day, villagers from nearby Verzé tore down fences that the lord had erected around land that was disputed between the lord and the village, and they refused to pay seigneurial dues. Within days, the whole Mâconnais was in open revolt against local lords. Like most collective violence in early modern Europe, this antiseigneurial revolt was controlled and directed against specific, often symbolic, targets. Groups of peasants generally attacked castles, most of which contained only servants and seigneurial agents, since the lords and their families had left for the city.[1] Crowds of angry peasants often forced lords to hand over their archives, which they then burned. They also frequently attacked symbols of seigneurial authority, like pigeon houses and weathervanes.[2]

The violent stage of antiseigneurial revolt in the region lasted only about a week, and the repression was swift and harsh, with about thirty hangings. Open violence against lords in the summer of 1789 did not spread to the rest of the province and was basically limited to regions of poor winemaking, where landless vine workers were left penniless by low wine prices. Still, antiseigneurial revolts sprang up periodically all over France from 1789 to about 1793, and at least a third of Burgundian bailliages experienced some antiseigneurial group violence during the Revolutionary decade.[3]

We know from other sources that by 1789 many people were angry with lords and the system that supported them. The best source for evaluating peasant opinion toward lords and seigneurialism are the parish *cahiers de doléances*. In 1972 George V. Taylor argued that the *cahiers* were conservative, and that according to them, people wanted minor reforms as opposed to fundamental changes.[4] Recently, however, historians have rediscovered that many of the *cahiers* in fact demanded radical change that would have deeply transformed French society. John Markoff shows that there was widespread criticism of lords and seigneurial authority, that many *cahiers* demanded the suppression of many dues and rights, and that a few wanted seigneurialism itself to be abolished.[5] Philippe Grateau has also suggested that the *cahiers* go a long way toward conceptualizing radical change in all kinds of ways.[6]

In northern Burgundy some *cahiers* not only expressed anger against an individual lord, but also called into question the legitimacy of seigneurial authority in a more general way. The inhabitants of Aignay-le-Duc, for example, demanded that all seigneurial rights be redeemable (that peasants be able to free themselves from annual dues with a one-time payment). Additionally, they noted their desire to: "abolish the ridiculous and miniscule rights due to certain lords, such as the obligation of a festive meal at weddings, the requirement to lower the chain on a bridge certain days of the year, and other rights of this sort, useless to lords and devouring their vassals (we cannot see how it would be possible to remain seriously attached to a pettiness so unfit for the century in which we live)."[7]

The inhabitants of Blaisy asked the Estates-General to inquire as to the abolition of "all harmful rights, and those contrary to public liberty."[8] The seigneurial right of *mainmorte* received special scorn in the parish *cahiers* of the province. From Chaudenay-le-Château we hear: "A vile slave becomes free through the first step he makes in France and a Frenchman becomes a slave who has the misfortune of being born in a region where this abominable custom exists."[9]

By 1789 peasants all over France were angry about seigneurialism and the payments they had to make to lords. When asked their opinion about the state of the kingdom, country dwellers everywhere complained about their lords, and a few months later many joined antiseigneurial crowds, tore down castles, burned archives, attacked symbols of seigneurialism, forced lords to feed them and give them drink, and refused to pay dues. Explaining why peasants revolted against lords in 1789 is more difficult than it first seems. The obvious answer, that peasants revolted because things were unbearable, besides being tautological (we know it was unbearable only because people refused to bear it), is questionable as a causal explanation. Some form of seigneurialism had existed in France for many centuries. Something, in other words, must have changed to cause French peasants to call the system into question so thoroughly.

Explanations of peasant antiseigneurial revolt in 1789 can be divided into two schools of thought, both of them originating in the nineteenth century. The explanation that historians today probably find most convincing was suggested by Alexis de Toqueville. Tocqueville noticed that, of continental European nations, France had the weakest seigneurial system and the strongest antiseigneurial sentiment. If revolts were caused simply by exploitation, we would expect Prussian peasants to have revolted long before French country dwellers. Emmanuel Le Roy Ladurie, paraphrasing Tocqueville, expressed the relation between revolt and seigneurialism as follows: "the more the seigneurie is archaic, the less it is contested."[10]

How do we go from the least exploitative lords to the strongest antiseigneurial anger? For Tocqueville the answer lay in one of the processes of modernization that characterized the early modern era: state centralization. To see how centralization led to revolt, we first have to understand Tocqueville's view of seigneurialism as a reciprocal and mutually beneficial contract. Peasants accepted the loss of freedom and the annual payments because they got something in return. Initially they received military protection, but by the early modern period lords' contribution was limited to the arbitration of disputes, relief for the poor, patronage, and a measure of safety through seigneurial police officers. As the central government grew stronger during the seventeenth and eighteenth centuries, lords found themselves deprived of power. The removal of the most important aristocrats to Versailles, the beginnings of a bureaucratic state, efforts to replace venal officeholders with provincial intendants, the development of a more effective tax-collection apparatus, a more centralized system of poor relief, and the strengthening of the royal justice system–these all made traditional elites less powerful. The central state had gradually replaced lords as the most important political force in local life. Peasants revolted, then, because by the late eighteenth century they were getting nothing in return for their payments and services to the lord. Seigneurial institutions had become obsolete.

The other explanation for peasant revolt is simpler, and perhaps more intuitive. It also links antiseigneurial revolt to modernization, but this explanation is basically economic, in opposition to Tocqueville's political explanation. The "seigneurial reaction" theory posits that lords became more exploitative over the course of the seventeenth and eighteenth centuries. They did this partly to make up for losses sustained by inflation, and partly because, since they were becoming capitalists, paternalistic seigneurialism no longer made sense to them. Peasants in 1789 resented their seigneurs more than ever, then, simply because lords were making them pay more than ever before.

Perhaps the best-known articulation of the seigneurial reaction thesis is that of Marc Bloch.[11] In his history of French agriculture, Bloch says that monetary inflation through the late medieval and early modern period had led to an effective reduction of the value of seigneurial dues, which were fixed by custom.[12] The strategy of French lords, claims Bloch, was twofold: the reinvigoration of old seigneurial dues and the invention of new ones, and a closer management of the domain.[13] From the seventeenth century lords began rewriting their *terriers* periodically. These manuals of seigneurial dues, rights, and privileges provided legal proof of the lord's prerogatives, since his peasants had to sign the document and thereby legitimated the demands contained in it.

The redrawing of *terriers* became increasingly common in the eighteenth century, with an informal legal industry and professional literature to help lords ensure that they missed no rights or dues. Given the complication of seigneurial law and local tradition, Bloch says that the commissioners drawing up the *terriers* frequently not only revived ancient rights that had ceased being observed and discovered new implications for old rights and dues but also invented entirely new privileges. Lords also worked hard in the eighteenth century to reconstitute their estates, paying closer attention to their land and forest resources. The result of these changes was that by 1789 most French peasants faced a class of seigneurial landowners who controlled more land and collected more dues than at any time since the fourteenth century. Other historians have given support to the thesis of the seigneurial reaction. Georges Lefebvre's study of the peasants of the Nord in the Revolution concludes that in the Hainaut and the Cambrésis lords were "determined to resuscitate rights fallen into disuse or that had remained hitherto unproductive," while a more recent text on the peasantry in the Revolution rehearses the same arguments.[14]

Historians of rural northern Burgundy have tended to accept the notion of a seigneurial reaction. Pierre de Saint Jacob posits a heightening of seigneurial extraction through the invention of new seigneurial dues and reinvigoration of old ones, and especially through lords' tighter control over common land and forests.[15] Robert Forster also saw evidence of a seigneurial reaction in his study of the Saulx-Tavanes family and their administration of their Burgundian seigneuries.[16] In order to support a lavish lifestyle in the court of Versailles, this family increased its revenue from land rents, forests, and seigneurial dues, making this family highly unpopular in its villages by 1789. Jean Bart's general account of the Revolution in Burgundy notes that "it is certain that the desire of lords, of their officers or their *fermiers,* to increase land rents and seigneurial dues coincides with the general movement of prices and the economic evolution of the century."[17] The only historian of rural Burgundy in the late eighteenth century who is skeptical of the seigneurial reaction thesis is Hilton Root. In his *Peasant and King in Burgundy,* he describes a process that could almost be described as seigneurial antireaction, arguing instead that the French state protected peasants from the designs of greedy lords.[18] The state did this because seigneurial extractions competed with royal taxes for money from peasants' pockets. Root describes a Tocquevillian situation where the growth of the central state, with its fiscal apparatus, took authority from Burgundian lords and protected ordinary citizens from lordly oppression.

In 1972 William Doyle published an important revisionist article that questioned the notion of an aristocratic reaction, the idea that in the eighteenth century French nobles became more exclusive.[19] As part of his argument Doyle criticized the seigneurial reaction thesis. His main criticism was that although historians of rural France could show that in the late eighteenth century lords were much concerned with the collection of dues and protection of their rights, no one had proven that this was a new thing. Doyle suggested that lords had always looked out for their rights, and even in the seventeenth century commonly rewrote their *terriers* whenever a seigneurie changed hands.[20] Statistical work was needed, Doyle said, comparing seigneurial dues in seigneuries over a long period of time, in order to establish that late eighteenth-century lords were more exploitative than their parents and grandparents, and that this led to the Revolution of 1789. Although other parts of the aristocratic reaction thesis have been solidly debunked,[21] it has proven more difficult to assemble evidence that allows comparison of lordly incomes over a long period. Forster's work is exceptional in this regard, demonstrating with impressive exactitude that the revenue of the Saulx-Tavanes family increased over the eighteenth century and especially in its last decades, but we have no way of knowing that this family was representative. Saint Jacob examined an incredible number of archival documents and undoubtedly understood seigneurialism in northern Burgundy better than anyone. Still, his evidence for a seigneurial reaction is unsystematic, being primarily based on *terriers* and seigneurial usurpation of common land. What is lacking, in other words, is evidence that most villagers in most northern Burgundian seigneuries were paying a greater proportion of their income to the lord than their parents or grandparents had.

An analysis of seigneurial justice in northern Burgundy allows us to investigate the seigneurial reaction and Tocquevillian theses of antiseigneurial revolt. I approach the question from two different perspectives. The first is to draw a portrait of the ways the central state affected life in the province's villages, especially through the provincial intendant. The goal is to see whether the provincial intendant had indeed, by the late eighteenth century, become the primary political force in village life, replacing the seigneurial judge and effectively limiting the power of lords. If, as Root argues, this was the case, the declining usefulness of lords as a source of protection, patronage, and paternalism in the lives of villagers will help us understand peasant sentiment in 1789. The second perspective from which to examine the question is through the cases tried in seigneurial courts. If there was indeed a seigneurial reaction in the province during the eighteenth century, we would expect the number of times that lords sued peasants to increase and for seigneurialism itself to become increasingly visible in the local courts of northern Burgundy.

The triangular relationship among the central state, lords, and peasants looks a great deal like that suggested by partisans of the seigneurial reaction thesis. I see little reason to accept the notion that lords had become irrelevant by the eighteenth century, or that the central state had replaced lords as the primary political force in the village. The growth of the central state, at least inasmuch as it concerned village affairs, occurred through the co-opting of seigneurial justice rather than the creating of a parallel system of royal administration that took over its jurisdiction. Far from withering away, seigneurial authority may even have increased over the course of the eighteenth century. This is difficult to evaluate, but I demonstrate that lords were suing more peasants by the 1780s than they had earlier in the century. They were pursuing peasants for nonpayment of dues, but the greatest increase was in the number of peasants sued for trespass and other offenses in seigneurial forests and fields. Certainly the inflation of the twin price revolutions of the sixteenth and eighteenth centuries meant that seigneurial dues like the *cens* and the seigneurial *taille* were much less valuable by the late eighteenth century than they had been earlier.[22] This provided incentive for lords to concentrate more attentively on their revenue as landlords. Still, I am reluctant to apply the notion of a seigneurial reaction to the situation in the province, because despite a few high-profile cases, there was little invention of new dues or rediscovery of old ones. This undoubtedly occurred but was not likely to increase substantially the total amount of money peasants paid to lords. Seigneurs increasingly turned toward the modern exploitation of their land to get more revenue, rather than seeking to increase the *cens* that their peasants paid.

The Provincial Intendant, the Seigneurial Judge, and Village Affairs

One of the changes involved in the construction of a modern state is a move away from a judicial state toward an administrative one, as the central government increasingly decides matters that previously had fallen to judges. For France during the ancien régime this involved a process whereby provincial intendants were given power of decision over matters that had been decided by ordinary judges. Sebastien Evrard has recently argued that by the second half of the eighteenth century the intendant of the *généralité* of Dijon had developed into a modern bureaucrat whose power was administrative rather than properly judicial. In stark contrast to what he sees as an abusive, hidebound ordinary judicial system run by judges who cared for nothing but their personal revenue, the intendants were enlightened, effective administrators.[23] Hilton Root goes further still. He claims that Burgundy's royal intendants took over the policing of village political matters to the detriment of the province's judges, and he posits that the motive behind this transfer of authority was a ministerial antiseigneurialism that saw lords as competitors for limited peasant tax revenue. The king and his agents did what they could to oppose the claims and exactions of lords, and by the eighteenth century, according to Root, the central state had replaced the seigneur as the primary political force in local village affairs. Root's main evidence comes from court cases between village communities and seigneurs, cases that required the intendant's permission before going to court. The royal intendant's role in these cases reveals, says Root, that the French state supported the claims of village communities against lords and pushed for more political autonomy for villages.[24]

But did provincial intendants really want to limit seigneurial authority over villages? And were they in a position to do so effectively by the second half of the eighteenth century? Did the central state protect peasants from rapacious seigneurs, thus rendering obsolete and illegitimate seigneurial authority in the eyes of those subject to it? While this may have been the case in some parts of France, the actual situation in northern Burgundy looks rather different from that suggested by Root. Villages remained much more closely under the supervision of the local seigneurial court than under that of the provincial intendant; the seigneur's personal authority over village life remained little affected over the course of the eighteenth century; intendants did not intervene in *triage* or other disputes to protect common land; and the Parlement of Dijon was, by the 1780s, working hard to limit still further the small amount of authority the intendant had over village affairs.

The provincial intendant of the *généralité* of Dijon had three main responsibilities that impacted village life and sometimes brought him into jurisdictional conflict with the provincial parlement. The province's magistrates never contested the first responsibility, oversight over local finances. The second, conducting lease auctions of commons, brought about a conflict with the parlement, which defended the exclusive right of seigneurial judges to conduct such auctions. Despite the king's open support of the intendant, this dispute, which included the issuing of contradictory royal edicts and parlementary general *arrêts,* was still not settled when the royal coup d'état and the revolt of the parlements began in 1788.

But it was the intendant's third responsibility over village affairs that brought him into most open conflict with the Dijon Parlement. The intendant was entitled (indeed, required) to "verify" all court cases involving village communities before the litigants presented their case to a judge. It was here that the intendant's authority most directly challenged the jurisdiction of the parlement (and seigneurial judges)–and it is in the supposed authority to end court cases between villages and lords that Root sees the central state's protection of village autonomy. But the magistrates of the provincial parlement successfully insisted that the intendant's role in judicial affairs was limited to the simple verification of the paperwork provided by villages, and they demanded that the intendant not decide any of these cases. There was also a legal loophole that meant that if the intendant rejected a village court case as unfounded, the parties could pursue the case anyway, which further discouraged the intendant from intervening in village affairs. Even in the decades before the French Revolution, then, villages interacted as a community much more often with the seigneurial judge than with the intendant, and the state's authority over local communities remained primarily judicial rather than administrative or bureaucratic.

There was no question that oversight of village finances belonged solidly to the intendant and his staff. After about 1770 most villages submitted annual fiscal reports to the intendant (sometimes, after a lapse, for five or six years combined). This control of local finances was no mere formality, and successive intendants all took their responsibility seriously, frequently striking unnecessary expenses from the accounts and forcing village treasurers to pay for unnecessary expenses out of their own pockets.[25] After 1770 villages also needed the intendant's permission before contracting any debt or agreeing to any expense.[26]

By contrast, seigneurial judges only had the right to intervene on the collection side of village finances, leaving expenditures to the oversight of the intendant. The local judge did have a responsibility to make sure the community nominated two local assessors and collectors of royal taxes, and he had to swear them in as officers. The same judge settled any disputes that arose within the community over the assessment or collection of these taxes. But seigneurial judges could not authorize villages to tax themselves, approve village expenses, or authorize any purchases.

The second form of the intendant's authority over villages, the oversight of the leasing of common land, was linked to his jurisdiction over village finances. The practice of leasing village common land to the highest bidder put revenue into village coffers, which could not be spent without the intendant's permission. The intendant's control over the auctions of common land, however, came into conflict with the policing rights that seigneurial judicial officers had over village politics. Since it was often during the Grands-Jours that communities decided to lease their commons, it made sense for the seigneurial judge to oversee the process. Furthermore, the royal Waters and Forests ordinance of 1669 clearly stated that all leasing of this sort was to be done in open auction and overseen by the seigneurial judge.

In practice, communities did their leasing of commons both before the seigneurial judge and before the intendant or a subdelegate, although there was a preference for the seigneurial judge. In 1775, for example, the villagers of Bagnot leased their commons to Pierre Martin and François Gérard for 9 livres. The auction was done before the intendant's representative, probably in the nearby larger bourg of Baigneux-le-Juif.[27] A year earlier, in the village of Aisy and the hamlet of Pont-d'Aisy, it was the seigneurial judge who performed the auction. In this case a few villagers apparently tried to defraud the community. They presented the judge with a lease to Alexandre Ligeret for 24 livres. The judge and other community members, however, insisted on a public auction to see if anyone would offer a better price. In the end another inhabitant offered 77 livres for the lease, over three times the original amount.[28] In Epagny in 1751 the auction took place at the Grands-Jours, where Jean Brocard got the common land for nine years at 112 livres a year.[29]

While village communities continued sometimes to have the seigneurial judge perform the auction of common land, and sometimes to use the subdelegate of the intendant, the issue of jurisdiction over these auctions came to a head in the 1770s. In April 1778 the Dijon Parlement issued an *arrêt* that repeated a clause from the royal ordinance of 1669. Villages were forbidden to conduct their leasing auctions "other than before the local judges [*juges des lieux*], on threat of nullity and of a fine of 100 livres."[30] Although the parlement did not specifically mention the intendant in the *arrêt,* it was clear that it was directed against his authority. Three months later, the king attempted to settle the matter in favor of the intendant. Against the ordinance of 1669, a royal *arrêt de conseil* of July 1778 contrasted the good of communities, and especially the duty of the intendant to watch over village indebtedness. All leasing of commons was to be overseen by the intendant or subdelegate, who alone could be trusted to ensure that land brought in its true value.[31]

The Parlement of Dijon registered this decree without comment and ordered its execution, but the magistrates quickly remonstrated to the king.[32] The parlementaires began by praising the wisdom of the provision in the 1669 ordinance that common lands "can be leased after adjudication by the local judicial officers without fees in an assembly."[33] They described in detail two instances where the intendant ordered communities to have the subdelegate perform the auction, as a result "depriving the natural judges of the knowledge of a fact that is attributed to them to the exclusion of the *commissaire départi.*"[34] They argued that the intendant's job was the verification and liquidation of the debts of village communities, so that his responsibilities in overseeing commons should be limited to verifying the revenue and ensuring that the communities spent it wisely. To this remonstrance they received no answer from the king, and purely formulaic responses from the Prince of Condé and the keeper of the seals.[35] A year later, the provincial parlement issued its next volley in this dispute. Referring once again to the ordinance of 1669, the parlementary magistrates issued "interdiction to communities and to parties to use any auctions other than those done in the prescribed manner by the said article seven of section 25 of the said ordinance."[36] The *arrêt* still did not mention the intendant, but the "prescribed manner" according to the ordinance of 1669 involved adjudication before the "local justice."

Despite the king's support for the intendant, matters continued much the same up to the Revolution, with both seigneurial judges and subdelegates performing the leasing of communal lands. But seigneurial judges continued to read each year to their *justiciables* the parlement's *arrêt* of 1780 that ordered the leasing be done before the seigneurial judge. They also continued to perform the auctions through the 1780s.[37] It seems, in fact, that many country dwellers preferred using the services of the seigneurial judge for this. Out of 303 parish *cahiers de doléances,* 17 called for the abolition of the intendant and asked that the seigneurial judge take over his responsibilities with respect to village affairs. Of these, 10 *cahiers* explicitly requested that only the seigneurial judge be permitted to perform the adjudication of common land. Not a single *cahier* mentioned the leasing of commons without demanding the seigneurial judge be responsible for it.

A dispute between the parlement and the intendant in 1789 illustrates the problem of the higher costs of using the subdelegates for the leasing of commons. In that year the parlement ordered the imprisonment of a subdelegate for performing the auction of the right to take small wood from the communal forest to make stakes to hold up vines. The Dijon Parlement was angry not only because the subdelegate had performed the service but also because he had charged money for it. The intendant defended the collection of money by saying it was common for subdelegates to collect "modest honoraria" in affairs that brought revenue to the community.[38] In a pro-parlement pamphlet from 1789, the author noted that the public nature of the auctions in the village, before the seigneurial judge, removed intrigue. The fact that the judge did it for free meant that "the leasing party does not calculate, in a reduction of the price he offers, the costs of the auction."[39] The combined inconvenience of a trip to town, perhaps a trip involving the entire community, and payment for a service that was free in the local seigneurial court and frequently conducted in the village directly after the Grands-Jours doubtless contributed to the feeling that led to the common demand in parish *cahiers* for the suppression of the intendant.

The other way the intendant touched on village political life was through the requirement that all communities receive his permission before pleading any case in any court. Hilton Root sees this requirement as a way the central state could intervene to protect villages from overzealous lords, most notably to guard communal land from seigneurial usurpation. In reality, the intent of this law was to stop villages from suing when they had no chance of winning, thereby protecting village finances in the interest of royal taxes. This goal stopped well short of the kind of protection that Root suggests the law was used for, but even this was too much for the magistrates of the Dijon Parlement, who insisted that the intendant do nothing more than verify village unanimity and check their paperwork. For most of the eighteenth century the intendant saw records from all lawsuits involving village communities without judging, although after 1784 the intendant A. L. Amelot de Chaillou did intervene to end court cases that villages stood no chance of winning.

It was a matter of much disagreement whether the intendant had the right to halt the lawsuits that he verified. When Amelot took over as intendant in 1784, he began an extensive inquiry into this question of authorizations for court cases involving communities. "We were," he complained to the controller general, "accustomed to regard the authorizations of the *commissaire départi* as a formality."[40] The problem, according to an undated memo from the 1780s, was a contradiction between two royal edicts that defined the mission of the intendant. An *arrêt* from 1683 gave the intendant the authority to "judge and decide all cases, civil as well as criminal." However, the 1703 law that first required authorization for communities in court cases ordered the intendant to send these cases back to the ordinary judges, without deciding the matter.[41]

The Parlement of Dijon, of course, chose to enforce the 1703 law and denied the intendant even the right to refuse a community's request for permission, seeing this as the exercise of jurisdictionary authority that belonged to them. These magistrates maintained that the intendant's only job in these cases was to make sure that the community was unanimous in its desire to go to court. The magistrates complained in 1789 that Amelot had worked to change established practice with respect to the required authorization, turning it into a kind of jurisdiction: "the requests presented him by communities for a simple authorization, become in his hands the pretext for an evocation."[42]

The 1703 law required communities that wanted to go to court to provide the intendant with a deliberation of the village community and a consultation from a lawyer. The lawyer's written analysis of the case's merits had to conclude that the community's position was defensible, while the deliberation of the members of the community showed the intendant the village's unanimity in the decision to pursue the case. Parlement saw the intendant's authority in the control of court cases as limited simply to the verification of these two documents: the intendant's supporters "desire that he cannot refuse an authorization when presented with a deliberation of the community and a consultation from a lawyer, whoever he may be."[43] Amelot claimed the right to decide whether the case had merits, but the province's magistrates saw this as a usurpation of their jurisdiction and also decried the idea that one man, and not a Burgundian, could be supreme judge in these cases, with appeal only to the Royal Council.

The solution the intendant suggested soon after he came to power in 1784, which was subsequently implemented, provides further evidence that through the eighteenth century the intendants had limited authority over village court cases. The remedy to the "drawback of leaving the decision to a single man who can deceive himself or be deceived" was for the intendant Amelot to put together a council of three enlightened and skilled lawyers to examine the requests for "permission to plead." Together with these three Burgundian lawyers, Amelot suggested, he would then be able to halt meritless cases before they bogged down the court system and emptied village coffers. In a report prepared for the controller general by his staff, evaluating Amelot's proposal, the author noted that "the Parlement cannot find it inappropriate that the intendant take the necessary precautions not to authorize unfounded lawsuits." This reform was put into practice, and this council of lawyers did in fact reduce the number of court cases involving communities as well as the amount of money communities were paying for meritless court cases during last five years before the Revolution, or so an anonymous administrator claimed in the late 1780s.[44]

A recent work allows us to evaluate the effectiveness of the intendant's control through the required authorizations of village communities' going to court, both before and after the creation of the committee of lawyers in 1784.[45] Sebastien Evrard confirms that before 1784 the intendants' intervention in village court cases was purely formulaic; he estimates that a maximum of 3 percent of requests for permission to plead a court case were turned down before 1784.[46]

After the creation of the committee of lawyers in 1784, the intendant took a more activist role in village affairs, sometimes refusing to allow villages to pursue cases that they might lose, or encouraging the villages to settle their disputes out of court. In Evrard's sample of 427 requests for permission after the committee was put in place, the intendant turned down only 39 requests after consulting with his committee.[47] About 10 percent of cases submitted to the committee involved seigneurial rights, but unfortunately Evrard does not indicate how many of these the committee rejected. It is clear, however, that in cases involving seigneurial rights and dues the intendant did not decide the case, but rather sometimes decided not to allow the village to pursue the court case because of the committee's opinion that the community would lose.[48]

There was another problem that effectively rendered the intendant powerless in the face of ruinous court cases involving communities. The possibility that four or five of the principal inhabitants of the village could be sued as representatives of the community meant that, even had the Parlement of Dijon not actively opposed him, the intendant dared not frequently turn down requests for permission to go to court. Lawsuits against a village's wealthiest inhabitants were based on the legal fiction of communal solidarity, whereby each individual was held to be responsible for the community as a whole.[49] In general, this served to simplify the central government's collection of taxes, and it simultaneously gave local judges a great deal of authority over local politics. The unpublished memo from the early 1780s described the results of solidarity for communal court cases. Should a village community choose not to go to court (as defendant) or should it be forbidden by the intendant from doing so, the plaintiff simply brought suit against the four principal inhabitants of the village. These four then sued four other inhabitants of their village (or, of the same village), who then "denounce others and these finish by acting as guarantee for the whole community." The final result was the involvement of the whole community, not as a body, but individually, acting in guarantee for each other. A single case led to three or four others (all "*demandes en garantie*"), and the cost of the case to the community more than doubled. Since the community was not involved as a body, however, the intendant would be powerless to intervene.[50] In 1785 the Parlement of Dijon forbade the practice, ordering all legal practitioners to refuse to take on such cases, describing this use of *contrainte solidaire* as "irregular, expensive and unjust."[51] But since this applied only to cases where the intendant had already refused to allow a court case against the village to go forward, it would still be possible to circumvent the intendant's authority in this way.

In 1784 Antoine Chaignet, the *fermier* of the seigneurie of Ampilly-les-Bordes, sued the village community to collect the seigneurial *taille*. Since the village paid this in a lump sum to the lord (or his *fermier*), this was effectively a lawsuit against the community. But the *fermier* chose to sue only the elected village officers, and thus the intendant did not hear of the case and had no possibility of intervening.[52] It sometimes made good sense for plaintiffs to sue several representatives instead of the community. Of course, if the representatives reacted as the intendant described above, it could slow down the course of justice considerably, something few plaintiffs desired. In most cases, though, avoiding the intendant's permission would speed things up considerably, since communities were often painfully slow to assemble and deliberate, consult a lawyer, and send the papers to the intendant. In Meursault, for example, the parish priest began a lawsuit against the village in January 1785. The judge ordered the community to assemble and deliberate and then get permission from the intendant if the inhabitants decided to defend their case. It was not until May of that year, four court sessions later, that the villagers had decided to go ahead with the case. The last mention of the case was in July 1785, by which time the community still did not have the permission of the intendant.[53] Since no final judgment is to be found in the registers, the case presumably settled out of court.

The possibility of circumventing an intendant's refusal of permission to plead a case, combined with the narrow interpretation that the Parlement of Dijon placed on the intendant's jurisdiction, put the intendant in a position of little real authority over communal politics in other than financial affairs. Even if Burgundy's intendants had been truly antiseigneurial, a proposition for which I am not persuaded there is sufficient evidence, they had almost no authority to protect ordinary people from their lords. Even Root acknowledges that communities almost always lost in court cases versus their lords once the case went before the province's judges, a fact that reinforces the powerlessness of successive intendants to defend villagers against rapacious seigneurs.

Root claims that the central state, through provincial intendants, curtailed the power of lords in order to protect the central government's fiscal interests. This explains, he says, why intendants would defend the vitality of communal farming in the face of seigneurial attempts to usurp land and rights. In order to make this claim, Root seriously underestimates the very real fiscal threat posed by court cases to village finances and overestimates the ability of villages to pay these court costs.

Court costs could be considerable, sometimes all but bankrupting villages. A court case involving the village of Montot cost the community 136 livres 16 sols. This may not seem like much, but together with one other court case that year, the village paid out 184 livres in court costs. The total revenue of Montot that year was only 500 livres, so court costs made up about 35 percent of the village's expenses.[54] Some communities paid vast amounts of money for court cases: in the 1780s the tiny village of Fontaine-en-Duesmois had to pay 5,469 livres for legal fees in a case against the lord that it nevertheless lost.[55]

To raise the money to pay for these court cases, communities had two options: ask the intendant for permission to tax themselves through a *taille négociale,* self-imposed taxes raised by a village community, or raise money through the leasing of common land or forest resources. They could also borrow the money, but they would generally repay the loan through a *taille négociale.* Villages did not have the right to tax their own inhabitants regularly, but communal taxes were permitted under exceptional circumstances to meet specific needs–and official permission from the intendant was required to raise this money.[56]

How much revenue did northern Burgundian villages lose to legal practitioners in the form of local taxes to pay legal fees? There is an estimate in the undated report already cited. From January to July in an unspecified year (possibly 1782 or 1783) the intendant had ordered communal taxes to pay for court cases in the amount of 72,058 livres 18 sols 8 deniers.[57] But this amount seems either exaggerated or exceptional, since more reliable figures exist for each year from 1785 to 1788, when the taxes to pay legal fees for villages amounted to between 44,254 livres and 79,647 livres for the whole year.[58] Admittedly the figure was probably higher before 1784, when Amelot put in place a new procedure to discourage village court cases, but as only about 10 percent of court cases were ended by the intendant's intervention, it is unlikely that villages spent two to three times more money on court cases before the reform of 1784. Local taxes do not, however, tell the whole story of the costs of court cases. As noted, some villages decided to rent out common land or access to forests in order to raise the money required to litigate. Taken together, then, we could estimate that villages in the province spent between 100,000 and 250,000 livres a year on court fees. It is not surprising that the intendant was more concerned with reducing the number of court cases than with using his authority to help villages outwit their seigneurs.

Royal administrators were consistently more concerned with the high costs of court cases than with revenue lost through seigneurial usurpation of common land. This fact comes through clearly in a series of remonstrances and responses between the provincial Estates and the king. In 1776 the Estates remonstrated to the king on the subject of common land. After underlining the importance of commons for farming, the Estates said most villages lacked the paperwork to prove ownership of their land. This meant that when villages sued encroachers they had difficulty getting the land back, since testimony by witness that the village had used the land for thirty years was the best proof they could come up with. They suggested that all villages be ordered to put together a description of the lands they own, agree on the declaration in a general assembly, and then draw up an official declaration before a notary. Three copies of the declaration would be housed in the village, with the local seigneurial court, and in the archives of the Estates. The declarations could then be used in court cases to maintain the land owned by the village.[59]

If Root is right to suggest that intendants supported village court cases to retake common land seized by lords, we would expect the king to accept this suggestion, but he refused it. His reason? The reform would lead to multiple court cases, legal fees from which would ruin the villages. When he responded to the request a few years later, almost certainly after consulting with the provincial intendant, he noted that "the consideration of the multiple and ruinous court cases for communities, that the execution of a law such as that requested could bring about, has motivated His Majesty to suspend his decision on this article until such time as the Estates propose means that are not susceptible of the same disadvantages."[60] In 1781 the counselors of the Estates reported to the assembled orders, suggesting that if the communities limited their declaration to the land of which they are "currently in peaceable use and possession," the reform would actually make for fewer court cases rather than more.[61] But the Estates never presented this request to the king, dropping the matter after 1781.

The provincial intendant was much concerned with villages' high spending on court cases. It was this concern, rather than an attempt to minimize seigneurial power, that motivated A. L. Amelot de Chaillou to attempt to extend or reestablish his authority over village court cases after 1784. In a report he prepared justifying his authority over village court cases, the intendant never once mentioned the desire to protect villages from lords. Rather, his argument was based on his (exaggerated) estimate that villages spent 400,000 livres a year on court cases. What was worse, the report argued, was that villages lost at least 90 percent of the cases in which they were involved.[62]

The provincial intendants of the *généralité* of Dijon may have wanted to end seigneurial (and other) usurpation of common land. Because of legal difficulties involved in proving possession in the absence of written title, however, the court cases required to maintain village land holdings were expensive, sometimes prohibitively so. The last intendant in the province certainly wanted to protect village finances–but did so by limiting the number of cases involving communities, rather than supporting these cases. For a few short years he was successful in this, but he continually came up against the Dijon Parlement's jealous defense of its right to be the highest judge of all Burgundians. By 1788 the province's magistrates were again actively opposing what they saw as a usurpation of jurisdiction and working, in the words of the intendant, to keep him "reduced to signing, without examination, what is presented to him, to verifying at most the exterior form of a multitude of village practitioners."[63]

Was There a Seigneurial Reaction in Eighteenth-Century Northern Burgundy?

Tocqueville's explanation does not fit the northern Burgundian situation. The growth of the central state apparently was not accomplished by undermining seigneurial authority in a direct way. What of the seigneurial reaction thesis? The records of seigneurial courts in northern Burgundy show that there was an intensification of seigneurialism, but with some difference from the seigneurial reaction described by Bloch, Lefebvre, and Jones. As table 6.1 shows, during the 1750s in the courts studied, lords, their agents, and their *fermiers* initiated 82 lawsuits against peasants. In the 1780s there were 185 such lawsuits. Northern Burgundian lords, in other words, sued their peasants 2.3 times more often in the last decade of the ancien régime than their parents had in the 1750s.

The doubling of lawsuits initiated by lords and their agents is largely explained by prosecution for offenses in the forests and fields of lords, which increased by a factor of 5.5 over this period of forty years. Without forest and field lawsuits the number of seigneurial cases only increased from 61 to 69 between the 1750s and the 1780s, an increase that approximately parallels population growth. Lords, however, also sued more peasants for offenses of all kinds, a fact that is hidden by simply giving the number of lawsuits. During the 1780s lords in the sample sued three times as many peasants as they did in the 1750s, since lawsuits initiated by lords (and their agents) generally involved more defendants in the 1780s than in the 1750s. As we can see in table 6.2, the 185 seigneurial lawsuits in the 1780s involved 451 defendants, or three times as many as the 150 defendants tried in the 82 seigneurial cases in the same courts in the 1750s.

A crackdown by lords, field guards, and judges on forest use and pasturing in seigneurial forest and field was by far the most important element in the changes in the seigneurial system in the province, far more significant than any invention of new dues. Indeed, seigneurial judges came down hard

Table 6.1. Lawsuits involving lords

	Lawsuits in the 1750s	Lawsuits in the 1780s
Forest and field offenses	21	116
Seigneurial dues	47	43
Mainmorte	1	1
Hunting and fishing	2	12
Monopolies	2	6
Honorific privileges	2	2
Unknown	7	5
Total	82	185

Table 6.2. Villagers sued by seigneur

	Defendants in seigneurial lawsuits, 1750–59	Defendants in seigneurial lawsuits, 1780–89
Regular session	115	365
Annual assizes	35	86
Total	150	451

on pasture offenses in the lords' forests. In 1785 the guard of the forest of Meursault caught twenty-four villagers pasturing their animals in the seigneurial forest. These villagers had eight mares and ninety cows pasturing in the seigneurial forest. The judge sentenced them to pay 1,580 livres in fines and the same amount in damages for what looks a lot like an enclosure riot.[64] The normal sentence for cattle found in the forest under guard was 20 livres per head of cattle, plus whatever damages the animals had committed. The resulting combined fine and damages, often amounting to 40 livres, was a substantial amount of money, and an animal caught twice in the seigneurial forest could have cost its master more in fines and damages than it was worth.

The intensification of the lords' policing of their forests made good sense in the economic climate of the eighteenth century, especially in northern Burgundy. Labrousse's index of prices indicates that the price of wood almost doubled from 1750 to 1789.[65] Between 1729 and 1789 in the Burgundian village of Beaumont the price of wood increased from 48 to 160 livres per *arpent*.[66] Wood prices outstripped the rise in the price of grain by a considerable margin: the price of wheat, according to Labrousse, rose 56–66 percent between 1726–41 and 1785–89.[67] Rising wood prices provided incentive to lords increasingly to close off their forests to villagers and their animals. This was especially true in northern Burgundy, given the economic importance of the forest and the wood industry. The regions of the Morvan, the Châtillonais, and most of the western section of northern Burgundy were covered by vast forests. Villages in these regions exported significant quantities of wood to Paris.[68] Lords responded to higher prices by hiring more forest guards and offering them higher wages. In the 1780s the Saulx-Tavanes family increased the number of guards in its pay from five to eight and increased their salaries from 74 to 200 livres each.[69] In 1785 the baron of Pagny paid his two guards 713 livres a year, a considerable sum.[70]

Lords and villages sometimes fought over access to forests, and in some cases peasants had legal access rights to forests owned by the lord. In the village of Ancey, for example, the inhabitants possessed the formal right to pasture their animals in part of the seigneurial forest after the "fourth leaf fallen"–that is, after the harvest of the forest, the inhabitants had to wait until the newly planted trees had survived four years and were strong enough to "withstand the tooth of the cattle."[71] Lords sometimes extended the no-trespassing period on the pretext that the trees were not yet strong enough to withstand the teeth and hooves of cows and pigs, as in Senailly, where the closure of the forest was extended from the mandated five years to eleven years.[72]

But there is an important distinction between villages that possessed a formal access right to the seigneurial forest and villages where a de facto right existed based on the complicity of the lord. Few villages had a formal legal right of pasture in seigneurial forests; it existed in only two of the villages studied. It is much more difficult to address the possibility of the criminalization of forest trespass in cases where access had been tolerated by the lord. The steep rise in the value of wood over the eighteenth century certainly pushed lords to protect their forest resources more aggressively, and part of this effort probably involved keeping villagers out of forested land where before the lord and his guards had tacitly allowed them to enter.

Most seigneurs were absent from their seigneurie for most of the year, choosing to leave the daily running of their estates to their agents and judicial officers. Other absentee lords opted instead to lease their land, dues, and rights to a *fermier général*. Saint Jacob has argued that a large share of the responsibility for the "seigneurial reaction" goes to these rural bourgeois who brought agrarian capitalism to the countryside with a great deal of vigor.[73] The cases heard in fourteen seigneurial courts confirm the importance of seigneurial general tenants in maintaining seigneurial rights and protecting the property of lords, but they also suggest that the role of *fermiers* in the intensification of seigneurial rights should not be overestimated. *Fermiers* were not necessarily more "capitalist" than lords.

Table 6.3. Lawsuits involving *fermiers généraux* as plaintiffs

Type of case	1750s, regular session	1750s, assizes	1780s, regular session	1780s, assizes
Forest and field offenses	17	2	5	48
Dues and rights	12	10	17	4
Monopolies	1	0	3	0
Lease terms	4	0	5	0
Insult	0	0	1	0
Total	34	12	31	52

Table 6.3 presents the number and type of lawsuits that involved *fermiers* as litigants defending the rights, property, and dues of the seigneurie.[74] Over-tenants instigated close to half of the "seigneurial" lawsuits and court cases, often collaborating with the prosecutor and judge to bring charges against peasants who failed to pay or resisted their authority. Does this represent a large number? Answering this question requires knowing the proportion of seigneuries that were being run by *fermiers* rather than by lords and their agents. An accurate calculation of this proportion would require close analysis of general leases for all of the fourteen seigneuries studied–not only because a seigneur might switch from one mode of exploitation to the other but also because the terms of the lease could change from one tenancy to the next. Since the scattering of these leases in countless notarial archives renders this impractical, I chose instead simply to make a list of seigneuries that mention the existence of a general *fermier* at least once during the decade of the 1780s. Twelve of the fourteen seigneuries were leased out to a general *fermier* at least once from 1780 to 1789, as evidenced by the court cases and by other documents in communal and seigneurial records. This is an approximation, since several seigneuries included multiple villages; and while likely, it is not certain that all of the hamlets and villages were rented out to *fermiers*.

It seems likely, then, that the vast majority of lords leased out their land and rights to a general *fermier*, who frequently had recourse to the services of the seigneurial court against his neighbors and in defense of the seigneurie. But what is equally important is that *fermiers* initiated only about half of the "seigneurial" lawsuits and police cases–an equal number of cases were instigated either by the lord himself or by the *procureur d'office* operating in his interest. Moreover, the number of suits initiated by *fermiers* increased by about the same proportion as the number of lawsuits filed by seigneurs, as both categories of cases approximately doubled between the 1750s and the 1780s. This suggests that seigneurs and *fermiers* were enforcing the seigneurial system with about the same amount of rigor and brings some nuance to the notion that *fermiers* were the primary motive force behind the intensification of the seigneurie over the course of the eighteenth century.

Lords sued more people by the 1780s–but was it because lords had become more litigious or because peasants had become less submissive? This issue is difficult to resolve conclusively, but evidence from the court cases suggests that lords were quicker to defend their interests and more careful over their income than they had been earlier. Many of the lawsuits for seigneurial dues demanded payment of arrears dating back twenty-nine years or proof that the dues had been paid each year. Furthermore, many of these cases involved multiple defendants, sometimes as many as thirty people, who were forced by the court to provide receipts for past years.[75] When in 1785 Jean Baptiste Ginot inherited his father's estate, the lord of St. Aubin and Gamay sued the son for twenty-nine years of *cens* and other dues. Ginot claimed that his father had paid and that he only owed for the past three years. Since Ginot could not present a receipt, the judge sentenced him to pay 147 livres, or twenty-nine years of this seigneurial due.[76] The increasing frequency of large lawsuits directed against many villagers to collect dues in arrears indicates that lords were simply trying to catch anyone who had failed to keep the necessary receipts. Historians of popular culture have demonstrated the importance of honor, honesty, and justice to ordinary people's conception of the social world and their relations to others.[77] The egregious abuse of authority involved in double-charging those who had no receipts surely generated a great deal of ill-will among villagers, substantially out of proportion to the number of villagers actually sentenced to pay.

The importance of forest cases also strongly supports the contention that relations between lords and ordinary people changed in the late eighteenth century. While the incidence of wood theft may have increased over the century, it is unlikely that peasants stole or used six times more wood by the 1780s than they had in the 1750s. Those accused of illegal pasturing or wood theft did not claim a traditional communal right of access to the lord's forest. If the increase in seigneurial court cases were the result of a nascent antiseigneurialism, we would expect that by the 1780s some people might begin to justify their antiseigneurial actions, instead of throwing themselves (as they often did) on "the mercy of the court." Although people caught in the forest occasionally responded with violence toward the guard, the incidence of this behavior does not seem to have increased between 1750 and 1780 despite the steep increase in convictions for wood theft.[78]

The court records of seigneurial justices in northern Burgundy show that something changed between lords and peasants in the late eighteenth century. Lords became more attentive to their estates and used their courts increasingly to protect their revenue from both land and dues. The intensification of seigneurialism in the last decades of the eighteenth century, though, was different from Bloch's seigneurial reaction. The process was characterized primarily by the rigorous policing of the land that lords owned, without much evidence of the invention or even reinvigoration of seigneurial dues. The late eighteenth century saw northern Burgundian lords focusing their attention more explicitly on revenue from their land. By offering higher salaries to forest guards and remaining in close contact with their judicial officers, lords managed to increase their revenue from fines and, much more importantly, protect a resource that had become quite valuable.

Lords also became more attentive to their arable and pastoral land. Leases with general *fermiers* and account books from seigneuries support an extension of Robert Forster's conclusions concerning the Burgundian estates of the Saulx-Tavanes family. Forster shows that this family increased profit from its seigneuries by increasing land rents and administering the forests more carefully.[79] With inflation and a steady rise in the price of land and in the profitability of renting, the revenue from seigneurial dues became relatively less important to most lords. In a series of leases of the seigneurie of Billey and Villerrottin, the price of the lease increased by a factor of 2.7 between 1747 and 1786.[80]

Bloch was mistaken to suggest that the reinvigoration of old dues and outright invention of new ones was the main force transforming the seigneurie in the eighteenth century and leading to an increase in antiseigneurial sentiment among peasants.[81] There is no doubt that such invention and reinvigoration did happen in some cases. In regions where the forest was less economically important, modernizing, profit-oriented seigneurs may have devoted more energy than northern Burgundian lords to increasing their revenues from dues. In northern Burgundy, however, lords devoted a great deal more energy to protecting and increasing their income from their forests.

Tocqueville's claim that the growth of the central state left lords with no services to give their vassals obviously does not explain the northern Burgundian situation. Still, there might be some validity to his observation that antiseigneurial sentiment was strongest in those parts of Europe where seigneurial authority was weakest and most modern. E. Le Roy Ladurie has famously put forward this theory, based to a significant extent on Saint Jacob's presentation of the seigneurial reaction in northern Burgundy.[82] According to Le Roy Ladurie, seigneurial authority was less contested in northern Burgundy because feudalism remained more archaic there than in many parts of France.

On a national scale, how strong was seigneurial authority and the seigneurial system in northern Burgundy, and how intense was popular resentment to lords? And what was the relationship between the vitality of the system and the strength of the opposition to it? Firstly, although antiseigneurial rebellion in 1789 was not as strong in northern Burgundy as in some other parts of France, it was not as weak as some have claimed. Jean

Bart characterizes the Burgundian experience in the Revolution as about average in terms of violence and upheaval.[83] Was antiseigneurial sentiment moderated by the archaic nature of feudalism in the province? The claim seems tenuous–despite the continued existence of ancient rights like *mainmorte,* seigneurialism in the province was more modern than archaic, based largely on the drive for profit. Furthermore, revolt against lords needed more than simple antiseigneurial sentiment to get started, and regions with fewer revolts may merely be those with weaker traditions of opposition to authority. The presence or absence of antiseigneurial sentiment in parish *cahiers de doléances* is a poor predictor of antiseigneurial revolt.[84] Despite the fact that in Burgundy antiseigneurial revolt in 1789 was limited to a few wine-producing areas, we know from parish *cahiers* that peasants throughout the province strongly resented the strength of the feudal regime.

It may be that in northern Burgundy the rapidity and cheapness of the justice that peasants got in ordinary cases made them more accepting of seigneurial authority. The increased visibility, however, of seigneurial authority as lords and their agents took advantage of more efficient justice probably worked in the opposite direction. It is certain that in northern Burgundy there was a strong link between the strength of the seigneurial regime and the vitality and even popularity of the judicial system, but it is questionable whether this applies to other regions of France. In southwestern France, for example, while seigneurial authority seems to have been weaker than in most of France, seigneurial justice nevertheless remained important. By contrast, lords were powerful in Maine, but seigneurial justice was almost moribund.[85] It may be that the regional variety of France simply defies generalization, and that antiseigneurial sentiment in some regions sprang from the weakness and in other places from the strength of the seigneurie. In Burgundy, though, it is clear that the impulse to revolt against lords sprang at least in part from a noticeable increase in the visibility of lordly authority–but also that it was probably moderated by the lords' continued provision of a useful, even essential service for the litigious inhabitants of the province.

Conclusion

Where does this leave us in our search for the causes of peasant antiseigneurial sentiment and revolt in 1789? Firstly, people did not revolt against an institution that had been rendered obsolete by the rise of the state. Seigneurialism remained omnipresent in the lives of ordinary people, and the authority of lords to administer justice through personally appointed officers remained undiminished. Secondly, it seems unlikely that ordinary people in northern Burgundy were paying more money, or a higher proportion of their income, to their lord. No simple increase in the extent of exploitation is apparent in the records of the courts.

What changed to make ordinary people so opposed to the power of lords? First of all, the increase in lords' use of the courts to sue peasants made seigneurial authority, and the lords' commitment to the bottom line, more visible. Lords always knew the dues and rights that belonged to them and tried to collect, but by the end of the eighteenth century the chance that a tricky peasant could avoid paying had diminished because of the increased nearness of seigneurial justice to village life. The increase in the number of peasants who were sued over dues and of investigations by the court going back several years to catch those who had not paid the seigneurial land transfer fees or the *cens* surely generated a great deal of ill will among villagers, and especially among village leaders. More importantly, the tendency of lords to reserve their forests for their own private use and rigorously to pursue even minor thefts of firewood must be considered an important cause of peasant unrest. The *cahiers* are full of complaints that lords had usurped common land and excluded the village herd from his forests. And anecdotally, most of the peasant revolts discussed in the secondary literature (in this region) began with a dispute over forests.

Peasants revolted in 1789 against lords who had basically become capitalists–lords who, while determined to defend traditional rights that profited them, were focusing their energy on their property. Ordinary people clearly resented being excluded from forests as well as having to pay higher land rents. Still, complaints in the *cahiers* against "useless" seigneurial dues and rights, and violence directed against symbols and papers, suggest something more–that the institution of seigneurialism itself had been delegitimized in the eyes of ordinary people. The answer may lie neither in the land nor in the lords' record books, but in people's minds. We need to take seriously the possibility that Enlightenment ideas had percolated into the countryside and made forced service and payments determined by birth seem illegitimate and monstrous even to ordinary people.[86]

Chapter 7

A Popular Institution?

Seigneurial Justice in the *Cahiers de Doléances*

Over the course of the eighteenth century seigneurial justice changed both for the better and for the worse in northern Burgundy. On the one hand, administrators, magistrates, and judges agreed that it was important to simplify procedure for minor cases. They set in motion procedural reforms that allowed ordinary people to have their cases tried quickly and cheaply. They also strengthened and formalized the system of judicial checks that already existed and worked to ensure that judges remained in close contact with the villages. On the other hand, seigneurial justice became increasingly important in the administration and enforcement of the seigneurie and allowed absentee lords to ensure that their estates, rights, and dues were protected better than they had ever been before.

How did ordinary people react to these two changes in the way they experienced contact with the institution of seigneurial justice? To what extent were they aware of the changes that had been put in place? In 1789, at the end of a long period during which justice and seigneurial domination were inextricably linked, what were ordinary people thinking about seigneurial justice? I have already both illustrated the important ways the local seigneurial court influenced daily life and demonstrated that voluntary recourse to the court's authority was commonplace. I have argued that most ordinary people did not resent, hate, or fear seigneurial justice. Parish *cahiers de doléances* from 1789, however, allow us to see much more directly what ordinary people appreciated or disliked about the institution.

While there are many complaints about seigneurial justice in the parish *cahiers* of northern Burgundy, the most striking thing is how positive the *cahiers* are with respect to the institution.[1] While the majority had grievances about seigneurial justice and the judicial system, very few suggested abolition. People complained that these local courts were too distant from their lives and that lords used their courts to enforce unfair seigneurial dues. Still, the authors made it abundantly clear that so long as changes were made to curtail the authority of lords, the judicial system could continue to function much as it had in the last decades of the ancien régime. The authors of the *cahiers* made a crucial distinction between seigneurial justice as a judicial institution and as a seigneurial institution. They suggested several ways of curtailing the influence that lords had over their courts, showing that for ordinary people the most objectionable problem with seigneurial justice was the way that lords used their courts to protect their rights–that often the lord was in effect both plaintiff and judge in the court.

The Influence of Presiding Officers

In the spring of 1789 every parish in France assembled to draw up a list of grievances, its *cahier de doléances.* They also elected two representatives who would take their *cahier* to the bailliage or *sénéchaussée,* where those delegates would then write another *cahier,* this one to be taken to the Estates-General that was to be held later that year. This was one of the largest public consultations ever engaged in, and the surviving *cahiers* constitute an unparalleled source for evaluating popular opinion in 1789. There are, however, a host of difficulties involved in their interpretation. To what extent can statements in the *cahiers* be used to evaluate what ordinary people thought about seigneurial justice? The assemblies in which the communities drafted their *cahiers* were often presided over by the local seigneurial judge, whose presence may have made villagers reticent to state their true opinion on seigneurial justice (and many other subjects).[2] Markoff and Shapiro have demonstrated that the presence of seigneurial judges in the assemblies did not make villagers less likely to denounce seigneurial institutions and rights.[3] In the Burgundian bailliage of Semur-en-Auxois, where seigneurial judges chaired 44 percent of assemblies, the *cahiers* were nevertheless unanimous in denouncing their lords.[4] In fact, in Shapiro and Markoff's sample, assemblies presided over by a seigneurial officer were more likely to discuss and criticize the seigneurial system than those not so chaired.[5] Their conclusions mean that we can trust parish *cahiers* as sources for peasant opinion on the seigneurial system, but they tell us nothing about the trustworthiness of *cahiers* for comments on justice.

It is possible to compare the comments on seigneurial justice in those *cahiers* written in village assemblies presided over by seigneurial officers with the *cahiers* written in the absence of the judge, *procureur d'office,* and clerk. The *cahiers* themselves only rarely list the name of the president of the assembly, so generally we know their names only when the record of the election of representatives exists. The name of the president could be located for 229 of the *cahiers* from northern Burgundy. As we see in table 7.1, seigneurial officers presided over the majority of the village assemblies, but a substantial minority (about 40 percent) nevertheless took place in the absence of these officers. The documents sometimes explained the nonparticipation of the

Table 7.1. Influence of presiding seigneurial officers on the contents of parish *cahiers*

Presiding officer	President (%)	Mentioned seigneurial justice (%)	Specifically requested preservation (%)	Extend the authority of seigneurial courts (%)	Abolish (%)
Judge	74 (32)	32 (43)	1 (1)	15 (20)	6 (8)
Procureur d'office	25 (11)	13 (52)	2 (8)	7 (28)	0
Clerk	35 (15)	11 (31)	0	5 (14)	0
Subtotal, seigneurial officers	134 (59)	56 (42)	3 (2)	27 (20)	6 (4)
No relation to local court	95 (41)	44 (46)	4 (4)	17 (18)	3 (3)

seigneurial officer by specifying that he lived too far away or was absent. The heads of household of Barbirey, for example, met in the presence of Claude Faucillon, schoolmaster, "their natural secretary, having no judicial officers in the village."[6] In other instances, though, there was no such explanation, as in the case of Mâlain, presided over by Edme Mairet, royal notary from Sombernon, "expressly commissioned by the inhabitants."[7]

In table 7.1 we compare the contents of *cahiers* prepared in the presence of a seigneurial officer with those prepared before a notary, schoolmaster, or simple *practitien* who was not connected to the local seigneurial justice. The analysis takes into account four points of comparison: whether or not the document mentions seigneurial justice at all, requests for the extension of the authority of seigneurial judges, and specific demands either for the preservation or for the abolition of seigneurial justice. The two groups of *cahiers* are highly similar, and the few small differences do not support the notion that presiding seigneurial officers much influenced the contents of the *cahiers*. The *cahiers* written in assemblies presided over by seigneurial officers mentioned seigneurial justice slightly less often than those written outside of the presence of the officers, but the difference (about 4 percent) is not significant enough to suggest that peasants could not speak their mind when the judge was present.

We will see below that a significant proportion of parish *cahiers* requested the extension of the authority of seigneurial courts. But did they do so because they were encouraged, provoked, or even forced to do so by the presiding seigneurial officer? About a fifth of both types of *cahiers* requested that seigneurial courts be given the authority of other judicial or administrative institutions. *Cahiers* from officer-presided and notable-presided assemblies were strikingly similar. About the same proportion of *cahiers* in both categories mentioned seigneurial justice, and similar numbers of villages in both groups demanded the abolition, preservation, or extension of seigneurial justice. Judges allowed villagers to speak their mind not only about feudalism but also about seigneurial justice.

Cahiers de doléances nevertheless have to be treated with some caution. They do not reflect "raw" peasant opinion toward seigneurial justice, or indeed any other subject. The *cahiers* result from a series of exchanges and debates that took place in the spring of 1789. The projected audience for the *cahiers* (ostensibly the king, but also the nation) also affected both form and content. We should also not forget that village society was often deeply divided. The *cahiers,* then, reflect village politics, are the result of negotiation within the village community, and were prepared with a specific goal in mind. Still, they can provide us with a good indication of what many peasants were thinking in 1789 with respect to France's institutions and their future.

The Need to Preserve Seigneurial Justice

Ordinary northern Burgundians had much to say about their judicial system, and about seigneurial justice more specifically. Three-fifths of *cahiers* asked for some reform of the judicial system (183 out of 303). In these 183 *cahiers* there are 465 grievances about justice in total, an average of 2.6 complaints per *cahier* in those that mention the legal system. Of the 120 *cahiers* silent on judicial questions, 43 are purely local *cahiers* that simply listed their seigneurial dues and taxes and contained no real complaints or suggestions.[8] So of 260 "big-picture" *cahiers,* 183 talk about justice (70.4 percent). The fact that most *cahiers* contained references to the judicial system can also be seen in Régine Robin's analysis of the *cahiers* of one Burgundian bailliage, Semur-en-Auxois. Robin shows that a quarter of the common keywords in the *cahiers* referred specifically to the judicial system.[9] A number of parish *cahiers* simply requested the reform of civil and criminal procedure, without specifically referring to seigneurial justice. Still, 139 parish *cahiers* specifically mentioned seigneurial justice at least once (either by name, by referring to the "justice des lieux," or by referring to matters that were specific to the institution such as the new procedure for *mésus*). This means that 46 percent of the *cahiers* in the sample, or about half of "big-picture" *cahiers,* referred specifically to seigneurial justice. The frequency with which the *cahiers* spoke of seigneurial justice is not necessarily indicative of the degree to which ordinary people disliked the institution, however, as is revealed by an analysis of the grievances and comments, many of which specifically requested the preservation of the institution.

Table 7.2. Demands and grievances related to justice in parish *cahiers*

General (77)	
General legal reform is needed	39
Legal uniformity for the nation	2
Justice should be free	6
Justice should be cheaper	16
Punishments in criminal cases should be reduced	11
Other	3
Procedure (65)	
Procureurs postulants (local legal practitioners) are too greedy	5
Abolish debtor's prison	12
Impose time limits for the duration of cases	13
Restore the old (pre-1772) procedure for the trial of farming torts	3
All minor cases should be heard at the annual assizes	2
Simplify procedure	21
Other	9
Other institutions (118)	
Abolish all *tribunaux d'exception*	23
Reform the justice of intendants	1
Abolish intendants	12
Abolish intendants AND:	
1. Give their authority to seigneurial judges	17
2. Give their authority to a committee	7
Abolish the *Maîtrises des Eaux et Forets*	4
Abolish the *Maîtrises des Eaux et Forets* AND:	
1. Give their authority to seigneurial judges	20
2. Give their authority to the bailliage	8
Reform the *Maîtrises des Eaux et Forêts*	1

(cont'd)

Table 7.2. Demands and grievances related to justice in parish *cahiers*–*(cont'd)*

Other institutions (118)–*(cont'd)*	
Keep Parlement's authority as it is now	5
Parlement's authority should be limited to that of a court (no political role)	2
Abolish *jurés priseurs*	12
Abolish *justice prévôtale* in favor of seigneurial courts	1
Increase the authority of presidial courts	4
Allow arbitration in all cases	1
Seigneurial justice	
Abolish seigneurial justice	10
Maintain seigneurial justice	7
Distance to justice/residence of the officers (72)	
All officers should reside in the villages they judge	4
Procureur d'office and *greffier* should reside in the village	6
Greffier should reside in the village	5
Justice should be given "sur les lieux"	44
Should not have to go far away for probate	5
Justice should be further removed from the village	2
Geography of seigneurial justice is too complicated	3
Nearby lords should together nominate one set of officers between them	3
Police (25)	
Seigneurial forest guards should be more closely watched	6
Seigneurial forest guards should be trusted	1
Messiers should be believed on their unsubstantiated word	8
Village policing is too lax	5
Village policing is too strict	1
Police *cabarets* more closely (at Grands-Jours)	1
Royal laws should be posted in seigneurial courts	1
Grands-Jours should be held more frequently	2

(cont'd)

Complaints about justice specific to feudalism (15)	
Reduce fines for farming torts	2
Pay fines to the community, not the lord	2
Seigneurial rights are bad since judged by the "interested parties"	6
It is bad that the court is used to enforce seigneurial dues	3
Justice should be given exclusively in the king's name	2
Reduce control of the lord over the justice (23)	
All cases involving the lord should be heard in the bailliage	4
Seigneurial judges should be appointed permanently	14
The king should name all seigneurial judges	2
Two judges in all seigneurial courts (one named by lord, one by community)	3
Increase authority of seigneurial judges (31)	
Forbid appeal in minor cases	10
Give seigneurial judges authority over disputes concerning the *vingtième* tax	2
Village finances to be overseen by seigneurial judges, not the intendant	4
Commons should be under the seigneurial judge, not the intendant	10
Give seigneurial judge jurisdiction over all *mésus*	1
Abolish the 1787 reform (i.e., pro seigneurial justice)	4
Other complaints about seigneurial justice (27)	
Judges should get a decent salary	3
Officers of seigneurial courts should all be holders of university degrees	8
Seigneurial judges should consult with two important locals before deciding cases	1
Revoke 1772 criminal reform since it costs the crown money	1
Probate justice is too expensive	5
Probate justice is cheap enough	1
Litigants should have the choice of taking their suits to a royal court	3
Lords should be required to have a jail and/or a courthouse	5

The data in table 7.2 represent all of the comments concerning justice and the judicial system in the parish *cahiers*. Seigneurial justice was mentioned in the *cahiers* far more often than any other judicial institution. There were 210 grievances about seigneurial justice compared to 118 comments on all other judicial institutions combined. That people had more grievances, comments, and suggestions for seigneurial than for royal justice suggests seigneurial courts remained active and continued to affect the everyday lives of ordinary people down to the Revolution. Despite their frequent mention of seigneurial courts, the *cahiers* were much more favorable to them than to the other judicial institutions. Thirty-six *cahiers* demanded the suppression of the intendant and his subdelegates, and thirty-two called for the abolition of the *Maîtrise des Eaux et Forêts*. Twenty-three *cahiers* wanted all *tribunaux d'exception* (courts with a special jurisdiction over specific kinds of crimes or disputes) to be suppressed, and the strongest criticism was reserved for *jurés priseurs,* royal officers responsible for executing judicial seizures and sales.

People complained more often about seigneurial justice than about other judicial institutions but demanded its abolition less often. Furthermore, many of the complaints about other judicial institutions and officers demanded their jurisdiction and responsibilities be given to seigneurial judges. In twenty of the thirty-two demands for the abolition of the royal justice of the *Eaux et Forêts,* the local seigneurial judge was to take over the jurisdiction of these courts, and in seventeen of thirty-six demands for the suppression of the royal intendant, the seigneurial judge would receive his jurisdiction and oversight over village finances and forests. The villagers of Courcelles-Fremoy decided not to write a *cahier* at all, choosing rather simply to give authority to their representatives to participate in the reform of the kingdom. They had only one specific grievance: "with a unanimous voice they have charged their deputies to see that the following demand is inserted into the *cahier* of the bailliage, that the administration of the forests of communities be given to the ordinary local judges, or to royal judges in villages that belong to the royal domain."[10] In general, the *cahiers* make it clear that villagers resented the intervention of the intendant and the Waters and Forests officers as much as they appreciated the assistance of the seigneurial judge in regulating their affairs and especially in administering communal property.

The *cahiers* suggested other ways of increasing the authority of seigneurial judges. Ten *cahiers* would reduce the number of appeals by forbidding appeal of the decisions of seigneurial judges in minor cases. The parishioners of Moutier-St.-Jean asked that "the formalities of justice be simplified in procedure, that all cases be judged at most within two years, that judges of lords be sovereign up to 60 livres in principal."[11] Eighteen other suggestions, if followed, would have put seigneurial judges in control of disputes about the *vingtième* tax, village account books, communal forests, and serious *prévôtal* crimes. No fewer than 77 of the 483 grievances about justice would have given more authority to seigneurial judges!

Very few of even the most critical *cahiers* called into question the fairness of seigneurial courts–only five or six suggested that judges were unfair. Three asked that the community be allowed to nominate its own judge to hear cases in conjunction with the seigneurial judge.[12] Usually, as in the case of the village of Boux-sous-Salmaise, this request followed another for limitations on the number of cases appealed from seigneurial courts. Responding to the notion that appeal was needed because seigneurial judges might be inadequately trained or easily bribed, they suggested "forcing the judge to call to the audience two or three of the most learned villagers, whose opinions the judge will have to hear before passing judgment."[13] But even these *cahiers* were responding to an imagined objection and do not necessarily indicate a perception that seigneurial judges were unfair.

Most people thought seigneurial justice was fair, a substantial number of *cahiers* explicitly requested the extension of seigneurial justice, and the vast majority anticipated its preservation. A small minority of *cahiers* nevertheless requested abolition of the institution. Ten *cahiers* demanded the outright abolition of seigneurial justice, suggesting it be replaced with more powerful bailliages.[14] The *cahier* of Vaux asked for the "suppression of seigneurial courts, or the execution of the law given on the eighth of May 1788, and in the case that seigneurial justices subsist, that the officers be chosen by the *procureurs généraux* [of bailliages], that they be made permanent [*inamovibles*], or that while providing justice in the village, all parties be free to demand the removal of the case to the bailliage."[15] Two *cahiers* made the vaguer suggestion that in the future all justice should be rendered in the king's name, and two others wanted the king to nominate all seigneurial judges.[16] Of 303 parish *cahiers,* then, a mere 14 called for the abolition of the institution. The majority of *cahiers* foresaw the continuation of seigneurial justice, some explicitly demanded the preservation of the institution, and only a small minority asked for its suppression.

The preference of many villagers that seigneurial judges continue hearing their disputes does not mean they were entirely satisfied with the judicial system in general or with seigneurial justice in particular. What angered people most about the ancien régime judicial system was the distance they had to travel to get justice. The demand for closer justice is the most common of all legal grievances, being more frequent even than the call for general legal reform. Forty-four *cahiers* state that justice should be "given in the localities" ["rendue sur les lieux"].[17] The parish of Moux, in the bailliage of Saulieu, complained that inhabitants had to go to a distant town to see their judge and requested a "courthouse in the villages to render justice the most summarily possible by officers who will be forced to reside within the jurisdiction of the court."[18] A continuous judicial presence in the village, said the inhabitants of Lucenay-le-Duc, "would free the said inhabitants from having to go twelve leagues to request justice, which to them is quite onerous in cases of sealing of estates, *tutelles,* and settling of income for minor wards."[19] The wish for "justice in the localities" was surely a universal desire among both town dwellers and villagers in the eighteenth century; Ted Margadant has shown that during the Revolution many small towns argued for the preservation or implantation of local courts in order to preserve social order, keep the peace, and save inhabitants needless trips.[20]

The second main category of complaints–with forty-two grievances–was that lords used their courts to oppress the villagers. A common comment in the *cahiers* is that seigneurial dues and rights are unacceptable since always "judged by the interested parties."[21] The community of Marcellois requested the "suppression of all seigneurial right, *corvée,* customary chicken, *cens,* dues, all rights usurped by lords in times of ignorance, maintained by force and always increased by the seigneurial judges against the unfortunate inhabitants of the countryside, who are without fortune and without defenders."[22] A few parishes complained that fines handed out by the judge were a source of revenue for the lords and recommended lowering the fines or adjudging them to the profit of the community rather than to the lord. They decried the influence of a lord over his officers and the subservience of those under his direct authority who judged in the lord's interests.

Many *cahiers* simply pointed out the abuses resulting from the ownership of justice by lords, without proposing concrete reforms. This may reflect a common sentiment among ordinary villagers that their main duty was to summarize the problems and abuses that existed, leaving others (their deputies, those elected to represent the Third Estate at the Estates-General, the king) to find the solutions. A number of *cahiers* do, however, propose concrete solutions to this vexing problem. The most frequent remedy for this mixture of public and private power was that seigneurial judgeships be made permanent (fourteen suggest this). The *cahier* of Latrecey said that "it is necessary that His Majesty make seigneurial officers irremovable [*inamovibles*], except when, in serious cases that have been judicially investigated, the officers are found unworthy of their offices."[23] Other *cahiers* suggested that all cases involving the lord be heard in the bailliage, or that the community be allowed to nominate another judge who would hear these cases together with the seigneurial judge. The *cahier* of Boux-sous-Salmaise complained that most judges bought their offices from the lords, "so that in consequence they are in some ways forced to confirm by their judgments pretensions that are sometime founded on nothing but the cupidity of lords and the timidity, not to mention the stupidity, of their vassals." They asked that seigneurial judges no longer hear cases involving the lord.[24] These suggestions for reform would change the way that lords used seigneurial justice, without profoundly affecting the working of these local courts in nonseigneurial cases.

The authors of the *cahiers* also complained about judicial procedure in all ancien régime courts. Thirty-nine *cahiers* said general legal reform was needed. "That the reform of abuses relative to tribunals and to the administration of justice be promptly carried out," demanded the inhabitants of Baigneux-les-Juifs.[25] Twenty-one *cahiers* contained a demand that civil procedure be simplified, most commonly requesting "that procedure be shortened, both civil and criminal." Without suggesting concrete reform, the inhabitants of Voudenay L'Église complained that "the procedure prescribed by the civil code is too full of formalities; it costs immensely and serves only to eternalize lawsuits."[26] Thirteen *cahiers* suggested imposing strict time limits for the judging of cases. Six *cahiers* made the radical suggestion that justice should be free for all, while sixteen said that justice should be cheaper.

Bailliage Cahiers

Once each village had drawn up its *cahier de doléances,* the representatives elected by the village took that document to an assembly in the bailliage, where several delegates to the Estates-General would be elected. The bailliage assembly was also responsible to draw up one *cahier,* based on its deliberations and the reading of the parish *cahiers.* The delegates sent to represent the village at the bailliage were generally men who locally held a certain amount of respect and authority. Of 901 men sent to the bailliage assemblies in northern Burgundy, 11 percent were legal professionals,[27] while 46 percent of the representatives worked in agriculture, with the biggest single category being *laboureur* (33 percent). Merchants and bourgeois together made up about a third of representatives (33 percent), and a paltry 7 percent were artisans. The bailliage *cahiers* were the work of a rural elite. A coalition between the local farming elite of *laboureurs* and the rural merchants who supplied them accounts for no less than 60 percent of those elected.

A comparison of parish and bailliage *cahiers* is instructive. Anthony Crubaugh has argued that the high costs of civil justice discouraged the poor from going to court. He further cites evidence from *cahiers* that the inhabitants of Aunis and Saintonge criticized judges for ignoring the law in order to favor the wealthy over the poor.[28] If seigneurial courts indeed served the interests of the better-off, we would expect the authors of the bailliage *cahiers,* rural elites to a man, to have fewer complaints about the judicial system than the authors of the parish *cahiers.*

In northern Burgundy the elected representatives of the villages were no more satisfied with their judicial system than the average villager was, and they complained about most of the same things. In these eight bailliage *cahiers* there are a total of 76 demands concerning justice, or 9.5 demands per *cahier,* much higher than the 2.6 demands about justice found in the parish *cahiers.*

Furthermore, there are as many grievances about seigneurial justice in the bailliage *cahiers* as there are in the parish ones. In both data sets grievances about seigneurial justice make up slightly fewer than half of the grievances on justice (about 45 percent in both cases). The grievances on seigneurial justice are similar in both samples of *cahiers*.[29] Approximately the same proportion of demands would see seigneurial judges with jurisdiction over more cases, and approximately the same small proportion of *cahiers* called for abolition of the institution. Finally, the bailliage *cahiers* complained just as stridently that lords used their courts to enforce seigneurial dues and oppress their peasants, which is to be expected given the large number of peasant representatives who participated in the preparation of these documents.

There are, however, important differences between the two sets of *cahiers*. On the one hand, parish *cahiers* contained almost four times as many grievances about procedure as did bailliage *cahiers*. Of the judicial grievances in parish *cahiers*, 14 percent called for simplified and rationalized procedure, whereas only 4 percent of general Third Estate justice grievances mentioned the reform of procedure. This suggests that the village leaders were less hurt by slow and costly procedure than most people in the village. In fact, no bailliage Third Estate *cahier* asked that justice be given "in the localities," or that an officer of the court be forced to reside locally. On the other hand, 24 percent of bailliage grievances called for general legal reforms, while only 16 percent of parish grievances mentioned general reform–a difference that is indicative of a greater degree of literacy in the bailliage assemblies than in the parish meetings, where demands were more practical.

National Comparison

Throughout France, as in northern Burgundy, parish *cahiers* made frequent mention of seigneurial justice. It is true that in Charente-Maritime only 15 percent of parish *cahiers* spoke of seigneurial justice at all, but this was in a region of weak seigneurial authority, and other studies have found a more significant presence of the institution in the *cahiers*.[30] In the bailliage of Quingey in Franche-Comté, for example, 40 percent of parish *cahiers* mentioned the institution, while eight out of fourteen parish *cahiers* (57 percent) in the bailliage of Saint-Calais in Maine spoke of seigneurial justice.[31] In a national sample, 36 percent of parish *cahiers* mentioned seigneurial justice, which makes the institution the most frequently discussed element of the seigneurie.[32] In northern Burgundy, as we have seen, about half of peasant *cahiers* mentioned seigneurial justice, a figure that is likely only slightly above average for the kingdom.

While peasant *cahiers de doléances* in northern Burgundy mentioned seigneurial justice about as often as in most other parts of France, the content of these *cahiers* is rather different from those of other regions of France that have been studied. The main difference is the frequency with which the *cahiers* anticipated the preservation rather than requesting the abolition of the institution. As we have seen, in northern Burgundy only a small minority requested abolition; the vast majority of the *cahiers* that mentioned seigneurial justice foresaw its continuation, with reforms. Giffard indicates that the majority of Breton peasant *cahiers* requested the abolition of seigneurial justice, while a minority preferred reform, and only a very small number explicitly requested maintaining the institution. Marion finds the same pattern generally in France.[33] In Aunis and Saintonge, there were almost three times as many explicit requests for the abolition of seigneurial justice as for its conservation, although if we add those *cahiers* that implicitly foresaw its preservation, the proportions are about equal.[34] In the bailliages of Troyes and Chartres, the most common grievance about the judicial system was a request for the abolition of seigneurial justice, which appears in 22 percent of parish *cahiers*.[35] Most authoritative on the question are Markoff and Shapiro, who demonstrate that a majority of *cahiers* that discussed seigneurial justice did indeed request its abolition.[36] Those foreseeing or explicitly requesting its preservation nevertheless made up a substantial minority.[37]

Peasant *cahiers* from northern Burgundy seem to be appreciably more optimistic about seigneurial justice than those from other parts of France. There are no *cahiers,* for example, that complain, as do the inhabitants of La Chapelle Huon in the bailliage of Saint-Calais, that "the majority and even almost the totality [of seigneurial courts] do not have enough officers to run them," or from Saint-Sulpice in the Dordogne that "the judge is ignorant, the clerk is whatever legal practitioner shows up, who can barely sign, the *procureur* is a schemer who generally fills all of the functions himself."[38] Still, the reforms that northern Burgundian *cahiers* request are not dissimilar to those suggested elsewhere. Markoff argues that with respect to seigneurial justice peasants were most concerned with "the curtailment of the lords' opportunities for income and power."[39] A village in northern Burgundy that specified that seigneurial courts should be preserved, adding that justice should be given in the name of the king and that lords should not be able to fire judges, was expressing largely the same idea as Lavenay in Saint-Calais, which requested that the king "suppress subaltern [i.e., seigneurial] courts; form jurisdictions by parish rather than by fief in royal justices."[40] The twin desires for justice that was closer to the village and for the reduction of the authority of lords over justice was surely almost universal among French peasants by 1789.

The parish and Third Estate assemblies of northern Burgundy had many complaints to make and suggestions to offer on the nation's and the province's legal system. But how thorough were the changes that they had in mind? After a fruitless search for Enlightenment ideology, Roger Chartier concluded that those who wrote the parish *cahiers* were much more concerned with "the criticism and minute reform of institutions than by the affirmation of the new values of the eighteenth century."[41] The idea that the parish *cahiers* of 1789 were obsessed with inconsequential reforms rather than substantive change stretches back to a seminal article by George V. Taylor. As part of his attack on the social interpretation of the Revolution, Taylor argued that parish *cahiers* were more conservative than radical–the authors did not challenge private property, and there was no evidence that people were conceiving of the revolt against seigneurial authority.[42]

Several recent works, however, have challenged the notion that the *cahiers* were largely conservative. John Markoff has presented the strongest evidence of peasant radical sentiment. He acknowledges that peasant *cahiers* were unconcerned by arbitrary authority and hindrances to economic growth (in contrast to nobles and Third Estate elites). Markoff describes the typical rural viewpoint, as expressed in the *cahiers:* the abolition of those seigneurial dues and rights that serve no visible purpose, the reform of those that do, and a fairer distribution of the burden of taxation.[43] Philippe Grateau shows that, although the *cahiers* seldom use the major watchwords of the Enlightenment, "the peasant of 1789 clearly belongs to his century. He too dreams of liberty and equality, but he expresses the desire in his own words, with a language that is closer to that of notaries than to that of the philosophes."[44]

While the *cahiers* of northern Burgundy were generally favorable to seigneurial justice, and few requested abolition, the changes they did suggest are more substantial than "minute" reform. The typical solution for the problems of seigneurial justice would keep much of the old judicial structure in place but would wrest control of seigneurial justice from the hands of the lords. With permanent judgeships it would have become significantly more difficult for lords to influence the outcome of cases. It would also mean that judges would report far less frequently to the lords and would be able fairly to decide lawsuits initiated by lords against village communities and peasant individuals. Although the same courts would continue to have the same jurisdiction over the same kinds of cases, the institution would in fact be radically transformed by curtailing the power of lords over the judges.

Conclusion

The picture we get from reading these *cahiers* is a complex one. When the king sought their opinion on the state of the kingdom of France, country dwellers naturally began to reflect on their judicial system. The comments in the *cahiers* that are specific to seigneurial justice are, on balance, more positive than negative and largely confirm that the institution functioned relatively effectively to resolve the disputes of ordinary people and keep the peace within the village. Parish assemblies did not generally call into question the fairness of seigneurial justice in cases not involving the lord. In contrast to those of some other regions of France, the peasant *cahiers* of northern Burgundy do not generally denounce judges, prosecutors, and clerks as greedy, illiterate, and incompetent. There are no fewer than seventy-seven demands that, if followed, would have increased the authority of seigneurial judges. Thirty-seven *cahiers* would give the authority of the intendant or *maîtrises* to seigneurial judges. Ten *cahiers* asked that seigneurial judges be declared sovereign to a specified amount, reducing the number of appeals. Two requested more complete police powers for seigneurial officers, and one even wanted the abolition of *prévôtal* justice and the transfer of that authority to seigneurial judges.[45] The wish to give the powers of the Waters and Forests courts and the provincial intendant to the seigneurial judge is especially important in this respect, as these were the other two main institutions that had authority over village property, finances, and affairs. The *cahiers* demonstrate the extent to which ordinary people perceived seigneurial justice as local justice and even an instrument whereby the community regulated its own affairs–this is why they requested that they only have to do with the seigneurial judge for all kinds of community affairs.

There was, however, one element that interfered with the effective regulation of communal affairs by seigneurial judges in northern Burgundian villages–the power of lords over largely competent and just legal officers. The peasant *cahiers* confirm that justice was an important tool of seigneurial authority. The authors of the *cahiers* claimed that lords used their own courts to enforce unfair dues. The threat of destitution meant, they argued, that lords could bend judges to their will. The perspective on seigneurial justice in parish *cahiers* is based on a complex distinction between the court as legal institution and the court as seigneurial institution. A full quarter of the comments on seigneurial justice decried the way the lord could use seigneurial justice to force payment of exorbitant and unfair dues and fines, but virtually no one called into question the fairness of seigneurial justice in cases that did not involve the lord.

Conclusion: Lords, Judges, and the Self-Regulating Village

Seigneurial courts functioned as the lowest rung of the state structure in eighteenth-century northern Burgundy. A primary responsibility of the institution was to see to the enforcement of royal edicts and parlementary general *arrêts,* which is why the Parlement of Dijon ordered seigneurial judges to read aloud in the village royal edicts it registered and general *arrêts* it issued that affected village life. The village community was subject to the watchful eye of the seigneurial judge on a regular basis. Local judges oversaw tax collection in the village, both through their influence over the nomination of assessors and collectors and by hearing cases when individuals challenged their *taille* assessments. The local seigneurial court was the institution of the state that was closest to the village, and ordinary people had contact with the seigneurial judge far more frequently than with royal judges, the intendant and his subdelegates, the Waters and Forests court, the *élus* of the provincial Estates, or even the royal tax collection officers. Ordinary people appreciated the seigneurial judge's intervention more than that of the other institutions, which came under attack more often and more aggressively than seigneurial justice in the parish *cahiers de doléances.*

The relative popularity of seigneurial justice compared to all other institutions of the central state points to the main theme of this book, namely that seigneurial justice functioned effectively to allow village communities to regulate themselves. When the direct interest of the seigneur was not involved, the local judge helped keep the peace and maintain a degree of harmony within the many hundreds of small villages in northern Burgundy. Ordinary people did not perceive the seigneurial court as an outside authority that would impose its will on them, but rather primarily as a means of bringing a degree of coercion in order to enforce the will of the community.

One role of the local seigneurial court was to ensure the smooth functioning of the village community by regulating communal life even when there were no disputes. In northern Burgundy the daily functioning of agriculture required active and continual collaboration between the court and the village to ensure that common land did not disappear to encroachers and to protect seeded individual fields throughout the year. The village economy–based as it was on a combination of informal loans between neighbors, the delivery of goods on credit, and the use of more formal instruments of credit in the place of cash–likewise depended on frequent recourse to the court. Probate justice protected the interests of heirs, creditors, and minors and helped enforce the wishes of the deceased and the extended family in terms of the devolution of property and the care of children. In all of these essential services the seigneurial judge worked in cooperation with those involved–families, individuals, neighbors, and the village community. The intervention of the court helped reduce the number of disputes that divided ordinary northern Burgundians, thereby making life more livable in these face-to-face communities where neighbors inevitably knew what went on next door.

The other role of the court was, of course, to resolve those disputes that disrupted village life. In these instances the seigneurial judge generally acted to help the community find balance and restore a measure of harmony. Criminal justice primarily dealt with minor violent or property disputes between neighbors. Villagers resolved most of their violent confrontations or criminal property disputes without going to court, primarily because of the relatively high costs associated with criminal justice. When they did go to court over criminal disputes, however, the local seigneurial judge generally avoided escalating the conflict by focusing on restitution, reimbursement of damages for time lost, and a public apology. In civil cases, always far more numerous than criminal cases, judges helped families settle their inheritance troubles, ensured that servants and day laborers got what they had been promised, and helped restore honor lost through public insults. When disputing, people could choose to go to court; to invoke the help of a neighbor, friend, or social superior; to hammer out a compromise; or to use binding arbitration. None of these ways of working through problems could have functioned without the possibility and threat of recourse to official justice in the person of the local seigneurial judge; in northern Burgundy village communities required the assistance of the seigneurial court to regulate their own affairs.

The use that villages, families, and individuals made of the local seigneurial court together with the active intervention of judges in village affairs suggest a new way of thinking about village communities in early modern France. We can proceed by posing a series of questions about peasant communities: Did villages seek to regulate their own affairs without the intervention of outside authorities? To what extent were they able to do so? And finally, did ordinary people perceive seigneurial justice as a state institution that was likely to impose urban, elite, civilizing justice?

There can be little question that peasant communities clung to the ideal of self-regulation, valuing the right to determine their own affairs. In northern Burgundy village communities did indeed have a great deal of control over the institutions of local life. They decided how to use common land and determined who had access to communal resources and under what circumstances. It was villagers who policed the enforcement of communal agriculture through the election each year of unpaid *messiers, vigniers,* and *prud'hommes*. The community chose its *syndic*, schoolmaster, vestry officers, and forest guard. Villages were also largely responsible to divide the tax burden as they saw fit.

In communities of only several hundred inhabitants communal behavioral norms strongly influenced the way people acted. The Christian ideals of neighborliness and honesty were of significant importance. The idea of social place in this traditional society was significant, as was the common understanding that everyone was entitled to defend his or her honor and property. There were collective means of coercion–gossip, the advice of one's elders, the opinion of the parish priest, the cold shoulder, threats and violence from groups of young men, and shaming through shivarees–all of which worked to control the activities of any who threatened to disrupt the village or violate norms.

Communities valued their ability to decide their own affairs, and village opinion held that families and individuals were better off if they could avoid falling into conflict. When conflict arose they also felt that people should resolve their disputes among themselves, or with the help of a neighbor or village elder. The gulf between ideal and reality was, however, significant, and most ordinary people realized it was not possible for villages to maintain order and peace on their own. Villages were too divided by factions to be able entirely to regulate their own affairs. The stakes of communal agriculture were too high and attempts by villagers to get a bit more pasture, wood, and hay than their share were too common for the community to be able to get along without appeal to the authority of a nonresident, nonstakeholding judge. Villagers understood that recourse to an outside authority that possessed some coercive power was essential to the smooth running of village communities.

The bourg of Sombernon devoted a significant part of its *cahier de doléances* to questions of justice. The inhabitants argued that the maintenance of seigneurial justice was crucial, explicitly criticizing the reform of 1788 for the way it weakened seigneurial courts. If they were forced to take all of their disputes to the bailliage, the costs of justice would at least double. "Being exempt from neither discord nor death," the two things that obliged them to use the courts, they demanded the preservation of seigneurial justice. While the inhabitants decried the existence of discord, they nevertheless explicitly acknowledged its inevitability and the inability of communal institutions to end it: "discord, this fury that rules all too often [*que trop partout*], frequently comes to trouble the peace and union that exists among us, by raising debates that we cannot resolve without the help of justice."[1] While few other *cahiers* were as specific about the fact that village institutions could not maintain order on their own, all of the villages that mentioned seigneurial justice in their *cahier* implicitly acknowledge the necessity of having some sort of state-backed dispute-resolving institution close to the village.

The frequent demand for seigneurial officers that met in the village was an implicit admission of the community's need for outside help to manage its affairs. Take, for example, the *cahier* of Aisey-le-Duc, the seat of a large seigneurial justice that sat over six villages and several hamlets. The fact that the clerk lived more than a league from the village caused "delay in court sessions, a slow-down in reports for farming torts, and the loss of reimbursements for damages."[2] The village of Puits complained that "it is very expensive for the inhabitants to travel often more than three leagues to obtain the justice that is due them."[3] In St.-Thibault the villagers spoke of costs that "ruin those who are forced to have court cases."[4]

Villages needed outside help to maintain order. Ordinary people appreciated the role of the court and perceived it primarily as a way of enforcing village norms. There was only one way in which the courts sought to discipline the behavior of villagers that was likely to be unpopular. As we have seen, however, the attempt to end the public consumption of alcohol was entirely ineffective, and peasants resisted it vigorously. In the *cahiers* many villages requested the abolition of the intendant, the Waters and Forests court, and *jurés priseurs*. They did not, however, ask that villages be given exclusive control over the local finances, forests, and property that these institutions controlled. Rather they indicated that the local seigneurial judge could more effectively, more cheaply, and more equitably oversee their property and their rights.

Northern Burgundian villages may have used the local court to regulate themselves to a greater extent than was the case in other regions. Elsewhere communities may have had sufficient authority to maintain order more effectively on their own. In southern France where villages were substantially larger and seigneurs less powerful than in northern Burgundy, local notables may have been able to enforce communal norms informally, appealing to the local court more rarely. Anne Zink demonstrates that villages in southern France seldom used the court against local usurpers of common land, while the same thing was ubiquitous in northern Burgundian villages.[5] In western France the desire to avoid judicial institutions may have been very strong, whether because of a spirit of independence that came from living in comparative isolation or because of the enduring strength of communal religious observation. Bernard Schnapper's analysis of litigation rates in the nineteenth century places Brittany as one of the least litigious regions of France, partially vindicating the arguments of Le Goff, Sutherland, and Quéniart.[6] More generally, it seems possible that in Protestant regions of Europe recourse to local justice may have followed quite different patterns when consistories remained active.[7]

All over Europe in the early modern period, there were nevertheless powerful forces that made it difficult for villages to regulate themselves without some help from the outside. The strongest of these was without doubt the need to regulate communal farming. The ubiquity of credit in the local, regional, and national economy was another powerful force encouraging the use of the local court, as was the necessity to see to the transfer of property between generations. Before administrative centralization, enclosure, the imposition of strict limitations on the liberty of testators, and the widespread use of cash, most villages could not hope to regulate their own affairs. Through their desire to master their own affairs coupled with the recognition that disputes and conflicts that required outside intervention were an inevitable part of life, the villages of northern Burgundy are representative of many other agricultural communities in early modern Europe. What may have been specific to northern Burgundy was just how effectively these local courts worked to settle these disputes, and how popular they were when settling cases not involving the seigneur.

Not everything seigneurial judges did was directed toward allowing the local community to function in ways that ordinary people wanted. The judicial officers were employees of the seigneur, and as such they saw to the protection of his rights and property. It is true that only a very small percentage of court cases directly involved the lord or one of his representatives, but statistics such as this obscure the important activity of the officers in administering the seigneurie. Judges and *procureurs d'office* corresponded regularly with their employers, informing them of offenses committed in their fields and forests, and passing on reports from lower seigneurial officers like forest guards and clerks. They frequently looked after the collection of the *lods et ventes* on property transfers. As soon as the seigneurial forest guard deposited his reports with the clerk, the court prosecuted the offense in the lord's interest, without even waiting for an official go-ahead. Since all deaths had to be reported to the court, and because the judge had to release the estate before the heirs could divide it, probate justice was an effective way of ensuring that the lord collected on all *mainmorte* cases.

Seigneurial courts became the crucial tool in the intensification of the seigneurial regime that occurred in the late eighteenth century. By the last decade of the ancien régime, lords were suing their vassals much more frequently than during the middle of the century, sometimes in a catchall effort to double-charge vassals who had lost receipts. Despite population growth of only about 16 percent, the number of peasants sued by their lords tripled between the periods 1750–59 and 1780–89. Above all, lords used seigneurial courts increasingly aggressively to defend their private property.

There was, then, an effort by lords to collect their dues and squeeze every possible penny from their land. This was slightly different from the "seigneurial reaction" that many historians have posited as an explanation for the causes of peasant antiseigneurial sentiment, in that it is doubtful that most peasants by the late eighteenth century were paying significantly more dues to their seigneur than their parents or grandparents had. The invention of new dues that did occur was most likely simply part of the everyday attempts by lords to get what they could from inattentive peasants, rather than representing something new in the late eighteenth century. Most lords who wanted to increase their revenue sensibly focused their attention on a rigorous collection of preexisting dues and especially a more efficient exploitation of their land and forest.

It is difficult, of course, to make a direct link between the incidence of court cases involving the lord and antiseigneurial revolt in 1789. But there is plenty of evidence that by 1789 ordinary country dwellers resented the way lords used their courts to enforce the seigneurial system. In parish *cahiers de doléances* the main criticism people had of seigneurial justice was that lords appointed the judges who then decided, often unfairly, cases between lords and vassals. Seigneurial justice did help foment the Revolution since the institution gave lords a way of limiting peasant ill will and ensuring the collection of dues. It also made seigneurial authority more visible to ordinary people through the massive increase in court cases involving wood theft and trespass.

In the last decades of the eighteenth century, northern Burgundian lords changed the way they used the institution, relying more heavily on the regular intervention of the judicial officers. Seigneurial justice also changed in more positive ways, however. Indeed, a major preoccupation of this book has been to document the ways transforming change could occur under the cover of institutional continuity. We see this in the way the new emphasis placed on the assizes transformed the experience of going to court. These reforms also brought about a change in popular attitudes toward seigneurial justice, as ordinary people increasingly came to accept the court's role in administering village life, while simultaneously challenging the lord's ownership of the right of justice.

The important ways seigneurial justice in northern Burgundy changed for the better in the second half of the eighteenth century demonstrates the impressive capacity for reform that existed in France by the eighteenth century. Burgundian elites all shared the desire to shorten procedural formalities in local courts and to make justice cheaper, and they were able to implement such changes despite the paralysis that accompanied many attempts at reform by the late eighteenth century.

Despite the resounding success of the procedural changes implemented within the province, it is unlikely that seigneurial justice could have been reformed in a way that could have satisfied its critics. By the second half of the eighteenth century, a large number of people became critical of the link between justice and seigneurialism. Both ordinary people and jurists agreed that the influence of seigneurs over justice was illegitimate. For jurists the problem was that seigneurial justice diminished the authority of the sovereign. For ordinary people this mattered too, but they were more concerned with the fines, fees, and dues they had to pay to the lord because of the intervention of judicial officers.

The link between justice and seigneurialism was, ironically, precisely what allowed these local courts to function effectively. The desire of lords to have effective administrators of their estates ensured that all courts in northern Burgundy had officers. The authors of the important procedural reforms of the 1760s and 1770s were almost all high justice seigneurs who were protecting their own revenue from their seigneuries by ensuring the functioning of local justices. The lords' self-interest is what assured the survival of seigneurial justice in northern Burgundy and led to significant reforms that benefited ordinary people as well.

The changes that peasants suggested in their *cahiers de doléances* most frequently involved diminishing the control lords had over justice. This is understandable given the role the court played in administering the seigneurie. What the authors of the *cahiers* apparently did not understand, however, was that justice would likely have ceased to interest most lords and many officers if this were the case. Making the judiciary independent from the corrupting influence of the seigneur would have reduced the income of judicial officers and therefore required an infusion of money, which the monarchy simply did not have in the 1780s. Furthermore, the parlements would not have accepted the threat to the property of lords that would have resulted from the requested reforms, as is amply demonstrated by the remonstrances of parlements to the edict of 1788.[8] The reforms to seigneurial justice that peasants requested in the *cahiers* were, in fact, more radical than they realized and would have required substantial constitutional change to implement. Whether the Revolution they helped begin actually gave villagers more and better justice than seigneurial justice provided in the last decades of the eighteenth century remains an open question for northern Burgundy.[9] But despite their appreciation for the regulatory and dispute-settlement role of local seigneurial courts, there can be little doubt that ordinary people had in fact asked for a judicial revolution.

Appendix A

Regulations read out in the Grands-Jours during the 1780s
(the *arrêts* cited are from the Parlement of Dijon unless otherwise stated)

Do not swear or blaspheme (royal ordinances of 1560, 1566, 1606, 1666).

Do not work on Sundays or holidays without permission from the lord, his officers, or the priest (*arrêt* of 12 Dec. 1697).

No dances or public games without permission of the lord or his officers.

No gambling or games of chance, even disguised. Threat of arbitrary fines. All debts contracted for gambling are null and void (royal ordinance of 1629, *arrêts* of 1710, 1730, 1732, 1774).

No lotteries to be held (300-livre fine and confiscation) (*arrêt* of 8 Aug. 1775).

Inhabitants are not to go to *cabarets* within one league of their domicile. *Cabaretiers* are not to serve locals. The owners will be fined 50 livres and are to be responsible for the fines of misbehaving locals they served.

No gatherings at the time of weddings. Fifty-livre fine for anyone carrying a gun around the time of a wedding. Cannot force the couple to pay anything (*arrêts* of 1705, 1718).

No gatherings on roads and in public places. No insults, mistreatment, or hindering of those who do commerce in grain and flour (*arrêt* of 1775).

No carrying of arms.

No hunting or trapping (*arrêts* of 1716, 1731, 1740, 1766, 1767, 1768).

When wolves are seen, the officers of the local court are to assemble the community and organize a hunt. The guns are to be distributed to men between twenty and sixty years old (*arrêt* of 1766).

Dogs are not to run free unless they have a stick of a foot and a half in length, of one-inch diameter, around their neck–threat of 10-livre fine (*arrêt* of 1768).

No fishing without permission. Do not pollute rivers with chalk and other substances. When rivers freeze over, do not cut holes in the ice and light fires (to fish).

Règlements généraux qui s'observent dans tout le ressort de la cour, et dont on fait lecture à la tenue des Grands-Jours, Nouvelle Édition: Revue, corrigée et augmentée (Dijon: Causse, 1786).

When the village owns the right of fishing, the right is to be auctioned off by the seigneurial judge in the presence of the *procureur d'office* and the village officers. The money should be used to repair the church or for other pressing needs of the community. Those who acquire the right of fishing are forbidden from passing it on to others.

No bonfires in forests and heaths–threat of corporal punishment and arbitrary fine and damages (royal ordinance of 1669).

No pasture in forests until after the fourth leaf fallen (Custom of Burgundy).

Do not steal the fruit from trees, under pretext of a traditional usage right (royal ordinance of 1669).

No sheep or goats in forests, heaths, unused land, or on the banks of forests (i.e., in empty land where communal rights exist de facto) (royal ordinance of 1669).

Do not peel bark or wood to tie together sheaves of wheat (royal ordinance of 1669, *arrêt* of 1769).

All inhabitants (i.e., all heads of households) are to attend each communal assembly (threat of 3 livres 5 sol fine). The village officers are to submit the names of the absent to the seigneurial court (1687 royal declaration).

Lords must have officers in their courts. When a position becomes vacant, they are to replace him within a month. Once a year the officers must have Grands-Jours. Everyone is to attend the Jours, without causing any disturbances, making noise, or leaving before the end of the assizes (*arrêt* of 1768).

Parish vestry-boards are to submit their accounts to the officers of the court each year after the Grands-Jours. Priests are not to have access to the money of the parish, which should be administered by the *fabriciens-receveurs-comptables* (*arrêt* of 1772).

Anyone who finds a lost article or animal must report it to the seigneurial court (Custom of Burgundy).

Do not harvest on other people's land (*arrêt* of 1764).

Communities must keep their roads in good shape. All seeded land bordering on roads or common land must be enclosed (i.e., or the owner cannot demand payment of damages from wandering animals).

There are to be no separate herds of animals (*arrêts* of 1608, 1609, 1622, 1656, 1660, 1670, 1676, 1679, 1683, 1697, 1700, 1732, 1733, 1735, 1740, 1771).

No animals are to pasture unless under guard.

No animals are to pasture in meadows between 25 March and the first cutting of hay (*arrêts* of 1771, 1774).

No pigs, sheep, goats in meadows at any time.

The communal shepherd must keep sick animals separate from the others (*arrêt* of 1714).

No geese in seeded fields or meadows.

No harvesting at night. Do not bring the harvest in until the tithe has been estimated (or at least call the tithe collectors three times loudly and in an intelligible voice).

No one (not even tithe collectors) can pass through planted fields.

No gleaning except by the old and infirm (and even then, only after the removal of all grain, tithes, and seigneurial dues). No one who is able to work should glean (royal edict of 1554, *arrêts* of 1760, 1778).

No gleaning until after the Feast of St. Rémy (1 October)(*arrêt* of 1760).

No horses or cattle in the vines at any time of the year. Local judicial officers should pursue any who do so. Do not plant beans, peas, or cabbages in the vines (*arrêt* of 1749).

No harvesting of grapes until after the *ban de vendanges,* which should be done by four experts named in an assembly of landowners, *cultivateurs,* and *forains* (nonlocal landowners) (*arrêt* of 1740).

No gleaning in vines until three days after the grape harvest is finished.

Chimneys must be maintained in good shape. *Procureurs d'office* should inspect each chimney twice a year and submit reports to the judge.

Fours banaux (communal/seigneurial ovens) should be maintained in good shape, and the lessees must heat them on the customary days. Those villagers subject to this right should not bake their dough anywhere else.

Do not carry fire in the streets. No bonfires during *veillées.* No candles in barns and stables.

Do not store manure or straw in the streets.

Any community wishing to go to court must first assemble and deliberate and then get permission from the intendant (royal declaration of 1703).

When two or more villages share rights of communal pasture over one piece of land, none of these can subtract the land from these rights without the consent of the others.

All caterpillar nests must be destroyed.

Clerks of seigneurial courts may not let the reports of pasture offenses committed in the communal forest be taken from their archives. The inhabitants must pursue any who harm the communal forests (and *procureurs d'offices* should ensure they do so) (*arrêt* of 1773).

Do not trespass in the gardens and orchards of others. Do not tear down fences or hedges.

Local tax assessors (*asséeurs*) should pass on to the local collectors only the tax rolls that have been verified by the *receveur chargé de la vérification.* Tax rolls are not subject to stamp or other paper taxes (*arrêt* of 1758).

When communities tax themselves for public works, the lord only pays taxes on his land (not on his income from seigneurial rights) (*arrêt* of 1769).

Messiers must submit reports of any *mésus* within ten days or be held personally responsible. Those selected by the community must accept (cannot refuse) the job (*arrêt* of 1771).

Messiers must not overlook any contraventions or give permission to pasture in any forbidden place.

Forest guards are personally responsible for any offenses they fail to report within two days (royal ordinance of 1669).

Anyone can enclose his land (royal edict of 1770).

Any *mésus* committed without violence is to be settled at the Grands-Jours. Describes the procedure to be used (royal ordinance of 1773).

Procedure for tax disputes (*procès en surtaux*). Only have three months to submit a disagreement with an assessment. Costs and procedure will be limited (royal declaration of 1773).

Each bailliage has a *conservateur des hypothèques.* He holds a list of mortgages (or liens). Debtors should present letters from their creditors to establish that they have paid the debts (these are required before selling the land) (royal edict of 1771).

People can take their cases to the royal or seigneurial judge, as they choose (*arrêt* of 1768).

Pregnant women must make a declaration (either to a notary or to the seigneurial judge).

Those held prisoner because their community has not paid all its taxes are to be paid on the following scale for each day spent in prison on behalf of the community: 50 sols for a *laboureur,* 40 sols for an artisan, 36 sols for a *manouvrier.* In addition, the community must pay 25 sols per day for his food (*arrêt* of 1766).

All *messiers, vigniers,* and other village officers must submit a report within ten days of any contravention to regulations (not just farming offenses, but also any against morality or anything else) (*arrêt* of 1771).

Appendix B

Class Justice? Statistical Tests

The following tests are designed to bring some statistical rigor to the question of whether seigneurial courts in northern Burgundy administered a kind of class justice, basically allowing the wealthy to sue the poor. Plaintiffs and defendants in the fourteen seigneurial courts studied were matched to their tax assessments, which were then used as a proxy for wealth levels. These assessments of plaintiffs and defendants were then subjected to a paired t-test. The null hypothesis in all cases was that the mean tax assessment (and so, approximate level of wealth) of plaintiffs was significantly different from the mean tax assessment of defendants (that on average, plaintiffs were from a significantly different social stratum than defendants). In all cases the test results indicated that the null hypothesis should be rejected.[1] There was, in other words, no significant difference between the wealth levels of plaintiffs and defendants.

The graphs that follow the statistical tests can be used more impressionistically to show the same thing. These graphs present the tax assessments of defendants plotted against the assessments of plaintiffs, with each point representing one court case. A class-justice model would lead us to expect the points to be clustered in a vertical line toward the high end of the x-axis (plaintiffs). In fact, there is little pattern, although many of the points are lower than the average assessments (of about 20 livres), and most are lower than 40 livres for both plaintiffs and defendants.

Table B.1 Paired t-test for null hypothesis: "Plaintiffs were significantly wealthier than defendants"

	Mean		Standard deviation				
	Plaintiff	Defendant	Plaintiff	Defendant	p-value	t	° of freedom
1750s, regular session	25.9	25.7	17.7	16.2	0.867	0.168	188
1750s, assizes	22.9	24.2	11.8	9.4	0.561	0.586	39
1780s, regular session	29.3	25.7	25.7	21.9	0.119	1.564	200
1780s, assizes	20.5	19.6	14.5	14.4	0.411	0.824	179

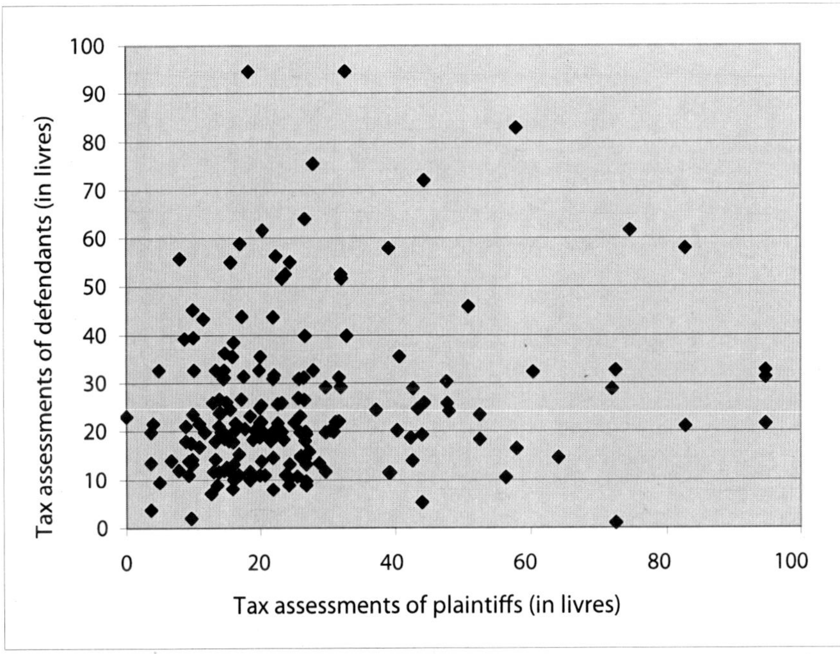

Figure B.1. Tax assessments of litigants, 1750–59, regular session

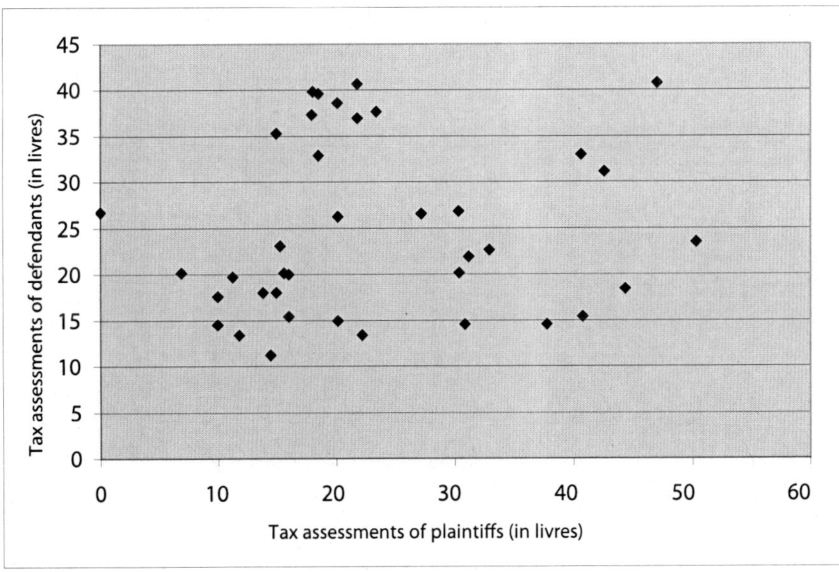

Figure B.2. Tax assessments of litigants, 1750–59, Grands-Jours

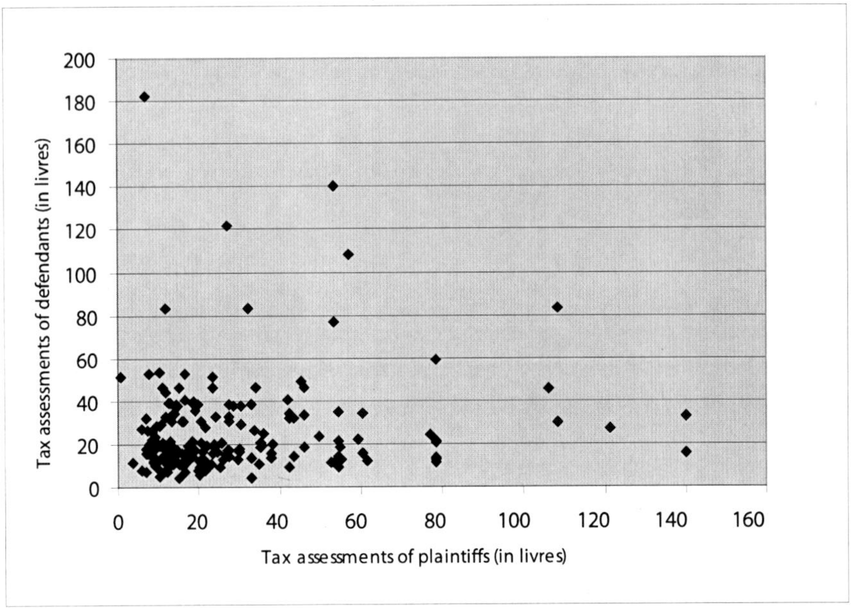

Figure B.3. Tax assessments of litigants, 1780–89, regular session

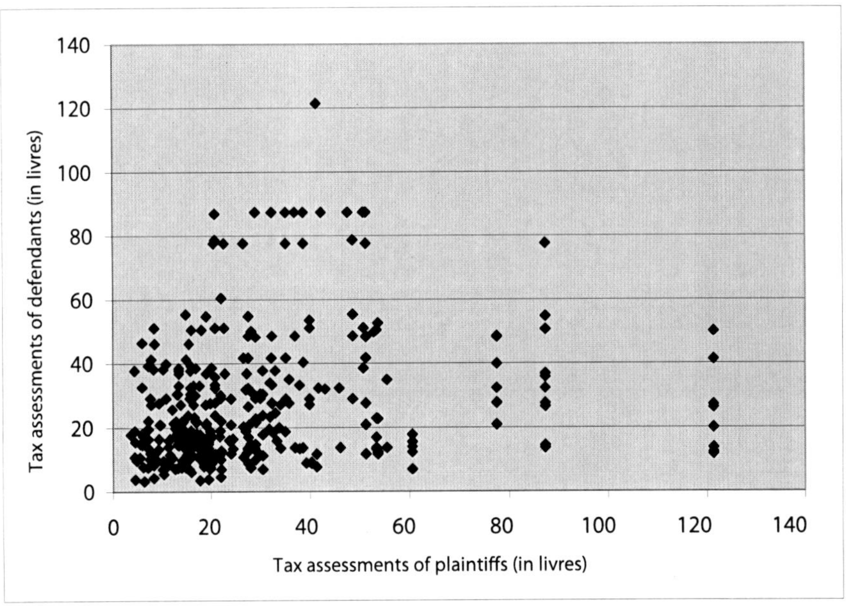

Figure B.4. Tax assessments of litigants, 1780–89, Grands-Jours

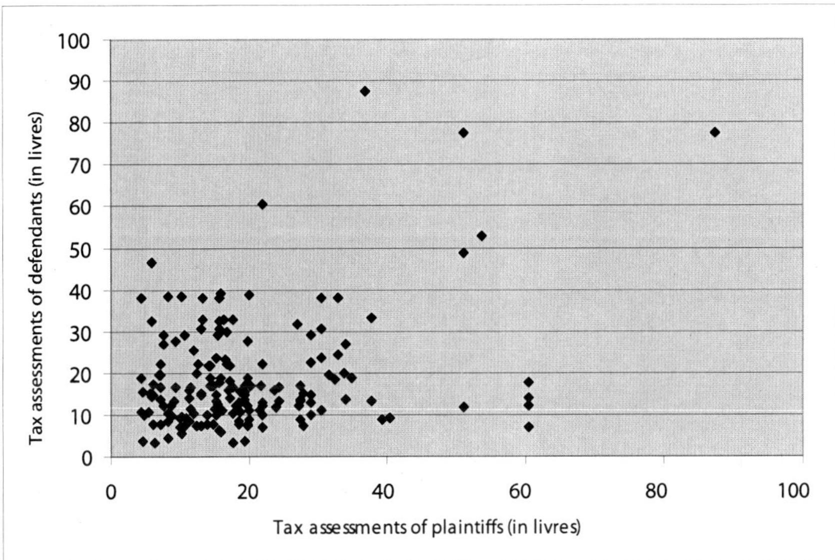

Figure B.5. Tax assessments of litigants, 1780–89, Grands-Jours, *mésus* cases excluded

Notes

Preface

1. Thomas Kuehn, *Law, Family, and Women: Toward a Legal Anthropology of Renaissance Italy* (Chicago: University of Chicago Press, 1991), 1–2.

Introduction

1. For examples of rural histories that place the seigneurie at the center, Annie Antoine, *Fiefs et villages du Bas-Maine au XVIIIe siècle: Étude de la seigneurie et de la vie rurale* (Mayenne: Éditions universitaires de l'Ouest, 1994); Anne Zink, *Clochers et troupeaux: Les communautés rurales des Landes et du Sud-Ouest avant la Révolution* (Talence: Presses universitaires de Bordeaux, 1997); Anthony Crubaugh, *Balancing the Scales of Justice: Local Courts and Rural Society in Southwest France, 1750–1800* (University Park: Pennsylvania State University Press, 2001); Michel Brunet, *Le Roussillon: Une société contre l'État, 1780–1820* (Perpignan: Minuprint, 1990); Michel Brunet, *Les pouvoirs au village: Aspects de la vie quotidienne dans le Roussillon du XVIIIe siècle* (Perpignan: Minuprint, 1990).

2. There are exceptions: both Hilton Root and Jean Gallet see the royal government working hard to limit the authority of lords. Hilton Root, *Peasants and King in Burgundy: Agrarian Foundations of French Absolutism* (Los Angeles: University of California Press, 1987), 1–20; Jean Gallet, *Seigneurs et paysans en France, 1600–1793* (Rennes: Presses universitaires de Rennes, 1999), 167–90.

3. Anatoli Ado, *Paysans en Révolution: Terre, pouvoir et jacquerie, 1789–1794* (Paris: Société des Études robespierristes, 1996), 23–25; John Markoff, *The Abolition of Feudalism: Peasants, Lords, and Legislators in the French Revolution* (University Park: Pennsylvania State University Press, 1996), 66–143; Gilbert Shapiro and John Markoff, *Revolutionary Demands: A Content Analysis of the* Cahiers de Doléances *of 1789* (Stanford: Stanford University Press, 1998).

4. Guy Lemarchand, "Troubles populaires au XVIIIe siècle et conscience de classe: Une préface à la Révolution Française," *Annales historiques de la Révolution française* 279 (1990): 36; Jean Nicolas, *La rébellion française: Mouvements populaires et conscience sociale, 1661–1789* (Paris: Éditions du Seuil, 2002), 151–220.

5. Rather than cite the many dozens of works on rural history and seigneurialism, I refer the reader to my bibliography.

6. The seigneurie was held to be made up of two components: justice and fief. The fief basically includes the land and all rights attached to it, but there was another complex of rights, dues and authority that derived from the lord's right of justice.

See Gallet, *Seigneurs et paysans,* 20–30. For an analysis from the eighteenth century, Pierre Jacquet, *Traité des justices des seigneurs, et des droits en dépendants, conformément à la jurisprudence actuelle des différents tribunaux du royaume, suivi des pièces justificatives qui ont trait à la matière* (Paris: Louis Cellot, 1764), 16–18.

7. Most of the classic histories of ancien régime peasants contain very little on seigneurial justice (Goubert and Roche on the Beauvaisie, or Le Roy Ladurie on Languedoc, for example).

8. André Chenal, *Étude sur le présidial d'Orléans, 1551–1790* (Orléans: Imprimerie de A. Gout, 1908), 13–20. Royal *présidial* courts were supposed to have at least nine judges (and each decision rendered as a court of last resort required seven sitting magistrates to hear the case). Although some courts had considerably more judges (as many as 15, as in the case of the *présidial* of Besançon), it seems unlikely that the royal infrastructure could deal with the volume of litigation likely to be produced by openfield agriculture and a local economy that ran on credit. Other works on *présidiaux* include Jean Malmezat, *Le bailli des montagnes d'Auvergne et le présidial d'Aurillac comme agents de l'administration royale* (Paris: Librairie du Recueil Sirey, 1941); Sylvain Soleil, "Le siège présidial d'Angers (1551–1790): Contribution à l'histoire administrative et judiciaire" (doctoral thesis, Université de Rennes, 1995); Édouard Everat, *La sénéchaussée d'Auvergne et siège présidial de Riom au XVIIIe siècle* (Paris: E. Thorin, 1885).

9. These figures are from *capitation* tax rolls for 1746. Departmental Archives of the Côte d'Or (hereafter cited as ADCO), C 5644. For the number of seigneurial judges in the Dijon bailliage, see below, chapter 1.

10. For example, Crubaugh, *Balancing the Scales of Justice,* 44; Brigitte Maillard, "Les hautes justices seigneuriales, agents actifs des régulations sociales dans les campagnes de la moyenne vallée de la Loire au XVIIIe siècle," in François Brizay, Antoine Follain, and Véronique Sarrazin, eds., *Les justices de village: Administration et justice locales de la fin du Moyen Âge à la Révolution* (Rennes: Presses universitaires de Rennes, 2002), 292–93.

11. André Giffard, *Les justices seigneuriales en Bretagne aux XVIIe et XVIIIe siècles* (Paris: Arthur Rousseau, 1902), 22–25, 219–22.

12. Abel Poitrineau, "Aspects de la crise des justices seigneuriales dans l'Auvergne du XVIIIe siècle," *Revue historique de droit français et étranger* 39 (1961): 554; see also A. Achard, *Une ancienne justice seigneuriale en Auvergne: Sugères et ses habitants* (Clermont-Ferrand: Impr. De Bussac, 1929), 162–63.

13. Henri Sée, *Les classes rurales en Bretagne du XVIe siècle à la Révolution* (Paris: V. Giard et E. Brière, 1906), 117–27.

14. Pierre de Saint Jacob, *Les paysans de la Bourgogne du nord au dernier siècle de l'Ancien Régime* (Paris: Société Les Belles lettres, 1960), 125–27. Also Jean Bastier, *La féodalité au siècle des lumières dans la région de Toulouse (1730–1790)* (Paris: Bibliothèque nationale, 1975), 136–37. Bastier is much more optimistic about seigneurial justice than Saint Jacob, but he does conclude that the right of justice allowed lords to influence local political matters.

15. Poitrineau, "Aspects de la crise," 569–70; also A. Combier, *Les justices seigneuriales du bailliage de Vermandois sous l'Ancien Régime* (Paris: Albert Fontemoing, 1897), 17–19, 30; Bataillon admits that most judges were legally competent, but criticizes the accumulation of judicial offices and low wages, which he blames for many of the problems associated with seigneurial justice: Jacques-Henri Bataillon,

Les justices seigneuriales du bailliage de Pontoise à la fin de l'Ancien Régime (Paris: Librairie du Recueil Sirey, 1942), 54–59; and perhaps most negative, Achard, *Ancienne justice seigneuriale,* 167.

16. Combier, *Justices seigneuriales,* 93; Emmanuel Guillaume, *Justice seigneuriale et vie quotidienne dans la vallée du Mont-Dore au XVIIIe siècle* (Clermont-Ferrand: La française d'édition et d'imprimerie, 1992), 82; Crubaugh, *Balancing the Scales of Justice,* 50.

17. Raymond Delaporte, *La sénéchaussée de Châteauneuf-du-Faou, Huelgoat et Landeleau et les juridictions seigneuriales du ressort* (Paris: A. Pedone, 1905), 193; Albert Esmein, *Cours élémentaire de l'histoire du droit français* (Paris: Larose, 1898), 416.

18. Marcel Marion, *Le garde des sceaux Lamoignon et la réforme judiciaire de 1788* (Paris: Hachette, 1905), 15.

19. Pierre Lemercier, *Les justices seigneuriales de la région Parisienne de 1580 à 1789* (Paris: F. Loviton et Compagnie, 1933), 230–78.

20. Bastier, *Féodalité au siècle des lumières,* 108–9.

21. Alain Blanchard, book review of Brizay, Follain, and Sarrazin, *Les justices de village,* originally published in *Histoire et sociétés rurales,* available at the Web site of the Association de l'histoire du village (Villannelle), http://perso.orange.fr/villanelle/Activites/Colloques/cr_justices.htm.

22. Olwen Hufton, "Le paysan et la loi en France au XVIIIe siècle," *Annales: Économies, sociétés, civilisations* 38 (1983): 679–701.

23. Giffard, *Justices seigneuriales en Bretagne,* vi.

24. Zoë A. Schneider, "The Village and the State: Justice and the Local Courts in Normandy, 1670–1740" (PhD diss., Georgetown University, 1997).

25. Soleil, "Le siège présidial d'Angers (1551–1790); Sylvain Soleil, "Le maintien des justices seigneuriales à la fin de l'Ancien Régime; faillite des institutions royales ou récupération? L'exemple angevin," *Revue historique de droit français et étranger* 74 (1996): 83–100.

26. Brizay, Follain, and Sarrazin, *Les justices de village.*

27. Benoît Garnot, "Une réhabilitation? Les justices seigneuriales dans la France du XVIIe siècle," *Histoire, économie et société* 24, no. 2 (2005): 221–32.

28. Zink, *Clochers et troupeaux,* 163–88.

29. Fabrice Mauclair, "La justice seigneuriale de la duché-pairie de La Vallière (1667–1790)" (doctoral thesis, Université de Tours, 2006).

30. Crubaugh, *Balancing the Scales of Justice.*

31. This characterization is taken from Le Roy Ladurie's analysis, which is substantially based on Saint Jacob's work. Emmanuel Le Roy Ladurie, "Révoltes et contestations rurales en France de 1675 à 1788," *Annales: Économies, sociétées, civilisations* 29 (1974): 10–12.

32. The exception is Root, *Peasants and King.*

33. See especially his conclusions. Saint Jacob, *Les paysans de la Bourgogne du nord,* 567–74. Saint Jacob relies significantly on the work of his mentor, Gaston Roupnel, especially with respect to the loss of property from the village to the city. Gaston Roupnel, *La ville et la campagne au XVIIe siècle: Études sur les populations du pays dijonnais* (Paris: Armand Colin, 1955, c. 1922), 75–90.

34. Régine Robin, *La société française en 1789: Semur-en-Auxois* (Paris: Plon, 1970), 153–55.

35. Robert Forster, *The House of Saulx-Tavanes: Versailles and Burgundy, 1700–1830* (Baltimore: Johns Hopkins University Press, 1971), 203–10.

36. Jean Bart, *La liberté ou la terre: La mainmorte en Bourgogne au siècle des Lumières* (Dijon: CNRS, 1984), 213–41.

37. Root, *Peasants and King,* 1–20.

38. For my own analysis of the (frankly limited) role of the provincial Intendant in village life, see below, chapter 6.

39. In general the rule seems to have been that depositions in summary cases belonged in the judicial calendar, while those in nonsummary cases generated a separate *procès-verbal.* Interrogations of the accused are always recorded in the form of a *procès-verbal.*

40. The handwriting is also much harder to read in the registers than in the *procès-verbaux.*

41. But the same case might not reappear for several months, with no indication of why the delay was longer than the expected fortnight.

42. ADCO B2 734/2, seigneurial justice of Meursault, Grands-Jours 21 Aug. 1780.

43. ADCO B2 734/1, seigneurial justice of Meursault, sessions 30 May 1753, 20 June 1753, 8 Aug. 1753.

44. ADCO B2 734/2, seigneurial justice of Meursault, sessions 27 Mar. 1786, 8 May 1786, 22 May 1786.

45. Population figures are taken from ADCO L 496, Amelot census, 1786. Provincial averages (and a demonstration of the accuracy of the Amelot census) can be found in Christine Lamarre, "La population de la Bourgogne à la fin du XVIIIe siècle à travers le dénombrement Amelot (1786)," *Annales de Bourgogne* 55 (1983): 65–99.

46. The convention generally governing the naming of agricultural professions in eighteenth-century Burgundy was as follows: *journaliers* were agricultural day laborers, *manouvriers* were farmers who exploited too little land or were to poor to have their own plough, and *laboureurs* were wealthy enough to possess their own plough and the animals to pull it. In addition, tax records often specify whether a farmer owned or rented his land by adding either "*propriétaire*" or "*pour autrui*" after the profession.

47. John Mackrell, "Criticism of Seigniorial Justice in Eighteenth-Century France," in John Bosher, ed., *French Government and Society, 1500–1850* (London: Athlone Press, 1973), 139–40.

Chapter 1

1. The following account is based on ADCO 29F 50, "Mémoire pour Etienne-Philibert Debadier écuyer, seigneur de Jullenay et du Fourneau, lieutenant civil au bailliage de Saulieu, intimé: Contre les habitants dudit Jullenay . . . ," *mémoire* 1741.

2. Giffard, *Justices seigneuriales en Bretagne,* 39. Giffard also notes that about half of these courts were middle and low justices, and that on average there was about one high justice for two parishes.

3. Poitrineau, "Aspects de la crise," 554.

4. Pierre Goubert and Daniel Roche, *Les français et l'ancien régime: La société et l'état* (Paris: A. Colin, 1984), 273–76. For a more nuanced view that takes into account geographical variation within France, see Jean Gallet, *Seigneurs et paysans,* 215–16.

5. There is also a possibility that some of the records of seigneurial courts were destroyed as a result of the law of 17 June 1793 requiring the destruction of "titres féodaux." For a description of the results of this law, see A. Ado, "La lutte autour de l'application de la loi du 17 juillet 1793 sur l'abolition des droits féodaux," in *La grande Révolution française* (Moscow: Sciences sociales aujourd'hui, 1989), 89–118; Albert Soboul, "De la pratique des terriers au brûlement des titres féodaux (1789–1793)," *Annales historiques de la Révolution française* 36 (1964): 149–58. Both focus primarily on the destruction of documents like *terriers* that described seigneurial rights.

6. Soleil, "Le siège présidial d'Angers," 210–11.

7. Giffard, *Justices seigneuriales en Bretagne,* 36–70; Crubaugh, *Balancing the Scales of Justice,* 7.

8. In 1790 the intendant Amelot de Chaillou prepared a report for departmental administrators that listed several administrative projects he had begun but not yet finished, such as an in-depth study of village finances. He makes no mention of any judicial investigation. ADCO C 56, *mémoire* 20 Oct. 1790.

9. "Mémoire sur l'administration de Messieurs les Intendants de Bourgogne par le Sieur Acher de Montorval ancien premier secrétaire de cette intendance," 1780. ADCO 1 Mi 270 (R1), microfilm of National Archives (hereafter cited as AN), H1 185, no. 99.

10. This figure is surprisingly accurate. The Amelot census of 1786 gives a total of 1,105,468 inhabitants of the province. ADCO L 496, Amelot *recensement.*

11. "Mémoire sur l'administration . . . ," ADCO 1 Mi 270 (R1).

12. See, for example, Bibliothèque Municipale de Dijon (hereafter cited as BM Dijon), fonds Saverot 16, 48, *arrêt* 4 Jan. 1768, "Arrêt de règlement, qui juge qu'en matière profane, l'action en complainte possessoire s'exerce ou pardevant le juge seigneurial des lieux, ou pardevant le juge royal, au choix du demandeur; le premier saisi est compétent." This parlementary *arrêt* specifies that the act was to be printed and sent into all bailliages and then from each bailliage into "all of the inferior and seigneurial justices that depend on the court," where it was to be read and published at the next session of the assizes.

13. BM Dijon, MS 1307, "Recueil," vol. 4, *arrêt* 11 May 1767.

14. ADCO B2 424/2, seigneurial justice of Aisy, Pont d'Aisy, letter 30 Nov. 1783.

15. *Almanach de la province de Bourgogne, et particulièrement de la ville de Dijon, pour l'année bissextile 1780* (Dijon: Frantin, 1780), 78–98. While this list does not indicate the area for which the courts and officers are listed, it is in fact a list of the seigneurial justices for the bailliage of Dijon. See C. Lamarre, "Carte de la province de Bourgogne au XVIIIe siècle," *Annales de Bourgogne* 55 (1983): 145–80. Lamarre's map and list of parishes is to a large extent based on *Nouvel état général et alphabétique des villes, bourgs et paroisses, villages, hameaux et écarts en dépendant compris dans les Etats du duché de Bourgogne* . . . (Dijon: Defay, 1783).

16. The figures for the number of adults are probably a little high. Christine Lamarre shows that in 1786, 32 percent of the province's inhabitants were under

the age of fifteen. About another quarter of the population was between the ages of fifteen and thirty. Furthermore, villages had a lower proportion of adults than did cities. This means the number of inhabitants of marriageable age and above may have been close to half in many rural communities.

17. See below, chapter 4, for total number of civil and criminal cases in the fourteen courts studied.

18. Crubaugh, *Balancing the Scales of Justice,* 10–11.

19. The assizes seem to have remained important primarily in eastern France. Serge Dotenwill, “Le rôle des assises et règlements de seigneurie dans la régulation sociale aux XVIIe et XVIIIe siècles: Le cas du Centre-Est de la France,” in Brizay, Follain, and Sarrazin, *Les justices de village,* 219–38. In some parts of France, particularly the west, the main purpose of the assizes was to force the villagers to acknowledge the authority of the lord. In cases where *justice foncière* and high justice were held by different lords, these assizes would not necessarily allow peasants to identify the seigneurial court they lived under. Even in these cases, however, it was almost certainly common knowledge in the village. Annie Antoine, “Justice foncière et contrôle social,” in Brizay, Follain, and Sarrazin, *Les justices de village,* 270–72.

20. ADCO B2 242/1, *cahier* of Thoisy-le-Désert, Crécey. For the other two, see ADCO B2 254/1, *cahier* of Moux; ADCO B2 254/1, *cahier* of St. Léger de Foucheret.

21. There are exceptions: crimes committed on royal roads would be tried directly in a royal court, while criminal acts committed on or immediately around the *Canal de Bourgogne* were tried in the provincial Estates.

22. Jacquet, *Traité des justices de seigneur,* 58.

23. Méllenet, “Coutumes générales du duché de Bourgogne, Comté de Charollais, et terres d’outre Saône qui n’usent de droit écrit,” 66, BM Dijon MS 2241. The document is not dated, but Méllenet was born in 1661 and died in 1722. Special thanks to Chris Corley for this reference.

24. ADCO 32F 1295, “Question à décider entre M le marquis . . .” The place of residence was generally accepted to be the parish in which a person celebrated Easter Mass, but payment of taxes as well as public knowledge also mattered.

25. Archives Municipales de Dijon (hereafter cited as AM Dijon), C 32 règlement des droits de justice de la ville sur Fontaine-lès-Dijon.

26. ADCO G 789 seigneurial papers of the Autun Cathedral, *bornage* from 1762.

27. Seigneurial papers entered the departmental archives in three ways. During the Revolution the papers of émigrés were seized by authorities for burning, but most were kept (these are housed in series E). During the last two centuries, and especially in the last few decades as interest in family history has exploded in France (as elsewhere), many noble families or current owners of *châteaux* have donated their papers to the state (most of these are housed in series F and J). Ecclesiastical seigneuries, owned by religious orders, saw all their papers seized, along with their land, during the Revolution (these are in series G and H).

28. In the *présidial* of Saintes, 90 of 197 seigneurial justices had their appeals judged in another seigneurial court, forcing litigants sometimes to go through many layers of appeal. Crubaugh, *Balancing the Scales of Justice,* 11.

29. Daguesseau, "Idée générale ou plan abrégé de l'usage que l'on pourrait faire des Estats envoyés par les Intendants pour faire former un meilleur arrangement des sièges ordinaires de la Judicature," printed in Paule Combe, *Mémoire inédit du chancelier Daguesseau sur la réformation de la justice, avec une étude préliminaire* (Valence: Imprimeries réunies, 1928), 171–73.

30. Boucher d'Argis cites a Burgundian example where cases went through seven levels of jurisdiction. From Dannemoine appeals went to the seigneurial justice of Vessanes, then through the seigneurial courts of Carizey, Flogny, and Tonnerre–from there appeals went to the bailliage of Sens and finally to parlement. Boucher d'Argis, *Cahier d'un magistrat du Châtelet de Paris, sur les justices seigneuriales et l'administration dans les campagnes* (Paris: Clousier, 1789), 3–15.

31. The exception would be cases that were evoked from the Parlement of Dijon into the Royal Council to be decided by the king. This was, however, very rare. See Albert N. Hamscher, "Parlement and Litigants in the King's Councils during the Personal Rule of Louis XIV: The Example of Cassation," in Mack P. Holt, ed., *Society and Institutions in Early Modern France* (Athens: University of Georgia Press, 1991), 209.

32. Villages suggested, for example, that appeal from seigneurial courts be forbidden in cases worth less than 50 livres. ADCO B2 254/1, *cahier* of Bard.

33. BM Dijon MS 769, "Registre des arrêts du parlement," vol. 4, deliberation of 14 Aug. 1690. The list included the "Marquisats de Chausin et Laperriere, celui de Seurre, le comté de Noyers, le Bailliage temporal de Châlon, le comte de Montreal, celui de Pontvelle, le Marquisat de Bagé, St. Rambert, St. Srolin, Vavambon, Tressort, Meximieux, Valromey, Montreval, Montellier, le Comté de St. Grivier, celui de Pontdain, le duché de Pontdevaux," and several others, unnamed.

34. ADCO B2 27/278 and 279, Parlement *arrêts-minutes,* Grand Chambre, 1785. Also ADCO B2 27/240 and 241, Parlement *arrêts-minutes,* Grand Chambre, 1755; B2 46/41 Parlement *arrêts définitifs,* Tournelle, 1785; ADCO B2 46/32 Parlement *arrêts définitifs,* Tournelle, 1755.

35. ADCO B2 118/42 and 43, *qualités* for Dijon bailliage, 1785; ADCO B2 118/21 *qualités* for Dijon bailliage, 1755.

36. See, for example, Goubert and Roche, *Les français et l'ancien régime,* 273–76.

37. I consulted the text of the edict in *Recueil des déclarations, édits, lettres patentes et arrêts du Conseil d'État du Roi, registrés au Parlement de Dijon* (Dijon: Ressayre, 1707–89). Most studies of crime in the eighteenth century contain some description of the reform of 1772. See, for example, Nicole Castan, *Justice et répression en Languedoc a l'époque des lumières* (Paris: Flammarion, 1980), 117–22. A complete explanation of how the central government implemented this reform will have to await the publication of Al Hamscher's study of legal fees in the ancien régime.

38. The figures given here for parlement and bailliages come from the final judgments of these courts and so exclude all crimes that started in court and ended before a final judgment (while the figures from seigneurial courts include all criminal trials that continued past initial summons). It is doubtful, however, that many major crimes were put out of court in parlement, since it was mandatory for parlement to hear appeals of all capital cases from seigneurial courts. The case, then, would either end with a confirmation, modification, or repeal of the decision of the seigneurial

judge. Doubtless in the bailliage, however, many more minor criminal affairs began in court and then were settled informally.

39. Eric Wenzel, "Le monitoire à fin de révélation sous l'Ancien Régime: Normes juridiques, débats doctrinaux et pratiques judiciaires dans le diocèse d'Autun (1670–1790)" (doctoral thesis, Université de Bourgogne, 1999), 117, 301–8.

40. This is true with the caveat that after 1772 most major criminal cases were investigated by the seigneurial court and then passed on to the royal court for judgment.

41. Guyot, *Répertoire universel et raisonné de jurisprudence civile, criminelle, canonique et bénéficiale; ouvrage de plusieurs jurisconsultes, mis en ordre et publié par M Guyot, écuyer, ancien magistrat* (Paris: Visse, 1784), 74–75, s.v. "bailli, bailliage," written by Boucher d'Argis.

42. Ibid., 615, s.v. "Juges des Seigneurs," written by M. H., *avocat au Parlement,* and M. Merlin.

43. Middle and low justices did have financial ceilings, and centuries of inflation had stripped them of all authority. By the eighteenth century middle and low justice had fallen into disuse; there may have been a handful of active low and middle justices in northern Burgundy, but their judicial activity was limited almost exclusively to fines for police matters rather than civil affairs between individuals. My research in the archives of northern Burgundy did not uncover any active middle or low justices, although I did not undertake a rigorous search for such courts. There may have been a few instances where the fines were handed out by a low justice and civil and criminal cases were heard in another local high justice. For an explanation of high, middle, and low justice, see Jean Bouhier, *Les coutumes du duché de Bourgogne avec les anciennes coutumes, tant générales, que locales, de la même province, non encore imprimées, et Les observations de M. Bouhier, Président à Mortier honoraire au Parlement de Bourgogne, & de l'Académie Française* (Dijon: Arnaud Jean-Baptiste Auge, 1742–1746), 2:16–31.

44. The amount involved was available for 370 of 1,008 cases in regular session in the 1780s and 295 of 964 cases in the 1750s.

45. ADCO B2 1048, seigneurial justice of the St. Bénigne religious chapter, 1 Apr. 1786.

46. ADCO B2 734/2, seigneurial justice of Meursault, 27 Apr. 1789.

47. "Observations générales sur la population de l'ancienne généralité de Dijon, document présenté par Pierre Bodineau," *Mémoires de la Société pour l'histoire du droit et des institutions des pays bourguignons, comtois et romands* (hereafter cited as *MSHDB*) 52 (1995): 193–203.

48. ADCO B2 101/3, bailliage of Dijon, deliberations of the community of *procureurs,* deliberation of 18 Jan. 1782.

49. ADCO B2 111/46, bailliage of Dijon, civil and criminal sentences; B2 118/42–43, bailliage of Dijon, civil *qualités* for 1785.

50. ADCO L 496, Amelot census.

51. See chapter 6 for a fuller discussion of litigation rates and the problems associated with them.

52. The original edict was given in 1693. "Edit du Roi, concernant les officiers des justices seigneuriales, donné à Versailles au mois de mars 1693," in Jacquet, *Traité des justices de seigneur,* appendix, xiii–xviii. The edict says that much disorder had slid into the administration of justice, the result of hiring untrained judges without

character. Seigneurial judges were to be sworn in at the royal court of their choice. In February 1766 the Parlement of Dijon issued an *arrêt* ordering execution of this edict. The parlementaires cited the failure of the original edict as their reason for reissuing it. "Arrêt du Parlement qui ordonne que l'édit du mois de Mars 1693, concernant la prestation de serment par tous ceux qui possèdent des Offices de Judicature, sera exécuté selon sa forme et teneur." BM Dijon, fonds Saverot 16.

53. ADCO B 12123–12144, Parlement of Dijon, *enregistrement des édits et lettres patentes,* 1700–89. For the bailliage of Arnay-le-Duc, B2 235/66–89, *sentences et procès-verbaux,* 1709–90.

54. *Almanach de la province de Bourgogne,* 78–98.

55. I used tax rolls from the following cities and villages: Aignay-le-Duc, Arc-sur-Tille, Beaumont, Boussenois, Bretigny, Champagne-sur-Vingeanne, Crécey, Dijon, Fixey, Fixin, Fleury-sur-Ouche, Fontaine-Française, Gemeaux, Genlis, Gissey-sur-Ouche, Issurtille, Mâlain, Messigny, Mirebeau, Orville, Pontailler, Pont-de-Pany, St. Julien, Salives, Saulx-le-Duc, Selongey, Sombernon, Spoy, Talant, Ursy, Velars, Velars-sur-Ouche, Viévigne, and Villey-sur-Thil. The thirty-four officers I list as unknown either were not found in the tax rolls of the city or village where the *Almanach* placed them or were simply listed as *greffier, procureur d'office,* or judge.

56. Arguing in court was a privilege reserved for *avocats.* David A. Bell, *Lawyers and Citizens: The Making of a Political Elite in Old Regime France* (Oxford: Oxford University Press, 1994), 30. On *procureurs,* see Louis Groustel, *Essai sur la profession de procureur* (Dijon: n.p., 1749).

57. A word on the difference between "*procureur d'office*" and "*procureur fiscal*": Eric Wenzel suggests that purists insisted that "fiscal" referred to those working in high justice courts, while "d'office" was for middle and low justice. I have not seen this distinction made in the writing of legal theorists. In any case, by the eighteenth century all active seigneurial courts were high justices. Wenzel, "Le monitoire à fin de révélations," 117. An anonymous manuscript written by a magistrate of the Parlement of Dijon and dated 1748 claims that the parlement in 1658 passed a general *arrêt* forbidding the use of the title *procureur fiscal,* insisting rather on the title *procureur d'office.* BM Dijon MS 2292, "Recueil alphabétique d'arrêts et de délibérations secrètes du Parlement de Dijon avec des notes sur beaucoup d'arrêts et délibérations par M . . . ," s.v. "procureur d'office." The same manuscript, with the slightly different title "Recueil des délibérations secrètes du Parlement de Bourgogne" and the addition of the date 1748, can be found in the ADCO B 12071/8, Parlement of Dijon. While "*procureur fiscal*" does occasionally appear in documents from the eighteenth century, in northern Burgundy *procureur d'office* is indeed much more common.

58. On venality of royal offices the standard work is Roland Mousnier, *La vénalité des offices sous Henri IV et Louis XIII* (Paris: Presses universitaires de France, 1971). On the eighteenth century see William Doyle, *Venality: The Sale of Office in Eighteenth-Century France* (Oxford: Clarendon Press, 1996). On the illegality of venality of seigneurial offices, see Charles Loyseau, *Les oeuvres de M. Charles Loyseau, Parisien: Contenans les cinq livres du droit des offices, avec autres livres, tant des seigneuries, des orders, du déguerpissement et délaissement par hypothèque, que la garantie des rentes, et des abus des justices de village* (Paris: Pierre Rocolet, 1640), 544–45.

59. Giffard said that in Brittany many judges owned their offices, and that in some big seigneuries the judgeship was actually an inheritable right. Giffard, *Justices*

seigneuriales en Bretagne, 88–90. In Normandy it seems that venality of seigneurial offices was also quite common. Schneider, "Village and the State," 300–302, 400.

60. Mauclair, "Justice seigneuriale de La Vallière," 279–81.

61. ADCO B 12135, register of Parlement; 7 Dec. 1765. One case hints vaguely about "fees" the judge paid, but these could have been something as simple as stamp taxes on the contract granting him the office.

62. Article 27 of the Ordinance of Roussillon specified that a seigneurial judge could be removed without justification so long as he had neither purchased the office nor been given it in return for services rendered. See Esmein, *Cours élémentaire,* 419. On one hand, Loyseau held that normally a lord could remove his officers without good reason, but that it was much more difficult to destitute an officer who had bought the office. Venality was not only a source of revenue for the lord but also a form of protection for the officer. On the other hand, Loyseau also recognized that in reality lords often freely fired even judges who had purchased their offices. Loyseau, *Oeuvres,* 569.

63. Henry Forestier, "Petits documents: Ce qu'était la situation du procureur fiscal d'une petite justice de l'Auxerrois au XVIIIe siècle," *Annales de Bourgogne* 10 (1938): 139–40.

64. ADCO E 1410, *manuel* of the seigneurie of Foncegrive.

65. ADCO B 12135, *registres* of Parlement.

66. Benoît Garnot, citing C. Lamarre, who used the lists provided in the *Almanach,* claims that in 1769 fully 40 percent of officers (judges, *procureurs d'office,* and clerks) in the bailliage of Dijon resided in the village they judged. This is based, however, on a misreading of Lamarre, who shows that of 269 seigneurial officers within the bailliage of Dijon, 166 lived in Dijon. She gives no indication of what proportion of the remaining 103 lived in a village they judged. Benoît Garnot, "Justices seigneuriales et régulation sociale: L'exemple bourguignon au XVIIIe siècle," in Brizay, Follain, and Sarrazin, *Les justices de village,* 199; Christine Lamarre, "Quelques observations sur le fonctionnement des bailliages en Bourgogne et Lyonnais au XVIIIe siècle," in Benoît Garnot and Rosine Fry, eds., *Ordre moral et délinquance de l'antiquité au XXe siècle, actes du colloque de Dijon* (Dijon: Éditions universitaires de Dijon, 1994), 431.

67. Schneider, "Village and the State," 484–593.

68. ADCO E Dépôt 14/17, communal archives, Ampilly-lés-Bordes, *État des sections;* ADCO C 6887, tax rolls, Ampilly-lés-Bordes.

69. In one case it is the widow of the judge who is listed in the 1787 tax rolls, and since these lists do not exist for earlier years, it is impossible to say if his widow acquired the land before or after his death. She is listed as "veuve du Sieur Jérôme Louhet, bourgeoise à Auxonne." ADCO C 6452, tax rolls, Villerrottin.

70. ADCO C 6036, tax rolls, Montot.

71. "Délibération des procureurs au bailliage du Charollet du 18 mai 1775," recorded in the registers of the Dijon Parlement, *Recueil d'arrêts du Parlement de Dijon,* vol. 5. The officials of the bailliage of Charolles agreed with their deliberation, which was then put into effect.

72. ADCO B2 101/3, bailliage of Dijon, deliberations of the community of *procureurs,* deliberation of 26 Jan. 1782.

73. ADCO B2 101/3, bailliage of Dijon, deliberations of the community of *procureurs,* deliberation of 26 Dec. 1786.

74. This figure is highly approximative, being based on distances cited in leagues in Abbé Claude Courtépée and Edme Beguillet, *Description générale et particulière du duché de Bourgogne, précédé de l'abrégé historique de cette province,* 5 vols. (Dijon: Frantin, 1774–85). The location of the *chef-lieu* to which villagers would have traveled can be found in *Nouvel état général et alphabétique des villes.* I verified the distances using twenty-first-century cartographic software, and Courtépée and Beguillet's estimates seem to be conservative (that is, they underestimated the distances).

75. For an explanation of the dispute-resolving functions of the annual assizes (Grands-Jours), see below, chapter 3.

76. Cited in O. Morel, *Les assises ou Grands-Jours dans les justices seigneuriales de Bresse à la fin de l'Ancien Régime (1768–1788)* (Bourg: Imprimerie du Courrier de l'Ain, 1935), 6.

77. "Arrêt du Parlement concernant les Assises de Bresse," *Recueil d'Arrêts du Parlement de Dijon.,* vol. 5 (BM Dijon, MS 1308, 29 Apr. 1771).

78. ADCO G 1449, private seigneurial papers, seigneurie of Montot, leases of the seigneurie. The leases here are dated 7 Apr. 1709, 5 Sept. 1732, 7 Sept. 1741, 1 Sept. 1750, 14 Sept. 1759, 4 Apr. 1777.

79. ADCO E 1410, *manuel* of the seigneurie of Foncegrive.

80. Even this exceptionally well paid position could hardly have supported a judge, since 500 livres was still less than the amount tithe-holders were required to pay parish priests. ADCO 10F 867, private seigneurial papers, barony of Pagny. This folder contains lists of receipts given to the lord for the wages. For example: "Je, soussigné, déclare avoir reçu du Sieur Vaurey, bourgeois à Pagny-Chateau [the seigneurial agent] la somme de 300 livres pour l'année échue le décembre dernier des gages que Madame la Duchesse de Châtillon a attribué à la place de lieutenant en son bailliage [some large seigneurial courts in Burgundy had the right to refer to themselves as seigneurial bailliages] de Pagny, dont elle m'a honoré. À Seurre le 10 février 1786. Signé Poireau."

81. Livre de travail de M. Jean Finot, avocat à Semur. BM Dijon, MS 1942. Thanks to Robert Schwartz for pointing this document out to me.

82. *Réflexions sur les réformes dans l'administration de la justice* (n.p., 1788), 2.

83. See Jeremy Hayhoe, "Droit, pratique et seigneurie: Le travail quotidien de Jean Finot, avocat, juge et agent seigneurial à Semur-en-Auxois," *Revue historique du droit français et étranger* 85, no. 3 (2007).

84. ADCO B2 101/3, bailliage of Dijon, deliberations of the community of *procureurs,* deliberation of 18 Jan. 1782, containing a copy of the *mémoire* sent to the Parlement of Dijon.

85. *Réflexions sur les réformes,* 2–4.

86. Jérôme Pétion de Villeneuve, "Les lois civiles et l'administration de la justice ramenées à un ordre simple et uniforme," in *Oeuvres de Jérôme Pétion, membre de l'Assemblée Constituante, de la Convention Nationale, et Maire de Paris* (Paris: Garnery, 1793), 1:188.

87. Hayhoe, "Droit, pratique, seigneurie."

88. Leonard R. Berlanstein, *The Barristers of Toulouse in the Eighteenth Century (1740–1793)* (Baltimore: Johns Hopkins University Press, 1975), 23–27.

89. Frédérique Pitou, *La robe et la plume: René Pichot de la Graverie, avocat et magistrat à Laval au XVIIIe siècle* (Rennes: Presses universitaires de Rennes, 2003), 85–126.

90. See below, chapter 5, for a description of contemporary criticisms of seigneurial justice.

91. *Nouvel état général et alphabétique des villes,* s.v. "Sainte-Sabine."

Chapter 2

Epigraph. ADCO 10F 1146, private seigneurial papers, barony of Pagny, correspondence from 1727.

1. ADCO B 12145, Dijon Parlement, *registres.*

2. Giffard, *Justices seigneuriales en Bretagne,* 226–52; Poitrineau, "Aspects de la crise," 560, 569; Zink, *Clochers et troupeaux,* 165–66.

3. ADCO G 1449, seigneurial papers for Montot.

4. "Édit du Roi, concernant les frais des procédures en matière criminelle dans les Justices seigneuriales," in *Recueil du Parlement de Dijon,* volume for Maupeou years, 03–1772.

5. This general *arrêt* was subsequently repeated at least twice. BM Dijon MS 1307, Recueil des arrêts du Parlement, vol. 4, 5 Dec. 1765; vol. 5, 23 Sept. 1775 and 16 Oct. 1779.

6. ADCO C4, intendant, justice. This was a (rare) example of the exercise of the right of *prévention,* which allowed royal courts to take cases from seigneurial courts only if the seigneurial court failed to pursue the case. Jean Riollot, *Le droit de prévention des juges royaux sur les juges seigneuriaux* (Paris: Rousseau, 1931).

7. ADCO 10F 831, private papers, barony of Pagny, "État des frais de la procédure instruite en la justice de Pagny contre André Truchart et consorts en 1769."

8. It is important to emphasize again that these figures are the amounts paid by the lord to prosecute criminal cases and do not reflect the amounts that the judicial officers were paid.

9. See below, chapter 3.

10. ADCO B2 SUP 23 écrous, bailliage of Arnay-le-Duc; ADCO B2 SUP 276, écrous, bailliage of Beaune. The list is actually much longer than 153 (554 *écrous* for the 1780s in these two bailliage prisons), but I excluded soldiers locked up for contravening military law at the request of the prevotal court of the *maréchaussée,* mostly deserters.

11. ADCO L 176–correspondence of districts to the department, "Mémoire de l'état des prisons et hôpitaux du District de Châtillon-sur-Seine."

12. The situation is apparently different in the Touraine, where many seigneurial courts had both a prison and a courthouse in the village. The justices of St.-Christophe and Château-la-Vallière within the *duché-pairie* of La Valière both had two-story buildings with the courtroom above the prison. Mauclair, "Justice seigneuriale de La Vallière," 170–85.

13. BM Dijon MS 2241, Méllenet, "Coutumes générales du duché de Bourgogne."

14. Edme La Poix de Fréminville, *Traité général du gouvernement des biens et affaires des communautés d'habitants des villes, villages et parroises du Royaume* (Paris: Gissey, 1760), 577.

15. On confiscation for criminal acts, see Pascal Bastien, "La 'seconde punition': Quelques remarques sur la confiscation des biens dans la coutume de Paris au XVIIIe siècle," in Benoît Garnot, ed., *Justice et Argent: Les crimes et les peines pécuniaires du XIIIe au XXIe siècle* (Dijon: Éditions universitaires de Dijon, 2005), 271–80.

16. Antoine d'Espeisses, *Les oeuvres de M. Antoine d'Espeisses, advocat et jurisconsulte de Montpellier,* vol. 3, *Où toutes les plus importantes matières du Droit Romain sont méthodiquement expliquées, et accommodées au Droit Français; confirmées par les arrêts des cours souveraines et enrichies des plus utiles doctrines des auteurs anciens et modernes* (Lyon: Jean-Antoine Huguetan & Marc-Antoine Ravaud, 1664), 119–27. D'Espeisses adds that creditors and family members with rights of usufruct over the property (but not claims of inheritance) preceded the lord in distribution of the property.

17. Jean Bart, *Histoire du droit privé de la chute de l'Empire romain au XIXe siècle* (Paris: Montchretien, 1998), 325–35; Marc Pena, "Des libéralités accordées aux bâtards en ancien droit français," *MSHDB* 52 (1995): 49–81.

18. ADCO B2 46/41 criminal *arrêts définitifs* for the Tournelle (for 1785), 13 Oct. 1785. Bastien was suspected of having "done violence to *des personnes du sexe* in their homes."

19. François de Boutaric, *Traité des droits seigneuriaux et des matières féodales* (Toulouse: Jean-François Forest, 1767), 512–60; d'Espeisses, *Oeuvres,* 3:129–40.

20. Mining rights, on the other hand, belonged to the king. D'Espeisses, *Oeuvres,* 3:129–32.

21. Boutaric, *Traité,* 565–66.

22. This also explains the rights of confiscation and bastardy. By committing a crime heinous enough to merit capital punishment, the criminal effectively cut himself off from the human community and as a wild beast became property of the lord. By the same token, an illegitimate child seemed similarly to be the result of a union that had more to do with uncontrolled nature than with proper human relations.

23. See ADCO B2 1032/1, seigneurial justice of St. Bénigne, sessions 30 Dec. 1754, 15 Jan. 1755, 18 Jan. 1755, 8 Feb. 1755, 20 Feb. 1755. In this case the *fermier* refused to take charge of a wandering horse because it was covered in sores. They later found the horse's owner, who had to pay for the horse's upkeep and treatment.

24. ADCO 1H 856, order of St. Bénigne, seigneurial papers, statement of the revenue of the *ferme,* 17 Apr. 1789.

25. Although in some parts of France hunting may have been a domanial right, attached to the land rather than to justice (and therefore belonging also to the feudal lord who has no rights of justice), in Burgundy it was clear that it was attached to justice. See, for example, Jean Henriquez, *Code des seigneurs hauts-justiciers et féodaux* (Paris: Nyon, 1780), 242.

26. Boutaric thought that all nobles were allowed to hunt on their own land. This may have been tolerated in some instances but was still illegal. Boutaric, *Traité,* 532.

27. ADCO B2 452/1, justice of Belleneuve.

28. Giffard, *Justices seigneuriales en Bretagne,* 239–45; Crubaugh, *Balancing the Scales of Justice,* 61–76.

29. Ordinance of 1667, titre 24, art. 11; cited in Edme La Poix de Fréminville, *La pratique universelle pour la rénovation des terriers et des droits seigneuriaux* (Paris: Despilly, 1762), 1:443. See also Disson, *Précis des ordonnances, édits, déclarations, lettres-*

patentes et règlements, dont les dispositions sont le plus en usage dans le ressort du Parlement de Bourgogne (Dijon: Jean-Baptiste Capel, 1781), s.v. "Juges des Seigneurs."

30. Forster, *House of Saulx-Tavanes,* 61–108. See Crubaugh, *Balancing the Scales of Justice,* 61–75, for a helpful analysis of the interaction between lords and prosecutors.

31. ADCO 10F 1146, private seigneurial papers, barony of Pagny, correspondence from 1727.

32. ADCO 44F 285, private papers of the family of Perrard, correspondence from 1737.

33. ADCO B2 734/2, justice of Meursault, Auxey-le-Grand, Auxey-le-Petit, session 14 Jan. 1785.

34. These letters are spread throughout documents that are virtually uninventoried in series E, F, and J.

35. ADCO 35F 284, private seigneurial papers, Thenissey, "État des extraits délivrés à M. le marquis de Clugny."

36. ADCO 10F 867, private seigneurial papers, barony of Pagny, receipts for 1785–86.

37. ADCO 10F 1153, private seigneurial papers, barony of Pagny, letter 27 May 1781.

38. This suggestion, the *procureur d'office* said, would bring about "the condemnation of the delinquents to the legal expenses." ADCO 10F 1153, private seigneurial papers, barony ofPagny, letter 27 May 1781.

39. ADCO E 24/8, seigneurial papers, Saffre, letter 20 Oct. 1763.

40. ADCO 18J 1, Vaillant de Meixmoron papers, seigneurie of Agencourt, letter 8 Oct. 1777.

41. The case is more complicated than simple rebellion against a well-established seigneurial right. The *terrier* made no mention of the lord's right to a monopoly on the grape harvest for the first day. The lord and his agent claimed that this was an implicit right, that "these things are due even when the *terrier* does not specify them [*ces choses sont dues sans que le terrier en fasse mention*]." The inhabitants argued this was not an implicit right attached to justice, but rather one that had to be established by title. ADCO 18J 1, private seigneurial papers of Agencourt, letter 8 Oct. 1777.

42. Archives de la ville de Beaune, *Les cahiers de doléances du tiers état beaunois* (n.p., n.d.).

43. For a comparison of rates of litigation between lords and peasants, see Bastier, *Féodalité au siècle des lumières,* 124–27; Zink, *Clochers et troupeaux;* Sée, *Classes rurales en Bretagne,* 125; Giffard, *Justices seigneuriales en Bretagne,* 245–52. In the southwest, Crubaugh has found percentages of cases involving lords that seem about as high as those in northern Burgundy, but overall caseloads were substantially lower in the courts analyzed by Crubaugh, so per capita lawsuits involving lords would be lower too. Crubaugh, *Balancing the Scales of Justice,* 61–68.

44. Seventy of these cases were for theft of wood, and sixty-seven involved pasture offenses.

45. Nicolas, *Rébellion française,* 154.

46. ADCO B2 1220/7, seigneurial justice of Senailly, session 25 June 1788.

47. ADCO B2 458/3, seigneurial justice of Billey, sessions 13 Jan. 1759, 15 Jan. 1759, 21 Jan. 1759, 30 Jan. 1759, 15 Feb. 1759, 7 May 1759.

48. Hamish Graham, "Exercice d'équilibre. Gardes forestiers, autorité seigneuriale et société rurale au XVIIIe siècle," in Claire Dolan, ed., *Entre justice et justiciables: Les auxiliaires de la justice du Moyen Âge au XXe siècle* (Quebec: Les presses de l'Université Laval, 2005), 213–14.

49. See "Ordonnance des Eaux et Forêts de 1669," Titre XXX (Des Chasses), art. 3, in Isambert et al., eds., *Recueil général des anciennes lois françaises* (Paris: Belin-Leprieur, 1829), 18:295–96.

50. ADCO E 852, private seigneurial papers of Fontaine-en-Duesmois, "État des revenues et situation de la terre de Fontaine-en-Duesmois," 10 Mar. 1777; ADCO B 10918, Chambre des Comptes, *reprise de fief et dénombrement,* Flée and Allerey, 9 Dec. 1702.

51. ADCO C 8068, contrôle des actes, bureau de Baigneux-les-Juifs, 1783. I also looked through the records of other *bureaux,* without finding a single *retrait féodal* from the late eighteenth century.

52. See, for example, ADCO E 2084 bis, "Manuel des cens, seigneurie of La Motte et Belleneuve," written in the 1740s. This document lists some cases of *retrait féodal* to justify the disappearance of a few land parcels from the *cens* roll. Robert Schwartz describes the highly successful use of *retrait féodal* by Nicolas Philippe Berbis over the village of Tart-le-Bas. Robert M. Schwartz, "The Noble Profession of Seigneur in Eighteenth-Century Burgundy," in Jay Smith, ed., *The French Nobility in the Eighteenth Century: Reassessments and New Approaches* (University Park: Pennsylvania State University Press, 2006).

53. ADCO B2 1220/7, seigneurial justice of Senailly. Senailly (including the nearby hamlet of St. Germain-lès-Senailly) in 1786 had a population of 762. ADCO L 496, Amelot census of 1786. I have no way of knowing its population in the 1750s, but in 1757 tax rolls there were 94 hearths. ADCO C 7373, tax rolls of Senailly, 1757.

54. ADCO B2 423/1, seigneurial justice of Aisy-sous-Thil. In 1786 the population of Aisy (including the outlying hamlet of Pont-d'Aisy) was 325. ADCO L 496, Amelot census of 1786. In 1758 there were 71 hearths in the tax rolls. ADCO C 7228, tax rolls of Aisy and Pont-d'Aisy, 1758.

55. ADCO B2 734/2, seigneurial justice of Meursault, sessions 10 July 1786, 24 July 1786, 11 Dec. 1786, 8 Jan. 1787.

56. ADCO B2 1220/7, seigneurial justice of Senailly, session 7 May 1789.

57. ADCO 1H 1721, religious order of St. Bénigne, seigneurial papers, Epagny, "Manuel et déclaration des terres, droits et revenues de la seigneury d'Epagny conforme aux précédentes dont la dernière est de 1750," undated.

58. ADCO B2 1077/1, seigneurial justice of Ampilly-lès-Bordes, sessions 7 Feb. 1784, 8 May 1784.

59. Personal communication, based on James Collins's analysis of ADCO C 4824, *recherches de feux,* bailliage de Châtillon. The data for Fontaine-en-Duesmois come from this document.

60. ADCO B2 1077/1, seigneurial justice of Ampilly-lès-Bordes, sessions 7 Feb. 1784, 8 Apr. 1784.

61. ADCO 1H 802, religious order of St. Bénigne, seigneurial papers, Saulon-la-Chapelle, folder of receipts for *cens* owed and paid for the eighteenth century. For Bussy-le-Grand, the *recherche des feux* indicates that the inhabitants paid 280 livres in seigneurial *taille* and "*cens* that are a similar amount." ADCO C 4824, *recherche des feux,* bailliage of Châtillon.

62. At the end of twenty-nine years the seigneurial due did not expire. Unlike almost all other kinds of rights and property, seigneurial dues were considered "imprescriptible" and thus never expired. Lords were forbidden from collecting dues beyond twenty-nine years in the past, but the failure to collect dues over a long period did not extinguish them in the sight of the law. This is why some *cahiers* from 1789 requested that seigneurial rights be made "prescriptible" after thirty years (i.e., that they expire through nonuse). See, for example, ADCO B2 135/1, *cahiers de doléances,* Dijon bailliage, *cahier* of the Third Estate of Dijon. Jean Bart, *La Révolution française en Bourgogne* (Clermont-Ferrand: La Française d'édition et d'imprimerie, 1996), 52–53.

63. ADCO B2 734/2, seigneurial justice of Meursault, sessions 3 Jan. 1785, 24 Jan. 1785, 14 Feb. 1785, 28 Feb. 1785, 14 Mar. 1785, 23 May 1785, 8 Aug. 1785, 20 Mar. 1786, 8 May 1786, 22 May 1786.

64. ADCO 1H 1721, religious order of St. Bénigne, "Manuel et déclaration des terres."

65. ADCO B 10918, Chambre des Comptes, *reprise de fief* for Allerey, 9 Dec. 1702.

66. ADCO G 1447, seigneurial papers of the religious order of Messieurs de la Sainte Chapelle de Dijon, declarations of tithe for Montot, 1730.

67. Markoff, *Abolition of Feudalism,* 157–58.

68. ADCO B2 1077/1, seigneurial justice of Ampilly-lés-Bordes, session 23 July 1783. The low amount of the fine suggests that Languereau presented evidence of extenuating circumstances, such as the threat of inclement weather.

69. Saint Jacob, *Paysans de la Bourgogne du nord,* 119.

70. Ibid., 32–38, 43–44.

71. There is no judgment of the court, since the *fermier* did not know who was responsible for the "thefts." The court used a *monitoire* to encourage witnesses to come forward. Several inhabitants were eventually fingered by the twenty-five witnesses who testified, but the judge's interrogation centered around the wood theft rather than the *tierce.*

72. Six days of *corvées* per year was the maximum that the Parlement of Dijon allowed. A few seigneurial documents mention numbers higher than six, but Saint Jacob indicates that the extra days were probably not collected. Saint Jacob, *Paysans de la Bourgogne du nord,* 113.

73. ADCO 1H 908, religious order of St. Benigne, seigneurial manual of Bellefond, 1771; ADCO C 2459, *reprises de fief,* Billey and Villerrottin, 1732; Archives of the Hôpital-Général de Dijon, B1/11, leases of the seigneurie of Ancey, 14 June 1778.

74. ADCO B2 734/2, seigneurial justice of Meursault, sessions 24 Jan. 1785, 31 Jan. 1785, 14 Feb. 1785, 16 Jan. 1786.

75. ADCO B2 1220/7, seigneurial justice of Senailly, sessions 27 Jan. 1757, 3 Mar. 1757.

76. ADCO E 96, private seigneurial papers, Meursault, seigneurial *manuel,* undated.

77. Saint Jacob, *Paysans de la Bourgogne du nord,* 120–22.

78. For example, ADCO 1H 803, religious order of St. Bénigne, seigneurial papers for Savigny-le-Sec, lease of the seigneurial flour mill, 20 June 1789.

79. Brunet, P*ouvoirs au village,* 87–115.

80. ADCO B2 1048/2, seigneurial justice of the chapter of St. Bénigne, sessions 19 Feb. 1780, 12 July 1780, 27 July 1780, 27 June 1781. Six inhabitants of Messigny found themselves in court in a suit brought by the miller. They justified their use of another mill by the claim that the flour was poorly milled and that the mill shut down over the summer. No fewer than twelve people in the village corroborated this in testimony, but the judge apparently chose to believe the seventeen other witnesses who said they had used the mill all summer and were content with the service.

81. Saint Jacob, *Paysans de la Bourgogne du nord,* 121.

82. ADCO B2 458/4, seigneurial justice of Billey, Grands-Jours of 5 Aug. 1789.

83. ADCO B2 605/1, seigneurial justice of Fontaine-en-Duesmois, Grands-Jours of 17 June 1782.

84. G. Gudin de Vallerin has written several articles on the influence of *mainmorte* on social structure. See his "Mainmorte et communauté de famille en Auxois, de la fin du XVIIe siècle jusqu'au début du XIXe siècle," *MSHDB* 37 (1980): 229–43; "Les doubles mariages en Auxois au XVIIIe siècle," *Annales de Bourgogne* 52 (1980): 213–25. See also Michel Petitjean and Françoise Fortunet de Loisy, *Les contrats de mariage à Dijon et dans la campagne bourguignonne de la fin du XVIIIe siècle au milieu du XIXe siècle* (Dijon: Éditions universitaires de Dijon, 1980).

85. Bart, *Liberté ou la terre,* 1–2.

86. Ibid., 2–3.

87. The three seigneuries of *mainmortables* were Senailly (including the hamlet of St. Germain), Aisy-sous-Thil (and the hamlet of Pont d'Aisy), and Flée (including the hamlet of Allerey).

88. ADCO B2 1221/1, seigneurial justice of Senailly, sessions 20 Feb. 1751, 4 Mar. 1751, 18 Mar. 1751.

89. In this case the estate was worth approximately 75 livres. See the auction of this estate to a certain Pochat for 75 livres. ADCO B2 1221/1, seigneurial justice of Senailly, session 18 Mar. 1751.

90. BM Dijon MS 1931, "Lettres addressées par Chartraire de Montigny à son homme d'affaires M. Finot, avocat à Semur-en-Auxois," letter 5 Aug. 1789, sent from Paris.

91. ADCO B2 1220/7, seigneurial justice of Senailly, session 16 Mar. 1789.

92. ADCO B2 1021/2, seigneurial justice of Senailly, Inventaire du greffe, 1784. See also ADCO B2 1021/1 for the various *procès-verbaux d'échute de mainmorte.* For the examples cited, the *échute* of Philibert Moreau is dated 12 Feb. 1739, and that of Nicolas Canian le jeune is from 13 Jan. 1766.

93. For example, ADCO B2 1221/1, seigneurial justice of Senailly, session 29 Nov. 1759.

94. Antoine, *Fiefs et villages du Bas-Maine,* 238.

Chapter 3

1. Saint Jacob, *Paysans de la Bourgogne du nord,* 58–59; Gallet, *Seigneurs et paysans,* 168–80.

2. Crubaugh, *Balancing the Scales of Justice,* 27.

3. In fact, the preponderance of minor crimes seems to be greater in northern Burgundy than in most other parts of France. Crubaugh, for example, finds that 17 percent of crimes in his sample were filed by the public party, which generally occurred only for major crimes. In northern Burgundy the proportion is well under 10 percent, which testifies to a higher willingness to use the courts, a result of the courts' here working better. Crubaugh, *Balancing the Scales of Justice,* 93.

4. ADCO B2 457/3, seigneurial justice of Billey, Villerrottin, sessions 21 Sept. 1751, 24 Sept. 1751, 10 Oct. 1751, 13 Oct. 1751, 24 Dec. 1751, 4 Jan. 1752, 26 Jan. 1752. In the end, the court sentenced the seventy-two-year-old vagabond to a whipping, two hours in the stocks, branding with a V (for *voleur*), a fine of 1,000 livres, and banishment from the territory of the seigneurial court of Villerrottin for six years.

5. ADCO B2 452/1, seigneurial justice of Belleneuve, session 11 May 1784.

6. An *arrêt* of the Dijon Parlement, for example, from 1763, "forbids all judges . . . from condemning [the accused] to pay the legal expenses, when the public party is the sole party." BM Dijon, MS 1306, "Recueil d'arrêts du Parlement de Dijon," vol. 3, *arrêt* 9 Mar. 1763.

7. ADCO 10F 831, barony of Pagny, "État des frais."

8. BM Dijon, MS 1306, "Recueil d'arrêts du Parlement de Dijon," vol. 3, *arrêt* 9 Mar. 1763.

9. ADCO 10F 1153, private seigneurial papers, barony of Pagny, letter 27 May 1781.

10. ADCO B2 439/1, seigneurial justice of Bagnot, sessions 20 Oct. 1787, 22 Oct. 1787, 15 Dec. 1787, 18 Jan 1788.

11. ADCO B2 457/3, seigneurial justice of Billey and Villerrottin, sessions 27 Aug. 1756, 28 Aug. 1756, 29 Aug. 1756, 31 Aug. 1756, 15 Sept. 1756, 26 Oct. 1756.

12. This case required three sessions, including the hearing of witnesses. ADCO B2 439/1, seigneurial justice of Bagnot, sessions 29 July 1780, 26 Aug. 1780, 15 Dec. 1780.

13. Ibid., sessions 18 Jan. 1752, 21 Jan. 1752, 14 Feb. 1752.

14. It was, however, comparatively rare for criminal cases, except thefts in seigneurial forests treated as police matters, to be settled at the assizes, which were reserved for minor cases. ADCO B2 1048, seigneurial justice of the *prieuré* of St. Bénigne, Grands-Jours (assizes) 30 Aug. 1783.

15. The breakdown of the crimes in the courts sampled here is strikingly similar to that discovered over a seventy-five-year period in one Burgundian seigneurial court. See Xavier Debilly, "La petite délinquance au XVIIIe siècle: L'exemple d'Ampuis," in Benoît Garnot, ed., *La petite délinquance du Moyen Age à l'époque contemporaine* (Dijon: Éditions universitaires de Dijon, 1998), 154–57.

16. Grosjacques testified that he and the woman (the daughter of Ambroise Dalais, another local, who was accused of reselling Grosjacques's stolen goods) had discussed marriage, that he had given her 10 livres in pledge, but that he had not discussed it with her father. The father testified that Grosjacques broached the subject with him, to which he responded that "he would never have her." It is possible that Dalais and his daughter led Grosjacques, who comes across as a bit simple, to break into the basement of Antoine Febvre with promises of marriage. After the investigation in the seigneurial court, as per the edict of 1772, the case was sent to

the bailliage, where Grosjacques was sentenced to a lifetime in the galleys. ADCO B2 604/2, seigneurial justice of Foncegrive, sessions 3 Jan. 1785, 4 Jan. 1785, 7 Jan. 1785, 8 Jan. 1785, 29 Jan. 1785. Also ADCO B2 111/46, bailliage of Dijon, criminal *arrêts,* judgment 6 July 1785.

17. ADCO B2 602/1, seigneurial justice of Flée, sessions 22 Nov. 1759, 13 Dec. 1759, 20 Dec. 1759.

18. ADCO B2 604/1, seigneurial justice of Foncegrive, sessions 13 Oct. 1757, 14 Oct. 1757, 17 Nov. 1757, 3 July 1758.

19. ADCO B2 605/1, seigneurial justice of Fontaine-en-Duesmois, sessions 27 Nov. 1782, 30 Nov. 1782.

20. Wood thefts vastly outnumber all other criminal offenses, but since most were settled summarily at the assizes (for no more than a few sols in legal fees), only those tried using criminal procedure are counted here.

21. ADCO B2 604/2, seigneurial justice of Foncegrive, sessions 5 Apr. 1781, 9 Apr. 1781, 21 July 1781, 7 Sept. 1781. Since the court used inquisitorial procedure (and the threat of corporal punishment), the only plaintiff was the public prosecutor and the lord paid the court costs. The court records never stated the costs when the lord was footing the bill, but with eighteen witnesses, interrogations of the accused, and several days of sessions, the costs were probably almost as high as the fines.

22. Benoît Garnot, "La violence et ses limites dans la France du XVIIIe siècle: L'exemple bourguignon," *Revue historique* 606 (1998): 250.

23. ADCO B2 603/2, seigneurial justice of Foncegrive, session 24 Apr. 1784.

24. For a list of insults commonly found in defamation cases in northern Burgundy, see Benoît Garnot, "Deux approches des procès pour injures en Bourgogne au XVIIIe siècle," in Garnot, *La petite délinquance du Moyen Age,* 431–41.

25. ADCO B2 1048, justice of religious chapter St. Bénigne, sessions 22 Nov. 1786, 29 Nov. 1786, 7 Dec. 1786, 5 Jan. 1787. In the records, the court clerk recorded the insults as "g . . . et p . . ." (for "garce et putain"); clerks commonly abbreviated very severe insults.

26. ADCO B2 1048, justice of religious chapter of St. Bénigne, sessions 15 Nov. 1780, 20 Dec. 1780.

27. ADCO B2 1252/2, seigneurial justice of Ancey, sessions 16 Nov. 1756, 17 Nov. 1756, 7 Dec. 1756.

28. ADCO B2 604/2, seigneurial justice of Foncegrive, sessions 11 Oct. 1787, 11 30 Oct. 1787.

29. ADCO B2 1252/2, seigneurial justice of Ancey, sessions 16 Nov. 1756, 17 Nov. 1756, 7 Dec. 1756.

30. Ibid., sessions 22 Nov. 1757, 29 Nov. 1757, 28 Jan. 1758, 21 Mar. 1758.

31. ADCO B2 604/2, seigneurial justice of Foncegrive, sessions 19 June 1784, 10 July 1784, 20 July 1784, 23 July 1784, 24 July 1784. The *plaintes* are dated 19 June 1784.

32. Indeed, filing a countersuit was a common strategy in civil cases.

33. ADCO B2 457/3, seigneurial justice of Billey, Villerrottin, depositions 6 Dec. 1754.

34. This is my translation of "ledit Burgiard qui boutenait sa culotte et prenait à témoin les assistants pour la main dans la culotte." B2 457/3, seigneurial justice of Billey, Villerrottin, sessions 27 Aug. 1756, 28 Aug. 1756, 29 Aug. 1756, 31 Aug. 1756, 15 Sept. 1756, 26 Oct. 1756.

35. Le Goff and Sutherland argue that village communities in Brittany primarily regulated themselves by settling the disputes of inhabitants informally. In fact, the popularity of the counter-Revolution can be partly attributed to the attempts of the Revolutionary state to impose its judicial authority on villages. T. J. A. Le Goff, and D. M. G. Sutherland, "The Revolution and the Rural Community in Eighteenth-Century Brittany," *Past and Present* 62 (1974): 96. This vision of the rural community is central to Howard Brown's interpretation of the Revolution in general and the Directory in particular. Howard Brown, *Ending the French Revolution: Violence, Justice, and Repression from the Terror to Napoleon* (Charlottesville: University of Virginia Press, 2006). See also Nicole Castan, *Les criminels de Languedoc: Les exigences d'ordre et les voies du ressentiment dans une société pré-révolutionnaire, 1750–1790* (Toulouse: Publications de l'Université de Toulouse-le Mirail, 1980), 14; Steven G. Reinhardt, *Justice in the Sarladais, 1770–1790* (Baton Rouge: Louisiana State University Press, 1991), xviii, 56–64; Benoît Garnot, "L'ampleur et les limites de l'infrajudiciaire dans la France de l'Ancien Régime (XVIe–XVIIe–XVIIIe siècles)," in Benoît Garnot, ed., *L'infrajudiciaire du Moyen Age à l'époque contemporaine* (Dijon: Éditions universitaires de Dijon, 1996), 70; Bruce Lenman and Geoffrey Parker, "The State, the Community, and the Criminal in Early Modern Europe," in V. A. C. Gatrell, Bruce Lenman, and Geoffrey Parker, eds., *Crime and the Law: The Social History of Crime in Western Europe since 1500* (London: Europa, 1980), 15.

36. Lenman and Parker, "State, Community, and Criminal," 11–48.

37. Edme La Poix de Fréminville, *Dictionnaire ou traité de la police générale des villes, bourgs et seigneuries de la campagne* (Paris: Les associés, 1775), iv–v; Loyseau, *Oeuvres,* 88–90; Charles de Secondat Montesquieu, *The Spirit of the Laws,* trans. Anne M. Cohler, Basia Carolyn Miller, and Harold Samuel Stone (Cambridge: Cambridge University Press, 1989), 517.

38. La Poix de Fréminville, *Traité général,* 637–53; Daniel Jousse, *Traité de l'administration de la justice* (Paris: Debure père, 1771), 1:178–80.

39. ADCO B2 451/1, seigneurial justice of Belleneuve, 29 Oct. 1759.

40. ADCO B2 1222/7, seigneurial justice of Senailly, St. Germain, Grands-Jours 6 Oct. 1754.

41. ADCO B2 605/1, seigneurial justice of Fontaine-en-Duesmois, session 12 May 1755.

42. *Règlements généraux pour les justices seigneuriales, corrigés et augmentés par un Avocat de cette ville, en l'année 1779* (Dijon: Capel, 1779); *Règlements généraux qui s'observent dans tout le ressort de la cour, et dont on fait lecture à la tenue des Grands-Jours: Nouvelle Édition: Revue, corrigée et augmentée* (Dijon: Causse, 1786).

43. Elsewhere in France the same person assessed and collected local taxes, whereas in Burgundy these functions were separated.

44. ADCO B2 607/18, seigneurial justice of the barony of Gemeaux, session 15 May 1757, also Grands-Jours 7 June 1757.

45. Some local positions likely provided ways to earn small amounts of money. Tax collectors were generally paid for their work, and *syndics* received money for trips they made for the village. The job of *messier,* however, was very onerous. The position required a great deal of time spent patrolling the fields, and the *messiers* were held civilly responsible for any damage for which they did not find the animals that had committed the offense.

46. BM Dijon, MS 1308, "Recueil d'arrêts du Parlement de Dijon," vol. 5, *arrêt* 26 Mar. 1768 (cited in *Règlements généraux pour les justices seigneuriales*).

47. ADCO B2 603/2, seigneurial justice of Foncegrive, sessions 17 Jan. 1783, 19 Feb. 1783, 5 Apr. 1783, 8 May 1783, 26 July 1783.

48. Most notably, Saint Jacob, *Paysans de la Bourgogne du nord,* 377–79; also Robin, *La société française en 1789,* 153; Root, *Peasants and King,* 162–63, 178; Bart, *La Révolution française en Bourgogne,* 50–52; Arlette Brosselin, *La forêt bourguignonne (1660–1789)* (Dijon: Éditions universitaires de Dijon, 1987), 111–14.

49. ADCO B2 423/1, seigneurial justice of Aisy, Grands-Jours 12 May 1789. They did a survey of the common land in 1765. ADCO E Dépôt 10/33, communal archives of Aisy, *bornage des communaux,* 19 Sept. 1765.

50. ADCO B2 1252/2, seigneurial justice of Ancey, Grands-Jours 12 Apr. 1755.

51. See, for example, ADCO B2 603/2, seigneurial justice of Foncegrive, Grands-Jours 22 Dec. 1785.

52. The number of households that were headed by women in seventeenth-century France varied from about 3 percent to about a third. There was a significant increase in the number of such households over the seventeenth century, and by the last decades of the century the respective percentages for the bailliages of Dijon, Auxonne, and Autun were 15.3, 18.0, and 12.7. James B. Collins, "The Economic Role of Women in Seventeenth-Century France," *French Historical Studies* 16 (1989): 444–52.

53. This phrase is the one used in all written deliberations of assembled communities. See, for example, ADCO E Dépôt 439/15, Montot communal archives, deliberation, 8 Aug. 1785.

54. ADCO B2 605/1, seigneurial justice of Fontaine-en-Duesmois, Grands-Jours 7 May 1788.

55. ADCO B2 603/2, seigneurial justice of Foncegrive, Grands-Jours 22 Dec. 1785.

56. ADCO B2 604/2, seigneurial justice of Foncegrive, village deliberation 23 July 1785.

57. ADCO B2 1252/2, seigneurial justice of Ancey, Grands-Jours 23 Aug. 1756.

58. In the context of these small villages, most taverns were simply a living room of an inhabitant. The informality of most rural *cabarets* made it still more important that owners get permission. Consumption of wine at home, among friends, was not forbidden or regulated, but the moment money changed hands for the wine, the place of consumption became a *cabaret.* This is why in 1780 Claude Babel justified having given wine to villagers, without official permission, by saying that "the drinkers who were at his place were his relatives and they did not pay for the wine." The judge apparently believed him, since he threw the case out. ADCO B2 1252/3, seigneurial justice of Ancey, Grands-Jours 12 Sept. 1780.

59. ADCO B2 458/4, seigneurial justice of Billey, Grands-Jours 7 Sept. 1786.

60. ADCO B2 451/1, seigneurial justice of Belleneuve, session 16 Jan. 1755.

61. These figures come from tax records.

62. ADCO B2 734/2, seigneurial justice of Meursault, Grands-Jours 10 Aug. 1784.

63. ADCO B2 617/24, seigneurial justice of Gemeaux, session 20 Sept. 1781. Gemeaux was not listed above in the villages with a butcher, since it was not one of the fourteen courts studied closely.

64. This was part of parlement's entrenchment of seigneurial justice in the 1760s and 1770s. BM Dijon, MS 1308 "Recueil d'arrêts du Parlement de Dijon," vol. 5, *arrêt* 19 Dec. 1770.

65. Judith A. Miller, *Mastering the Market: The State and the Grain Trade in Northern France, 1700–1860* (Cambridge: Cambridge University Press, 1999), 2–3, 50.

66. ADCO B2 423/1, seigneurial justice of Aisy, Grands-Jours 6 Oct. 1784.

67. BM Dijon, MS 1308, "Recueil des arrêts du Parlement," *arrêt* 12 Jan. 1778. The original *arrêt* is cited in La Poix de Fréminville, *Dictionnaire ou traité de la police générale,* s.v. "cabarets."

68. ADCO B2 1032, justice of religious chapter of St. Bénigne, Messigny, Grands-Jours 15 Sept. 1755. The court fined the two *échevins* 10 livres each for their "disobedience and rebellion to justice."

69. ADCO B2 SUP 76, seigneurial justice of Chazilly, Grands-Jours 3 Oct. 1786.

70. ADCO B2 601/2, seigneurial justice of Flée, session 27 Jan. 1753.

71. For a stimulating discussion of taverns in early modern Germany as a battleground for the struggle between elites and the people, see Ann B. Tlusty, *Bacchus and Civic Order: The Culture of Drink in Early Modern Germany* (Charlottesville: University of Virginia Press, 2001), 3–5, 102; see also James Van Horn Melton, *The Rise of the Public in Enlightenment Europe* (Cambridge: Cambridge University Press, 2001), 225–50.

72. ADCO B2 1253/1, seigneurial justice of Ancey, session 19 Nov. 1754. People often conducted business in taverns, usually formalizing a contract with a shared drink. Tlusty, *Bacchus and Civic Order,* 103–13.

73. ADCO B2 604/2, seigneurial justice of Foncegrive, session 7 Mar. 1785, 9 Mar. 1785.

74. For a fuller description of the court's role in policing and enforcing the rules of communal farming, see Jeremy D. Hayhoe, "Litigation and the Policing of Communal Agriculture in Eighteenth-Century Northern Burgundy, 1750–1790," *Agricultural History Review* 50 (2002): 25–50.

75. ADCO B2 439/1, seigneurial justice of Bagnot, Grands-Jours 2 Sept. 1755.

76. ADCO B2 607/7, seigneurial justice of Gemeaux, session 23 May 1758.

77. Ibid.

78. The eight courts were the justice of the *prieuré* of Larrey (justice of religious chapter of St. Bénigne) and the seigneurial justices of Bagnot, Ampilly-les-Bordes, Lanthes, Billey, Ancey, Foncegrive, and Fontaine-en-Duesmois.

79. Population figures from ADCO L 496, Amelot census, 1786, Billey. Court records: ADCO B2 458/4, seigneurial justice of Billey.

80. ADCO B 11073, Chambre des Comptes, *reprise de fief,* Billey, 14 Dec. 1769.

81. Although he acknowledges that civil justice ("justice contentieuse civile") remains virtually unstudied, Garnot argues that policing and probate were the two main activities of seigneurial judges. Garnot, "Les justices seigneuriales dans la France," 226; Crubaugh, *Balancing the Scales of Justice,* 24–26.

82. ADCO B2 423/1, seigneurial justice of Aisy, Pont d'Aisy, *renonciation de succession;* 4 Jan. 1783, *scellé* 5 Oct. 1782, *inventaire* 12 Nov. 1782; ADCO B2 423/2, seigneurial justice of Aisy, Pont d'Aisy, regular session 31 Jan. 1783.

83. Voisin, "Institution du Droit Français, relativement aux Maximes Générales du Royaume et aux usages particuliers, soit de la Bourgogne, soit des Pays de Droit Ecrit, qui ressortissent au Parlement de Bourgogne," unpublished manuscript, BM Dijon MS 1515, 125–26. Jean Bouhier, "Observations de la Coutume de Bourgogne, par M. le Président Bouhier," in Joly de Bevy, ed., *Oeuvres de jurisprudence de M. Bouhier, Président à Mortier au Parlement de Dijon* (Dijon: Frantin, 1787)," 473–78. The nominations were generally unanimous (presumably based on the stated wishes of either the deceased or surviving parent), but when there was disagreement the judge seems to have taken the opinion of the majority. See, for example, ADCO B2 668/1, seigneurial justice of Lanthes, tutelle of 22 Nov. 1783.

84. This was an unwritten customary usage–the Custom was silent on the matter. See BM Dijon, fonds Saverot 16/48, "Certificats d'usages donnés par les Avocats du Parlement de Dijon," *certificat* 22 Jan. 1703. The lawyers state that in the duchy of Burgundy, "the *tutelle* does not end at the age of puberty, as it does in regions of written law, regardless of the fact that there are no precise mentions of this point in the Custom, and that the Written Law, which we have to follow in cases not decided by the Custom, is contrary; they also certify that the *tutelle* lasts until the age of 25." See also Bouhier, "Observations de la Coutume de Bourgogne," 467–72.

85. Thanks to Jean Bart, of the Université de Bourgogne, for clarifying this for me.

86. Voisin, "Institution du Droit Français," BM Dijon, MS 1515, 124.

87. ADCO B2 606/1, seigneurial justice of Fontaine-en-Duesmois, 2 May 1756.

88. ADCO B2 668/1, seigneurial justice of Lanthes, 21 Feb. 1787. Also *scellé* of 2 Jan 1787.

89. See, for example, ADCO B2 668/1, seigneurial justice of Lanthes, 4 Mar. 1787.

90. ADCO B2 SUP 308, seigneurial justice of Aisy, Pont-d'Aisy, *vente de fruits pendants par racines,* 12 July 1750.

91. Voisin, "Institution du Droit Français," BM Dijon, MS 1515, 130.

92. See, for example, ADCO B2 457/3, seigneurial justice of Billey, Villerrottin, sessions 28 June 1758, 7 Jul 1758, 14 July 1758.

93. ADCO B2 SUP 76, seigneurial justice of Chazilly-le-Haut, Chazilly-le-Bas, emancipation of 24 Oct. 1789.

94. The issue of majority was highly complicated in Burgundy. No theorists doubted that marriage emancipated, but many parlementaires (most notably Jean Bouhier) held that other than marriage, only leaving home emancipated. A forty-year-old spinster or bachelor living at home would then still need permission to write a will or sign any document. Chris Corley clarified this matter for me. For more on this question, see his "Parental Authority, Legal Practice, and State-Building in Early Modern France," (PhD diss., Purdue University, 2001).

95. Bouhier, "Observations de la Coutume," 472.

96. The inventory did not include land and buildings (immovables), the most significant part of the estate to be divided. All of the goods, cash, and money owed to or by the estate are listed.

97. ADCO B2 606/1, seigneurial justice of Fontaine-en-Duesmois, sessions 4 June 1750, 20 June 1750, 11 Aug. 1750.

98. ADCO B2 603/2, seigneurial justice of Foncegrive, *tutelle* 4 June 1751.

99. ADCO B2 457/4, seigneurial justice of Billey, Villerrottin, session 26 Apr. 1780. See also *inventaire* 7 May 1781, *vente* 8 May 1781, *tutelle* 11 Apr 1781, *distribution des deniers* 21 May 1781, 12 Jan 1782.

100. ADCO B2 605/1, seigneurial justice of Fontaine-en-Duesmois, *homolgation de testament,* 4 June 1789. See also *aposition de scellé,* 1 Dec. 1788.

101. ADCO B2 603/2, seigneurial justice of Foncegrive, sessions 15 Mar. 1751, 17 Apr. 1751, 21 Apr. 1751.

102. ADCO B2 SUP 75, seigneurial justice of Chazilly-le-Haut, Chazilly-le-Bas, *homolgation de testament* 27 May 1751. See also *aposition de scellé* 8 Oct. 1750.

103. This was determined through working in the records of the registration of legal acts. A search through all the registered acts for the years 1756, 1766, and 1785–86 found only forty contracts involving Messigny inhabitants that were not done by the local notary, and none of these involved inheritance affairs. ADCO C 8795–C 8797, bureau of Dijon, *contrôle des actes,* 1785–86; ADCO C 8712–C 8715, bureau of Dijon, *contrôle des actes,* 1756; ADCO C 8741–C 8744, bureau of Dijon, *contrôle des actes,* 1766.

104. ADCO 5Mi 10R27, Mcfm *état civil* for Messigny, 1724–1792. This includes only those who died in Messigny proper, excluding those from the attached hamlet of Vantoux. For the wills, ADCO 4E 5/132–141, Forneron notaire, minutes for 1780–89.

105. ADCO 4E 5/134, Forneron *notaire,* minutes for 1782, testament 5 Dec. 1782.

106. Ibid., testament 18 Nov. 1782.

107. ADCO 4E 5/135, Forneron *notaire,* minutes for 1783, testament 26 Sept. 1783.

108. ADCO 4E 5/139, Forneron *notaire,* minutes for 1787, testament 30 Nov. 1787.

109. ADCO 4E 5/137, Forneron *notaire,* minutes for 1785, testament 5 Nov. 1785. Paulette Poncet-Cretin discusses the importance of such peace-seeking phrases, although she does not associate them with female will-writers. Paulette Poncet-Cretin, “La pratique testamentaire en Bourgogne et en Franche-Comté de 1770 à 1815” (doctoral thesis, Université de Bourgogne, 1973), 22.

110. Jean Yver, *Égalité entre héritiers et exclusion d’enfants dotés: Essai de géographie coutumière* (Paris: Sirey, 1966), 13.

111. This is based on a small sample. In the 1750s only thirty-three inheritance disputes reached a final settlement in court (I show in chapter 4 that many inheritance disputes settled out of court, due to the shame involved in airing family linen in public) and listed final court costs. There were twenty-two such cases in the 1780s.

112. These figures come from the “distributions des deniers de l’hoirie.” The value of the estate (again, excluding land and buildings) is from the total brought in by the sale, while the cost of the settlement is the amount the court took from the

revenue of the sale. Apart from funeral costs paid to the priest, the court officers were paid before any other creditors.

113. ADCO B2 1252/2, seigneurial justice of Ancey, sessions 17 Feb. 1757, 1 Mar. 1757, 18 Mar. 1757, 26 Mar. 1757.

114. *Règlements pour les fonctions et droits des officiers, greffiers, procureurs, huissiers et notaires des provinces de Bourgogne, Bresse et Bugey* (Dijon: A. de Fay, 1724), 13–30.

115. "Arrêt du Parlement contenant nouveau règlement sur les fonctions et les droits des Officiers des Justices inférieures," 7 Dec. 1747, Recueil d'arrêts du Parlement de Dijon, vol. 3, BM Dijon, MS 1306.

116. Of 337 and 482 estates sealed in the sample in the 1750s and 1780s, 47 and 66, respectively, had auctions of the estates.

117. In many cases the nomination of guardians took place months after the death, with people frequently waiting until the Grands-Jours. The assembled family members all knew who had looked after the minors and the property since the death and simply rendered official what already existed.

118. ADCO B2 SUP 76, seigneurial justice of Chazilly-le-Haut, Chazilly-le-Bas, *tutelle* 3 Feb. 1751.

119. ADCO B2 1134/6, seigneurial justice of Chambolle and Morey, session 18 Dec. 1786.

120. BM Dijon, MS 1306, Recueil des arrêts du Parlement, vol. 3, *arrêt* 7 Dec. 1747.

121. Mauclair, "Justice seigneuriale de La Vallière," 390–93.

122. Anthony Crubaugh indicates that revolutionary justices of the peace were paid a salary (initially 600 livres, raised to 900 in 1793). Revolutionaries paid lip-service to the idea that justice should be free, but in practice this does not seem to have been the case. Crubaugh argues that JPs dispensed cheaper justice than seigneurial courts but does not provide figures about how much justice cost in the Revolution. Crubaugh, *Balancing the Scales of Justice,* 132, 146, 206–7.

Chapter 4

1. See William L. F. Felstiner, Richard L. Abel, and Austin Sarat, "The Emergence and Transformation of Disputes: Naming, Blaming, Claiming . . ." *Law and Society Review* 15 (1980–81): 632.

2. Marc Galanter, "Reading the Landscape of Disputes: What We Know and Don't Know (and Think We Know) about Our Allegedly Contentious and Litigious Society," *UCLA Law Review* 31 (1983): 12–14.

3. Michael J. Saks, "Do We Really Know Anything about the Behavior of the Tort Litigation System–and Why Not?" *University of Pennsylvania Law Review* 140 (1992): 1173.

4. Galanter notes that "the master pattern of American disputing is one in which there is actual or threatened invocation of an authoritative decision-maker. This is countered by a threat of protracted or hard-fought resistance, leading to a negotiated or mediated settlement." Galanter, "Reading the Landscape of Disputes," 26–27.

5. This is a point made persuasively by Jonathan Dewald in *Pont-St.-Pierre, 1398–1789: Lordship, Community, and Capitalism in Early Modern Europe* (Los Angeles: University of California Press, 1987), 129–37.

6. For a similar view of the relationship between litigation and extrajudicial dispute settlement, see the innovative discussion in Hervé Piant, "Le tribunal de l'ordinaire: Justice et société dans le prévôté de Vaucouleurs (v. 1670–1790)" (PhD thesis, Université de Bourgogne, 2000), 214–36. A fascinating analysis of the extrajudicial function of Protestant consistories in Geneva that places the institution within a range of both formal and informal modes of dispute resolution can be found in Christian Grosse, "'Pour bien de paix': La régulation des conflits par les consistoires en Suisse romande (XVIe–XVIIe siècles)," in Jean-Luc Chabot, Stéphane Gal, and Christophe Tournu, eds., *Figures de la médiation et lien social* (Paris: Harmattin, 2006), 85–107.

7. Felstiner, Abel, and Sarat, "Emergence and Transformation of Disputes," 633–36. See also Galanter, "Reading the Landscape of Disputes," 13. In his evaluation of the dispute-centered approach to litigation, David M. Trubek points out that deciding what a dispute is can be difficult indeed. David M. Trubek, "The Construction and Deconstruction of a Disputes-Focused Approach: An Afterword," *Law and Society Review* 15 (1980–81): 735.

8. Isabelle Carrier, "L'art de louvoyer dans le système judiciaire de l'Ancien Régime: Le procureur et la procédure civile," in Dolan, *Entre justice et justiciables,* 479–90.

9. Daniel Lord Smail, *The Consumption of Justice: Emotions, Publicity, and Legal Culture in Marseille, 1264–1423* (Ithaca: Cornell University Press, 2003), 87.

10. Gregory Hanlon, "Justice in the Age of Lordship: A Feudal Court in Tuscany during the Medici Era (1619–66)," *Sixteenth Century Journal* 35, no. 4 (2004): 1005–33.

11. Castan, *Justice et répression,* 15–48.

12. Jean Quéniart, *Le Grand Chapelletout: Violence, normes et comportements dans la Bretagne rurale au XVIIIe siècle* (Rennes: Éditions Apogée, 1993), 144, 170.

13. ADCO B2 602/2, seigneurial justice of Flée, session 17 Mar. 1790.

14. On the equality of the Burgundian legal Custom, see Jean Bart, "L'égalité entre héritiers dans la region dijonnaise à la fin de l'Ancien Régime et sous la Révolution," *MSHDB* 29 (1968–69): 65–78.

15. Poncet-Cretin, "Pratique testamentaire," 131.

16. ADCO 4E 5/141, Forneron *notaire, partage* 11 Oct. 1789.

17. ADCO B2 SUP 77, seigneurial justice of Chazilly-le-Haut, session 10 Sept. 1751.

18. ADCO B2 1252/3, seigneurial justice of Ancey, session 14 Aug. 1759.

19. Jeffrey Merrick, "Fathers and Kings: Patriarchalism and Absolutism in Eighteenth-Century French Politics," *Studies on Voltaire and the Eighteenth Century* 308 (1993): 281–301.

20. ADCO B2 734/1, seigneurial justice of Meursault, session 8 Jan. 1755. The widow apparently saw reason, since the case ended that day. With no judgment of the court, and no further sessions, the parties probably settled the dispute amicably.

21. ADCO B2 439/1, seigneurial justice of Bagnot, sessions 31 July 1753, 16 Nov. 1753, 1 Feb. 1754.

22. Piant, "Tribunal de l'ordinaire," 200–206, quotation is from 201.

23. Christopher W. Brooks, *Lawyers, Litigation, and English Society since 1450* (London: Hambledon Press, 1998), 63–128; Lenman and Parker, "State, Community, and Criminal," 16.

24. Craig Muldrew, *The Economy of Obligation: The Culture of Credit and Social Relations in Early Modern England* (London: St. Martin's Press, 1998), 203.

25. Brooks, *Lawyers, Litigation and English Society,* 10–12. Again, these are cases in the advanced stage of pleading, rather than complaints.

26. Muldrew, *Economy of Obligation,* 243–46.

27. Brooks, *Lawyers, Litigation, and English Society,* 29–33.

28. Richard Kagan, *Lawsuits and Litigants in Castille, 1500–1700* (Chapel Hill: University of North Carolina Press, 1981), xx–xxii and passim.

29. Dewald, *Pont-St.-Pierre,* 254.

30. John A. Dickinson, "L'activité judiciaire d'après la procédure civile: Le bailliage de Falaise, 1668–1790," *Revue d'histoire économique et sociale* 2 (1976): 152.

31. Colin Kaiser, "The Deflation in the Volume of Litigation at Paris in the Eighteenth Century and the Waning of the Old Judicial Order," *European Studies Review* 10 (1980): 309–36.

32. Mauclair, "Justice seigneuriale de La Vallière," 563–64; Michèle Raffeau, "Une seigneurie nivernaise: La terre d'Huban," (doctoral thesis, Université de Bourgogne, 1981), 262.

33. These reforms are described in detail in chapter 5.

34. John R. Wunder, *Inferior Courts, Superior Justice: A History of the Justices of the Peace on the Northwest Frontier, 1853–1889* (Westport, CT: Greenwood Press, 1979), 158–59.

35. William E. Nelson, *Dispute and Conflict Resolution in Plymouth County, Massachusetts, 1725–1825* (Chapel Hill: University of North Carolina Press, 1981), 52–53.

36. Bernard Schnapper, "Pour une géographie des mentalités judiciaires: La litigiosité en France au XIXe siècle," *Annales: Économies, sociétés, civilisations* 23 (1979): 399–419.

37. Such cases made up 16 percent of cases tried by the JPs analyzed by Anthony Crubaugh. Crubaugh, *Balancing the Scales of Justice,* 164.

38. Schnapper does not provide a national average for JPs, but he does indicate that in 1856–60 there were nationally 3.6 times as many cases heard by JPs as in the civil tribunals. Since he gives a national average for litigation before the civil tribunals, multiplying the two figures provides a national average for JPs. Schnapper, "Pour une géographie des mentalités judiciaires," 411–12.

39. This data had to be inferred from the map provided in Schnapper, "Pour une géographie des mentalités judiciaires," 411.

40. ADCO B2 1042, seigneurial justice of the religious chapter of St. Benigne, Messigny session 16 Jan. 1751.

41. See chapter 1.

42. The best analysis of the *bail à cheptel,* for any region of France, is Françoise Fortunet's *Charité ingénieuse et pauvre misère: Les baux à cheptel simple en Auxois aux XVIIIe et XIXe siècles* (Dijon: Éditions universitaires de Dijon, 1985).

43. Marc Lindimer, "Messigny et Vantoux: Étude Démographique, 1690–1790" (Master's thesis, Université de Bourgogne, 1997), 30–31. The rate for the period

1661–1740 was only slightly lower, with 56 percent of marriages uniting two inhabitants of Messigny.

44. Gilles Postel-Vinay, *La terre et l'argent: L'agriculture et le crédit en France du XVIIIe au début du XXe siècle* (Paris: A. Michel, 1998).

45. See the court case where the judge ordered Meunier to repay Villereau the money in question. ADCO B2 668/1, seigneurial justice of Lanthes, session 21 Jan. 1785.

46. That is, it means assuming that neighbors sued over the same kinds of things as inhabitants of two different villages.

47. ADCO B2 734/1, seigneurial justice of Meursault, sessions 24 Nov. 1751, 15 Dec. 1751, 19 Jan. 1752.

48. ADCO B2 457/4, seigneurial justice of Billey, Villerrottin, sessions 29 Apr. 1783, 16 May 1783.

49. ADCO B2 SUP 76, seigneurial justice of Chazilly-le-Haut, Chazilly-le-Bas, session 20 Aug. 1781.

50. ADCO B2 1252/2, seigneurial justice of Ancey, Grands-Jours 23 Aug. 1756.

51. For an excellent discussion of *séparation de biens* and *séparation de biens et de corps,* see Julie Hardwick, "Seeking Separations: Gender, Marriages, and Household Economies in Early Modern France," *French Historical Studies* 21 (1998): 157–80.

52. ADCO B2 118/42, Dijon bailliage, *qualités,* 18 May 1785.

53. Sometimes *manouvriers* and *journaliers* are difficult to distinguish, although theoretically *manouvriers* were small farmers who leased most of their land while *journaliers* were property-less day laborers. People listed in tax rolls as *journalier* may have occasionally given their profession as *manouvrier* to the clerk.

54. Unfortunately, Crubaugh gives no indication of how he defined "frequent litigants," and it is not clear how to compare his data to the occupations of all litigants that I present in table 4.5. Crubaugh, *Balancing the Scales of Justice,* 35.

55. Mauclair, "Justice seigneuriale de La Vallière," 498–500.

56. Michel Heichette, *Société, sociabilité, justice: Sablé et son pays au XVIIIe siècle* (Rennes: Presses universitaires de Rennes, 2005), 25–27. The figures cited by Heichette, however, are based solely on the *procès-verbaux* and thereby include only criminal and major civil cases.

57. Crubaugh, *Balancing the Scales of Justice,* 224.

58. This is true for civil cases but does not apply to cases involving the lord. I argued above that seigneurial courts did exacerbate tensions between lords and their vassals.

59. Hervé Piant, "La confiance perdu: Hommes de loi, délinquants et opinion publique à Vaucouleurs au XVIIIe siècle," in Benoît Garnot, ed., *Juges, notaires et policiers délinquants: XIVe–XXe siècle* (Dijon: Éditions universitaires de Dijon, 1997), 67.

60. Yves Jeanclos, *L'arbitrage en Bourgogne et en Champagne du XIIe au XVe siècle: Étude de l'influence du droit savant, de la coutume et de la pratique* (Dijon: Centre de recherche historique, 1977), 11.

61. Projet ARTFL, "Dictionnaires d'autrefois," http://www.lib.uchicago.edu/ARTFL/projects/dicos/onlook.html. The untranslated definitions are from the *Dictionnaire de l'académie française:* "Celui que des personnes choisissent de part et d'autre pour terminer leur différend. Prendre, nommer, choisir quelqu'un pour

arbitre. Convenir d'arbitres. Se rapporter de quelque chose à des arbitres. Sortir d'une affaire par arbitres. Compromettre entre les mains d'arbitres"; from the *Dictionnaire critique de la langue française* (1787), s.v. "arbitre": "juge choisi par les parties, qui lui donnent pouvoir de terminer leur différend"; s.v. "arbitrateur": quelqu'un choisi "pour terminer un différend à l'amiable." See Grosse, "'Pour bien de paix,'" 85.

62. Schneider, "Village and State," 672–73.

63. BM Dijon MS 1307, "Recueil d'arrêts du Parlement de Dijon," vol. 4, *arrêt* 20 Mar. 1766.

64. ADCO B2 254/1, bailliage of Saulieu, *cahier* of Ogny.

65. ADCO B2 24, Dijon Parlement, *registres des audiences d'instruction.*

66. ADCO B2 24/266, Dijon Parlement, *registres des audiences d'instruction* for 1755; ADCO B2 24/306, Dijon Parlement, *registres des audiences d'instruction* for 1785. Of 233 cases in these registers (108 in 1785 and 125 in 1755), 59 were ratifications of arbitrations (25.3 percent).

67. ADCO B2 24/306, Dijon Parlement, *registres des audiences d'instruction* for 1785, session 14 Feb. 1785.

68. Ibid., session 13 Aug. 1785.

69. For the one overturned arbitration, ADCO B2 24/266, Dijon Parlement, *registres des audiences d'instruction* for 1755, 30 Apr. 1755.

70. ADCO B2 136 bis, Dijon bailliage, records of arbitration; ADCO B2 163 bis, Beaune bailliage, records of arbitration; ADCO B2 183 bis, St. Jean-de-Losne bailliage, records of arbitration; ADCO B2 208, La Montagne (a sub-bailliage of Châtillon-sur-Seine), records of arbitration; ADCO 221/1 bis, bailliage of Semur-en-Auxois, records of arbitration.

71. ADCO B2 1048, seigneurial justice of the religious chapter of St. Bénigne, Larey, session 27 Feb. 1784.

72. In addition, of course, André had to turn the property over to her. ADCO B2 136 bis, Dijon bailliage, records of arbitration, 23 June 1788.

73. ADCO B2 183 bis, St. Jean-de-Losne bailliage, arbitration records, 18 Mar. 1771.

74. ADCO B2 1048, seigneurial justice of the religious chapter of St. Bénigne, Bellefond, sessions 29 May 1782, 14 Sept. 1782.

75. ADCO B2 734/2, seigneurial justice of Meursault, sessions 11 Dec. 1786, 8 Jan. 1787, 29 Jan. 1787, 12 Feb. 1787, 12 Mar. 1787, 30 Apr. 1787, 14 May 1787, 18 June 1787, 31 Dec. 1787, 14 Apr. 1788, 16 June 1788, 23 June 1788. The final decision of the arbitrators is not in the records of the seigneurial court. Possibly the "délai" granted by the judge extended into the Revolutionary period, or perhaps the judge saw the arbitration record without having the clerk copy it or noting that the had seen it.

76. ADCO B2 1077/1, seigneurial justice of Ampilly-lès-Bordes, sessions 30 July 1785, 19 Nov. 1785, 26 Nov. 1785, 1 Apr. 1786, 2 Dec. 1786.

77. Zoë Schneider, "Women before the Bench: Female Litigants in Early Modern Normandy," *French Historical Studies* 23 (2000): 24–25.

78. Jeanclos says that women arbitrators were always ecclesiastics–a trusted nun or abbess might make a good choice. Also, since laypeople could not arbitrate cases involving ecclesiastics, an abbess might arbitrate between other female ecclesiastics. Jeanclos, *L'arbitrage en Bourgogne,* 71–85.

79. ADCO B2 226/1, bailliage of Semur-en-Auxois, arbitrages, 9 June 1773. For Finot's work as a judge, see Hayhoe, "Droit, pratique et seigneurie."

80. Schneider makes this same point, noting that in the late seventeenth and early eighteenth centuries there was a marked tendency increasingly to nominate lawyers. Schneider, "Village and State," 674.

81. Eric Wenzel, "Le clergé diocésain d'Ancien Régime au coeur de l'infrajustice: L'exemple de la Bourgogne aux XVIIe et XVIIIe siècles," in Benoît Garnot, ed., *L'infrajudiciaire du Moyen Age à l'époque contemporaine* (Dijon: Éditions universitaires de Dijon, 1996), 248.

82. Castan, *Justice et répression,* 16; Reinhardt, *Justice in the Sarladais,* 56–64.

83. ADCO B2 SUP 77, seigneurial justice of Chazilly-le-Haut, Chazilly-le-Bas, sessions 23 Apr. 1750, 30 Apr. 1750, 16 July 1750.

84. ADCO B2 457/4, seigneurial justice of Billey, Villerrottin, sessions 4 Oct. 1782, 8 Oct. 1782, 18 Oct. 1782.

85. Françoise Maréchal and her daughter, Laurence Moissenet, both testified describing the meeting around a table in their house, but Jacques Moissenet (Françoise's husband) did not. All of these attempts to bring peace were made by village women.

86. ADCO B2 604/2, seigneurial justice of Foncegrive, sessions 11 Oct. 1787, 30 Oct. 1787. Deposition 11 Oct. 1787. The consensus of the witnesses seems to be that neither party was really at fault, and that both brought scandal to the region.

87. ADCO B2 734/1, seigneurial justice of Meursault, sessions 26 Nov. 1755, 3 Dec. 1755, 17 Dec. 1755. Deposition 3 Dec. 1755.

88. ADCO B2 1252/2, seigneurial justice of Ancey, sessions 29 Oct. 1754, 6 Nov. 1754, 19 Nov. 1754, 26 Nov. 1754, 11 Dec. 1754. The depositions of the witnesses (sixteen of them, ten for Roux on the first date and six for the Carrés) are dated 19 and 26 Nov. 1754. Fremyet and the Carré brothers simply agreed publicly to rehabilitate his reputation and to pay the costs of the court case to that point (64 livres 7 sols 10 deniers).

89. ADCO B2 546/2, seigneurial justice of Corgengoux, letter from Lenef to Gondier, 27 May 1718.

90. ADCO B2 1252/3, seigneurial justice of Ancey: first case 24 May 1780, 31 May 1780; second case 23 June 1781.

91. ADCO B2 439/1, seigneurial justice of Bagnot: first case 9 Aug. 1788; second case 6 Feb. 1789.

92. Galanter, "Reading the Landscape of Disputes," 24–25.

93. ADCO B2 1220/7, seigneurial justice of Senailly, St. Germain, sessions 29 Jan. 1756, 5 Feb. 1756.

94. ADCO B2 734/2, seigneurial justice of Meursault, session 14 Feb. 1785.

95. Ibid., session 30 Jan. 1786.

96. ADCO B2 SUP 77, seigneurial justice of Chazilly-le-Haut, Chazilly-le-Bas, session 5 Sept. 1754.

97. ADCO B2 601/2, seigneurial justice of Flée, sessions 30 Apr. 1757, 5 May 1757, 18 May 1757.

98. ADCO B2 604/2, seigneurial justice of Foncegrive, sessions 27 Feb. 1789, 16 May 1789. It might seem that this simple inheritance dispute hardly involved much animosity and so hardly required third-party intervention. This is not the case,

however. Ladey and Normand had a great deal of animosity toward each other. In 1785 they had been involved in a court case over a violent beating that Ladey gave Normand, an assault that was apparently the continuation of a debt and a prior court case. After the resolution of the 1785 case it is likely that relations between the two remained strained–but this inheritance dispute in 1789 would have threatened to bring everything into the open again and disrupt broader community relations. For a discussion of the Lady-Normand fight, see above, chapter 3.

99. Jean Bart thinks the *bureaux de paix* were ineffective in towns and cities but suggests that when mediating between country dwellers they were successful in halting about half of all disputes. See his "La justice de paix du canton de Fontaine-Française à l'époque révolutionnaire," *MSHDB* 26 (1965): 213. Anthony Crubaugh estimates that in La Rochelle the overall rate of success for conciliations in the *bureaux de paix* was about 36 percent; he has examples where success was as low as 9 percent, and as high as 63 percent. Crubaugh, *Balancing the Scales of Justice,* 189. In the town of Arc-sur-Tille, the JP managed to reconcile the parties in only two of fifty-eight attempted conciliations. Christophe Breugnot, "La justice de paix dans le canton d'Arc-sur-Tille à l'époque révolutionnaire" (D.E.A. thesis, Université de Bourgogne, 1994), 99–102.

100. Dewald, *Pont-St.-Pierre,* 129–37.

101. I place "amicably" in quotation marks because it seems to me risky to assume that private arrangement was necessarily friendlier than a court case. For various reasons, people may often have agreed to terms that nevertheless seemed unjust to them. And even if they may have felt that the settlement was equitable, anger against the other for having provoked the disagreement may have remained, especially since many of these disputes sprang up in times of grief after the death of a relative. In their *cahier de doléances,* the inhabitants of Blancey complained that the slowness of official justice sometimes forced them to accept poor terms in a settlement: "a poor and miserable creditor suffers by being unable to pursue a rich debtor who employs the tricks of chicanery to frustrate the poor out of the money owed him, and who uses these tricks to force a settlement that is as unjust as it is cruel." ADCO B2 242/1, bailliage of Arnay-le-Duc, *cahiers de doléances, cahier* of Blancey.

102. The figures I give do not take into account cases that may have been dropped before the first session, as no records exist that allow for this to be evaluated.

103. Brooks, *Lawyers, Litigation, and English Society,* 12.

104. Crubaugh, *Balancing the Scales of Justice,* 51–52, and passim; Schneider, "Village and State," 673–80.

105. ADCO B2 457/4, seigneurial justice of Billey, Villerrottin, session 20 Apr. 1787.

106. A few of the "unsettled" cases may have resulted from discouraged plaintiffs dropping the case because of the legal hassles involved in going to court. Dropping a case, of course, can be seen as an out of court settlement–avoidance as settlement. The majority of unsettled cases, though, hardly involve long delays and a high number of court sessions before being dropped. It is highly unlikely that, in the example cited above, Jeanne Claude Roussey dropped her request for about 200 livres simply because the judge told her once to come back in a week.

107. ADCO B2 604/2, seigneurial justice of Foncegrive, session 27 June 1786.

108. Jean-Paul Poisson, *Notaires et société: Travaux d'histoire et de sociologie notariales* (Paris: Economica, 1990); Phillip T. Hoffman, Gilles Postel-Vinay, and Jean-Laurent Rosenthal, *Priceless Markets: The Political Economy of Credit in Paris, 1660–1870* (Chicago: University of Chicago Press, 2000).

109. Alfred Soman, "L'infra-judiciaire à Paris, d'après les archives notariales," *Histoire, économie et société* 1 (1982): 369–75; Soman, "Justice et infrajustice en France (XVIe–XVIIIe siècle)," in Garnot, *L'infrajudiciaire du Moyen Age à l'époque contemporaine,* 77–86.

110. ADCO 4E 5/132–141, Forneron *notaire,* minutes for 1780–89; ADCO 4E 5/116–120, Mathieu *notaire,* minutes for 1750–59; ADCO 4E 5/121–132, Berrué *notaire,* minutes for 1760–79. Note that there is a gap in the run of notarial documents here from 1774 to 1778. The number of accommodations in this decade, then, was actually a good deal higher than the figures cited in the table, probably about double.

111. ADCO 4E 5/139, Forneron *notaire,* accommodation, 19 June 1787.

112. ADCO 4E 5/119, Berrué *notaire,* accommodation, 4 Nov. 1757.

113. ADCO 4E 5/121, Berrué *notaire, partage et testament,* 13 Jan. 1760.

114. ADCO 4E 5/137, Forneron *notaire, transaction sur procès,* 23 Nov. 1785.

115. S. Poirey, "Le retrait lignager dans le duché de Bourgogne (XVIe–XVIIIe siècle)," *MSHDB* 54 (1997): 156–58.

116. ADCO 4E 5/132, Forneron *notaire, supplément de vente,* 3 Nov. 1780.

117. In 90 percent of 91 declarations of pregnancy from Is-sur-Tille and Grancey-le-Château the woman demanded a copy, usually saying that she intended to use it to get what was due her. M.-C. Straboni, "Recherches sur la sexualité illégitime: Les déclarations de grossesse dans les 2 cantons ruraux actuels d'Is-sur-Tille et de Grancey-le-Chateau de 1750 à 1751" (D.E.A. thesis: Université de Bourgogne, 1975–76), 77–78. See also Hayhoe, "Illegitimacy, Inter-generational Conflict, and Legal Practice," 673–84.

118. ADCO 4E 5/123, Berrué *notaire, déclaration de grossesse,* 9 Jan. 1763.

119. The notary used the phrase in the testaments of Anne de Serry and Anne Drouard in 1785. ADCO 4E 5/137, Forneron *notaire,* testaments 5 Nov. 1785 and 24 Feb. 1785.

120. Robert C. Ellickson, *Order without Law: How Neighbors Settle Disputes* (Cambridge: Harvard University Press, 1991), 4, 53–59.

121. Ibid., 240–49, 249 for the quotation.

Chapter 5

1. Peter Jones, *Reform and Revolution in France: The Politics of Transition, 1774–1791* (Cambridge: Cambridge University Press, 1995), 107–38; Michael Kwass, *Privilege and the Politics of Taxation in Eighteenth-Century France: Liberté, Égalité, Fiscalité* (Cambridge: Cambridge University Press, 2000), 23.

2. On the *présidiaux,* see André Chenal, *Étude sur le présidial d'Orléans,* 152–53; on the 1772 reform of criminal procedure for seigneurial courts, Castan, *Justice et repression,* 117.

3. Combe, *Mémoire inédit du chancelier Daguesseau,* 108–10; John A. Carey, *Judicial Reform in France before the Revolution of 1789* (Cambridge, Harvard University Press, 1981), 2–6. Carey argues that legal reformers in the eighteenth century failed to distinguish between traditional reforms based on legal precedent and modern reforms based on theoretical justifications–attempts to innovate often fortified the institution.

4. *Protestations du Parlement de Bourgogne du 4 Juin 1788.* BM Dijon, Fonds Delmasse 606.

5. Several historians have remarked on the revitalization of Burgundian seigneurial justice in the late eighteenth century, including Saint Jacob (who links it to the seigneurial reaction), but none have seen it as a coherent policy of the Dijon Parlement. C. Lamarre, "Quelques observations sur le fonctionnement des bailliages," 432; Albert Colombet, "Une justice seigneuriale à la fin de l'Ancien Régime: Vantoux et ses Grands Jours," *MSHDB* 3 (1936): 195–207; Garnot, "L'ampleur et les limites de l'infrajudiciaire," 74; Saint Jacob, *Paysans de la Bourgogne du nord,* 412–34.

6. The following analysis is heavily indebted to Mackrell, "Criticism of Seigniorial Justice," 123–45; see also J. Q. C. Mackrell, *The Attack on "Feudalism" in Eighteenth-Century France* (London: Routledge, 1973).

7. Gallet, *Seigneurs et paysans,* 167–90.

8. The edition cited is Loyseau, *Oeuvres* (Paris: Pierre Rocolet, 1640).

9. See, for example, *Avis au Tiers-Etat de Bourgogne, concernant les justices seigneuriales* (n.p., 1789). All of the writer's arguments are drawn from Loyseau.

10. Indeed, Loyseau's global vision of the state and public authority escaped most of his contemporaries, not just those who wrote about seigneurial justice. See Brigitte Basdevant-Gaudemet's seminal study of Loyseau's thought: *Aux origines de l'État moderne: Charles Loyseau, 1564–1627: Théoricien de la puissance publique* (Paris: Economica, 1977), 282. Much of the following analysis of Loyseau's work is drawn from Basdevant-Gaudemet. A useful presentation of Loyseau's *Discours de l'abus des justices de village,* especially with respect to the reception of his ideas, can be found in François Brizay and Véronique Sarrazin, "Le *Discours de l'abus des justices de village:* Un texte de circonstance dans une œuvre de référence," in Brizay, Follain, and Sarrazin, *Les justices de village,* 109–22.

11. The phrase used by Loyseau is "puissance publique." Loyseau, *Oeuvres,* 508. Basdevant-Gaudemet, *Loyseau,* 118–27.

12. David Parker has shown that historians have overemphasized the importance of king-as-lawmaker in the construction of the ideology and practice of absolutism. He shows that in reality the king was limited by Roman and customary law, and especially religion and ideas of natural justice. David Parker, "Sovereignty, Absolutism, and the Function of the Law in Seventeenth-Century France," *Past and Present* 122 (1989): 36–74.

13. Loyseau, *Oeuvres,* 511–12.

14. Ibid., 512.

15. Loyseau, "Livre des seigneurs," in *Oeuvres,* 100.

16. Loyseau writes at length about the problem of the firing of judges by lords. Judges are officers, not commissioners–proof of this can be found in the fact that a judge does not automatically end his term upon the death of a lord or the transferral of the seigneurie. This means that in theory a lord could only remove a judge from

office if he failed to fulfill his judicial duties. Unfortunately, "as in several other points of jurisdiction, usage has overcome reason," and in reality lords practice "*destitution à volonté*." Loyseau also attacks arbitrary removal from a practical perspective, noting that lords possess enough power over villagers, "without [giving them] this authority over them, to be able to fire them at will, when they do not make the lords win all their cases, and render justice to their fantasy." Loyseau, *Oeuvres,* 558–79.

17. Boucher d'Argis, *Cahier d'un magistrat du Châtelet de Paris,* 2.

18. Daguesseau, "Idée générale ou plan abrégé de l'usage que l'on pourrait faire des Estats envoyés par les Intendants pour faire former un meilleur arrangement des sièges ordinaires de la Judicature," in Combe, *Mémoire inédit du chancelier Daguesseau,* 163–83. The manuscript, kept in the Bibliothèque nationale, is undated. Combe dates it at 1738.

19. Ibid., 163–65.

20. Ibid., 173.

21. A concise presentation of the distinction as seen by Bodin can be found in Quentin Skinner, *The Foundations of Modern Political Thought* (Cambridge: Cambridge University Press, 1978), 294–97. The citation, which is from Bodin's *Of Sovereignty,* is taken from 295. See also James Collins, *The State in Early Modern France* (Cambridge: Cambridge University Press, 1995), 10–11.

22. *De l'administration de la justice dans les campagnes* (n.p., 1789), 2. Another author writes that "court cases last for centuries; they go through five or six degrees of jurisdiction, pass before the eyes of a hundred different judges, the litigants are consumed in legal fees; the offence . . . is forgotten; the property in question, is dissipated, eaten by *gens de loi,* before there is any definitive solution." Pétion de Villeneuve, "Les lois civiles et l'administration de la justice," 164.

23. Fouquau de Pussy, *Idées sur l'administration de la justice dans les petites villes et bourgs de France, pour déterminer la suppression des jurisdictions seigneuriales* (Paris: n.p., 1789), 4.

24. Filled with flights of fancy, the author adds that this would provide opportunities for talented young men in the provinces and stem their flight to Paris, thus providing husbands for peasant girls and ending prostitution in the countryside. Ibid., 77–81.

25. Ibid., 85–88.

26. See also Challan, *Réflexions sur l'administration de la justice, sur la formation de tribunaux ordinaires et municipaux, afin de rendre la justice gratuite, et d'éviter les abus qui règnent spécialement dans les justices seigneuriales* (Paris: n.p., 1789). Challan also calls for reimbursement of the right of justice.

27. S.-N.-H. Linguet, *Nécessité d'une réforme dans l'administration de la justice et dans les lois civiles en France, avec la réfutation de l'Esprit des lois* (Amsterdam: n.p., 1764), 58–59.

28. A. Cocahe-Zilgien, "Un génie méconnu du XVIIe siècle: L'avocat Linguet (1736–1794), incendiaire, réactionnaire et visionnaire," *Annales africaines de la Faculté de droit et des sciences économiques de Dakar* 1 (1960): 83–122.

29. Ibid., 98–99.

30. Linguet, *Nécessité d'une réforme,* 7–8.

31. Darline Gay Levy, *The Ideas and Careers of Simon-Nicolas Henri Linguet: A Study in Eighteenth-Century French Politics* (Urbana: University of Illinois Press, 1980), 25–30.

32. M. Mézard, *Essai sur les réformes à faire dans l'administration de la justice en France* (n.p., 1788), 81.

33. Durand Echeverria, *The Maupeou Revolution: A Study in the History of Libertarianism: France, 1770–1774* (Baton Rouge: Louisiana State University Press, 1985), 136.

34. Doyle, *Venality,* 262–67. Doyle notes that "however pernicious, abusive, or ridiculous it might be, venality could not be destroyed because it was too expensive to buy out" (267).

35. Loyseau, *Oeuvres,* 569. Note that his discussion of seigneurial justice comes up within the context of offices and venality.

36. Ibid., 568.

37. Bouhier, *Coutumes,* 93, 107. The quotation from the Ordinance of Roussillon is likewise taken from Bouhier, *Coutumes,* 93.

38. P. L. F. Jouye Desroches, *Rapport présenté au nom du Comité de Judicature, sur le remboursement des officiers des ci-devant justices seigneuriales* (Paris: Imprimerie nationale, 1791), 3–4. See also Viellart, *Opinion présentée au comité des droits féodaux, sur l'abolition des justices seigneuriales, et des droits qui en dérivaient* (Paris: Imprimerie nationale, 1790), 4.

39. Keith Michael Baker, *Inventing the French Revolution: Essays on French Political Culture in the Eighteenth Century* (Cambridge: Cambridge University Press, 1990), 170.

40. David Parker, "Absolutism, Feudalism, and Property Rights in the France of Louis XIV," *Past and Present* 179 (2003): 91–93.

41. Poitrineau, "Aspects de la crise," 568–69.

42. Schneider, "Village and State," 1–20; Soleil, "Le maintient des justices seigneuriales," 93–95.

43. BM Dijon, MS 1306, "Recueil d'Arrêts du Parlement de Dijon" (hereafter cited as "Recueil"), vol. 3, *arrêt général* 3 July 1747.

44. BM Dijon, MS 1308, "Recueil," vol. 5, *arrêt* 7 July 1774.

45. "Recueil," *arrêt* 29 Mar. 1768. The court had issued a similar *arrêt* several years earlier. In 1728 Parlement had "made very express prohibitions to the said Claude Martin to perform the functions of the clerk in the justice of the said Rochetaillé, as long as he runs a *cabaret,* on threat of having his judicial acts and procedures declared null and void, and being sentenced to pay damages and interests to the litigants so affected." BM Dijon, MS 1305, "Recueil," vol. 2, *arrêt* 4 Aug. 1728.

46. BM Dijon, MS 1306, "Recueil," vol. 3, *arrêt* 6 Aug. 1764.

47. BM Dijon, MS 1308, "Recueil," vol. 5, *arrêt* 14 Mar. 1776.

48. BM Dijon, MS 1309, "Recueil," vol. 6, *arrêt* 1 Mar. 1788.

49. See also BM Dijon, MS 1306, "Recueil," vol. 3, *arrêt* 3 July 1756. The culprit here was the justice of the Doyenne de Paray.

50. BM Dijon, MS 1306, "Recueil," vol. 3, *arrêt* 9 Mar. 1763.

51. BM Dijon, MS 1308, "Recueil," vol. 5, separate *arrêts* 23 Sept. 1775, 16 Oct. 1779.

52. BM Dijon, MS 1307, "Recueil," vol. 4, *arrêt* 19 Feb. 1766.

53. BM Dijon, MS 1307, "Recueil," vol. 4, *arrêt* 20 Mar. 1766.

54. BM Dijon, MS 1308, "Recueil," vol. 5, *arrêt* 26 Mar. 1768: "Arrêt du Parlement qui ordonne à tous les seigneurs Justiciers du ressort de la cour, d'instituer des officiers pour l'exercise de leurs justices."

55. BM Dijon MS 1308, "Recueil," vol. 5, *arrêts* 13 Feb. 1772 and 1 Mar. 1770.

56. BM Dijon, MS 1308, "Recueil," vol. 5, *arrêt* 17 Dec. 1772.

57. BM Dijon, MS 1308, "Recueil," vol. 5, *arrêt* 28 Dec. 1773.

58. *Règlements généraux pour les justices seigneuriales.*

59. The record from the Grands-Jours of the seigneurial justice of Senailly, for example, from 1781, contains the following phrase: "we have had read the general regulations (*règlements généraux*) printed by Causse in 68 articles." ADCO B2 1220/7, seigneurial justice of Senailly, St. Germain, Grands-Jours 30 May 1781. Prior to the publication of this (and several other) small handbook(s), seigneurial judges did read out police *arrêts,* but the choice of *arrêts* was at their discretion.

60. *Règlements généraux qui s'observent dans tout le ressort de la cour.*

61. ADCO 18J 30, undated correspondence. The last phrase cited is ambiguous, since the original "depuis le rétablissement de la justice" could also be rendered "reestablishment of justice." It is unclear, therefore, whether the author means to describe thereby the process of judicial reform or whether his local justice had become inactive and had been resuscitated.

62. ADCO 18J 33 letter from Poulin fils aîné *avocat* 9 Apr. 1776.

63. ADCO C 3341, provincial Estates, folder on jurisprudence, Déclaration du Roi sur les instances en surtaux, 31 Dec. 1773. The policy of the Estates toward the question of *surtaux* court cases can be reconstructed from the registers of remonstrances. See, for example, C 3331, provincial Estates, *cahiers de remontrances,* 1731–1758.

64. ADCO C 3332, provincial Estates, *cahier de remontrances des États,* remonstrance of 1773, art. 5.

65. Ibid., *cahier des remontrances* for 1761–76, remonstrances for 1773, art. 6, "Instances en mésus."

66. ADCO C 3341, provincial Estates, folder on jurisprudence, Déclaration du Roi sur les mésus, 31 Dec. 1773.

67. BM Dijon, MS 1308, "Recueil," vol. 5, *arrêt* 30 Dec. 1773.

68. In 1769 the Second Chamber of the Estates deliberated as follows: "The honorable gentlemen will not be admitted with a deliberative voice unless they are twenty-five years old and have provided a *reprise de fief ou arrière fief* with at least middle and low justice, situated in the duchy and county of Burgundy and surrounding regions, the said *reprise de fief* done in person or by a legal representative or guardian." A *reprise de fief* was an official document required whenever a seigneurie changed hands. It listed the property and rights that made up the seigneurie. ADCO C 3046, *cahier des carnots du 2e Etat,* 1769, art. 6.

69. AM Dijon C14, jurisdiction folder, 29 July 1778.

70. Albert Colombet, *Les parlementaires bourguignons à la fin du XVIIIe siècle* (Lyon: Bosc, 1936), 118–51, 156–85.

71. Ibid., 103–4.

72. Ibid., 67–77.

73. I recorded the *capitation* records for the years 1746 and 1787. ADCO C 5644, Parlement, *capitation,* 1746; ADCO B 12155, Parlement, *capitation,* 1787. For these same years I also recorded the names of everyone who owned a seigneurie, as well as the name of the seigneuries in question from the *vingtième* rolls. For 1787: ADCO C 5483,

bailliage of Beaune, 1787; ADCO C 5836, bailliage of Arnay-le-Duc, 1787; ADCO C 5837, bailliage of Autun and Montcenis, 1787; ADCO C 5839, bailliages of Auxerre and Auxonne, 1787; ADCO C 5841, bailliage of Avallon, 1787; ADCO C 5842, bailliage of Bar-sur-Seine, 1787; ADCO C 5845, bailliage of Châlon, 1787; ADCO C 5844, bailliage of Charolles, 1787; ADCO C 5848, bailliage of Châtillon, 1787; ADCO C 5852 bailliage of Nuits, 1787; ADCO C 5856, bailliage of Semur-en-Auxois, 1787; ADCO C 5857, bailliage of Semur-en-Brionnais, 1787; ADOC C 5851, bailliage of Dijon, 1787. For 1746, I used the following manuscript (which was drawn up using the *dixième* rolls for 1746): BM Dijon MS 1159, "État des seigneurs de la province de Bourgogne, des terres et seigneuries qu'ils y occupent et du dixième qu'ils en payent au Roi en l'année 1746, ledit État distribué par bailliage et chef-lieu."

74. Jean-Luc Poisot, "Le recrutement du Parlement après 1775: Les origines sociales des nouveaux conseillers" (Master's thesis: Université de Bourgogne, 1977), 67–68, 88. Thanks to Jean Bart for providing me with a copy of this master's thesis.

75. Colombet, *Parlementaires,* 61–62.

76. Daguesseau, "Idée générale," 163–82.

77. Jean Bart, "La pénétration du droit bourguignon en Bresse à la fin de l'Ancien Régime," *MSHDB* 25 (1964): 75–76; Jean Bart, "Du droit bourguignon au droit français," *MSHDB* 49 (1977): 13–14, 20.

78. Julian Swann, "Power and Provincial Politics in Eighteenth-Century France: The Varenne Affair, 1757–1763," *French Historical Studies* 21 (1998): 441–76; M. de la Cuisine, *Le Parlement de Bourgogne depuis son origine jusqu'à sa chute* (Dijon: A. Durant, 1857), 3:220–40; Stéphane Pannekoucke, "L'affaire Varenne (1760–1763): Jeux de clientèle et enjeux de pouvoir entre Versailles, Paris et Dijon," *Annales de Bourgogne* 78 (2006): 33–68.

79. For a description of the legal reforms of 1788, see Jean Egret, *The French Prerevolution, 1787–1788,* trans. Wesley D. Camp (Chicago: University of Chicago Press, 1977), 144–78.

80. See the anonymous pamphlet *Avis au Tiers-Etat de Bourgogne.*

81. Egret, *Prerevolution,* 154–56.

82. *Protestations du Parlement de Bourgogne du 4 Juin 1788,* BM Dijon, Fonds Delmasse 606.

83. *Arrêté de la Chambre des Comptes de Bourgogne et Bresse,* BM Dijon, Fonds Delmasse 609 (9 June 1788).

84. Jean Bastier, "Le parlement de Toulouse et les justices subalternes au XVIIIe siècle," in Jacques Poumarède and Jack Thomas, eds., *Les Parlements de Province: Pouvoir, justice et société du XVe au XVIIIe siècle* (Toulouse: Framespa, 1996), 407–8.

85. Éric Gasparini, "Justice seigneuriale et régulation sociale: L'exemple de quelques seigneuries comtoises dans la seconde moitié du XVIIIe siècle," in Brizay, Follain, and Sarrazin, *Les justices de village,* 262–64; Soleil, "Le siège présidial d'Angers," 211; Soleil, "Le maintien des justices seigneuriales," 83–100; Sylvain Soleil, "Les justices seigneuriales et l'État monarchique au XVIIIe siècle: L'incorporation par le droit," in Brizay, Follain, and Sarrazin, *Les justices de village,* 325–39.

86. These authors, of course, all argue that the reform attempts were ineffective. Giffard, *Justices seigneuriales en Bretagne,* 44–48, 291; Poitrineau, "Aspects de la crise," 552; Crubaugh, *Balancing the Scales of Justice,* 7.

87. ADCO 18J 34, letter from M. de Prey Aug. 8, 1778. The author of the letter was clearly engaged in some kind of dispute with the seigneurial judge, as de Prey had already written to Parlement in 1776 complaining about the judge's refusal to hear farming disputes at the assizes.

88. Cited in Nicolas Delasselle, "Une justice seigneuriale à Coulanges-la-Vineuse et au Val-de-Mercy au XVIIIe siècle" (Master's thesis: Université de Bourgogne, 1992), 145–48. These villages were in southern Burgundy, now the department of the Yonne.

89. The best description of the procedure followed in seigneurial courts, emphasizing its oral nature, is Mauclair, "La justice seigneuriale de La Vallière," 125–30.

90. This figure includes only those cases judged in regular session. At the assizes, parties presented their own cases without representation. Since by the 1780s about half of all cases were tried at the assizes, we can say that over 50 percent of cases in seigneurial courts involved no legal representation.

91. The *sergent* was an officer of the seigneurial court. He was usually a local man, preferably someone with basic literacy skills. His main responsibilities were to deliver summons, assist the court at auctions, and sometimes carry out court-ordered seizures of goods.

92. ADCO C 1402, intendant, village files, Senailly, 1774.

93. ADCO B2 601/2, seigneurial justice of Flée, sessions 9 Dec. 1751, 23 Dec. 1751, 2 Mar. 1752, 20 July 1752, 15 Mar. 1753, 5 Apr. 1753, 12 Apr. 1753.

94. Most recently, Crubaugh, *Balancing the Scales of Justice,* 44.

95. "Ordonnance civile touchant la réformation de la justice," April 1667, in Isambert et al., *Recueil général des anciennes lois françaises,* 18:103, 128–31.

96. Daniel Jousse, *Nouveau commentaire sur l'ordonnance civile du mois d'avril 1667* (Paris: Debure l'aiîné, 1753), 204.

97. ADCO B2 101/3, bailliage of Dijon, deliberations of the *procureurs,* deliberation, 18 Jan. 1782, containing a copy of a *mémoire* sent to the Parlement of Dijon relative to the *arrêt* of 3 July 1781. See also the deliberations of 15 Apr. and 6 May 1783 relative to the possibility of pursuing the matter to the Royal Council. The *procureurs* of the bailliages of Saint-Jean-de-Losne, Charolles, Arnay-le-Duc, Belley, Nuits, Autun, Beaune, Saulieu, Châlon-sur-Saône, and Semur-en-Brionnais approved the pursuit of the matter to the Royal Council, while those of Bourg, Montcenis, Semur-en-Auxois, Gex, Châtillon-sur-Seine, and Avallon opposed such an action. Those of Auxonne and Bourbon-Lancy failed to answer the letters sent to them on the subject. They selected two members to present their case in Paris. Much correspondence is exchanged, but it all led nowhere, and by the spring of 1789 the *procureurs* had spent 6,942 livres 7 sols 6 deniers, with nothing to show for it.

98. Ibid., bailliage of Dijon, *délibérations des procureurs.*

99. Ibid., deliberation 25 June 1783.

100. ADCO B2 1032, B2 1048 seigneurial justice of the religious chapter of St. Bénigne. Based on 100 cases from the 1750s. I counted only those that began after 1752, since many of the cases picked up in 1750–51 had in fact begun in 1749 or before. The sample from 1782–90 contained 185 cases where the date of the summons was known.

101. All of the percentages listed here are proportions of the number of cases that had a final settlement, rather than all cases.

102. C.-E. Labrousse, *Esquisse du mouvement des prix et des revenus en France au XVIIIe siècle* (Paris: Dalloz, 1933), 137–48.

103. Kagan, *Lawsuits and Litigants,* 42–45.

104. Wunder, *Inferior Courts, Superior Justice,* 155–56.

105. Crubaugh, *Balancing the Scales of Justice,* 50.

106. Piant, "Prévôté de Vaucouleurs," 450.

107. Mauclair, "Justice seigneuriale de la La Valière," 518, 556.

108. Pierre de Saint Jacob has pointed to the importance of the assizes in northern Burgundy, and he even noticed the reinvigoration of the assizes in the last twenty years of the ancien régime. He correctly underlined the importance of the assizes in policing the seigneurie and protecting seigneurial rights but failed to notice the important increase in civil cases being tried at the assizes. Saint Jacob, *Paysans de la Bourgogne du nord,* 407–10.

109. The Grands-Jours were to be done by village rather than by court. The larger seigneurial court of the religious chapter of St. Bénigne, in other words, had to have separate annual assizes in the villages of Bellefond, Epagny, Larey, Messigny, Sauley, Saulon-la-Chapelle, and Savigny-le-Sec.

110. Since the records of the Grands-Jours were often on loose paper, it is theoretically possible that some may be missing from the records. But it is generally possible to see from the other records of the court whether assizes were held in the village in question. When the court skipped a year, for example, the judge at the next assizes handed out fines for two years. In years without assizes, the local officers (*syndics, messiers, prud'hommes*) had to appear before the judge at his weekly session to be sworn in.

111. ADCO B2 457/2, seigneurial justice of Corgengoux, Mazerotte, and Parney, probate inventory of Claude Caillet, 19 Feb. 1733.

112. For a description of the prereform procedure to be used in *mésus* cases, see Lucan, *Traité des mésus à l'usage du duché de Bourgogne avec les Arrêts de Règlement rendus à ce sujet* (Dijon: Causse, 1772).

113. ADCO B2 734/1, seigneurial justice of Meursault, sessions 9 Aug. 1752, 23 Aug. 1752.

114. ADCO B2 734/2, seigneurial justice of Auxey, Grands-Jours 21 Aug. 1780.

115. ADCO 1F 301/1, private papers, undated letter.

116. ADCO 18J 21, private papers, Jacquinot notes, 1791.

117. Crubaugh, *Balancing the Scales of Justice,* 168–72.

118. I do not argue that the legal reforms of the Revolution were unimportant or ineffectual. There seems little doubt that the Revolutionary legal system, until at least the early nineteenth century, made it easier to settle inheritance disputes, debts, and other cases. Only for *mésus* do I contend that the Revolution made it more difficult (and only in northern Burgundy). For a study of a Burgundian JP that concludes that the institution worked well in rural areas, see Jean Bart, "Justice de paix du canton de Fontaine-Française," 213. See also Christophe Breugnot, "La justice de paix dans le canton d'Arc-sur-Tille à l'époque révolutionnaire" (D.E.A. thesis: Université de Bourgogne, 1994), 104. Although active, these institutions look a good deal less vibrant than Crubaugh's.

119. ADCO B2 1048, seigneurial justice of the religious chapter of St. Bénigne, village of Epagny, Grands-Jours 29 Aug. 1780.

120. ADCO B2 603/2, seigneurial justice of Foncegrive, Grands-Jours 22 Dec. 1785.

121. ADCO B2 1048, seigneurial justice of the religious chapter of St. Bénigne, village of Messigny, Grands-Jours 4 Sept. 1783.

122. James C. Scott, *Weapons of the Weak: Everyday Forms of Peasant Resistance* (New Haven: Yale University Press, 1985), xv–xix; Scott, *Domination and the Arts of Resistance: Hidden Transcripts* (New Haven: Yale University Press, 1990), 1–14.

123. Regular court sessions were also public, but it seems unlikely that a large number of villagers regularly attended court, especially since the sessions were frequently held in town.

124. ADCO B2 1252/2, seigneurial justice of Ancey, Grands-Jours 12 Aug. 1755.

125. ADCO B2 1048, seigneurial justice of the religious chapter of St. Bénigne, village of Messigny, Grands-Jours 4 Sept. 1783.

126. Ibid., village of Savigny-le-Sec, Grands-Jours 4 Sept. 1788.

127. ADCO B2 1252/3, seigneurial justice of Ancey, Grands-Jours 13 Aug. 1759.

128. ADCO B2 1048, seigneurial justice of the religious chapter of St. Bénigne, village of Epagny, Grands-Jours 24 Aug. 1784.

129. Ibid., village of Messigny, Grands-Jours 4 Sept. 1783.

130. These figures include the civil side of *mésus,* which were, after all, lawsuits over very minor torts. It excludes, however, the fines handed out for *mésus,* which were always much more numerous.

131. Jean Richard is highly skeptical of the use of tax rolls by social historians. In the Burgundian bailliage of Châtillon-sur-Seine he found evidence of villagewide conspiracies to defraud the taxman. Some villages in the middle of the century (his examples are from the 1740s and 1750s) underreported the number of households in order to lower the global amount of taxes owed by the village. In 1741, for example, the village of Bremur listed between eleven and fifteen hearths from 1733 to 1747. By 1752, after an investigation by authorities, the figure was up to twenty-six hearths. The beggar listed in the rolls of Beaulieu at 25 livres *taille* certainly did not pay it himself. Richard says that in many villages the tax rolls presented to the crown were almost entirely fictive and that villages divided the tax burden among themselves in a way that had no relation to what the state thought it knew. See his "A propos d'une source documentaire: De faux rôles des tailles en Châtillonnais (1741)," *Annales de Bourgogne* 55 (1983): 34–38. While this type of abusive practice certainly occurred, it was an anomaly. Richard himself acknowledged that the administration undertook reforms after 1750 that probably curtailed some of the worst abuses. My comparison of tax rolls to the list of those appearing in courts reveals that in the sample used here there is no significant exclusion of those who were better off (or of anyone, for that matter).

132. ADCO B2 1252/3, seigneurial justice of Ancey, Grands-Jours 4 Sept. 1786.

133. See, for example, ADCO B2 603/2, seigneurial justice of Foncegrive, Grands-Jours 18 Dec. 1780.

134. ADCO B2 1252/3, seigneurial justice of Ancey, Grands-Jours 7 Sept. 1785.

Chapter 6

1. Taken from Bart, *La Révolution française en Bourgogne,* 122–40.

2. On the 1789 antiseigneurial revolt, see Markoff, *Abolition of Feudalism,* 218–29, and Ado, *Paysans en Révolution,* 102–9, 125–50. On the destruction of archives, see Soboul, "De la pratique des terriers," 149–58.

3. Markoff, *Abolition of Feudalism,* 347.

4. George Taylor, "Revolutionary and Nonrevolutionary Content in the *Cahiers* of 1789: An Interim Report," *French Historical Studies* 7 (1972): 479–502.

5. Markoff, *Abolition of Feudalism,* 69–78; Markoff, "Peasant Protest," *Comparative Studies of Society and History* 34 (1990): 416.

6. Philippe Grateau, *Les cahiers de doléances:* Une relecture culturelle (Rennes: Presses universitaires de Rennes, 2001), 19.

7. ADCO B2 209 bis, bailliage of Châtillon-sur-Seine, *cahier* of Aignay-le-Duc.

8. Ibid., *cahier* of Blaisy.

9. ADCO B2 242/1, bailliage of Arnay-le-Duc, *cahier* of Chaudenay-le-Château.

10. Le Roy Ladurie, "Révoltes et contestations rurales," 12.

11. Before Bloch, P. Sagnac suggested that revolutionary antiseigneurial sentiment was caused by an intensification of the seigneurial regime. Sagnac, *Quomodo jura dominii aucta fuerint regnant Ludocivo XVI* (Paris: Marchesou, 1898).

12. Marc Bloch, *French Rural History: An Essay on its Basic Charasteristics* (Los Angeles: University of California Press, 1970), 126–49.

13. According to feudal theorists, the seigneurie was composed of two parts: the fief, which was essentially a form of public authority; and the *domaine,* which was the physical estate, the land that the lord owned.

14. Georges Lefebvre, *Les paysans du Nord pendant la Révolution Française* (Paris: A. Colin, 1972 [c. 1924]), 163; Peter Jones, *The Peasantry in the French Revolution* (Cambridge: Cambridge University Press, 1988), 42–59.

15. Saint Jacob, *Les paysans de la Bourgogne du nord,* 420–34.

16. Forster, *House of Saulx-Tavanes,* 207.

17. Bart, *La Révolution française en Bourgogne,* 52.

18. Root, *Peasants and King,* 15.

19. William Doyle, "Was there an Aristocratic Reaction in Pre-Revolutionary France?" *Past and Present* 57 (1972): 97–122.

20. Jean Meyer had suggested in 1966 that there was nothing new about the revision of *terriers* and the scrupulous attention late eighteenth-century lords paid to their estates. Meyer, *La noblesse bretonne an XVIIIe siècle* (Paris: Imprimerie nationale, 1966), 784–85.

21. Notably in Guy Chausinand-Nogaret, *The French Nobility in the Eighteenth Century: From Feudalism to Enlightenment* (Cambridge: Cambridge University Press, 1985), 84–130.

22. David Hackett Fischer, *The Great Wave: Price Revolutions and the Rhythms of History* (Oxford: Oxford University Press, 1996).

23. Sébastien Evrard, *L'intendant de Bourgogne et le contentieux administratif au XVIIIe siècle* (Paris: De Broccard, 2005), 15.

24. Root, *Peasants and King,* 1–15.

25. These village accounts are classified by village for the late eighteenth century. They are housed in series C in the ADCO.

26. ADCO C 3523, provincial Estates, folder on jurisprudence, "Arrêt du conseil . . ." 4 Sept. 1770. Communities, the *arrêt* orders, "may not conduct transactions, nor other acts or contracts that directly or indirectly alienate the goods of the said community without first having obtained the written authorization of the intendant." This was a reform requested by the provincial Estates in their remonstrances of 1770.

27. ADCO C 1453, intendant, Bagnot, 26 June 1775.

28. ADCO B2 423/2, seigneurial justice of Aisy, Pont-d'Aisy, session 3 July 1774.

29. ADCO B2 1032, seigneurial justice of the *prieuré* of Larrey, session 14 Aug. 1751.

30. BM Dijon, MS 19178, *Recueil des déclarations, édits, lettres patentes et arrêts du Conseil d'État du Roi, enregistrés au Parlement de Dijon,* vol. 14, *arrêt* 8 Apr. 1778.

31. ADCO C 3523, provincial Estates, folder on jurisprudence, royal *arrêt* 31 July 1778.

32. BM Dijon, MIC 433, microfilm of registers of Parlement remonstrances, 1761–82, Remontrances au sujet de l'amodiation des biens communaux, 15 Mar. 1779.

33. Ibid.

34. Ibid.

35. Condé answered: "I will employ myself in this occasion, as in all others, to the success of that which you desire." Ibid.

36. BM Dijon, MS 1308, "Recueil," vol. 5, 17 Mar. 1780.

37. See, for example, ADCO B2 1048, seigneurial justice of the religious chapter of St. Bénigne, session 6 Apr. 1784. For evidence that courts read this *arrêt* to the villagers each year at the Grands-Jours, see ADCO B2 451/2, seigneurial justice of Belleneuve, Grands-Jours 21 Oct. 1782.

38. ADCO C3, intendant, handwritten *mémoire* 31 Mar. 1789.

39. *Remontrances . . . sur un arrêt du Conseil, en date du 14 Février 1789* (Dijon, 1789). BM Dijon, Fonds Delmasse 399.

40. AN H/1/200/2, *pays d'Etats,* Bourgogne, *mémoire sur les abus dans les procès des communautés,* 1784–87.

41. ADCO C 3519, provincial Estates, folder on jurisdictional disputes, undated *mémoire* (from after 1781 based on internal evidence).

42. ADCO C 3, intendant, justice, unpublished *mémoire* for the intendant, 31 Mar. 1789. This document was prepared in response to another pamphlet prepared for the Parlement of Dijon. Although I have been unable to find the original pro-parlement document, the author of this report cites extensively from it. The quotation is drawn from marginal citations from the original.

43. ADCO C 3519, provincial Estates, folder on jurisdictional disputes, undated *mémoire.*

44. AN H/1/200/2, pays d'Etats, Bourgogne, undated *mémoire.*

45. Indeed, the creation of the committee of lawyers by Amelot is at the heart of Evrard's argument that the monarchy was working toward a modern conception of administrative law. Evrard, *L'intendant de Bourgogne,* 18–23, 143–45, 254–58.

46. In the first six months of 1784, before the committee was created, Evrard found 138 requests and only three refusals. Ibid., 290.

47. There is no archive that contains all of the requests for permission to plead. Evrard estimates he found about two-thirds of the requests. Ibid., 349.

48. By contrast, the intendant did "judge" cases involving village finances, deciding things like whether the seigneur, other privileged inhabitants, and nonresident landowners should have to contribute to construction and repairs in the public space of the village. Ibid., 309–11.

49. There were attempts to abolish *contrainte solidaire* by royal edict, but these were largely ineffective in most of France, including Burgundy. See Marie-Laure Legay, "1775: L'abolition de la contrainte solidaire en France," in Garnot, *Justice et argent,* 195–96.

50. ADCO C 3519, provincial Estates, folder on jurisdictional disputes, undated *mémoire.*

51. BM Dijon, MS 1309, "Recueil," vol. 6., *arrêt* 4 Mar. 1785.

52. ADCO B2 1077/1, seigneurial justice of Ampilly-lés-Bordes, sessions 7 Feb. 1784, 8 May 1784.

53. ADCO B2 734/2, seigneurial justice of Meursault, sessions 3 Jan. 1785, 24 Jan. 1785, 28 Feb. 1785, 11 Apr. 1785, 23 May 1785, 18 July 1785.

54. ADCO E Dépôt 439/15, communal archives of Montot, village accounts, 1 Apr. 1787.

55. ADCO C 1360, intendant, accounts for Fontaine-en-Duesmois, 28 May 1788.

56. Pierre d'Orgéval Dubouchet, *La taille en Bourgogne au XVIIIe siècle* (Dijon: Pornon, 1938), 105–10.

57. ADCO C 3519, provincial Estates, folder on jurisdictional disputes, undated *mémoire.*

58. ADCO C 360, intendant, register of *impositions négociales.*

59. ADCO C 3332, provincial Estates, *cahier des remontrances,* 1776, art. 7. See also ADCO 1F 460, Administration de la province de Bourgogne considéré comme pays d'État, chap. 62, "Conservation des biens communaux." This undated *mémoire,* likely written in the early 1780s (certainly after 1779 from internal evidence), described the same problems as the remonstrance cited.

60. ADCO C 3333, provincial Estates, *cahier des remontrances,* 1779, art. 9.

61. ADCO C 3012, provincial Estates, *décrets des Etats,* 1781, *Remontrances des conseillers et procureurs syndics,* "Usages et communaux."

62. ADCO C 3519, provincial Estates, folder on jurisdictional disputes, undated *mémoire.*

63. Ibid.

64. ADCO B2 734/2, seigneurial justice of Meursault, session 13 June 1785.

65. The increase was by a factor of 1.9. Labrousse, *Esquisse du mouvement des prix,* 348.

66. Forster, *House of Saulx-Tavanes,* 73. An *arpent* was a measure of land approximately equal to a hectare.

67. Labrousse, *Esquisse,* 137–48.

68. Saint Jacob, *Paysans de la Bourgogne du nord,* 7–19, 272–73.

69. Forster, *House of Saulx-Tavanes,* 73–75.

70. ADCO 10F 867, private seigneurial papers, barony of Pagny, receipt 8 Jan. 1785.

71. ADCO B2 1252/2, seigneurial justice of Ancey, session 11 Sept. 1786.

72. ADCO B2 1220/7, seigneurial justice of Senailly, St. Germain, sessions 7 May 1782, 10 May 1782. The court ordered experts to visit the forest in question, who concluded that the trees were strong enough. The judge then ordered the lord to allow the animals into the forest.

73. Saint Jacob, *Paysans de la Bourgogne du nord,* 428–32. Saint Jacob dates the participation of *fermiers* in the seigneurial reaction from after 1760. While wealthier than most other villagers, few northern Burgundian *fermiers* could aspire to the wealth and social position enjoyed by *fermiers* in the cereal plains around Paris. See Michel Moriceau, *Les fermiers de l'Ile de France, XVe–XVIIIe siècle* (Paris: Fayard, 1994).

74. I have excluded, in other words, simple debt cases involving *fermiers,* primarily nonpayment for hay, wheat, and other goods delivered.

75. Twenty-nine was the maximum number of years' worth of arrears for which a lord could demand payment.

76. ADCO B2 734/2, seigneurial justice of Meursault, sessions 3 Jan. 1785, 24 Jan. 1785, 14 Feb. 1785, 28 Feb. 1785, 14 Mar. 1785, 23 May 1785, 8 Aug. 1785, 20 Mar. 1786, 8 May 1786, 22 May 1786.

77. Heichette, *Société, sociabilité, justice,* 284; William Beik, *Urban Protest in Seventeenth-Century France: The Culture of Retribution* (Cambridge: Cambridge University Press, 1997), 33–35; Nicolas, *La rébellion française,* 482.

78. On attitudes toward guards, see Hamish Graham, "Exercice d'équilibre," in Dolan, *Entre justice et justiciables,* 219, 224–45; Philippe Crémieu-Alcan, "Huissiers et gardes forestiers en Guyenne au XVIIIe siècle à travers les délits forestiers: Une même difficulté à faire le 'dû de leur charge?'" in Dolan, *Entre justice et justiciables,* 248–49, 258–59; A. Corvol, "Les délinquances forestières en Basse-Bourgogne depuis la réformation de 1711–1718," *Revue historique* 526 (1978): 366–67.

79. Forster, *House of Saulx-Tavanes,* 54–108.

80. In 1747 the lord leased the seigneurie to Claude Macherat for 750 livres per year for nine years. In 1786 Jacques Macherat and Claude Robin paid 2,000 livres and six measures of beets for the same seigneurie. ADCO E 1552, private seigneurial papers of Montot and Villerrottin, leases 27 Feb. 1747, 12 Mar. 1754, 1 Dec. 1761, 3 Dec. 1767, 8 July 1786.

81. David Parker suggests that the intensification began much earlier, during the seventeenth century, and that in many ways it was led by the monarchy. See Parker, "Absolutism, Feudalism, and Property Rights," 91–92.

82. Le Roy Ladurie, "Révoltes et contestations rurales," *Annales: Economies, sociétés, civilisations* 29 (1974): 12.

83. Bart, *La Révolution française en Bourgogne,* 10.

84. John Markoff, "Peasant Grievances and Peasant Insurrection: France in 1789," *Journal of Modern History* 62 (1990): 473.

85. Zink, *Clochers et troupeaux,* 165–84; Antoine, *Fiefs et villages du Bas-Maine,* 259–84.

86. Grateau, *Les cahiers de doléances,* 334.

Chapter 7

1. The following analysis is based on 303 parish *cahiers*, almost complete series from four northern Burgundian bailliages. This includes *cahiers* from the following bailliages: 94 parishes from Châtillon-sur-Seine (ADCO B2 209 bis), 122 from Semur-en-Auxois (B2 226/1), 48 from Arnay-le-Duc (B2 242/1), 36 from Saulieu (B2 254/1), and a handful from the bailliage of Beaune (B2 161/3).

2. According to article 25 of the electoral law of 24 January 1789, all parish assemblies were to be presided over by the "juge du lieu," or in his absence by any public officer. In Roger Chartier's sample the proportion of assemblies chaired by an "homme de loi" varies from as high as 98 percent in the bailliage of Orléans to 77 percent in the bailliage of Troyes. See Roger Chartier, "Cultures, lumières, doléances: Les cahiers de 1789," *Revue d'histoire moderne et contemporaine* 21 (1981): 68–70.

3. Markoff, *Abolition of Feudalism*, 20–26; Shapiro and Markoff, *Revolutionary Demands*, 150–56.

4. Régine Robin, "Quatrième État et cahiers de doléances dans le bailliage d'Auxois en 1789," *Bulletin de la Commission d'histoire économique et sociale de la Révolution française* (1966), 31–33; cited in Shapiro and Markoff, *Revolutionary Demands*, 153.

5. Shapiro and Markoff see the presidency of a seigneurial officer as evidence of a strong seigneurial regime, which would plausibly make it more likely that people would complain about the seigneurial system. Shapiro and Markoff, *Revolutionary Demands*, 153–55.

6. ADCO B2 242/1, bailliage of Arnay-le-Duc, *cahier* of Barbirey.

7. Ibid., *cahier* of Mâlain.

8. The only nonlocal demand that these *cahiers* occasionally contain is for a fairer system of taxation.

9. Robin, *La société française en 1789*, 315–16.

10. ADCO B2 226/1, bailliage of Semur-en-Auxois, *procès-verbal d'assemblée* for Courcelles-Fremois.

11. ADCO B2 254/1, *cahier* of Moutier St. Jean.

12. The strongest criticism of the *cahiers* that call for a second judge is that of Verrey-sous-Salmaise, which begins the suggestion with: "justice belonging only to the lords, it is badly administered toward the inhabitants [la justice apartenant seul aux seigneurs, elle se rend si mal envers les habitants]." ADCO B2 209 bis, *cahier* of Verrey-sous-Salmaise.

13. Ibid., *cahier* of Boux-sous Salmaise.

14. Not all these *cahiers* are as negative as they seem at first, however. The inhabitants of Villiers-les-Hauts demanded the suppression of all seigneurial courts. They then went on, however, to say that justice will be given by royal courts, and that the number of these courts are to be multiplied. They also asked "that justice be given in the localities as soon as there is a courthouse, and not elsewhere by loan of territory." Their main complaint with seigneurial justice in fact was the "too common abuses of influence that stem from the favour and interest of lords in the decisions of those who depend on them." The abolition of seigneurial justice, in other words, for this village means the divorce of justice and fief–a demand that is implicit in all *cahiers* that call for the permanence of seigneurial judgeships.

15. ADCO B2 209 bis, *cahier* of Vaux.

16. In other words, the lord would still pay for the courts and get any revenue, but he could not remove the officers, or even name those favorable to him.

17. The most common formulation for this demand is: "that lords who have [the right of] justice will be forced to have it rendered in the localities as much as possible, or at least in the nearest towns [que les seigneurs qui ont la justice seront tenus de la faire rendre sur les lieux autant que faire se pourra sinon dans les villes les plus prochaines]." See, for example, ADCO B2 226/1, *cahier* of Eringes.

18. ADCO B2 254/1, *cahier* of Moux.

19. ADCO B2 226/1, *cahier* of Lucenay-le-Duc.

20. Ted W. Margadant, *Urban Rivalries in the French Revolution* (Princeton: Princeton University Press, 1992), 147–55.

21. See, for example, Verrey-sous-Salmaise. The feudal system "produces abusive lawsuits, that are always judged by judges with an interest in conserving [seigneurial rights and dues] [donne lieu a des procès vicieux et toujours jugés par des juges intéressés à les conserver]." ADCO B2 209 bis.

22. ADCO B2 226/1, *cahier* of Marcelois.

23. ADCO B2 209 bis, *cahier* of Latrecey.

24. Ibid., *cahier* of Boux-sous-Salmaise.

25. Ibid., *cahier* of Baigneux-les-Juifs.

26. ADCO B2 242/1, *cahier* of Voudenay L'Église.

27. See the *procès-verbaux* of the bailliage assemblies. These were separate from the *cahiers* and in some cases exist where the *cahiers* themselves seem to have disappeared. In all cases they gave the names and professions of the representatives from each parish. I used the *procès-verbaux* for the following bailliages: Auxonne (ADCO B2 135/1), Nuits (ADCO B2 173/1), St. Jean-de-Losne (ADCO B2 183/1), Saulieu, Avallon (both in ADCO B2 254/1), Arnay-le-Duc (ADCO B2 242/1), and Semur-en-Auxois (ADCO B2 226/1).

28. Crubaugh, *Balancing the Scales of Justice*, 128–29.

29. This corroborates the claim made by John Markoff that while on many subjects general Third Estate and parish *cahiers* differed markedly, on the subject of seigneurial justice there was a basic agreement between them. Markoff, *Abolition of Feudalism*, 50–52.

30. Crubaugh, *Balancing the Scales of Justice*, 121–22. Crubaugh's analysis also draws on J.-N. Luc, *Paysans et droit féodaux en Charente-Inférieur pendant la Révolution française* (Paris: C.T.H.S., 1984).

31. François Vion-Delphin and François Lassus, eds., *Le bailliage de Quingey en 1789: Les cahiers de doléances* (Besançon: Les Belles lettres, 1989); Jean Arnould, "Les cahiers de doléances dans le bailliage secondaire de Saint-Calais pour les États-Généraux de 1789," http://www/aglossa.net/ecrits/cahiers_saint_calais.htm.

32. In a table, Markoff cites 36 percent as the proportion of peasant *cahiers* that mention seigneurial courts in general, but there are also 17 percent of *cahiers* under the heading "seigneurial courts, miscellaneous," and it is unclear if these two figures should be added together to get the percentage of peasant *cahiers* that mention seigneurial justice. Markoff, *Abolition of Feudalism*, 111–12.

33. Giffard, *Justices seigneuriales en Bretagne*, 268–85; Marion, *Dictionnaire des institutions de la France aux XVIIe et XVIIIe siècles* (Paris: A. Picard, 1923), s.v. "justice," 321.

34. Eleven *cahiers* explicitly requested abolition, four explicitly requested conservation, and eight implicitly foresaw the conservation of seigneurial justice. Crubaugh, *Balancing the Scales of Justice*, 124.

35. J. M. Constant, "Les idées politiques paysannes: Étude comparée des cahiers de doléances (1576–1789)," *Annales: Économies, sociétés, civilisations* 37 (1982): 720.

36. Shapiro and Markoff, *Revolutionary Demands*, 393.

37. Markoff, *Abolition of Feudalism*, 116–17.

38. Arnould, "Les cahiers de doléances," *cahier* of La Chapelle Huon. The selection from Saint-Sulpice is taken from Marion, *Dictionnaire des institutions*, s.v. "justice," 321.

39. Markoff, *Abolition of Feudalism*, 117.

40. Arnould, "Les cahiers de doléances," *cahier* of Lavenay.

41. Chartier, "Cultures, lumières, doléances," 82.

42. Taylor, "Revolutionary and Nonrevolutionary Content," 469–96.

43. Markoff, "Peasant Protest," 413–54. See also John Markoff, "Literacy and Revolt: Some Empirical Notes on France in 1789," *American Journal of Sociology* 91 (1986): 323–49. Here Markoff suggests literacy had only a slight effect on the incidence of rural revolt in 1789. See also James B. Collins, *The Ancien Régime and the French Revolution* (Toronto: Thompson Learning, 2002), 65–67. Comments from James Collins on my presentation of the *cahiers* of northern Burgundy were instrumental in causing me to take seriously the radical nature of the *cahiers*.

44. Grateau, *Les cahiers de doléances*, 143.

45. *Prévôtal* courts had authority over certain very serious crimes like counterfeiting and highway robbery, as well as all crimes involving royal roads or committed by vagabonds. See Ian Cameron, *Crime and Repression in the Auvergne and the Guyenne, 1720–1790* (Cambridge: Cambridge University Press, 1981).

Conclusion

1. ADCO B2 242/1, bailliage of Arnay-le-Duc, *cahiers de doléances*, *cahier* of Sombernon.

2. ADCO B2 209 bis, bailliage of Châtillon, *cahiers de doléances*, *cahier* of Aisey-le-Duc.

3. ADCO B2 226/1, bailliage of Semur-en-Auxois, *cahiers de doléances*, *cahier* of Puits.

4. ADCO B2 226/2, bailliage of Semur-en-Auxois, *cahiers de doléances*, *cahier* of St.-Thibault.

5. Zink, *Clochers et troupeaux*, 85–94.

6. Schnapper, "Pour une géographie des mentalités judiciaires," *Annales* 23 (1979): 406; Le Goff and Sutherland, "Revolution and the Rural Community," 96–119; Quéniart, *Le Grand Chapelletout*, 31–35.

7. In Puritan colonial New England some villages managed to keep the peace almost entirely without using the local court, while others did not. Nelson, *Dispute and Conflict Resolution in Plymouth County*, 4.

8. *Protestations des Présidents et Conseillers du Parlement de Dijon, qui se sont trouvés en lad. ville, le 9 Mai 1788*, BM Dijon, Fonds Delmasse 604; *Protestations du Parlement de Bourgogne, du onze Juin 1788*, BM Dijon, Fonds Delmasse 608; *Protestations du Parlement de Bourgogne du 4 Juin 1788*, BM Dijon, Fonds Delmasse 606; *Arrêté de la Chambre des Comptes de Bourgogne et Bresse du 9 juin 1788*, BM Dijon, Fonds Delmasse 609. Most of the bailliages in the province also published short reactions to the new law, affirming their determination to follow the parlement in its resistance to the forced registration. The list of protesting bailliages includes Autun, Auxonne, Beaune, Châtillon-sur-Seine, Dijon, Mâcon, Montcenis, Nuits, Saulieu, and Semur-en-Brionnais. See BM Dijon, Fonds Delmasse 588, 589, 592, 590.

9. The only comparison of ancien régime and Revolutionary justice remains Crubaugh, *Balancing the Scales of Justice*, but the contrast between the two institutions is unlikely to be nearly as great in northern Burgundy.

Appendix B

1. Note that for the 1780s Grands-Jours cases I have removed *mésus* cases. Because of their high number they overwhelm other trends in the data if left in.

Bibliography

Archival and Manuscript Sources

Archives Départementales de la Côte d'Or (ADCO)

Chambre des Comptes
B 10470–11118 *Reprises de fief, Aveux et dénombrements.*

Parlement
B2 24/265 *audiences d'instruction.*
B2 27/240–241, 278–279 Tournelle, *arrêts-minutes* (civil).
B2 46/32, 41 Tournelle, *arrêts définitifs* (criminal).
B2 50/24 Chambre des Requêtes, *procès-verbaux,* sentences (civil).
B 12123–12145 *enregistrement des édits et lettres patentes.*
B2 12160–12161 *épices.*
B 12155 *capitation* rolls.
B 12071/8 Recueil des délibérations secrètes du Parlement de Bourgogne.

Bailliages
Dijon
B2 101/3 *délibérations des procureurs.*
B2 111/38, 39, 46 *sentences criminelles.*
B2 118/21, 42–43 *qualités civiles.*
B2 133/1 oaths of judges.
B2 135/1 *cahiers de doléances.*
B2 136–137 bis *sentences arbitrales.*

Semur-en-Auxois
B2 195/2 *assises, plumitifs.*
B2 211/1 *cahiers de doléances, délibérations.*
B2 216/19, 23 *sentences criminelles.*
B2 218/11 *qualités civils.*
B2 226/1 *cahiers de doléances.*

Arnay-le-Duc
B2 235/66–89 *sentences, procès-verbaux.*
B2 242/1 *cahiers de doléances.*
B2 SUP 23 *écrous.*

Auxonne
B2 142/82–83, 99–100 *sentences.*

Beaune
B2 156/37–38, 59 *sentences criminelles.*
B2 163/1 bis *cahiers de doléances.*
B2 SUP 276 *écrous.*

Nuits
B2 167/90 *sentences criminelles.*
B2 173/1, 173/1 bis *cahiers de doléances.*

St. Jean-de-Losne
B2 177/10–11, 22–24 *sentences criminelles.*
B2 183/1 bis *cahiers de doléances.*

Châtillon-sur-Seine
B2 201/32, 34–45 *sentences criminelles.*
B2 202/17–29 *procès-verbaux.*
B2 209 bis *cahiers de doléances.*

Saulieu
B2 246/5, 8 *sentences criminelles.*
B2 254/1 *cahiers de doléances.*

Seigneurial courts
B2 423–424 Aisy-sous-Thil, Pont d'Aisy.
B2 438–439 Bagnot.
B2 451 Belleneuve.
B2 457–458 Billey, Villerrottin.
B2 546 Corgengoux.
B2 601–602 Flée.
B2 603–604 Foncegrive.
B2 605–606 Fontaine-en-Duesmois.
B2 607–617 Barony of Gemeaux.
B2 668–669 Lanthes.
B2 734–737 Meursault, Auxey-le-Grand, Auxey-le-Petit.
B2 763 Montot.
B2 1032–1048 *prieuré* of St. Bénigne.
B2 1077–1078 Ampilly-les-Bordes.
B2 1134, Chambolle and Morey.
B2 1220–1222 Senailly.
B2 1252–1253 Ancey.
B2 SUP 75–77 Chazilly-le-Haut, Chazilly-le-Bas.

Intendant

C 3 justice, jurisdiction.
C 4 justice.
C 56 correspondence.
C 327 *ter* justice, bailliage officers.
C 396 justice.
C 397 judicial fees.
C 458–C 5857 Intendant, political, and fiscal files divided by village.

Estates-General of Burgundy

C 3002–3014, *décrets.*
C 3046 *Deuxième Etat, cahier des carnots.*
C 3052 *Troisième Etat, cahier des carnots.*
C 3304–3307 *alcades des Etats.*
C 3330–3335 remonstrances.
C 3341 jurisdiction.
C 3354 correspondence.
C 3365–3367 correspondence.
C 3519–3523 jurisdiction conflicts.
C 3526 communal affairs.
C 3854–3856 roads.
C 4401 local roads (*finérots*).

Taxes

C 5836–C5857 *vingtièmes* rolls.
C 5644 *capitation,* 1746.
C 5905–7375 *taille* rolls by village.

Other

C 2178–2181 Bureau des Finances, Chambre des Domaines, *jugements définitifs.*
C 2459 Chambre des Domaines, summary of rights, Billey, Villerrottin.
C 8068 *Contrôle des actes, bureau* of Baigneux-les-Juifs, 1783.

Notaries

4E 5/116–120 Mathieu, Dubreuil, Berrué; 5/132–141 Forneron; 59/27 Bouzerand; 94/74 Gauvain; 53/2108 Ranfer; 19/67 Mourey.

Miscellaneous

E24–E3080 private seigneurial papers.
1F–44F private family papers.
1F 460 Administration de la province de Bourgogne considéré comme pays d'État.
G 789 Cathedral of Autun, seigneurial papers.
G 1446–1451 Montot, seigneurie, justice.
1H 762–1721 religious order of St. Bénigne, *prieuré* of Larey, seigneurie.
1J 2214/2 correspondence of the Nyel familly.

11J Pasquinelli-Dorland-Dornand papers.
18J Vaillant de Meixmoron papers.

Revolution

L 176, department of the Côte d'Or, correspondence with the districts.
L 496 1786 census.
L 1274 1793 census.
L 1314 district of Arnay-le-Duc, list of archives of abolished seigneurial justices.
L 1435 district of Beaune, list of archives of abolished seigneurial justices.

Microfilmed Sources

1 Mi 270 (R1) microfilm of AN, H1 185, no 99. "Mémoire sur l'administration de Messieurs les Intendants de Bourgogne par le Sieur Acher de Montorval ancien premier secrétaire de cette intendance," 1780.
1 Mi 285–301 (R1) Prince de Condé, correspondence. Microfilm of Musée Condé, Cabinet des livres. Manuscrits 1399–1416.
5Mi 10R27 Messigny, état civil, 1724–1792.

E Dépôt (Communal Archives Deposited in the ADCO)

E Dépôt 10 Aisy, Pont d'Aisy; 14 Ampilly-les-Bordes; 16 Ancey; 45 Bagnot; 77 Billey; 283 Foncegrive; 340 Lanthes, le Meix; 439 Montot; 585 Saulon-la-Chapelle; 590 Savigny-le-Sec; 595 Belleneuve; 701 Villerrottin.

Archives Nationales (AN)

E/3703/2 controller general, correspondence.
F/10/215 agriculture.
H/1/1440 petitions sent to the administration.
H/1/1441 *placets et mémoires,* 1781–92.
H/1/193/5, 195/3, 200/2, 204/6 *pays d'Etats,* Burgundy.
H/1/207/1 Estates-General of 1789.
O/1/512 instructions sent out to the provinces.
O/1/586 cities of Burgundy.
U/1074 Parlement of Paris, correspondence with the Parlement of Dijon.

Archives Municipales de Dijon (AM Dijon)

C13 justice, jurisdiction conflicts.
C14 justice, jurisdiction conflicts.
C31–32 justice, jurisdiction conflicts.

Archives de l'Hôpital-Général de Dijon

B1/7 Ancey, seigneurie, sales.
B1/11–16 leases, *terriers, manuels.*
B9/14 *terrier, manuel.*

Bibliothèque Municipale de Dijon (BM Dijon)

Bailliage protests concerning the edict of May 9 1788. Fonds Delmasse 588–92.
Correspondance concernant Chartraire de Montigny . . . MS 1943.
Documents divers, intéressant Essarois, Echalot, Éppoisses et Forléans . . . MS 1868.
Dossier concernant la situation financière de Chartraire de Ragny . . . 1750–1801. MS 1940.
État des seigneurs de la province de Bourgogne . . . 1746. MS 1159.
"Institutions du Droit François relativement aux Maximes Générales du Royaume et aux usages particuliers, soit de la Bourgogne, soit des Pays de Droit Écrit, qui ressortissent au Parlement de Bourgogne." Unpublished book manuscript written by Voisin. MS 1515.
Legal *mémoires,* facta, *arrêts.* Fonds Saverot 15–16.
Lettres addressées par Chartraire de Montigny à son homme d'affaires M. Finot, avocat à Semur-en-Auxois. MS 1931.
Livre de travail de M. Jean Finot, avocat à Semur. MS 1942.
Méllenet. "Coutumes générales du duché de Bourgogne, Comté de Charollais, et terres d'outre Saône qui n'usent de droit écrit." MS 2241.
Parlementary protests concerning the edict of 9 May 1788. Fonds Delmasse 604–9.
Pièces de procédure provenant d'études d'avocats et procureurs de la région de Semur, Montbard, Saulieu, Vitteaux . . . MS 1949.
Recueil alphabétique d'arrêts et de délibérations secrètes du Parlement de Dijon avec des notes sur beaucoup d'arrêts et délibérations par M–. MS 2292.
Recueil d'arrêts du Parlement de Dijon ("Recueil"), 6 volumes. MS 1304–9.
Recueil provenant de la famille Finot. MS 1960.
Registre des arrêts du parlement. 6 vols. MS 769. MIC 573.
Registres des Remontrances du Parlement de Dijon. MIC 443.
Remontrances du Parlement de Dijon. Fonds Delmasse 399.
Traité des tailles suivant les usages du Ressort du Parlement de Bourgogne. 1759. MS 316.

Published Primary Sources

Almanach de la province de Bourgogne, et particulièrement de la ville de Dijon, pour l'année bissextile 1780. Dijon: Frantin, 1780.
Archives de la ville de Beaune. *Les cahiers de doléances du tiers état beaunois.* n.l, n.d.
d'Argenson. *Considérations sur le gouvernement ancien et présent de la France.* Amsterdam: n.p., 1765.

Arnould, Jean. "Les cahiers de doléances dans le bailliage secondaire de Saint-Calais pour les États-Généraux de 1789," http://www.aglossa.net/ecrits/cahiers_saint_calais.htm.

Avis au Tiers-Etat de Bourgogne, concernant les justices seigneuriales. N.p., 1789.

Boucher d'Argis. *Cahier d'un magistrat du Châtelet de Paris, sur les justices seigneuriales et l'administration dans les campagnes.* Paris: Clousier, 1789.

——. *Règles pour former un avocat, tirées des plus célèbres auteurs anciens et modernes.* Paris: n.p., 1778.

Bouhier, Jean. "Conférence de la Coutume du Duché de Bourgogne." In *Oeuvres de jurisprudence de M. Bouhier,* edited by Joly de Bevy. Dijon: Frantin, 1787.

——. *Les coutumes du duché de Bourgogne avec les anciennes coutumes, tant générales, que locales, de la même province, non encore imprimées, et Les observations de M. Bouhier, Président à Mortier honoraire au Parlement de Bourgogne, & de l'Académie Française.* 2 vols. Dijon: Arnaud Jean-Baptiste Auge, 1742.

——. "Observations de la Coutume de Bourgogne, par M le Président Bouhier." In *Oeuvres de jurisprudence de M. Bouhier, Président à Mortier au Parlement de Dijon,* edited by Joly de Bevy. Dijon: Frantin, 1787.

Boutaric, François de. *Explication de l'Ordonnance de Louis XIV Roi de France et de Navarre sur les matières civiles.* N.p., 1743.

——. *Traité des droits seigneuriaux et des matières féodales.* Toulouse: Jean-François Forest, 1767.

Bretonnier, Bartholemy. *Recueil par ordre alphabétique des principales questions de Droit, qui se jugent diversement dans les différents tribunaux du royaume.* 2 vols. Paris: Martin, 1752.

Camus, Armand-Gaston. *Lettres sur la profession d'avocat, et sur les études nécessaires pour se rendre capable de l'exercer.* Paris: n.p., 1772.

Certificats d'usages donnés par les Avocats du Parlement de Dijon. N.p, n.d.

Challan. *Réflexions sur l'administration de la justice, sur la formation de tribunaux ordinaires et municipaux, afin de rendre la justice gratuite, et d'éviter les abus qui règnent spécialement dans les justices seigneuriales.* Paris: n.p., 1789.

Courtépée, Claude, and Edme Beguillet. *Description générale et particulière du duché de Bourgogne, précédé de l'abrégé historique de cette province.* 5 vols. Dijon: Frantin, 1774–85.

De l'administration de la justice dans les campagnes. N.p., 1789.

Disson. *Précis des ordonnances, édits, déclarations, lettres-patentes et règlements, dont les dispositions sont le plus en usage dans le ressort du Parlement de Bourgogne.* Dijon, Jean-Baptiste Capel, 1781.

Doléances du tiers-état cultivateur, dignes sur toutes les autres d'être prises en considération par le souverain, les ministres et la nation entière. Dijon: Frantin, 1789.

Dunod, M. F. I. *Observations sur les titres des droits de justice, des fiefs, des cens, des gens mariés et des successions, de la coutume du comté de Bourgogne, avec des traités à l'usage de la même province sur les institutions contractuelles, la puissance paternelle, les sociétés tacites, les baux à cheptel et une dissertation sur les incendies.* Besançon: Cl. Jos. Daclin, 1756.

——. *Traités de la mainmorte et des retraits.* Paris: Veuve Dupuis, 1760.

d'Espeisses, Antoine. *Les oeuvres de M. Antoine d'Espeisses, advocat et jurisconsulte de Montpellier.* 3 vols. Lyon: Jean-Antoine Huguetan & Marc-Antoine Ravaud, 1664.

Fouquau de Pussy. *Idées sur l'administration de la justice dans les petites villes et bourgs de France, pour déterminer la suppression des juridictions seigneuriales.* Paris: n.p., 1789.

Garnier, J., ed. *Chartes de communes et d'affranchissements en Bourgogne.* vol. 1. Dijon: J.-E. Rabutot, 1867.

Gauret, Jacques. *Stile universel de toutes les cours et jurisdictions du royaume pour l'instruction des matières civiles.* Paris: Les associés, 1693.

——. *Stile universel de toutes les cours et jurisdictions du royaume, pour l'instruction des matières criminelles.* Paris: Les associés, 1703.

Grappin, Pierre Philippe. *Dissertation sur l'origine de la main-morte dans les provinces qui ont composé le premier Royaume de Bourgogne.* Besançon: J. M. Couché, 1779.

Groustel, Louis. *Essai sur la profession de procureur.* Dijon: n.p., 1749.

Guyot. *Répertoire universel et raisonné de jurisprudence civile, criminelle, canonique et bénéficiale; ouvrage de plusieurs jurisconsultes, mis en ordre et publié par M Guyot, écuyer, ancien magistrat.* Paris: Visse, 1784.

Henrion de Pansey. *Dissertations féodales.* 2 vols. Paris: Théophile Barrois, 1789.

——. "Justices de paix." In *Oeuvres judiciaires du président Henrion de Pansey.* Paris: Gennequin ainé, n.d.

Henriquez, Jean. *Code des seigneurs hauts-justiciers et féodaux.* Paris: Nyon, 1780.

Les inconvéniens des droits féodaux. London: n.p., 1776.

Isambert, Jourdan, and Decrussy, eds. *Recueil général des anciennes lois françaises, depuis l'an 420, jusqu'à la Révolution de 1789.* 29 vols. Paris: Belin-Leprieur, 1829.

Jacquet, Pierre. *Traité des justices des seigneurs, et des droits en dependants, comformément à la Jurisprudence actuelle des différents tribunaux du royaume.* Paris: Louis Cellot, 1764.

Jousse, Daniel. *Nouveau commentaire sur l'ordonnance civile du mois d'avril 1667.* Paris: Debure l'aîné, 1753.

——. *Traité de l'administration de la justice.* 2 vols. Paris: Debure père, 1771.

Jouye Desroches, P. L. F. *Rapport présenté au nom du Comité de Judicature, sur le remboursement des officiers des ci-devant justices seigneuriales.* Paris: Imprimerie nationale, 1791.

La Poix de Fréminville, Edme. *Dictionnaire ou traité de la police générale des villes, bourgs et seigneuries de la campagne.* Paris: Les associés, 1775.

——. *La pratique universelle pour la rénovation des terriers et des droits seigneuriaux.* 5 vols. Paris: Despilly, 1762.

——. *Traité général du gouvernement des biens et affaires des communautés d'habitants des villes, villages et parroises du Royaume.* Paris: Gissey, 1760.

Le Trosne, Guillaume-François. *De l'administration provinciale, et de la réforme de l'impôt.* Basle: n.p., 1779.

Linguet, S.-N.-H. *Nécessité d'une réforme dans l'administration de la justice et dans les lois civiles en France, avec la réfutation de l'Esprit des Lois.* Amsterdam: n.p., 1764.

Loyseau, Charles. *Les oeuvres de M. Charles Loyseau, Parisien: Contenans les cinq livres du droit des offices, avec autres livres, tant des seigneuries, des ordres, du déguerpissement et délaissement par hypothèque, que la garantie des rentes, et des abus des justices de village.* Paris: Pierre Rocolet, 1640.

Lucan. *Traité des mésus à l'usage du duché de Bourgogne avec les Arrêts de Règlement rendus à ce sujet.* Dijon: Causse, 1772.

Mézard, M. *Essai sur les réformes à faire dans l'administration de la justice en France.* N.p., 1788.

Nouvel état général et alphabétique des villes, bourgs et paroisses, villages, hameaux et écarts en dépendant compris dans les Etats du Duché de Bourgogne, comtés et pays adjacents. Dijon: Defay, 1783.

"Observations générales sur la population de l'ancienne généralité de Dijon, document présenté par Pierre Bodineau." *MSHDB* 52 (1995): 193–203.

Le Parlement outragé. Dijon: n.p., 1761.

Pétion de Villeneuve, Jérôme. "Les lois civiles et l'administration de la justice ramenées à un ordre simple et uniforme." In *Oeuvres de Jérôme Pétion, membre de l'Assemblée Constituante, de la Convention Nationale, et Maire de Paris,* vol. 1. Paris: Garnery, 1793.

Preuves des faits énoncez dans la réponse du Parlement de Dijon à la request présentée au conseil par le Elus des Etats de la province de Bourgogne. où l'on fait voir que lesdits élus n'ont ni la connaissance de la voyerie, ni aucune autre juridiction contentieuse quelconque. N.p., n.d.

Prévot de la Jannés, M. *Les principes de la jurisprudence française, exposés suivant l'ordre des diverses espèces d'actions qui se poursuivent en Justice.* Paris: Barrois, 1780.

Quelques idées sur les cahiers, rapidement proposées aux sages et discrètes personnes qui s'en occupent. Dijon: n.p., 1789.

Recueil des déclarations, édits, lettres patentes et arrêts du Conseil d'État du Roi, registrés au Parlement de Dijon. 14 vols. Dijon: Ressayre, 1707–89.

Réflexions sur les réformes dans l'administration de la justice. N.p., 1788.

Règlements généraux pour les justices seigneuriales, corrigés et augmentés par un Avocat de cette ville, en l'année 1779. Dijon: Capel, 1779.

Règlements généraux qui s'observent dans tout le ressort de la cour, et dont on fait lecture à la tenue des Grands Jours. Nouvelle Édiction. Revue, corrigée et augmentée. Dijon: Causse, 1786.

Règlemens pour les fonctions et droits des officiers, greffiers, procureurs, huissiers et notaires des provinces de Bourgogne, Bresse et Bugey. Dijon: A. de Fay, 1724.

Rétif de la Bretonne. *La vie de mon père.* Paris: Éditions Garnier Frères, 1970.

Saint Jacob, Pierre de, ed. *Documents relatifs à la communauté villageoise en Bourgogne.* Paris: Société les Belles lettres, 1962.

Viellart. *Opinion présentée au comité des droits féodaux, sur l'abolition des justices seigneuriales, et des droits qui en dérivaient.* Paris: Imprimerie nationale, 1790.

Vion-Delphin, François, and François Lassus, ed. *Le bailliage de Quingey en 1789: Les cahiers de doléances.* Besançon: Les Belles lettres, 1989.

Voltaire. *Raisons pour désirer une réforme dans l'administration de la justice.* N.p., 1771.

Secondary Works

Abel, Richard L. "A Comparative Theory of Dispute Institutions in Society." *Law and Society Review* 8 (1973): 217–347.

Achard, A. *Une ancienne justice seigneuriale en Auvergne: Sugères et ses habitants.* Clermont-Ferrand: Impr. De Bussac, 1929.

Ado, A. "La lutte autour de l'application de la loi du 17 juillet 1793 sur l'abolition des droits féodaux." In *La grande Révolution française,* 89–118. Moscow: Sciences sociales aujourd'hui, 1989.

——. *Paysans en Révolution: Terre, pouvoir et jacquerie, 1789–1794.* Paris: Société des Études robespierristes, 1996.

Antoine, Annie. *Fiefs et villages du Bas-Maine au XVIIIe siècle: Étude de la seigneurie et de la vie rurale.* Mayenne: Éditions régionales de l'Ouest, 1994.

——. "Justice foncière et contrôle social." In *Les justices de village: Administration et justice locales de la fin du Moyen Âge à la Révolution,* edited by François Brizay, Antoine Follain, and Véronique Sarrazin, 270–72. Rennes: Presses universitaires de Rennes, 2003.

Arbassier, Charles. *L'absolutisme en Bourgogne: L'intendant Bouchu et son action financière d'après sa correspondance inédite (1667–1671).* Paris: Picard, n.d.

Astarito, Tommaso. *Village Justice: Community, Family, and Popular Culture in Early Modern Italy.* Baltimore: Johns Hopkins University Press, 1999.

Aubin, Gérard. *La seigneurie en Bordelais d'après la pratique notariale (1715–1789).* Rouen, Publication de l'Université de Rouen, 1989.

Audran-Delhez, Christiane. "À la force! S'efforcer d'approcher les archives criminelles des justices seigneuriales en Bretagne (1515–1630)." In *La petite délinquance du Moyen Age à l'époque contemporaine,* edited by Benoît Garnot, 19–36. Dijon: Éditions universitaires de Dijon, 1998.

Augustin, Jean-Marie. "Les Capitouls, juges des causes criminelles et de police à la fin de l'Ancien Régime (1780–1790)." *Annales du Midi* 84, no. 107 (1972): 183–211.

Baehrel, René. *Une croissance: La Basse-Provence rurale de la fin du seizième siècle à 1789: Essai d'économie historique statistique.* Paris: Éditions de l'École des hautes études en science sociale, 1988 [1961].

Baker, Keith Michael. *Inventing the French Revolution: Essays on French Political Culture in the Eighteenth Century.* Cambridge: Cambridge University Press, 1990.

Bart, Jean. "Les archives judiciaires du Parlement de Dijon." In *Case Law in the Making: The Techniques and Methods of Judicial Records and Law Reports.* Vol. 1, *Essays,* edited by Alain Wijffels, 249–65. Berlin: Dunker & Humbold, 1997.

——. "L'égalité entre héritiers dans la région dijonnaise à la fin de l'Ancien Régime et sous la Révolution." *MSHDB* 29 (1968–69): 65–78.

——. *Histoire du droit privé de la chute de l'Empire Romain au XIXe siècle.* Paris: Montchretien, 1998.

——. "La justice de paix du canton de Fontaine-Française à l'époque révolutionnaire." *MSHDB* 26 (1965): 193–216.

——. *La liberté ou la terre: La mainmorte en Bourgogne au siècle des Lumières.* Dijon: CNRS, 1984.

——. *La Révolution française en Bourgogne.* Clermont-Ferrand: La Française d'édition et d'imprimerie, 1996.

Basdevant-Gaudemet, Brigitte. *Aux origines de l'État moderne: Charles Loyseau, 1564–1627: Théoricien de la puissance publique.* Paris: Economica, 1977.

Bastien, Pascal. "La 'seconde punition': Quelques remarques sur la confiscation des biens dans la coutume de Paris au XVIIIe siècle." In *Justice et Argent: Les crimes et les peines pécuniaires du XIIIe au XXIe siècle,* edited by Benoît Garnot, 271–80. Dijon: Éditions universitaires de Dijon, 2005.

Bastier, Jean. "L'affaire Sirven devant la justice seigneuriale de Mazamet." *Revue historique de droit français et étranger* 49 (1971): 601–11.

——. *La féodalité au siècle des lumières dans la région de Toulouse (1730–1790).* Paris: Bibliothèque nationale, 1975.

——. "Le parlement de Toulouse et les justices subalternes au XVIIIe siècle." In *Les Parlements de Province: Pouvoir, justice et société du XVe au XVIIIe siècle,* edited by Jacques Poumarède and Jack Thomas, 407–23. Toulouse: Framespa, 1996.

Bataillon, Jacques-Henri. *Les justices seigneuriales du bailliage de Pontoise à la fin de l'Ancien Régime.* Paris: Librairie du Recueil Sirey, 1942.

Beauchet-Filleau. *Mémoire sur les justices royales, ecclésiastiques et seigneuriales du Poitou.* Poitier: Impr. De F.-A. Saurin, 1845.

Beik, William. *Urban Protest in Seventeenth-Century France: The Culture of Retribution.* Cambridge: Cambridge University Press, 1997.

Bell, David A. *Lawyers and Citizens: The Making of a Political Elite in Old Regime France.* Oxford: Oxford University Press, 1994.

Benoit, Arthur. *Les plaids annaux de la baronnie de Sarreck (Meurthe): Étude sur les justices seigneuriales au XVIIIe siècle.* Metz: Rousseau-Pallez, 1869.

Berlanstein, Leonard R. *The Barristers of Toulouse in the Eighteenth Century (1740–1793).* Baltimore: Johns Hopkins University Press, 1975.

Bleton-Ruget, Annie. "L'infrajustice institutionnalisée: Les justices de paix des cantons ruraux du district de Dijon pendant la Révolution." In *L'infrajudiciaire du Moyen Age à l'époque contemporaine,* edited by Benoît Garnot, 291–312. Dijon: Éditions universitaires de Dijon, 1996.

Bloch, Marc. *French Rural History: An Essay on its Basic Charasteristics.* Los Angeles: University of California Press, 1970.

Bodineau, Pierre. "Les bureaux de l'Intendant de Bourgogne à la fin de l'Ancien Régime." *Actes du 109e congrès national des sociétés savantes: Histoire de la Bourgogne et questions diverses,* 77–96. Paris: C.T.H.S., 1984.

Bordes, Maurice. *L'Administration provinciale et municipale en France au XVIIIe siècle.* Paris: Société d'édition d'enseignement supérieur, 1972.

Brennan, Thomas. "Police and Private Order in Early Modern France." *Criminal Justice Review* 13 (1988): 1–14.

——. *Public Drinking and Popular Culture in Eighteenth-Century Paris.* Princeton: Princeton University Press, 1988.

Bressan, Thierry. "La critique de la condition mainmortable en France à la veille de la Révolution (1779–1789)." *Annales Historiques de la Révolution française* (1997): 75–91.

——. "L'idée d'affranchissement général dans la principauté de Montbéliard (seconde moitié du XVIIIe siècle)." *MSHDB* 54 (1997): 129–52.

——. "La mainmorte dans la France du XVIIIe siècle: Le cas des provinces du Centre." *Histoire et sociétés rurales* 6 (1996): 51–76.

Breugnot, Christophe. "La justice de paix dans le canton d'Arc-sur-Tille à l'époque révolutionnaire." D.E.A. thesis, Université de Bourgogne, 1994.

Brizay, François, Antoine Follain, and Véronique Sarrazin, eds. *Les Justices de village: Administration et justice locales de la fin du Moyen Âge à la Révolution.* Rennes: Presses universitaires de Rennes, 2002.

Brizay, François, and Véronique Sarrazin. "*Le Discours de l'abus des justices de village*: Un texte de circonstance dans une œuvre de référence." In *Les justices de village: Administration et justice locale de la fin du Moyen Age à la Révolution,* edited by François Brizay, Antoine Follain, and Véronique Sarrazin, 109–22. Rennes: Presses universitaires de Rennes, 2003.

Brooks, Christopher W. *Lawyers, Litigation, and English Society since 1450.* London: Hambledon Press, 1998.

Brosselin, Arlette. *La forêt bourguignonne (1660–1789).* Dijon: Éditions universitaires de Dijon, 1987.

Brown, Howard. *Ending the French Revolution: Violence, Justice, and Repression from the Terror to Napoleon.* Charlottesville: University of Virginia Press, 2006.

Brunet, Michel. *Les pouvoirs au village: Aspects de la vie quotidienne dans le Roussillon du XVIIIe siècle.* Perpignan: Minuprint, 1998.

——. *Le Roussillon: Une société contre l'État, 1780–1820.* Perpignan: Minuprint, 1990.

Burriat, Jean-Pierre, Catherine Ditte, and Luc Ferrand. "Introduction générale: Porter plaine: Stratégies villageoises et institutions judiciaires en Île-de-France (XVIIe–XVIIIe siècles)." *Droit et cultures* 19 (1990): 13–22.

Cameron, Ian. *Crime and Repression in the Auvergne and the Guyenne, 1720–1790.* Cambridge: Cambridge University Press, 1981.

Carey, John A. *Judicial Reform in France before the Revolution of 1789.* Cambridge: Harvard University Press, 1981.

Carrier, Isabelle. "L'art de louvoyer dans le système judiciaire de l'Ancien Regime: Le procureur et la procédure civile." In *Entre justice et justiciables: Les auxiliaires de la justice du Moyen Âge au XXe siècle,* edited by Claire Dolan, 479–90. Quebec: Presses de l'Université Laval, 2005.

Castan, Nicole. *Les criminels de Languedoc: Les exigences d'ordre et les voies du ressentiment dans une société pré-révolutionnaire, 1750–1790.* Toulouse: Publications de l'Université de Toulouse-le Mirail, 1980.

——. *Justice et répression en Languedoc a l'époque des lumières.* Paris: Flammarion, 1980.

Castan, Yves. "Gestion criminelle et protectorat judiciaire dans la France d'Ancien Régime: Le parlement de Toulouse au XVIIIe siècle." In *Les Parlements de Province: Pouvoir, justice et société du XVe au XVIIIe siècle,* edited by Jacques Poumarède and Jack Thomas, 329–40. Toulouse: Framespa, 1996.

——. *Honnêteté et relations sociales en Languedoc (1715–1780).* Paris: Plon, 1974.

——. "Mentalités rurale et urbaine à la fin de l'Ancien Régime dans le ressort du Parlement de Toulouse d'après les sacs à procès criminels (1730–1790)." In *Crimes et criminalité en France sous l'Ancien Régime 17e–18e siècles,* 109–86. Paris: A. Colin, 1971.

Chartier, Roger. "Cultures, lumières, doléances: Les cahiers de 1789." *Revue d'histoire moderne et contemporaine* 21 (1981): 68–93.

Chausinand-Nogaret, Guy. *The French Nobility in the Eighteenth Century: From Feudalism to Enlightenment.* Cambridge: Cambridge University Press, 1985.

Chenal, André. *Étude sur le présidial d'Orléans, 1551–1790.* Orléans: Imprimerie de A. Gout, 1908.

Clément, Christelle. "Les délits ordinaires dans le bailliage de Châtillon-sur-Seine au XVIIIe siècle: L'exemple des litiges de voisinage." In *La petite délinquance du Moyen Age à l'époque contemporaine,* edited by Benoît Garnot, 145–52. Dijon: Éditions universitaires de Dijon, 1998.

——. "Les juristes délinquants: Quelques exemples dans le bailliage de Châtillon-sur-Seine (1750–1755)." In *Juges, notaires et policiers délinquants: XIVe–XXe siècle,* edited by Benoît Garnot, 129–40. Dijon: Éditions universitaires de Dijon, 1997.

Cocahe-Zilgien, A. "Un génie méconnu du XVIIIe siècle: L'avocat Linguet (1736–1794), incendiaire, réactionnaire et visionnaire." *Annales africaines de la Faculté de droit et des sciences économiques de Dakar* 1 (1960): 83–122.

Cohen, Esther. *The Crossroads of Justice: Law and Culture in Late Medieval France.* New York: Brill, 1993.

Collins, James B. *The Ancien Régime and the French Revolution.* Toronto: Thompson Learning, 2002.

——. "The Economic Role of Women in Seventeenth-Century France." *French Historical Studies* 16 (1989): 444–52.

——. *The State in Early Modern France.* Cambridge: Cambridge University Press, 1995.

Colombet, Albert. "Le curé homme de confiance du seigneur." *Annales de Bourgogne* 17 (1945): 274–80.

——. "Une justice seigneuriale à la fin de l'ancien régime: Vantoux et ses Grands Jours." *MSHDB* 3 (1936): 195–208.

——. *Les Parlementaires bourguignons à la fin du XVIIIe siècle.* Lyon: Bosc, 1936.

Combe, Paule. *Mémoire inédit du chancelier Daguesseau sur la réformation de la justice, avec une étude préliminaire.* Valence: Imprimeries réunies, 1928.

Combier, A. *Les justices seigneuriales du bailliage de Vermandois sous l'Ancien Régime.* Paris: Albert Fontemoing, 1897.

Constant, Jean-Marie. "Les idées politiques paysannes: Étude comparée des cahiers de doléances (1576–1789)." *Annales. Économies, sociétés, civilisations* 37 (1982): 717–28.

Corley, Christopher. "Parental Authority, Legal Practice, and State-Building in Early Modern France." PhD diss., Purdue University, 2001.

Corvol, A. "Les délinquances forestières en Basse-Bourgogne depuis la réformation de 1711–1718." *Revue historique* 526 (1978): 345–88.

Crémieu-Alcan, Philippe. "Huissiers et gardes forestiers en Guyenne au XVIIIe siècle à travers les délits forestiers: Une même difficulté à faire le 'dû de leur charge?'" In *Entre Justice et Justiciables: Les Auxiliaires de la Justice du Moyen Âge au XXe Siècle,* edited by Claire Dolan, 248–59. Quebec: Presses de l'Université Laval, 2005.

Crubaugh, Anthony. *Balancing the Scales of Justice: Local Courts and Rural Society in Southwest France.* University Park: Pennsylvania State University Press, 2001.

——. "Local Justice and Rural Society in the French Revolution." *Journal of Social History* 34 (2000): 327–50.

Cuisine, M de la. *Le Parlement de Bourgogne depuis son origine jusqu'à sa chute,* vol. 3. Paris: A. Durant, 1857.

Dawson, Philip. *Provincial Magistrates and Revolutionary Politics in France, 1789–1795.* Cambridge: Harvard University Press, 1972.

Debilly, Xavier. "La petite délinquance au XVIIIe siècle: L'exemple d'Ampuis." In *La petite délinquence du Moyen Age à l'époque contemporaine,* edited by Benoît Garnot, 153–64. Dijon: Éditions universitaires de Dijon, 1998.

Delaporte, Raymond. *La sénéchaussée de Châteauneuf-du-Faou, Huelgoat et Landeleau et les juridictions seigneuriales du ressort.* Paris: A. Pedone, 1905.

Delasselle, Nicolas. "Les coups et blessures dans la délinquance traitée par les justices seigneuriales au XVIIIe siècle: Le passage du criminel au civil." In *La petite délinquance du Moyen Age à l'époque contemporaine,* edited by Benoît Garnot, 465–78. Dijon: Éditions universitaires de Dijon, 1998.

——. "L'infrajudiciaire dans les actes d'assemblées de douze paroisses de l'Auxerrois sous l'Ancien Régime." In *L'infrajudiciaire du Moyen Age à l'époque contemporaine,* edited by Benoît Garnot, 419–26. Dijon: Éditions universitaires de Dijon, 1996.

——. "Une justice seigneuriale à Coulanges-la-Vineuse et au Val-de-Mercy au XVIIIe siècle." Master's thesis, Université de Bourgogne, 1992.

Desan, Suzanne. *The Family on Trial in Revolutionary France.* Berkeley: University of California Press, 2004.

Dewald, Jonathan. *Pont-St-Pierre, 1398–1789: Lordship, Community, and Capitalism in Early Modern France.* Los Angeles: University of California Press, 1987.

Dickinson, John A. "L'activité judiciaire d'après la procédure civile: Le bailliage de Falaise, 1668–1790." *Revue d'histoire économique et sociale* 2 (1976): 145–68.

Dinges, Martin. "Négocier son honneur dans le peuple parisien au XVIIIe siècle: La rue, 'l'infrajudiciaire' et la justice." In *L'infrajudiciaire du Moyen Age à l'époque contemporaine,* edited by Benoît Garnot, 393–404. Dijon: Éditions universitaires de Dijon, 1996.

Ditte, Catherine. "La mise en scène dans la plainte: Sa stratégie sociale: L'exemple de l'honneur populaire." *Droit et cultures* 19 (1991): 23–48.

Dotenwill, Serge. "Le rôle des assises et règlements de seigneurie dans la régulation sociale aux XVIIe et XVIIIe siècles: Le cas du Centre-Est de la France." In *Les justices de village: Administration et justice locales de la fin du Moyen Âge à la Révolution,* edited by François Brizay, Antoine Follain, and Véronique Sarrazin, 219–38. Rennes: Presses universitaires de Rennes, 2003.

——. *Une seigneurie sous l'Ancien Régime: L'Étoile en Brionnais du XVIe au XVIIIe siècle (1575–1778).* Roanne: Horvath, 1973.

Doyle, William. *Venality: The Sale of Office in Eighteenth-Century France.* Oxford: Clarendon Press, 1996.

——. "Was There an Aristocratic Reaction in Pre-Revolutionary France?" *Past and Present* 57 (1972): 97–122.

Druard, Jean. *Le droit de chasse en Bourgogne sous l'Ancien Régime.* Dijon: Paul Berthier, 1924.

Duma, Jean. "Aristocratie et justice seigneuriale au XVIIIe siècle." In *Journées Régionales d'Histoire de la Justice: Poitiers, 13, 14 et 15 novembre 1997,* 53–72. Paris: Presses universitaires de France, 1999.

Echeverria, Durand. *The Maupeou Revolution: A Study in the History of Libertarianism: France, 1770–1774.* Baton Rouge: Louisiana State University Press, 1985.

Egret, Jean. *The French Prerevolution, 1787–1788.* Trans. Wesley D. Camp. Chicago: University of Chicago Press, 1977.

Ellickson, Robert C. *Order without Law: How Neighbors Settle Disputes.* Harvard: Harvard Univesity Press, 1991.

Ergene, Bogac A. *Local Court, Provincial Society, and Justice in the Ottoman Empire: Legal Practice and Dispute Resolution in Çankiri and Kastamonu (1652–1744).* Boston: Brill, 2003.

Esmein, Albert. *Cours elémentaire de l'histoire du droit français.* Paris: Larose, 1898.

d'Estaintot, Comte. *Un procès entre deux seigneurs haut-justiciers (Valmont et Cany-Caniel) au XVIIIe siècle.* Rouen: Lestringant, 1891.

Everat, Édouard. *La sénéchaussée d'Auvergne et siège présidial de Riom au XVIIIe siècle.* Paris: E. Thorin, 1885.

Evrard, Sebastien. *L'intendant de Bourgogne et le contentieux administratif au XVIIIe siècle.* Paris: De Boccard, 2005.

Falletti, L. "Le contraste juridique entre Bourogne et Savoie au sujet de la mainmorte seigneuriale." *MSHDB* 12 (1948–49): 117–41; 13 (1950–51): 139–76; 14 (1953): 131–58.

Farcy, J.-C. "Les archives judiciaires et l'histoire rurale: L'exemple de la Beauce au XIXe siècle." *Revue Historique* 524 (1977): 313–52.

Farr, James R. *Authority and Sexuality in Early Modern Burgundy (1550–1730).* Oxford: Oxford University Press, 1995.

Felstiner, William L. F. "Influences of Social Organization on Dispute Processing." *Law and Society Review* 9 (1974): 63–95.

Felstiner, William L. F., Richard L. Abel, and Austin Sarat. "The Emergence and Transformation of Disputes: Naming, Blaming, Claiming . . ." *Law and Society Review* 15 (1980–81): 631–54.

Fenet, Jean. "Un procès historique deux fois séculaire: La lutte entre le bailliage présidial de Bourg, et les seigneurs hauts-justiciers de Bresse, au sujet du ressort des justices seigneuriales de 1601 à la Révolution." *MSHDB* 2 (1935): 198–202.

Ferrand, Luc. "Villageois entre eux." *Droit et culture* 19 (1990): 49–72.

Fischer, David Hackett. *The Great Wave: Price Revolutions and the Rhythms of History.* Oxford: Oxford University Press, 1996.

Forestier, Henry. "Petits documents: Ce qu'était la situation du procureur fiscal d'une petite justice de l'Auxerrois au XVIIIe siècle." *Annales de Bourgogne* 10 (1938): 139–40.

Forster, Robert. *The House of Saulx-Tavanes: Versailles and Burgundy, 1700–1830.* Baltimore: Johns Hopkins University Press, 1971.

——. *The Nobility of Toulouse in the Eighteenth Century: A Social and Economic Study.* New York: Octagon Books, 1971.

Fortunet, Françoise. *Charité ingénieuse et pauvre misère: Les baux à cheptel simple en Auxois aux XVIIIe et XIXe siècles.* Dijon: Éditions universitaires de Dijon, 1985.

——. "Époisses à la fin de l' Ancien Régime: Une communauté immobile ou Révolution silencieuse?" *MSHDB* 46 (1989): 179–86.

François, Xavier. "Continuités et ruptures dans le régime des biens entre époux et les transferts de patrimoines à Villiers-sur-Tholon de 1650 à 1789." *MSHDB* 60 (2003): 203–16.

——. "Un usage charactéristique des mutations sociales des XVIIe et XVIIIe siècles: Le droit de bagues et joyaux en Bresse, Bugey, Valromey et Pays de Gex." *MSHDB* 56 (1999): 293–300.

Frêche, Georges. *Toulouse et la région Midi-Pyrénées au siècle des Lumières (vers 1670–1789)*. Paris: Éditions Cujas, 1974.

Galanter, Marc. "Reading the Landscape of Disputes: What We Know and Don't Know (and Think We Know) about Our Allegedly Contentious and Litigious Society." *UCLA Law Review* 31 (1983): 4–71.

Gallet, Jean. *Seigneurs et paysans en France, 1600–1793*. Rennes: Presses universitaires de Rennes, 1999.

Garnot, Benoît. "L'ampleur et les limites de l'infrajudiciaire dans la France d'Ancien Régime (XVIe–XVIIe–XVIIIe siècles)." In *L'infrajudiciaire du Moyen Age à l'époque contemporaine,* edited by Benoît Garnot, 69–76. Dijon: Éditions universitaires de Dijon, 1996.

——. "Le bon magistrat et les mauvais juges à la fin du XVIIe siècle." In *Juges, notaires et policiers délinquants: XIVe–XXe siècle,* edited by Benoît Garnot, 17–32. Dijon: Éditions universitaires de Dijon, 1997.

——. "Deux approches des procès pour injures en Bourgogne au XVIIIe siècle." In *La petite délinquance du Moyen Age à l'époque contemporaine,* edited by Benoît Garnot, 431–41. Dijon: Éditions universitaires de Dijon, 1998.

——. "Justices seigneuriales et régulation sociale: L'exemple bourguignon au XVIIIe siècle." In *Les justices de village: Administration et justice locales de la fin du Moyen Âge à la Révolution,* edited by François Brizay, Antoine Follain, and Véronique Sarrazin, 197–204. Rennes: Presses universitaires de Rennes, 2003.

——. "Une illusion historiographique: Justice et criminalité au XVIIIe siècle." *Revue historique* 283 (1989): 361–80.

——. "Une réhabilitation? Les justices seigneuriales dans la France du XVIIIe siècle." *Histoire, économie et société* 24, no. 2 (2005): 221–32.

——. "La violence et ses limites dans la France du XVIIIe siècle: L'exemple bourguignon." *Revue Historique* 606 (1998): 237–54.

Garreta, Jean-Claude. "Les archives du Parlement de Dijon: Étude des sources." *MSHDB* 23 (1962): 203–44.

Garrioch, David. *Neighbourhood and Community in Paris, 1740–1790*. Cambridge: Cambridge University Press, 1986.

Gasparini, Eric. "La justice seigneuriale en Gévaudan à la veille de la Révolution française: L'exemple du Fau de Peyre." *MSHDB* 56 (1999): 181–98.

——. "Justice seigneuriale et régulation sociale: L'exemple de quelques seigneuries comtoises dans la seconde moitié du XVIIIe siècle." In *Les justices de village: Administration et justice locale de la fin du Moyen Age à la Révolution,* edited by François Brizay, Antoine Follain, and Véronique Sarrazin, 259–68. Rennes: Presses universitaires de Rennes, 2003.

Gauthier, Gaston. *Les registres de deux basses justices seigneuriales (XVIe et XVIIIe siècles)*. Nevers: Publication de la Société nivernaise, 1897.

Giffard, André. *Les justices seigneuriales en Bretagne aux XVIIe et XVIIIe siècles*. Paris: Arthur Rousseau, 1902.

Godechot, Jacques. *Les institutions de la France sous la Révolution et l'Empire*. Paris: Presses universitaires de France, 1968.

Goody, Jack "Inheritance, Property, and Women: Some Comparative Considerations." In *Family and Inheritance: Rural Society in Western Europe, 1200–1800,* 10–36. Cambridge: Cambridge University Press, 1976.

Goubert, Pierre. "Les officiers royaux des présidiaux, bailliages et élections dans la société française du XVIIe siècle." *XVIIe siècle* 42–43 (1959): 54–75.

Goubert, Pierre, and Daniel Roche. *Les français et l'ancien régime: La société et l'état.* Paris: A. Colin, 1984.

Graham, Hamish. "Exercice d'équilibre. Gardes forestiers, autorité seigneuriale et société rurale au XVIIIe siècle." In *Entre justice et justiciables: Les auxiliaires de la justice du Moyen Âge au XXe siècle,* edited by Claire Dolan, 213–25. Quebec: Les presses de l'Universtié Laval, 2005.

Grateau, Philippe. *Les cahiers de doléances: Une relecture culturelle.* Rennes: Presses universitaires de Rennes, 2001.

Greenshields, Malcolm. "Women, Violence, and Criminal Justice Records in Early Modern Haute Auvergne (1587–1664)." *Canadian Journal of History* 22 (1987): 175–94.

Gresset, Maurice. *Gens de Justice à Besançon de la conquête par Louis XIV à la Révolution française (1674–1789).* Paris: Bibliothèque nationale, 1978.

Grosse, Christian. "'Pour bien de paix': La régulation des conflits par les consistoires en Suisse romande (XVIe–XVIIe siècles)." In *Figures de la médiation et lien social,* edited by Jean-Luc Chabot, Stéphane Gal, and Christophe Tournu, 85–107. Paris: Harmattan, 2006.

Gudin de Vallerin, G. "Les doubles mariages en Auxois au XVIIIe siècle." *Annales de Bourgogne* 52 (1980): 213–25.

——. "Mainmorte et communauté de famille en Auxois, de la fin du XVIIe siècle jusqu'au début du XIXe siècle." *MSHDB* 37 (1980): 229–34.

Guillaume, Emmanuel. *Justice seigneuriale et vie quotidienne dans la vallée du Mont-Dore au XVIIIe siècle.* Clermont-Ferrand: La française d'édition et d'imprimerie, 1992.

Gutton, Jean-Pierre. *La sociabilité villageoise dans l'ancienne France: Solidarités et voisinages du XVIe au XVIIIe siècle.* Paris: Hachette, 1979.

Hadeishi, Hajime Howard. "To Be or Not to Be, a Function of Income? Northern Burgundy, 1744–1789." PhD diss., University of California, LosAngeles, 1997.

Hamscher, Albert. "Parlement and Litigants in the King's Councils during the Personal Rule of Louix XIV: The Example of Cassation." In *Society and Institutions in Early Modern France,* edited by Mack P. Holt. Athens: University of Georgia Press, 1991.

Hanley, Sarah. "Engendering the State: Family Formation and State Building in Early Modern France." *French Historical Studies* 16, no. 1 (1989): 4–27.

——. "The Family, the State, and the Law in Seventeenth- and Eighteenth-Century France: The Political Ideology of Male Right versus an Early Theory of Natural Rights." *Journal of Modern History* 78, no. 2 (2006): 289–332.

——. "The Jurisprudence of the *Arrêts*: Marital Union, Civil Society, and State Formation in France, 1550–1650." *Law and History Review* 21, no. 1 (2003): 1–40.

Hanlon, Gregory. "Justice in the Age of Lordship: A Feudal Court in Tuscany during the Medici Era (1619–66)." *Sixteenth Century Journal* 35, no. 4 (2004): 1005–33.

Hardwick, Julie. "Seeking Separations: Gender, Marriages, and Household Economies in Early Modern France." *French Historical Studies* 21 (1998): 157–80.

Hayhoe, Jeremy. "Droit, pratique et seigneurie: Le travail quotidien de Jean Finot, avocat, juge et agent seigneurial à Semur-en-Auxois." *Revue historique du droit français et étranger* 85, no. 3 (2007).

——. "Illegitimacy, Inter-generational Conflict, and Legal Practice in Eighteenth-Century Northern Burgundy." *Journal of Social History* 38 (2005): 673–84.

——. "Litigation and the Policing of Communal Agriculture in Eighteenth-Century Northern Burgundy, 1750–1790." *Agricultural History Review* 50 (2002): 25–50.

Heichette, Michel. *Société, sociabilité, justice: Sablé et son pays au XVIIIe siècle.* Rennes: Presses universitaires de Rennes, 2005.

Henry, Philippe. *Crime, justice et société dans la principauté de Neuchâtel au XVIIIe siècle (1707–1806).* Neuchâtel: La Baconnière, 1984.

Houdaille, Jacques. "Quatre villages du Morvan: 1610–1870." *Population* 42 (1987): 649–70.

Hufton, Olwen. "Attitudes towards Authority in Eighteenth-Century Languedoc." *Social History* 3 (1978): 281–302.

——. "Le paysan et la loi en France au XVIIIe siècle." *Annales: Économies, Sociétés, Civilisations* 38 (1983): 679–701.

Jeanclos, Yves. *L'arbitrage en Bourgogne et en Champagne du XIIe au XVe siècle: Étude de l'influence du droit savant, de la coutume et de la pratique.* Dijon: Centre de recherche historique, 1977.

Jessenne, Jean-Pierre. *Pouvoir au village et Révolution: Artois 1760–1848.* Lille: Presses universitaires de Lille, 1987.

Jones, Peter. "Agrarian Radicalism during the French Revolution." In *Reshaping France: Town, Country, and Region during the French Revolution,* edited by Alan Forrest and Peter Jones, 137–51. Manchester: Manchester University Press, 1991.

——. *The Peasantry in the French Revolution.* Cambridge: Cambridge University Press, 1988.

——. *Reform and Revolution in France: The Politics of Transition, 1774–1791.* Cambridge: Cambridge University Press, 1995.

Jouneaux, Olivier. "Villageois et autorités." *Droit et cultures* 19 (1990): 101–18.

——. "Villageois et autorités locales aux XVIIe et XVIIIe siècles: L'exemple de villages viticoles de la périphérie parisienne." Doctoral thesis, Université de Paris X-Nanterre, 1994.

Jouvenot, R. "Mainmortables ou pas, mainmortables quand même." *MSHDB* 32 (1973–74): 257–82.

Kagan, Richard L. *Lawsuits and Litigants in Castile, 1500–1700.* Chapel Hill: University of North Carolina Press, 1981.

Kaiser, Colin. "The Deflation in the Volume of Litigation at Paris in the Eighteenth Century and the Waning of the Old Judicial Order." *European Studies Review* 10 (1980): 309–36.

Karsten, Peter. *Between Law and Custom: High and Low Legal Cultures in the Lands of the British Diaspora–the United States, Canada, Australia, and New Zealand, 1600–1900.* Cambridge: Cambridge University Press, 2002.

Kessel, Patrick. *La nuit du 4 Août 1789.* Paris: Arthaud, 1969.

Kuehn, Thomas. *Law, Family, and Women: Toward a Legal Anthropology of Renaissance Italy.* Chicago: University of Chicago Press, 1991.

Kwass, Michael. *Privilege and the Politics of Taxation in Eighteenth-Century France: Liberté, Égalité, Fiscalité.* Cambridge: Cambridge University Press, 2000.

Labrousse, C.-E. *Esquisse du mouvement des prix et des revenus en France au XVIIIe siècle.* Paris: Dalloz, 1933.

Lamarre, Christine. "Carte de la province de Bourgogne au XVIIIe siècle." *Annales de Bourgogne* 55 (1983): 145–80.

——. *Petites villes et fait urbain en France au XVIIIe siècle: Le cas bourguignon.* Dijon: Éditions universitaires de Dijon, 1993.

——. "La population de la Bourgogne à la fin du XVIIIe siècle à travers le dénombrement Amelot (1786)." *Annales de Bourgogne* 55 (1983): 65–99.

——. "Quelques observations sur le fonctionnement des bailliages en Bourgogne et au Lyonnais au XVIIIe siècle." In *Ordre moral et délinquance de l'antiquité au XXe siècle, actes du colloque de Dijon,* edited by Benoît Garnot and Rosine Fry, 429–36. Dijon: Éditions universitaires de Dijon, 1994.

Lefebvre, Georges. *Les paysans du Nord pendant la Révolution française.* Paris: A. Colin, 1972, c. 1924.

Legay, Marie-Laure. "1775: L'abolition de la contrainte solidaire en France." In *Justice et argent: Les crimes et les peines pécuniaires du XIII*[e] *au XXI*[e] *siècle,* edited by Benoît Garnot, 189–98. Dijon: Éditions universitaires de Dijon, 2005.

Le Goff, T. J. A., and D. M. G. Sutherland. "The Revolution and the Rural Community in Eighteenth-Century Brittany." *Past and Present* 62 (1974): 96–119.

Lemarchand, Guy. "Troubles populaires au XVIIIe siècle et conscience de classe: Une préface à la Révolution Française." *Annales historiques de la Révolution française* 279 (1990): 32–48.

Lemercier, Pierre. *Les justices seigneuriales de la région Parisienne de 1580 à 1789.* Paris: F. Loviton et Compagnie, 1933.

Lenman, Bruce, and Geoffrey Parker. "The State, the Community, and the Criminal: Law in Early Modern Europe." In *Crime and the Law: The Social History of Crime in Western Europe since 1500,* 11–48. London: Europa, 1980.

Le Roy Ladurie, Emmanuel. "Family Structures and Inheritance Customs in Sixteenth-Century France." In *Family and Inheritance: Rural Society in Western Europe, 1200–1800,* 37–70. Cambridge: Cambridge University Press, 1976.

——. "Révoltes et contestations rurales en France de 1675 à 1788." *Annales: Économies, sociétés, civilisations* 29 (1974): 6–22.

Lévêque, Pierre. "Problèmes de l'alphabétisation en Bourgogne sous la monarchie censitaire." In *Lire et écrire, l'alphabétisation des français de Calvin à Jules Ferry,* 153–86. Paris: Éditions de Minuit, 1977.

Levy, Darline Gay. *The Ideas and Careers of Simon Nicolas Henri Linguet: A Study in Eighteenth-Century Politics.* Urbana: University of Illinois Press, 1980.

Ligou, Daniel. "Les États de Bourgogne et les problèmes fiscaux à la fin du XVIIIe siècle." *Mélanges Antonio Marongiu: Etudes présentées à la Commission internationale pour l'histoire des assemblées d'états,* 97–128. Palermo: Instituto di storia medievale, Universita di Palermo, 1967.

——. "Le personnel de l'Intendance et des États de Bourgogne: Aux origines du fonctionnarisme moderne." *Actes du 111e Congrès national des sociétés savantes: Section d'histoire moderne et contemporaine: Les pouvoirs régionaux: Représentants et élus,* 65–77. Paris: C.T.H.S., 1987.

Lind, E. Allan, Robert J. Maccoun, Patricia A. Ebener, William F. Felstiner, Deborah R. Hensler, Judith Resnick, and Tom R. Tyler. "In the Eye of the Beholder: Tort Litigants' Evaluation of Their Experiences in the Civil Justice System." *Law and Society Review* 24 (1990): 953–96.

Lindimer, Marc. "Messigny et Vantoux: Étude Démographique, 1690–1790." Master's thesis, Université de Bourgogne, 1997.

Lisberney, Jean. "La justice de Fontaine-les-Dijon au XVIIIe siècle." *MSHDB* 5 (1938): 207–9.

Luc, J.-N. *Paysans et droit féodaux en Charente-Inférieure pendant la Révolution française.* Paris: C.T.H.S., 1984.

Mackrell, J. Q. C. *The Attack on "Feudalism" in Eighteenth-Century France.* London: Routledge, 1973.

——. "Criticism of Seigniorial Justice in Eighteenth-Century France." In *French Government and Society 1500–1850,* edited by John Bosher, 123–45. London, Athlone Press, 1973.

Maillard, Brigitte. "Les hautes justices seigneuriales, agents actifs des régulations sociales dans les campagnes de la moyenne vallée de la Loire au XVIIIe siècle." In *Les justices de village: Administration et justice locales de la fin du Moyen Âge à la Révolution,* edited by François Brizay, Antoine Follain, and Véronique Sarrazin, 285–95. Rennes: Presses universitaires de Rennes, 2002.

Maillet, J. "Les anciens coutumiers bourguignons et la dévolution ab intestat." *Revue historique de droit français et étranger* 40 (1962): 153–80.

Malmezat, Jean. *Le bailli des montagnes d'Auvergne et le présidial d'Aurillac comme agents de l'administration royale.* Paris: Librairie du Recueil Sirey, 1941.

Mann, Bruce H. *Neighbors and Strangers: Law and Community in Early Connecticut.* Chapel Hill: University of North Carolina Press, 1987.

Margadant, Ted W. *Urban Rivalries in the French Revolution.* Princeton: Princeton University Press, 1992.

Marion, Marcel. *Dictionnaire des institutions de la France aux XVIIe et XVIIIe siècles.* Paris: Picard, 1993, c. 1923.

——. *Le garde des sceaux Lamoignon et la réforme judiciaire de 1788.* Paris: Hachette, 1905.

Markoff, John. *The Abolition of Feudalism: Peasants, Lords, and Legislators in the French Revolution.* University Park: Pennsylvania State University Press, 1996.

——. "Peasant Grievances and Peasant Insurrection: France in 1789." *Journal of Modern History* 62 (1990): 445–76.

——. "Peasant Protest: The Claims of Lord, Church, and State in the *Cahiers de Doléances* of 1789." *Comparative Studies of Society and History* 34 (1990): 413–54.

Mauclair, Fabrice. "La justice seigneuriale de la duché-pairie de La Vallière (1667–1790)." Doctoral thesis, Université de Tours, 2006.

Maza, Sarah. *Private Lives and Public Affairs: The Causes Célèbres of Prerevolutionary France.* Berkeley: University of California Press, 1993.

Maurice, René. *Justice seigneuriale et justice royale: Moeurs et crimes à Lorient au XVIIIe siècle.* Lorient: Imprimerie du nouvelliste du Morbihan, 1939.

McCormick, Peter, and Ian Greene. *Inside the Canadian Judicial System: Judges and Judging.* Toronto: Lorimer, 1990.

McIntosh, Wayne. "Private Use of a Public Forum: A Long Range View of the Dispute Processing Role of Courts." *American Political Science Review* 77 (1983): 991–1010.

Melton, James van Horn. *The Rise of the Public in Enlightenment Europe.* Cambridge: Cambridge University Press, 2001.

Merrick, Jeffrey. "Fathers and Kings: Patriarchalism and Absolutism in Eighteenth-Century French Politics." *Studies on Voltaire and the Eighteenth Century* 308 (1993): 281-301.

Meuvret, Jean. *Le problème des subsistances à l'époque Louis XIV.* 6 vols. Paris: Éditions de l'École des hautes études en sciences sociales, 1987.

Meyer, Jean. *La noblesse bretonne an XVIIIe siècle.* Paris: Imprimerie nationale, 1966.

Miller, Judith A. *Mastering the Market: The State and the Grain Trade in Northern France, 1700–1860.* Cambridge: Cambridge University Press, 1999.

Morand, François. *Les derniers baillis et procureurs d'office ou fiscaux des justices seigneuriales ressortissant au siège de la sénéchaussée en Boulonnais.* Boulogne-sur-Mer: Imprimerie de Vte. C. Aigre, 1883.

Moreau, Henri. "Notes sur la situation des subdélégués de l'Intendant en Bourgogne au XVIIIe siècle." *Annales de Bourgogne* 26 (1954): 161–84.

——. "Notes sur les subdélégués de l'Intendant en Bourgogne: Le rôle des subdélégués au XVIIIe siècle: Justice, police et affaires militaires." *Annales de Bourgogne* 29 (1957): 225–56.

——. "Les subdélégués et l'administration des communautés: L'Exemple de la subdélégation de Beaune." *Annales de Bourgogne* 31 (1959): 99–109.

Morel, O. *Les assises ou Grands-Jours dans les justices seigneuriales de Bresse à la fin de l'Ancien Régime (1768–1788).* Bourg: Imprimerie du Courrier de l'Ain, 1935.

Moriceau, Jean-Marc. *Les fermiers de l'Île-de-France: XVe–XVIIIe siècle.* Paris: Fayard, 1994.

Mousnier, Roland. *Les institutions de la France sous la monarchie absolue, 1598–1789.* Paris: Presses universitaires de France, 1990 [1974].

——. *La vénalité des offices sous Henri IV et Louis XIII.* Paris: Presses universitaires de France, 1971.

Muchembled, Robert. "Lay Judges and the Acculturation of the Masses: France and the Southern Low Countries, Sixteenth to Eighteenth Centuries." In *Religion and Society in Early Modern Europe, 1500–1800,* edited by Kaspar von Greyerz, 56–66. London: G. Allen and Unwin, 1984.

——. *La violence au village: Sociabilité et comportements populaires en Artois du XVe au XVIIe siècle.* Paris: Brepols, 1989.

Muldrew, Craig. *The Economy of Obligation: The Culture of Credit and Social Relations in Early Modern England.* London: St. Martin's Press, 1998.

Mutel, A. P. "La justice de Saint-Etienne: Contribution à un essai de géographie des justices seigneuriales." *Revue historique de droit français et étranger* 1990: 471–88.

Nachison, Beth. "Absentee Government and Provincial Governors in Early Modern France: The Princes of Condé and Burgundy, 1660–1720." *French Historical Studies* 21 (1998): 265–98.

Nelson, William E. *Dispute and Conflict Resolution in Plymouth County, Massachusetts, 1725–1825.* Chapel Hill: University of North Carolina Press, 1981.

Nicolas, Jean. *La rébellion française: Mouvements populaires et conscience sociale, 1661–1789.* Paris: Éditions du Seuil, 2002.

Noël, J.-F. "Une justice seigneuriale en Haute-Bretagne à la fin de l'Ancien Régime: La Châtellenie de la Motte-de-Gennes." *Annales de Bretagne et des Pays de l'Ouest* 83 (1976): 127–64.

d'Orgéval-Dubouchet, Pierre. *La taille en Bourgogne au XVIIIe siècle.* Dijon: Pornon, 1938.

Pannekoucke, Stéphane. "L'affaire Varenne (1760–1763): Jeux de clientèle et enjeux de pouvoir entre Versailles, Paris et Dijon." *Annales de Bourgogne* 78 (2006): 33–68.

Papon, Charles. "Le système financier bourguignon dans la première moitié du XVIIIe siècle." Doctoral thesis, Université de Paris II, 2005.

Parker, David. "Absolutism, Feudalism, and Property Rights in the France of Louis XIV." *Past and Present* 179 (2003): 60–96.

——. "Sovereignty, Absolutism, and the Function of the Law in Seventeenth-Century France." *Past and Present* 122 (1989): 36–74.

Payen, Philippe. *Les arrêts de règlement du Parlement de Paris au XVIIIe siècle: Dimension et doctrine.* Paris: Presses universitaires de France, 1997.

Pena, Marc. "Des libéralités accordées aux bâtards en ancien droit français." *MSHDB* 52 (1995): 49–81.

Petitjean, Michel, and Françoise Fortunet de Loisy. *Les contrats de mariage à Dijon et dans la campagne bourguignonne de la fin du XVIIIe siècle au milieu du XIXe siècle.* Dijon: Éditions universitaires de Dijon, 1980.

Piant, Hervé. "La confiance perdu: Hommes de loi, délinquants et opinion publique à Vaucouleurs au XVIIIe siècle." In *Juges, notaires et policiers délinquants: XIVe–XXe siècle,* edited by Benoît Garnot, 67–88. Dijon: Éditions universitaires de Dijon, 1997.

——. "La petite délinquance entre infrajudiciaire, procédure civile et répression pénale: L'injure et sa réparation dans la prévôté de Vaucouleurs sous l'Ancien Régime." In *La petite délinquance du Moyen Age à l'époque contemporaine,* edited by Benoît Garnot, 441–54. Dijon: Éditions universitaires de Dijon, 1998.

——. *Une justice ordinaire: Justice civile et criminelle dans la prévôté royale de Vaucouleurs sous l'ancien régime.* Rennes: Presses universitaires de Rennes, 2006.

——. "Le tribunal de l'ordinaire: Justice et société dans la prévôté de Vaucouleurs sous l'Ancien Régime (v. 1670–1790)." PhD thesis, Université de Bourgogne, 2000.

Pitou, Frédérique. *La robe et la plume: René Pichot de la Graverie, avocat et magistrat à Laval au XVIIIe siècle.* Rennes: Presses universitaires de Rennes, 2003.

Poirey, S. "Le retrait lignager dans le duché de Bourgogne (XVIe–XVIIIe siècle)." *MSHDB* 54 (1997): 153–218.

Poisot, Jean-Luc. "Le recrutement du Parlement après 1775: Les origines sociales des nouveaux conseillers." Master's thesis, Université de Bourgogne, 1977.

Poisson, Jean-Paul. *Notaires et société: Travaux d'histoire et de sociologie notariales.* Paris: Economica, 1990.

Poitrineau, Abel. "Aspects de la crise des justices seigneuriales dans l'Auvergne du XVIIIe siècle." *Revue historique de droit française et étranger* 39 (1961): 552–71.

——. *La vie rurale en Basse-Auvergne au XVIIIe siècle (1726–1789).* Paris: Presses universitaires de France, 1965.

Poncet-Cretin, Paulette. "La pratique testamentaire en Bourgogne et en Franche-Comté de 1770 à 1815." Doctoral thesis, Université de Bourgogne, 1973.

Postel-Vinay, Gilles. *La terre et l'argent: L'agriculture et le crédit en France du XVIIIe au début du XXe siècle.* Paris: A. Michel, 1998.

Quéniart, Jean. *Le Grand Chapelletout: Violence, normes et comportements dans la Bretagne rurale au XVIIIe siècle.* Rennes: Éditions Apogée, 1993.

Raffeau, Michèle. "Une seigneurie nivernaise: La terre d'Huban." Doctoral thesis, Université de Bourgogne, 1981.

Ramsey, John F. "The Judicial Reform of 1788 and the French Revolution." In *Studies in Modern European History in Honor of Franklin Charles Palm,* edited by Frederick J. Cox, Richard M. Brace, Bernard C. Weber, and John F. Ramsey, 217–38. New York: Bookman Associates, 1956.

Reinhardt, Steven G. "Crime and Royal Justice in Ancien Régime France: Modes of Analysis." *Journal of Interdisciplinary History* 13 (1983): 437–60.

——. *Justice in the Sarladais, 1770–1790.* Baton Rouge: Louisiana State University Press, 1991.

Richard, Jean. "L'élaboration d'un cahier de doléances: Piere-Claude Perrot, curé de Brazey-en-Plaine." *Annales de Bourgogne* 32 (1960): 5–34.

——. "Le Parlement de Bourgogne et la monarchie au dernier siècle de l'Ancien Régime." *Annales de Bourgogne* 49 (1977): 27–39.

——. "A propos d'une source documentaire: De faux rôles des tailles en Châtillonnais (1741)." *Annales de Bourgogne* 55 (1983): 34–38.

Riollot, Jean. *Le droit de prévention des juges royaux sur les juges seigneuriaux.* Paris: Rousseau, 1931.

Robin, Régine. "Fief et seigneurie dans le droit et l'idéologie juridique à la fin du XVIIIe siècle." *Annales historiques de la Révolution Française* 43 (1971): 554–602.

——. "Quatrième État et cahiers de doléances dans le bailliage d'Auxois en 1789." *Bulletin de la Commission d'histoire économique et sociale de la Révolution Française* (1966), 25–35.

——. *La société française en 1789: Semur-en-Auxois.* Paris: Plon, 1970.

Root, Hilton L. *Peasants and King in Burgundy: Agrarian Foundations of French Absolutism.* Los Angeles: University of California Press, 1987.

Rosen, Deborah A. *Courts and Commerce: Gender, Law, and the Market Economy in Colonial New York.* Columbus: Ohio State University Press, 1997.

Roupnel, Gaston. *La ville et la campagne au XVIIe siècle: Études sur les populations du pays dijonnais.* Paris: Armand Colin, 1955 [1922].

Rousseau, Xavier. "Existe-t-il une criminalité d'Ancien Régime? Réflexions sur l'histoire de la criminalité en Europe?" In *Histoire et criminalité de l'antiquité au XXe siècle: Nouvelles approches: Actes du colloque de Dijon-Chenove, 3, 4, et 5 october 1991,* edited by Benoît Garnot, 123–66. Dijon: Éditions univesitaires de Dijon, 1992.

Ruff, Julius R. *Crime, Justice, and Public Order in Old Regime France: The* Sénéchaussées *of Libourne and Bazas, 1696–1789.* London: Croom Helm, 1984.

Sabean, David. "Aspects of Kinship Behavior and Property in Rural Western Europe before 1800." In *Family and Inheritance: Rural Society in Western Europe, 1200–1800,* 96–111. Cambridge: Cambridge University Press, 1976.

——. *Kinship in Neckarhausen, 1700–1870.* Cambridge: Cambridge University Press, 1998.

——. *Power in the Blood: Popular Culture and Village Discourse in Early Modern Germany.* Cambridge: Cambridge University Press, 1984.

——. *Property, Production, and Family in Neckarhausen, 1700–1870.* Cambridge: Cambridge University Press, 1990.

Saint Jacob, Pierre de. "La fin des impositions directes d'Ancien Régime en Bourgogne." *Annales de Bourgogne* 19 (1947): 249–59.

——. "Le mouvement de la propriété dans un village bourguignon à la fin de l'Ancien Régime." *Revue d'histoire économique et sociale* 27 (1948): 47–52.

——. *Les paysans de la Bourgogne du nord au dernier siècle de l'Ancien Régime.* Paris: Société Les Belles lettres, 1960.

——. "Le village: Les conditions juridiques de l'habitat." *Annales de Bourgogne* 12 (1941): 169–202.

Saks, Michael J. "Do We Really Know Anything about the Behavior of the Tort Litigation System–and Why Not?" *University of Pennsylvania Law Review* 140 (1992): 1147–292.

Salmon, J. H. M. "Renaissance Jurists and 'Enlightened' Magistrates: Perspectives on Feudalism in Eighteenth-Century France." *French History* 8 (1994): 387–402.

Schnapper, Bernard. "Pour une géographie des mentalités judiciaires: La litigiosité en France au XIXe siècle." *Annales: Economies, sociétés, civilisations* 23 (1979): 399–419.

Schneider, Zoë A. "The Village and the State: Justice and the Local Courts in Normandy, 1670–1740." PhD diss., Georgetown University, 1997.

——. "Women before the Bench: Female Litigants in Early Modern Normandy." *French Historical Studies* 23 (2000): 1–32.

Schulte, Regina. *The Village in Court: Arson, Infanticide, and Poaching in the Court Records of Upper Bavaria, 1848–1910.* Cambridge: Cambridge University Press, 1994.

Schwartz, Robert M. "The Noble Profession of Seigneur in Eighteenth-Century Burgundy." In *The French Nobility in the Eighteenth Century: Reassessments and New Approaches,* edited by Jay Smith. University Park, Pennsylvania State University Press., 2006.

Scott, James C. *Domination and the Arts of Resistance: Hidden Transcripts.* New Haven: Yale University Press, 1990.

——. *Weapons of the Weak: Everyday Forms of Peasant Resistance.* New Haven: Yale University Press, 1985.

Sée, Henri. *Les classes rurales en Bretagne du XVIe siècle à la Révolution.* Paris: V. Giard et E. Brière, 1906.

Shapiro, Gilbert, and John Markoff. *Revolutionary Demands: A Content Analysis of the* Cahiers de Doléances *of 1789.* Stanford: Stanford University Press, 1998.

Sharpe, J. A. "Enforcing the Law in the Seventeenth-Century English Village." In *Crime and the Law: The Social History of Crime in Western Europe since 1500,* 97–119. London, 1980.

Shigaki, Yoshiro. "La criminalité dans le Pays du Nord de la Bourgogne d'après les Archives des justices seigneuriales." *Shigaku-Zasshi* 26 (1977): 1–31.

——. "Les institutions de la justice seigneuriale dans la Bourgogne du Nord sous l'Ancien Régime." *Shigaku-Zasshi* 23 (1974): 27–53.

Sigmann, Jean. *La Révolution de Maupeou en Bourgogne (1771–1775): La caste parlementaire à la fin du XVIIIe siècle.* Besançon: J. Sigmann, 1935.

Skinner, Quentin. *The Foundations of Modern Political Thought.* Cambridge: Cambridge University Press, 1978.

Smail, Daniel Lord. *The Consumption of Justice: Emotions, Publicity, and Legal Culture in Marseille, 1264–1423.* Ithaca: Cornell University Press, 2003.

Smith, Roger Everett. "A Provincial Administration under the Bourbon Monarchy: The Government of Burgundy in the Eighteenth Century." PhD diss., Cornell Univeristy, 1975.

Soboul, Albert. "De la pratique des terriers au brûlement des titres féodaux (1789–1793)." *Annales historiques de la Révolution française* 36 (1964): 149–58.

Soleil, Sylvain. "Les justices seigneuriales et l'État monarchique au XVIIIe siècle: L'incorporation par le droit." In *Les justices de village: Administration et justice locale de la fin du Moyen Age à la Révolution,* edited by François Brizay, Antoine Follain, and Véronique Sarrazin, 325–39. Rennes: Presses universitaires de Rennes, 2003.

——. "Le maintien des justices seigneuriales à la fin de l'Ancien Régime; faillite des institutions royales ou récupération? L'exemple angevin." *Revue historique de droit français et étranger* 74 (1996): 83–100.

——. "Le siège présidial d'Angers (1551–1790): Contribution à l'histoire administrative et judiciaire." Doctoral thesis, Université de Rennes, 1995.

Soman, Alfred. "L'infra-judiciaire à Paris, d'après les archives notariales." *Histoire, économie et société* 1 (1982): 369–75.

——. "Justice et infrajustice en France (XVIe–XVIIIe siècle)." In *L'infrajudiciaire du Moyen Age à l'époque contemporaine,* edited by Benoît Garnot, 77–86. Dijon: Éditions universitaires de Dijon, 1996.

Starr, June. *Dispute and Settlement in Rural Turkey: An Ethnography of Law.* Leiden: Brill, 1978.

Straboni, M.-C. "Recherches sur la sexualité illégitime: Les déclarations de grossesse dans les 2 cantons ruraux actuels d'Is-sur-Tille et de Grancey-le-Chateau de 1750 à 1751." D.E.A thesis, Université de Bourgogne, 1976.

Swann, Julian. "Power and Provincial Politics in Eighteenth-Century France: The Varenne Affair, 1757–1763." *French Historical Studies* 21 (1998): 441–76.

——. *Provincial Power and Absolute Monarchy: The Estates General of Burgundy, 1661–1790.* Cambridge: Cambridge University Press, 2003.

Tackett, Timothy. "Collective Panics in the Early French Revolution, 1789–1791: A Comparative Perspective." *French History* 17 (2003): 149–71.

Tapié, Victor-Lucien. "Les officiers seigneuriaux dans la société française du XVIIe siècle." *XVIIe siècle* 42–43 (1959): 118–40.

Taylor, George. "Revolutionary and Nonrevolutionary Content in the *Cahiers* of 1789: An Interim Report." *French Historical Studies* 7 (1972): 479–502.

Thuillier, André. "Agriculture et agronomie en Morvan à la fin du XVIIIe siècle." *Annales de Bourgogne* 46 (1974): 5–23.

Tlusty, Ann B. *Bacchus and Civic Order: The Culture of Drink in Early Modern Germany.* Charlottesville: University of Virigina Press, 2001.

Tournerie, Jean-André. *Recherches sur la crise judiciaire en province à la fin de l'Ancien Régime: Le présidial de Tours de 1740 à 1790.* Tours: Études et travaux de la Faculté de Tours, 1975.

Trubek, David M. "The Construction and Deconstruction of a Disputes-Focused Approach: An Afterword." *Law and Society Review* 15 (1980–81): 727–48.

Vardi, Liana. "Peasants and the Law: A Village Appeals to the French Royal Council, 1768–1791." *Social History* 13 (1998): 295–314.

Varine-Bohan, Béatrice de. "La seigneurie de Marigny-sur-Ouche au XVIIIe siècle: Structures traditionnelles et conquête bourgeoise." Doctoral thesis, Université de Bourgogne, 1974.

Vernus, M. "La culture écrite et le monde paysan en Franche-Comté (1750–1860)." *Histoire et sociétés rurales* 7 (1997): 41–72.

Vignier, F. "La justice de Magny-sur-Tille." *MSHDB* 23 (1962): 278–88.

Vivier, Nadine. *Propriété collective et identité communale: Les biens communaux en France, 1750–1914.* Paris: Publications de la Sorbonne, 1998.

Wanner, Craig. "The Public Ordering of Private Relations, Part Two: Winning Civil Court Cases." *Law and Society Review* 9 (1975): 293–306.

Wenzel, Eric. "Le clergé diocésain d'Ancien Régime au coeur de l'infrajustice: L'exemple de la Bourgogne aux XVIIe et XVIIIe siècles." In *L'infrajudiciaire du Moyen Age à l'époque contemporaine,* edited by Benoît Garnot, 241–50. Dijon: Éditions universitaires de Dijon, 1996.

——. "Le droit, la moralité et Dieu: Deux légitimations de la pratique du monitoire dans la Bourgogne du XVIIe siècle." *MSHDB* 54 (1997): 235–42.

——. "Le monitoire à fin de révélation sous l'Ancien Régime: Normes juridiques, débats doctrinaux et pratiques judiciaires dans le diocèse d'Autun (1670–1790)." Doctoral thesis, Université de Bourgogne, 1999.

——. "La petite délinquance commerciale à travers l'activité des justices consulaires provinciales sous l'Ancien Régime." In *La petite délinquance du Moyen Age à l'époque contemporaine,* edited by Benoît Garnot, 333–41. Dijon: Éditions universitaires de Dijon, 1998.

Wolodkiewicz, Witold. "Antoine-Gaspard et André-Jean Boucher d'Argis: Deux juristes éclairés devant la Révolution." In *La Révolution et l'ordre juridique privé: Rationalité ou scandale? Actes du Colloque d'Orléans, 11–13 septembre 1986,* 187–204. Paris: CNRS, 1988.

Wunder, John R. *Inferior Courts, Superior Justice: A History of the Justices of the Peace on the Northwest Frontier, 1853–1889.* Westport, CT: Greenwood Press, 1979.

Yver, Jean. *Égalité entre héritiers et exclusion des enfants dotés: Essai de géographie coutumière.* Paris: Sirey, 1966.

Zink, Anne. *Azereix: La vie d'une communauté rurale à la fin du XVIIIe siècle.* Paris: S.E.V.P.E.N., 1969.

——. *Clochers et troupeaux: Les communautés rurales des Landes et du Sud-Ouest avant la Révolution.* Talence: Presses universitaires de Bordeaux, 1997.

——. *L'héritier de la maison: Géographie coutumière du Sud-Ouest de la France sous l'Ancien Régime.* Paris: Éditions de l'École des hautes études en sciences sociales, 1993.

Index

Abel, Richard L., 253n1
abolition, seigneurial justice, 137, 140, 195, 197, 202, 206. *See also* preservation, seigneurial justice
abuse, spousal, 78, 112
accomodation sur procès, 124–30; debts settled, 128
acts, royal legal: *arrêt de conseil* of July 1779 concerning leasing auctions of commons, 180; Civil Ordinance of 1667, 49, 140, 155; Declaration of 1773 on *mésus,* 148–49; Edict of 1772 concerning criminal cases begun in seigneurial courts, 30; Ordinance of Roussillon, 141; Waters and Forests Ordinance of 1669, 66, 179–80
Agencourt, 51
agriculture, 77; communal, 76–77, 81–83, 212–13; offenses 50; openfield, 81; professions among litigants, 113. *See also* fines
agronomists, 135
Aignay-le-Duc, 173
Aisey-le-Duc, 214
Aisy, 15, 26, 53, 77, 79, 86, 179–80
Almanach de la province de Bourgogne, 24, 34, 40
Amelot de Chaillou, A. L., 181–83, 185–86, 233n8. *See also* intendant
Ampilly-les-Bordes, 38, 54, 184
Ancey, 15, 56, 77, 78, 92, 122, 167, 189
Angers, 23
Antoine, Annie, 60
appeal, 29
arbitrateur, distinct from *arbitre,* 115
arbitration, 86, 114–20; business disputes, 118; continuation of court case, 119; limited to accounting operations, 118–19; ressemblance to formal justice, 114–15
Arnoult l'ainé, 35
arrangement, 71–72. *See also* settlement, out of court; *accomodation sur procès*
arrêt de conseil, See acts, royal legal
arrêts, general of the Parlement of Dijon, 24, 26, 32, 63, 72–75, 76, 79, 180, 184; 1718 on cabarets (reissued in 1778), 79; 1747 concerning legal fees in probate, 93; 1763 on judicial fees in criminal cases, 63, 144; 1766 on arbitration, 116–17; 1766 on oaths of seigneurial judges, 145; 1766 on the reporting of criminal cases in seigneurial courts, 145; 1768 on seigneurial justice, 149, 162; 1770 on wages of *huissiers* and sergeants, 146; 1772 concerning vestry boards, 146; 1772 concerning *prud'hommes,* 149; 1773 on village forest guards, 147; 1778 on leasing auctions of commons, 180; 1780 on leasing auction of commons, 181; 1781 concerning fees charged by *procureurs postulants,* 156–57. *See also* Parlement, Dijon
assault, 67
asséeur, 74
assemblies, family, 123–24
assizes, annual, 22, 26, 39, 46, 72–78, 143, 145, 168, 219–22; cases judged, 165–68; forum for minor disputes, 154; location, 73
auction, estate, 91–92
August 4, 1789, 141
authority, public, 137
autoregulation. *See* community, self-regulating
Autun, seminary, 45
Auvergne, 153
Auxey-le-Grand, Auxey le Petit, 15, 79, 163

aveux et dénombrements, 13
avocats, 33–36, 42; arbitrators, 119–20; community of, bailliage of Beaune, 51
avoidance, 90

Bagé, 144
Bagnot, 64, 79, 81, 179
Baigneux-les-Juifs, 53, 205
bail à cheptel, 107
bailliages, 29–32; Arnay-le-Duc, 2, 35, 37, 40; Autun, 31; Auxonne, 15; Beaune, 24; Bresse, 39; Charolles, 38; Chartres, 207; Châtillonais, 15, 189; Dijon, 2, 13, 34, 37, 107, 112, 157; grands, 152; Saulieu, 15, 24, 79; Troyes, 207. *See also* jurisdiction, complementarity between seigneurial and royal
Baker, Keith Michael, 141–42
banalités, 56–57
banc seigneurial, 47
Barbirey, 197
Bart, Jean, 57–58, 152, 175, 259n99
Basdevant-Gaudemet, Brigitte, 137, 261n10. *See also* Loyseau, Charles
bastardy, 47–48
Bastier, Jean, 4, 153
Bellefond, 56, 119
Belleneuve, 48, 62, 72
Besançon, 153
Billey, 15, 52, 56, 78, 192, 62
Blaisy, 173
blasphemy, 73
Bloch, Marc, 173–75, 192
Bodin, Jean, 138
bornage, 28. *See also* jurisdiction dispute
Boucher d'Argis, 29
Bouhier, Bénigne, 28
Bouhier, Jean, 87, 141
Boutaric, François de, 48
Boux-sous-Salmaise, 203–4
bread, prices, 79
Brittany, 23, 153
Brooks, Christopher, 125, 255n23
Brown, Howard, 248n35
bureaux de paix, 259n99
Burgundy, Custom of, 84, 99, 141
cabaret, 65, 68–69, 73, 78–81, 121
cahiers de doléances, 7, 26, 33, 39, 51, 59, 94, 116, 136, 142, 172–73, 181, 193, 195–210, 213–14; assemblies, influence of presiding officers, 196; general Third Estate, 205–6; grievances concerning justice, 202; national comparison, 206–8; preservation of seigneurial justice, 197
capitation, 150
Carrier, Isabelle, 98
Castan, Nicole, 99–100, 120
cens, 54
census, 1786 (Amelot census), 26
centralisation, state, 1, 8–9, 22, 29–30, 61, 174. *See also* Tocqueville, Alexis de
Chambolle and Morey, 93
Chambre des comptes, 153
champart, 55
Chanceaux, 144
Chapelle Huon, la, 207
Charente-Maritime, 206
Chartier, Roger, 207–8
Chartraire de Montigny, 42, 58
Chaudenay-le-Château, 173
Chazilly-le-Haut, Chazilly-le-Bas, 26, 43, 80, 93
children, minor, 84
city dwellers, as litigants in seigneurial courts, 106–7
clerks, 84; income of, 41; office leased to the highest bidder, 36
collector, taxes, 74–75
Collins, James, 54, 249n52
Colombet, Albert, 150
Combier, Albert, 4
common land, 76–77; leasing auctions, 178–81. *See also* agriculture, communal
communities, as litigants, 122; slow to deliberate, 184. *See also contrainte solidaire; surtaux, procès en;* intendant
community, self-regulating, 62–63, 71–72, 95, 131, 212
confiscation, seigneurial right, 47
contract enforcement, role of courts, 12
contrainte solidaire, 54, 75–76, 183–84

contrôle des actes, 53
controller general, 182–83
Corberon, 50
Corgengoux, 122, 163
Corley, Christopher, 251n94
correspondence, between lords and officers, 50–51
corvée, 56
costs, justice, 4, 40, 46, 62, 70, 72, 91–94, 124, 149, 160–61, 164; average overall, 167–68; comparison to other regions, 160–61; as deterrent, 64; for seigneur, 46; strategies to limit, 94; for village communities, 185
costs, of *procureurs postulants,* 156–58
costs, transaction, as factor influencing choice of controller of behavior, 131
courts, seigneurial, average size of, 24–26
crime, 46, 62–72
Crubaugh, Anthony, 6, 27, 61, 84, 113, 125, 154–55, 160–61, 205, 253n122, 259n99, 267n118, 276n9
curateur, 85–86

Daguesseau, Chancellor, 29, 137, 151–52
Debadier, Etienne Philibert, 21
debt, 108; judged at assizes, 165
defamation, 67. *See also* assault; insults
Dewald, Jonathan, 102, 124
Dickinson, John, 102
Dijon, Hôpital général, 15
Dijon, University of, 35, 164
dishonor, 98, 124
dispute; difficulty of defining, 11, 129; inheritance, 109–10, 166–67; necessity of an outside authority to facilitate resolution, 213; paternity, 129–30; relation to lawsuit, 96–98
distance, between court and village, 36–40, 203–4
dixième, 150
donations, à cause de mort, 89–90
Doyle, William, 140–41, 175–76
dues, seigneurial, 2. *See also taille seigneuriale, tierce, cens, champart*

échevin. See syndic
elections, Estates-General of 1789, 205–6
Ellickson, Robert, 130–31
emancipation, minors, 86–87
enclosure; edicts, 135–36; riot, 188
Enlightenment, 3, 43, 140, 207–8
Epagny, 54, 165, 180
épaves, 48
épices, 41
escalation, dispute, 70
Estates, provincial, Burgundy, 136, 147, 150
Estates-General of 1789, 139, 173
Evrard, Sebastien, 177, 183

family, cases settled informally, 112, 124–25
farming disputes, 154. *See also mésus*
Felstiner, William F., 253n1
fermier général, 46, 54, 56, 189–91
feudistes, 43
fields and forests, protection of, 72
fields, divided into micro-parcels, 163–64
figure, dark, 10
finances, village, 178
fines, 50, 81–83, 188; as income for lords, 82–83; for nonattendance of assizes, 26; for offenses in forests, 50. *See also mésus*
Finot, Jean, 40–42, 120
fishing, 48, 52
Flée, 53, 55, 80, 99
Follain, Antoine, 4
Foncegrive, 36, 39, 40, 66, 78, 80, 166
Fontaine-en-Duesmois, 15, 53, 54, 57, 65, 73, 77, 102, 185
Fontaine-lès-Dijon, 28
food, policing of, 78–80
forests, communal, 189, 202–3. *See also* guard, communal
formalities of justice, reduced, 148–49
Forster, Robert, 8, 49, 175–76, 192
Fouquau de Pussy, 139
Franche-Comté, 206
Fyot de la Marche, first president of the Parlement of Dijon, 151

Galanter, Marc, 253n2
Garnot, Benoît, 5, 84, 248n35
Gemeaux, barony, 76, 82
geography, jurisdiction, 3, 21
Giffard, André, 3, 21, 23–29, 207
Godran, Collège, 35
grain, trade, 79
Grands-Jours. See assizes, annual
Grateau, Philippe, 173, 208
Grosse, Christian, 254n6
guard; communal, 74, 146; seigneurial, 52
guardians. *See tuteur* and *curateur*

Hamscher, Albert, 235n37
Hanlon, Gregory, 98–99
herd, communal, 74
historiography; northern Burgundy, 7–9, 70–71; seigneurial justice, 3–7, 61–62, 98, 143
honor, 67–69, 191
Huban, barony, 102
Hufton, Olwen, 5
huissiers, 146
hunting, 48, 52

Igé, 172
imprescriptibility, seigneurial rights, 244n62
inamovibilité, 203–4. *See also* venality; Loyseau, Charles
income, judicial officers, 38–43, 92. *See also* Finot, Jean
indemnification, seigneurial rights, 136, 140–42
inheritance, 69, 109–110; accomodation, 126–32; arbitration, 117–18; complication of cases, 11; court costs, 91–94; disputes, dishonor of conducting in public, 124, 126, 128; estate auctions, 93–94; jurisdiction, personal, 28; Messsigny, 88–92; number of estates settled by courts, 84; settled at assizes, 166–68; theft from heirs, 65. *See also* bastardy; emancipation; *mainmorte;* justice, probate; *tuteur*
insults, list of, 67–68
intendants, 2, 9, 23–24, 157, 181, 202; authority over village affairs, 177–183. *See also* Root, Hilton; Evrard, Sebastien
intestate, 90–91, 99, 130
inventaire après décès, See inventory, probate
inventory, probate, 87–88

Jacquinot, Antoine, 164
Jeanclos, Yves, 115, 119
journaliers, 232n46
Joussanvaux, 28
judges; agreement with Parlement reforms, 154–55; income, 40–43; residence, 37; participation in extrajudicial settlements, 97, 119, 123–24; professional motivations, 42–43; professional training, 33–34
Jullenay, 21
jurés priseurs, 202
juridiction volontaire. See justice, probate
jurisdiction; complementarity of seigneurial and royal, 30–33; probate, 28; territorial or personal, 27–28
justice of the peace, 105, 259n99
justice, class biases, 168–70, 223–27
justice, probate, 9–10, 60, 83–94, 215

Kagan, Richard, 102, 160
King's Lynn, 101

La Poix de Fréminville, 72
La Rochelle, 23
laboureurs, 112, 232n46
Labrousse, C.-E., 188–89
Lamoignon, chancellor, 4
Land, dispute, 109; judged at assizes, 167
landlords, urban, 8
Lanthes, 15, 39
Larey, *prieuré,* 13–14
Latrecey, 204
Lavenay, 207
law, Roman, 87, 152
lawsuit, disputeless, 12
lawyers. *See avocats*

Le Goff, T. J. A., 214, 248n35
Le Roy Ladurie, Emmanuel, 173, 192–93
Lebrun, Charles-François, 140
Lefebvre, Georges, 175
Lenman, Bruce, 248n35
Lermercier, Pierre, 4
Linguet, S.-N- H., 139–40
Litigants' motivations, 98
litigation; craze of the sixteenth century, 101; inter-community, 106–7; rates, 32, 102–6
lods et ventes, 53–54
lords. *See* seigneur
Loyseau, Charles, 137–39, 141; *Discours sur les abus des justices des villages,* 137; *Traité des seigneuries,* 137
Lucenay-le-Duc, 204

Mackrell, John, 232n47, 261n5
Mâcon, 172
Maine, 60, 193, 206
mainmortable, excluded from being arbitrator, 119
mainmorte, 8, 57–59, 173, 215
majority, age of, 85
Mâlain, 197
manouvriers, 112, 232n46
maréchaussée, 62
Margadant, Ted, 204
Marion, Marcel, 207
markets, 72
Markoff, John, 173, 196, 207–8
Mauclair, Fabrice, 6, 94, 102, 113, 160–61
Maupeou revolution, 140, 144, 146
meat, prices, 79
mediation, 120–24; ratified by judges, 125
Meilly, 144
Méllenet, 47
messiers, 81–82, 212
Messigny, 31, 48, 79, 80, 89, 90, 91, 106–8, 126, 129, 166; *accomodation sur procès,* 126–30; inheritance patterns, 88–92
mésus, 82, 148–49, 158, 168–69; procedure, 163–65; ubiquity, 163
Meursault, 11, 15, 31, 50, 54, 55, 79, 123, 163, 184, 188
Meyer, Jean, 269n20
Mézard, M., 140
Miller, Judith, 79
minors, 85–86. *See also tutelle, compte de; curateur;* emancipation; *tuteur*
Mirebeau, marquisat, 35
mobility, geographic, 107
monarchy, absolute, 137
monitoire à fin de révélation, 30–31
Montorval, Sieur Archer de, 23
Montot, 15, 26, 38, 55, 102, 185
Montrevel, 36
Morvan, 189
Moutier-St.-Jean, 202
Moux, 203
Muldrew, Craig, 255n24

Nelson, William E., 105
Nicolas, Jean, 52
northern Burgundy, compared to other regions, 5, 153, 192–94, 214–15
notaries, royal, 35; judicial officers, 33–36; role in accomodations, 126
note, promissory, 31–32, 108

officers, judicial, 33–43; accumulation, 40; landowners in villages, 37–38; salaries of, 46
officials, village, elections of, 74–76. *See also asséeur,* collector, *messier, prud'homme, syndic*
orphans, 85. *See also curateur,* emancipation, *tuteur*
outcomes, cooperative, 131; *See also* Ellickson, Robert
ordinance, royal. *See* acts, royal legal

Pagny, barony, 40, 45–46, 50, 63, 189
Parker, David, 142, 261n12, 272n81
Parker, Geoffrey, 248n35
Parlement, Dijon, 13, 21, 34; appeals, 29–30, 116; arbitration, 115–17; determination to render justice more summary, 39, 136; emancipation, 86–7; judicial fees in seigneurial

Parlement, Dijon–*(cont'd)*
courts, 92, 95, 156–58; magistrates' ownership of seigneurial courts, 150–52; oversight over seigneurial justice, 39, 45, 74–75, 136, 143–45; police, alcohol, 79; provincial patriotism, 151–52; reform of seigneurial justice, 145–48; relations to the provincial intendant, 178–83, 186–87. *See also arrêts,* general of the Parlement of Dijon
partage, 89–90. *See also* inheritance
Pasilly, 46
passage, rights of, 167
patriotism, provincial, 152
persons, crimes against, 64
Pétion de Villeneuve, Jérôme, 42
proximity, physical, importance for generating certain kinds of lawsuits, 108
physiocrats, 135
Piant, Hervé, 101, 115, 160–61
Pichot de la Graverie, René, 43
Poitrineau, Abel, 3, 21
police, 72–83; and agreement of village community, 79
Pont-Audemer, 37
Postel-Vinay, Gilles, 108
pregnancy, declaration, 129–30
priest, 122
prison, 47
procedure, 6, 155–162; assizes, 162–64; oral nature of, 11, 62, 155; summary, 156
procuration, 88
procureur fiscal, 237n57
procureur syndic. See syndic
procureurs, 33–34; community of, 32, 51, 157
procureur d'office, 80, 237n57; income of, 38–39, 41–42; police responsibilities of, 72; professional training of, 35; role in administering seigneurie, 51
procureur postulant, 146, 154–55, 161–62
professionalization, judicial officers, 35
property, crimes against, 64
prud'homme, 75, 149, 163, 213
public party, plaintiff, 144

Quéniart, Jean, 99, 214
Quingey, 206

reaction, aristocratic, 175–76
reaction, seigneurial, 2, 174–77, 187–94, 215–16
reconciliation, as function of court, 97, 121
reform, general institutional, 135–36; general legal, 198–99, 205
Règlements généraux pour les justices seigneuriales, 147
Reinhardt, Steven, 120, 248n35
Remonstrances; Parlement of Dijon, 180; provincial Estates of Burgundy, 149, 186
representation, legal, 148. *See also procureur postulant*
reputation, 69, 124–25
restitution, 65, 66, 71, 64
retours, 163
retrait féodal, 53–54
retrait lignager, 128–29
revolt, antiseigneurial, 1–2, 52, 172–77, 193–94, 216–17
Richard, Jean, 268n131
roads, judicial oversight, 72
Robin, Régine, 8, 198
Root, Hilton, 8–9, 175, 177–87
Rougemont, 46

Sablé, 113
Saffres, 51
Saint Jacob, Pierre de, 3–4, 7, 57, 175–76, 189–90
Saint-Calais, 206
Sainte Chapelle de Dijon, 15
Saint-Sulpice, 207
Saks, Michael, 96
Sarat, Austin, 253n1
Saucy, 15, 28
Saulon-la-Chapelle, 15, 54
Saulx-Tavanes, 8, 175
Schnapper, Bernard, 105–06, 214
Schneider, Zoë, 5, 37, 116, 125, 143
Scott, James C., 166
Sée, Henri, 3, 8

seigneur, 15, 76, 141–43, 174, 216–17; absentee, 49; cases involving, 22, 45, 60, 187–88; correspondence with judicial officers, 49–51; costs of maintaining a seigneurial court 45–48, 62, 82; personal involvement in running of justice, 49–59, 204–5; primary political force in village, 177–79; right to revoke judicial office, 34–35; salaries paid to judicial officers 40, 46. *See also* reaction, seigneurial; revolt, antiseigneurial; sentiment, antiseigneurial
Semur-en-Auxois, 40, 120, 196, 198
Senailly, 15, 52–53, 58, 73, 123, 189
sentiment, antiseigneurial, 1–2, 7, 173–74, 191–93; in royal and ministerial circles, 142, 177, 184
separation, spousal, 112
sergeant, 146
service, domestic, 166
settlement, out of court, 66, 97. *See also* arbitration, mediation, *accomodation sur procès*
settlement, rates, 125–25
Shapiro, Gilbert, 196, 207
Smail, Daniel Lord, 98–99
Soleil, Sylvain, 5, 23, 143
Soman, Alfred, 126
Sombernon, 213
sovereignty, 136
St.-Thibault, 214
subdelegate, 179, 180, 202
surtaux, procès en, 147–49, 158
Sutherland, D. M. G., 214, 248n35
syndic, 54, 57, 74–76, 213

taille, assessments; as proxy for wealth levels, 168–70; judge's control over, 1247–48, 152
taille, seigneurial, 54, 184
tax records, methodological challenges, 268n131
Taylor, George V., 172–73, 208
terriers, 61–62, 174–75
testament, 89-90, 129–30
theft, wood, 66
Thoisy-le-Désert, 26
threat, of lawsuit, 126–127
tierce, 55
tithe, 54–55
Tocqueville, Alexis de, 1, 29–30, 173, 187, 192–93
Toulouse, 42
transcript, hidden, 166. *See also Scott, James C.*
trespass offense, in seigneurial forests, 177
triage, 76–77
tribunaux d'exception, 202
tuteur, 85–86, 167
tutelle, compte de, 86; settled by arbitration, 118

usurpation, as origin of seigneurial justice, 138–39, 142

Val-de-Mercy, 154
Varenne affair, 152
Vaux, 203
venality, 35–36, 137, 140–41
vendanges, 56
Verzé, 172
vestry board, 146
Villerrottin. *See* Billey
vingtième, 150, 202
Voudenay l'Église, 205

wages, farm labor, 166
Waters and Forests court, 157
Wenzel, Eric, 120
witch, as insult, 122
women; as arbitrators, 119–20; as guardians for minors, 85; excluded from assizes, 77; will-writers, 90
wood industry, importance in northern Burgundy, 189
wood, prices, 188–89
Wunder, John R., 160

Zink, Anne, 5–6, 214

Does one pick Burgundy when one has an axe to grind? esp. abt peasant lot?